ENDORSEMENTS FOR BATTLEFIELD BLESSINGS: *STORIES OF FAITH AND COURAGE FROM FIRST RESPONDERS*

"This is one of those must resources! It's realistic, practical and inspirational. It needs to be in the hands of every firefighter."

H. Norman Wright, Author, Therapist;
Director of Christian Marriage Enrichment

"I have been in the emergency service for fifty years, and this book of testimonies of those who serve and risk their lives daily is of very special importance to those who walk this walk. To know and trust in our Lord is the one thing giving us strength to go on. I sincerely believe every Christian in the emergency service should read this book and share it with all co-workers. May God bless you as you read this and give you His cover as you perform your duties."

Ed Stauffer, Founder and Executive Director
of the Federation of Fire Chaplains

"First responders serve in a profession where danger, tragedy, and loss of life and property require them to give selflessly as they face danger head on. This book, written by first responders will provide inspiration, encouragement and the assurance you can meet the challenges of your day in God's strength."

Bob Crum, co-founder Fellowship of
Christian Firefighters International

"Whether we're responding to a rollover, house fire, or forest inferno, firefighters and first responders face a lot of stress. Stress from danger, tragedy, and even home issues, affect all of us. We pray that this book will remind our brothers and sisters that we're all in this together, and especially that the Lord walks with us even through the 'valley of the shadow of death.'"

Rick Barton, Strike Team Leader, Line Safety Officer,
or Public Information Officer in every western state
as well as the southeast United States and Alaska.

"The unique joys and challenges of being an emergency responder create unique pressure and stresses. The daily devotions in *Stories of Faith and Courage from Firefighters and First Responders* help to maintain your focus and commitment to serving your fellow man. At the same time, it reminds you to allow our Lord to help carry those unique burdens for you. That is part of his commitment to you."

Jim Felix, VP Board of Directors Wildland Firefighter Foundation/Owner, Supply Cache; 25 year wildfire veteran

"Firefighters and first responders are on the front lines of extreme stress, danger, and tragedy every day as they serve and protect our communities. The devotional entries in this book are first hand testimonials from those who meet these challenges with God's strength and comfort. I believe these testimonials convey the Lord's encouragement and strength in a very special and unique way."

Chris Riley, MS, CFO, MIFireE; Fire Chief, City of Pueblo (CO); and President, Colorado State Fire Chiefs Association

Stories OF **Faith** AND **Courage** FROM

FIREFIGHTERS
&
FIRST
RESPONDERS

G. REYNOLDS & S. REYNOLDS

GOD & COUNTRY
PRESS

Battlefields & Blessings: Stories of Faith and Courage from Firefighters and First Responders
Copyright © 2010 by Gaius and Sue Reynolds
Published by God & Country Press, an imprint of AMG Publishers
6815 Shallowford Rd.
Chattanooga, Tennessee 37421

ISBN 978-0-89957018-1
First printing—August 2010
Cover designed by Michael Largent, Indoor Graphics, Inc., Chattanooga, TN
Interior design and typesetting by Reider Publishing Services,
    West Hollywood, California
Edited and proofread by Rich Cairnes and Rick Steele

Printed in Canada
16 15 14 13 12 11 10 –T– 7 6 5 4 3 2 1

Sue Reynolds, Missionary – Fellowship of Christian Firefighters International (FCFI), and Chaplain Gaius Reynolds, President – FCFI; Volunteer Firefighter – Livermore, CO, Fire Protection District

NO GREATER LOVE

GREATER LOVE has no one," heralded the headlines repeatedly after the Attack on America September 11, 2001.

That love was implicit in the selfless sacrifice hundreds of first responders made prior to, since, and on that fatal day.

You are considered a selfless hero because of your

> Bravery,
> Tradition,
> Brotherhood,
> Patriotism,
> Sacrifice,
> Courage,
> Empathy,
> Heroism,
> Service,
> Dedication,

and the list goes on.

Humbly, you may deny being a hero and say,
"I'm just doing what my job calls me to do."

You come from many and varied backgrounds. You strive to serve your communities, countries, and fellow citizens. Your role as a hero is forever imprinted on the minds of Americans as people witness many selfless acts of bravery. When others flee for safety, you run into danger, focusing on the job you're called to do—not on the danger ahead. Shift work, emergency call-outs, interrupted family life, and the inevitable danger are accepted norms in your life.

Fires destroy and often kill. Rescue calls represent sadness most people never encounter. Your responses often put you in life-threatening situations, yet you accept that as a constant in your life. Day in and day out, you face tragedy. Oftentimes your sleep is interrupted by visions of the destruction and loss, whether those images involve dragging a youth from a fire, arriving on scene to find it's too late to save a life, or seeing homes and other property reduced to ashes.

Yes, you are a living example that:

> "Greater love has no one than this,
> that he lay down his life for his friends" (John 15:13).

The devotionals that follow contain true-life experiences from first responders throughout the world. The consequences of sin and Satan's evil presence and threats are evident in the tragedies and losses first responders face.

The ability to handle the devastating heartbreak and destruction first responders encounter in their daily duties, without being destroyed within, can only come from a heart that belongs to God. The comfort God provides, the hope of life beyond our earthly existence—an eternal dwelling in God's loving presence—the promise that, despite the immensity of the tragedy, God has a plan and will comfort and bring good from the not-so-good occurrences is what makes the Christian emergency worker stand out from others. Bitterness, depression, futility, and anger are replaced by concern, joy, hope, and peace.

> "And the peace of God, which transcends all understanding, will
> guard your hearts and your minds in Christ Jesus" (Philippians 4:7).

May God's love and peace, which surpasses all understanding, be yours. As you go about your daily work routines and personal life, may you rely on God's promises and peace. May you draw strength for the challenges you face, as well as for the routine tasks you perform. *That is our, the compilers of these devotionals, prayer for you.*

Penny McGlachlin, with Sue Reynolds

THE TRUTH ABOUT THE FIREFIGHTER'S PRAYER

One man's prayer

ALVIN WILLIAM LINN, known by those who loved him as "Smokey," turned to God when tragedy struck. His granddaughter, Penny McGlachlin, would like the world to know who penned "The Fireman's Prayer," and why.

To many, "The Fireman's Prayer" is just thought of as a poem, nothing more. But it was much more; it was one man's actual prayer to his God about his family as he reflected on a tragic call and wondered, "What if those were my children in there?" It was this gut reaction that was the inspiration for his written prayer.

Following is Penny McGlachlin's sharing about her grandfather, a former Wichita, Kansas, firefighter, who went to be with his Lord in March 2004.

"Alvin William Linn earned the name 'Smokey' when he was fifteen and ran into his grandfather's burning barn and drove out his Model "T" truck. Smokey and the truck made it out in one piece, but the seat of his pants was smoking. This must have been a sign of things to come, because it wasn't the last time he would charge into a burning building.

"When I was about four, I thought my grandfather was born a fireman, lived at the station, and would only occasionally visit us at grandmother's house. I learned a few things on my visits to the station; one was that if you walk in front of a truck being cleaned, someone will inevitably hit the siren button (just to see how high you'll jump). My grandfather became one of the first Red Cross instructors in Wichita to teach and certify people for CPR and first aid. I was the only eight-year-old in my school that was certified in both, whether I wanted to be or not.

"A. W. 'Smokey' Linn wrote 'A Fireman's Prayer' after responding to a call involving children trapped inside a burning apartment building. The firefighters could see the children in the windows, but they couldn't rescue them due to iron bars installed by the apartment owner. All they could do was try to contain the fire. About one in the morning, Smokey found himself sitting at the station's kitchen table putting into words his emotions.

"The Fireman's Prayer is one man's prayer (a man who was more than a fireman) to his Lord and Savior. He was a husband, father, grandfather, and son who knew how precious and short life can be.

'Hear my prayer, O God; listen to the words of my mouth.' (Psalm 54:2)

When I am called to duty, God, whenever flames may rage,
Give me the strength to save some life whatever be its age.
Help me to embrace a little child before it's too late,
Or some older person from the horror of that fate.
Enable me to be alert and hear the weakest shout,
And quickly and efficiently to put the fire out.
I want to fill my calling and give the best in me,
To guard my neighbor and protect his property.
And if according to your will I have to lose my life,
Please bless with your protecting hand my children and my wife."

More Than A Fireman (Courtesy of Hugo Ferchau,
Gunnison County Fire Protection District)

Daniel A. Clegg, Rural-Metro EMT; Engineer/EMT–Indianapolis Fire Department (Retired); Fellowship of Christian Firefighters Regional Director / International Board Member

INVENTORY

Planning for a New Year

CAN IT BE another year is gone? Time marches on! Holidays can be hectic and keep us from taking time to "smell the roses," but relaxing amid the flurry of activities will help you focus on God's blessings. Resolve now to pray without ceasing, attend church regularly, and become an active witness in your home, church, firehouse, and community.

Year-end is a time for budgets, tax forms, and inventories. As you reflect on the past year and plan for a new one, why not take your own personal inventory?

- Is there anyone you need to forgive?
- Are you sympathetic?
- Do you seek to understand another person's point of view?
- Are you quick to acknowledge a fault of yours? Ask forgiveness?
- Do you find the advice and command of others trying?
- How do you submit?
- Is self-discipline irksome or a delight?
- Are you impatient in the routine of your duties?
- Are you tolerant of the shortcomings of others?
- How do you treat those who are unkind and unreasonable?
- Are you doing anything you'd condemn in others? Have you been pure?
- What are you like at home? Are you appreciative?
- Are you regarded by others as reliable?
- Are you given to faultfinding?
- Are you trustworthy, never breaking confidence? If you give your word, is it your bond?
- Is the reputation of another safe in your hands?

> "Love is patient, love is kind. It does not envy, it does not boast, it is not proud. It is not rude, it is not self-seeking, it is not easily angered, it keeps no record of wrongs. Love does not delight in evil but rejoices with the truth. It always protects, always trusts, always hopes, always perseveres. Love never fails."
> (1 Corinthians 13:4–8)

- Are you afraid of doing more than is necessary in duties, service, love, and in going the second mile?
- Do you object to interruptions, or meet them graciously?
- Do you have firm, unwavering conviction?
- How do you handle criticism?
- Do you have a bridled tongue? Or are you argumentative, always insisting on your own way?
- Do you make the right use of leisure time?
- Do you love to be alone with God?
- Are you faithful to Bible study, prayer, and service to your church?
- Are you committed to sharing Christ with the fire service and the community you serve?
- Does your life manifest God's love?

Prayer:
May the New Year find your love manifest in my life.

JANUARY 2

Craig Duck, Lieutenant, Engine Co. 11 – Washington, DC, Fire Department; Fellowship of Christian Firefighters International Atlantic States Regional Director / International Board Member

GODLY HERITAGE

How would George Washington feel if he walked into a firehouse today?

FIREFIGHTERS have a godly heritage to be proud of as well as to learn from. George Washington, Thomas Jefferson, and Ben Franklin are a few of the notable godly men who led the fire service.

A great debt is owed by the fire service and our nation to Firefighter George Washington. He belonged to the Friendship Company of Alexandria, Virginia, and purchased a hand pumper for the company. Throughout his distinguished military career, Washington stopped by local firehouses to visit with firefighters. Perhaps the General would talk about tactics common to the area on big fires, or just talk about the local heroes. One can easily assume that much of his greatness was due to his training and heroism on the fire ground, coupled with his trust in God. I wonder how he'd feel today to walk into a firehouse and witness the foul language all too often prevalent.

I challenge you to walk into any firehouse in America, listen to the conversation, and see how long it takes before you hear foul language, conversations about immoral acts, or fantasies about doing evil deeds. I believe those types of conversations will come out the majority of the time. Ungodly conversations might not be the only thing you witness; many firefighters have strayed far away from God and his Word.

Sin has not always abounded in American firehouses, but when confronted with it, Christian firefighters can take comfort in God's teachings and not be embarrassed or think they are less of a firefighter if they've trusted in God's plan of salvation. George Washington, in his farewell speech, said, "Of all the dispositions and habits which lead to political prosperity, religion and morality are indispensable supports . . . Let it simply be asked: Where is the security for property, for

> "We have obtained an inheritance, having been predestined according to His purpose who works all things after the counsel of His will, to the end that we who were the first to hope in Christ would be to the praise of His glory." (Ephesians 1:11, 12 NASB)

reputation, for life, if the sense of religious obligation desert the oaths which are the instruments of investigation in courts of justice? And let us with caution indulge the supposition that morality can be maintained without religion."

If George Washington walked into your workplace and listened to your conversation, would he be pleased or repelled? Morality and religion based on God's Word are the very foundations of our country. This is a heritage we should take into our places of business as well.

Prayer:
Help me be "salt and light" in my firehouse and to never be ashamed of the inheritance I have in you and what our forefathers stood for in the fire service and in their lives. Let my walk match your Word.

*Rick Barton, Fire Safety Officer; Rick Barton Ministries,
Gunnison, CO; Fellowship of Christian Firefighters
International Ambassador-at-Large*

WHAT'S SO "HAPPY" ABOUT A NEW YEAR?

Reviewing and Planning

WHAT DAY is it?" Ever asked that question? Have you noticed how on a busy project, hours and days seem to run together? Important things such as your anniversary, birthdays, dentist appointments, and even days of worship sneak up and sometimes slip by.

That's one reason I like ringing in the New Year. It forces me to stop the clock and review the past year and plan goals for the new one.

How was *your* past year? Did you accomplish the things you'd set out to do? Did you get the garage painted? Take that long overdue vacation? Lose twenty pounds? More importantly, did you spend time in your Bible each day, mend that broken relationship, and devote more quality time to your spouse and kids?

January is a great time for reflection and goal-setting. As some sage said, "If you fail to plan, you plan to fail." By writing down a list of goals for the upcoming year, you begin moving forward instead of treading water or just reacting to daily "emergencies." You may not reach all your goals this year, but you can reach some, and that's a good start. It seems popular to discount New Year's resolutions as a waste of time. But are they?

> "Commit your way to the Lord; trust in him and he will do this: He will make your righteousness shine like the dawn, the justice of your cause like the noonday sun." (Psalm 37:5, 6)

What would you really like to happen this year? Write it down—even better, have lunch with your spouse or family and make a list. Start with your spiritual goals such as reading through the New Testament or entire Bible. Consider a regular daily time for prayer and joining a small group or Bible study. Then, write out your family goals: planning date nights with your spouse or child or taking a trip with your spouse, boys, girls, or parents. Setting financial goals may be needed. Do you need to get out of debt, eliminate credit cards, increase your church giving, or start a savings account for vacations or school expenses? And don't forget about the household goals your spouse may have: a new window, painting the garage, etc.

All these examples are achievable goals if you commit them to the Lord Jesus! (Psalm 37:5). And even if you don't reach them all this year, they become part of your long-range thinking.

At the end of the year, review your list. I'll bet you'll do better than you thought you would.

Prayer:
*Lord, this year I want to use New Year's for something
more than party hats. After all, I don't look so hot in one anyway.
I want this to be a happy, Spirit-filled year.*

*H. Norman Wright, Author, Therapist; Director –
Christian Marriage Enrichment*

NIGHT SHIFT
God also works the night shift

NIGHTTIME: For most it's a time of rest when the body and mind slow down. As darkness intensifies, noises diminish and quiet takes over—at least for most people. Then there are those who work the night shift. When others sleep, they are hard at work. It could be a nurse, a baker preparing tomorrow's breads, or a road crew repairing damage while traffic isn't so intense. It's also the world's first responders: those police officers cruising the streets of a darkened city and the firemen and medics responding to a call.

Sleep can also be elusive for those who aren't on call or working. For some, grief, pain, loss, and hurts, whether physical or emotional, are constant companions. They try to sleep, but sleep won't come. If they fall asleep hoping for a reprieve from the pain, the pain follows them and troubles their dreams.

For first responders, perhaps the night shift is a combination of both. On-duty work keeps one active and awake. Off-duty, tragedies encountered or personal concerns have you on a night shift you didn't apply for.

There's someone else who works the night shift. His name is God. Have you ever thought about God working the late shift? While you're working nights, sleeping, or wrestling with lack of sleep, God is busy. He's ever-present and caring about you at all times. The psalmist's words can bring you comfort: "He will not let your foot slip—he who watches over you will not slumber" (Psalm 121:3).

5

The Psalms contain other guidelines and promises that speak about sleep and rest. They share that God sustains you when you sleep and he makes you "dwell in safety" (Psalms 3:5; 4:8).

Regardless of the cause of your night shift, God's at work. He's thinking about you. If you wonder where God is, he is here, always. He is aware of your circumstances and pain and monitors every second of your life. God is aware of your emptiness and seeks to fill it in a manner beyond your dreams. God is aware of your wounds and scars and knows how to bring about a healing deeper than you can imagine. God is aware of destruction and tragedy you may experience and is available to bring you healing and peace. Yes, God works the night shift.

> "How precious are your thoughts about me, O God! They are innumerable! I can't even count them; they outnumber the grains of sand! And when I wake up in the morning, you are still with me!"
> (Psalm 139:17, 18 NLT)

Prayer:
When the night shift keeps me wide awake, thank you, Lord, for always being there with me. Thank you that you are ever-present and that you care about my every circumstance, wound, scar, pain, and need.

JANUARY 5

Dwayne Clemmons, Adjunct Instructor – Virginia Department of Fire Programs; Founder – DMC Ministries; Author of Exploits, Jesus Rides in an Ambulance, and Utterances from the Throne Room; Volunteer in Fire and EMS for forty years in Virginia

GOD, OUR SENIOR PARTNER
Accomplishing great and mighty things

EVERY JANUARY there's a significant increase in gym memberships, weight-loss programs, and the purchase of exercise equipment. First responders frequently seek additional training to improve skills, increase opportunities for promotion, and make life changes. The beginning of a new year seems to present an excellent opportunity to achieve goals.

However, a bizarre thing happens in a large majority of cases. Those who spend hours deliberating on what to do, strategizing on how to do it, and many dollars in practical application either stop, postpone, or completely fail in achieving the desired results.

Is it because they didn't really intend to accomplish their goals? Could it be they didn't do enough research? Or, is it something even more common to man?

The answer lies, as always, in the Word of God. Matthew 26:41 says, "The spirit is willing, but the body is weak." We indeed have good intentions but often are overwhelmed by circumstances.

An old man once told me, "Yesterday is gone and tomorrow is only a promissory note. The only thing we have is today. We must release our past, forgive ourselves, and move on if we are to accomplish the plans and purposes God has for our life."

Paul, in Philippians 3:12–21, exhorts us to forget about what's behind us and look to what's ahead. Using himself as an example, Paul says he presses on toward the goal of heaven and Christ.

In Proverbs 3:5, 6, we're directed to submit all our thoughts, ideas, and plans to God. He's our senior partner. He's ready to guide, direct, and help us. When we trust

> "Trust in the Lord with all your heart and lean not on your own understanding; in all your ways acknowledge him, and he will make your paths straight." (Proverbs 3:5, 6)

and lean on him, he directs our paths. Success in attaining godly goals rests in this trust.

God ordered his angels to guard us wherever we go. If we stumble, they'll catch us; their job is to keep us from falling. We'll walk unharmed among lions and snakes, and kick young lions and serpents from the path. He will give us the best of care, but we must trust and lean on him.

Get over the past, focus on today, seek his face, pray, strive toward his calling, and you and God will accomplish great and mighty things in the year to come, and beyond.

Prayer:
Lord, as the New Year unfolds, I willingly trust and lean on you.
With you, I can achieve new goals and godly results.

Fire Chaplain John Kalashian, Caledonia, Wisconsin;
Founder/Director – Men with a Burden, a ministry to
the homeless men at the Milwaukee Rescue Mission;
Founder/President – Corvettes for Christ

ANNOYING NUISANCES

Reminders of another rescue call
almost two thousand years ago

THE ALARM came in. Without hesitation, lights flashed and siren wailed, and I was en route, courtesy of Caledonia Fire Department, to a fire. Enthralled as a six-year-old, I experienced my first ride in an emergency vehicle. My heart raced as the firefighter expertly maneuvered our truck. The surrounding cars created an annoying nuisance as they threatened our speedy arrival. The urge to accelerate was tempered by the existence of road hazards, intersections, pedestrians, and vehicles.

I began to prioritize the rescue response. *How fast can we get there? What will we find? How big is the fire? Will anyone need to be rescued? What should be done first?* Time spent in transit to a rescue call is oftentimes wisely spent planning our steps.

I'm reminded of another rescue call that occurred more than two thousand years ago. This rescue call was meticulously planned and put into action by God the Father and his Son, Jesus Christ. Just as firefighters willingly put their lives on the line when answering a call, Christ voluntarily sacrificed his life on the cross when he answered the alarm to save us from our sin.

> "Jesus answered, 'I am the way and the truth and the life. No one comes to the Father except through me.'" (John 14:6)

The Bible tells us, "For God so loved the world that he gave his one and only Son, that whoever believes in him shall not perish but have eternal life" (John 3:16).

Likewise—like those annoying nuisances of traffic and cars that can prevent or delay a firefighter's successful rescue—Satan enjoys placing obstacles in our lives to prevent or at least delay us from reaching the saving, outstretched arms of Jesus Christ. It's true we're all sinners: "For all have sinned and fall short of the glory of God" (Romans 3:23). The world we live in is full of additional hazards such as sexual immorality, alcoholism, self-righteousness, and pride. Often we try to find our own "fixes" to the obstacles in our lives, but God wants us to know he is "the

8

way and the truth and the life" (John 14:6). He promises to rescue us from our sin and worldly obstacles, if only we do one thing—make that "call" to him!

Don't let any of those annoying nuisances get in the way of a successful rescue by Jesus Christ. All you have to do is "respond" to the ultimate Responder, Jesus Christ.

Prayer:
*When the thief comes to destroy and kill, when I try
to "fix" the obstacles in my life, I call on you.*

*Sue Reynolds, Missionary – Fellowship of Christian
Firefighters International (FCFI), and Chaplain Gaius
Reynolds, President – FCFI; Volunteer Firefighter –
Livermore, CO, Fire Protection District*

"KILLER B'S"
Betrayed? Bitter? Bashful? Boastful?

THE YOUNG man, just turned eighteen, anxiously waited at the station doors for the chief. "I'm ready to volunteer. You said I had to be eighteen."

He assisted on calls, never missing one regardless of the hour, until he was finally voted onto the volunteer fire department. He spent his every spare moment at the volunteer firehouse just in case a call came in. He looked up to his fellow volunteers and thrived on the attention and affirmation he received.

The year after he joined the department there was a higher volume of calls than normal, especially fire calls. He never missed a one; often being the first to respond. At the annual appreciation dinner that year he was awarded the Rookie of the Year award.

One cold winter night the pagers rang out late at night. The historic church was on fire. Relentlessly, the volunteers attacked the fire—to no avail. When the fire investigators sought a cause, arson was suspected. Sites of other recent fires were investigated, and signs of arson were then found. It wasn't long until the young man was questioned and found guilty of arson.

9

He was a loner at school, had stopped taking his meds, and was self-medicating on the adrenaline flow from fighting fires and from his new camaraderie with the community's heroes. Other signs, if a person is knowledgeable on common traits of arsonists, were easily recognizable.

A prison sentence followed and a fire department and community struggled with multiple losses. They had cared for and reached out to the young man and now felt betrayed. Some were bitter. They "what-ifed" themselves in regard to their lack of insight. Church members wondered if they were too bashful about sharing God's love, and, if they'd witnessed more, could they have helped him? Some to this day harbor an unforgiving spirit.

> "Now forgive my sin once more and pray to the LORD your God to take this deadly plague away from me." (Exodus 10:17)

A failure to forgive, commonly resulting in bitterness, will hurt you more than the person you harbor that bitterness toward. Other killer "Bs," as a former pastor shared, are feelings of betrayal, bashfulness, and boastfulness. Have you felt betrayed? Bitter? Bashful? Or even boastful about your accomplishments? If there are "Killer Bs" in your life, identify them, understand they're more harmful to you than to others, and move on to forgiveness.

Prayer:
Bring to mind, Lord, any "Killer Bs" that are acting like a deadly plague in my life, keeping me from moving on to forgiving others, as you have forgiven me, and delaying the ultimate peace you have for me.

JANUARY 8

Chaplain Gerald E. Brock, Darlington County, SC,
Fire District Station 8; "Fear Not," the Fire Dog

PRAYING AGAINST OUR ENEMIES
Enemies that hinder, damage, and try
to destroy the ministry

THE INTERNET is a key communication channel. Many Christian Web sites provide encouraging articles and suggested prayers to help encourage and strengthen our walk with the Lord. One such Web site is

called "Kingdom Praying," with a page entitled "Praying against the enemies of missionaries." Christian firefighters with a
special mission field—their departments and
the communities they serve—will face many
and varied enemies that hinder, damage, and
try to destroy the ministry. The Bible makes

> "But the Lord is faithful, and he will strengthen and protect you from the evil one."
> (2 Thessalonians 3:3)

it clear our enemies are strong and powerful, but not as strong as the God
we serve. Our key to overcoming and destroying our enemies is prayer to
our awesome, mighty, powerful, and victorious Lord.

As a chaplain with the fire service, inspired by this Web site, I wrote
this personal prayer for my ministry. I keep it with my prayer journal and
urge you to do the same.

Dear God, please protect me from:

- Fear: Your Word makes it clear that perfect love (your love)
  drives out all fear (1 John 4:18).
- Loneliness: Let me always remember that you are always with
  me—even "to the very end of the age, you are the "— "strength
  of my heart and my portion" in times of loneliness; Psalm 73:26).
- Worry: Help me realize you are everything I need now and in
  the future (Matthew 6:25–34; Philippians 4:6–9).
- Doubt: Please strengthen my faith and help me remember to
  trust you in all circumstances (Romans 10:17; 8:28).
- Discouragement: May I be filled with your hope and know
  your joy and peace as I trust in you, and then may that hope
  overflow from me (Romans 15:13).
- Misunderstandings: May I always speak God's truth in love so
  that in all things others will understand and grow in "him who
  is the Head, that is, Christ" (Ephesians 4:15).
- Hopelessness: You are the God of all comfort. May I rest in
  your comfort when things seem hopeless, and then comfort
  others with that same comfort (2 Corinthians 1:3, 4).
- Persecution: I know that "everyone who wants to live a godly
  life in Christ Jesus will be persecuted," so I seek your comfort
  and protection from anyone who tries to stop me from spread-
  ing the Gospel (2 Timothy 3:12).

Prayer:
*Lord, I know the Enemy will try to keep me from sharing your
love and promises. I ask you for your continued protection
from each and every dart the Enemy hurls my way.*

Reverend Wayne Detzler, PhD, Chaplain (Retired) –
Charlotte, NC, Fire Department; Fellowship of
Christian Firefighters Regional Director

AMAZING GRACE IN DARK DAYS
When darkness is deepest

IT'S MY SON." The captain was desperate. "My son has fallen from a balcony, and he is so badly injured. He has severe head trauma." I went to be with the captain. Together we waited for feedback from the doctors. He had fallen on his head. The news was serious at best, fatal at worst.

For many days we got bits and pieces of information. A cluster of firefighters huddled outside the intensive care unit waiting to hear. None of it sounded good. We prayed with the captain for his son. Hope was dim, as dim as the darkness around us all. It appeared as if the young man would never be the same again.

"Keep praying," the captain urged me. "Don't give up." The captain welcomed our prayer and our companionship during these crisis days. We grew closer to him as he grew closer to the Lord. For him this was a "teachable moment," a time when he was open to the Lord as never before.

Weeks of rehab followed for his son. It all seemed so hopeless. But the young man did work his way back to mobility and to some degree of mental recovery. Somehow, afterward we lost touch, never seeing each other for several months. Due to the large size of the fire department, my path did not cross the captain's.

On another level, I had contact with the captain's ex-wife, the mother of his injured son. She was a firm believer who'd learned to lean on the Lord through the struggles of her life.

> "My grace is sufficient for you, for my power is made perfect in weakness."
> (2 Corinthians 12:9)

Then came the shock. We visited our former church and, to my utter amazement, there sat the injured son. This young man was sitting with his mother in services. He was speaking again and he was open to the Lord.

How did God work? Let's count the ways: The Lord reached our captain and caused him to pray. The Lord worked healing in the young man's body. Also, God opened the young man's heart to God's Word.

Finally, the Lord brought mother and son back together in the house of God. God used this tragedy for good and once again showed how sufficient his grace is.

Prayer:
Lord, help me to trust you, even in dark nights of the soul.

Chaplain Robert Osbourn, Sylacauaga, AL, Fire Department

FACING YOUR FEAR
Make this a year of prayer

MOTIVATED BY the serious bouts of anxiety experienced by one of my loved ones, I conducted research and discovered anxiety is America's number 1 mental health problem, and it's on the rise. According to the National Institute of Mental Health, each year, anxiety affects at least nineteen million, or 13 percent of all people ages eighteen to fifty-four. In addition, it impacts thirteen million youngsters ages nine to seventeen. The World Health Organization states that the odds of developing an anxiety disorder have doubled in the past four decades.

Has anyone at your station said, "I've been experiencing weird sensations" or, "I felt sure I was dying"? Have you noticed crew members with fainting spells, shaking hands, or excessive fears?

Emergency service careers are packed with demands and situations most people don't experience, much less on a regular basis. Stress, anxiety, frustration aren't foreign to first responders.

I enjoy and research many other subjects. In all my research, I've yet to find anything about anxiety being due to the lack of prayer. But is it?

Prayer has been removed from many vital functions in America. Politicians, afraid of prayer, removed it from the schools and public forums. Jesus' name isn't looked at the same as it was a hundred years ago. The Ten Commandments were removed from American courthouses. Are you allowed to openly pray at your station?

Scripture addresses prayer repeatedly. Jesus taught his disciples to pray in Luke 11:1–13, telling them to begin by giving praise to our kind, merciful, gracious God. He said to pray for his kingdom to come (for Christ to be enthroned for his rule on Earth and in your life), pray for bread (the

13

necessities of life, body, and spirit to be fed), and pray for forgiveness and deliverance from temptation.

Jesus prayed continually. He prayed at his baptism (Luke 3:21), for deliverance from temptation (Matthew 6:13), and when alone (Luke 5:16, 9:18, and Mark 1:35), and he spent an entire night in prayer (Luke 6:12). He said and demonstrated that prayer is the source of strength and the avenue to an intimate relationship with God.

> "Do not be anxious about anything, but in everything, by prayer and petition, with thanksgiving, present your requests to God."
> (Philippians 4:6)

The Bible says, "When you pray," not "*If* you pray." Sounds almost like a commandment to me.

In researching prayer in the Bible, I found the search extensive. I urge you to do some research on your own and as you do, be sure to make this a year of prayer. Especially when anxiety rears its ugly head—try prayer.

Prayer:
Lord, thank you for this intimate avenue of communication we have with you.

Captain Raul A. Angulo, Seattle Fire Department;
Fellowship of Christian Firefighters Regional Director /
International Board Member

RAGS
The junk we carry around with us

I'VE NEVER forgotten an analogy from Corrie ten Boom regarding rags. She said rags are pieces of junk we carry around in our lives that prevent our lights from shining brightly.

Such rags can take the form of hurt, anger, jealousy, bitterness, lack of forgiveness, fear, or unconfessed sin.

Firefighters carry flashlights for multiple reasons. But, if their flashlight takes four D-cell batteries, the batteries won't fit if rags are taking up space. The rags are an obstacle to the power source, and the bulb won't illuminate.

14

Some Christian firefighters make me wonder if they even have a bulb. A few seem to have dead batteries. Others have become silenced and paralyzed with the fear of being politically incorrect. They take Hebrews 12:14, "Make every effort to live in peace with all men and to be holy; without holiness no one will see the Lord," to mean, don't be confrontational or argumentative in the workplace; if being holy is how you want to live, do it quietly.

> "Peter and the other apostles replied: 'We must obey God rather than men!'" (Acts 5:29)

Jesus revealed that his lordship often results in conflict. "Do you think I came to bring peace on earth? No, I tell you, but division" (Luke 12:51). Close relationships may be torn apart when one chooses to follow Jesus and others refuse. There's no middle ground. Loyalties must be declared and commitments made, sometimes to the point of severing close relationships. Are you willing to risk your family's and friends' approval in order to gain eternal life?

On the job, your decision to be the light is going to ruffle feathers, and you run the risk of facing consequences. Worst-case scenario—you could get fired. As much as "tolerance" is preached in this politically correct society, if you choose to remove the rags and let your light shine brightly, you'll quickly realize it doesn't apply to you, a Christian.

In Acts 5:29, when the Sanhedrin tried to silence Peter for preaching the Gospel, Peter's response was, "We must obey God rather than men!" Furious, the Sanhedrin wanted to put Peter to death. Peter was eventually crucified in Rome; however, because he did not feel worthy to die in the same manner as his Lord Jesus, the Romans honored his request to be crucified upside down.

It takes courage to shine bright in a dark world. If your light is dim, get rid of the rags.

Prayer:
Lord, I turn my rags over to you. Help me to stand brightly and not let "political correctness" keep me from being a witness to your love and truth.

Reverend Wayne Detzler, PhD, Chaplain (Retired) –
Charlotte, NC, Fire Department; Fellowship of
Christian Firefighters Regional Director

WHEN THE PLANE CRASHED
All those lonely people

ALL THE lonely people, where do they all come from?" These words from the old Beatles song "Eleanor Rigby" have haunted my life and my ministry. The words surged through my mind on a chilly January day at Charlotte Douglas Airport. Never had I witnessed so much devastation, so much death. The silence seemed deafening.

A commuter plane was cleared for takeoff. It roared down the runway and lifted into a clear, blue sky. It should have turned south for the short hop to Greenville, South Carolina. Instead of climbing on course, the plane rolled. Desperate faces of young and old alike peered out the windows as the turboprop plane dove into the concrete of the airport. A horrendous crash turned to deathly silence.

All twenty-one people on board were dead. Some bodies were strewn across the small disaster scene. Most of them were trapped in the burned-out body of the aircraft, piled up in a heap, torn, twisted, and broken. Anxiously, I stood by until the FBI chaplain paged me to the scene.

For three days firefighters combed through the wreckage gently lifting the broken bodies. The FBI chaplain and I stood in silence observing the gruesome drama before us. Initial evidence and identification information were carefully preserved. One by one, the mutilated forms of passengers and crew were silently carried to a decontamination tent. Agony weighed down our hearts and minds, like the gloom of a thousand winters.

> "Even the very hairs of your head are all numbered." (Matthew 10:30)

One by one we debriefed the fire units as they left the scene. We assured them their reaction was normal even though the situation was abnormal. Later we visited all the involved fire stations to check how they were doing. One captain stands out in my mind. "I'm done," the captain said. "This is my third plane crash during my career. I can't stand another one."

When nameless people suffer, we are almost numb. We cannot take in the pain and tears. It's so good to know that God knows each one by name. In the face of horror and death it's comforting to know that the Lord is still in control.

J A N U A R Y   1 3

William Garvey, Writer/Photographer; Damage
Prevention Supervisor for a gas company in Michigan

THE LONGEST YEAR
This is it! I thought

MY LONGEST year as a gas company supervisor started with a gas leak resulting in a death. Emotions ran rampant and questions flooded my mind: "Did we do everything right?" "What else could we have done?" "What caused this leak?" The following fall we finally discovered that the fire was caused by damage to an old gas line.

In the summer of that year we received a call from 9-1-1—a call requiring the cooperation of fire and gas company crews. A local business was on fire and there was a strong smell of gas in the area. When we arrived, we cut the electric wires and shut the gas off to the building. A firefighter informed us a house around the block was on fire. We began a search for gas leaks and every home we checked was full of gas. In the next ten minutes we cut the power and turned off the gas to ten homes. As we worked I prayed, "Lord, give me strength."

When a young girl approached and asked if we could get her wheelchair-bound grandpa out of his house, we went into rescue mode. Inside the home, packed with people, gas smells permeated the air. "Get out!" I shouted. "Now!" Then I grabbed the man in the wheelchair and went out through the garage. As we cleared the home, I heard a loud boom and was thrown against the wall of the home.

This is it! I thought. But God wasn't ready to take us home yet. Then another house exploded. Again, praise God, no one was hurt.

Down the road I saw my boss. He was followed by an electric crew. They'd shut off the gas and electric to all the homes in the area.

This extensive gas leak was caused by a directional boring crew, who'd hit our gas main, along with the underground sewer line, causing gas to come up through people's toilets and drains.

17

As the firefighters finished their search, the word came that all was safe. We ended up losing three houses and a business, but by working side-by-side with firefighters everyone went home safe. Without our combined training and skill coupled with God's strength, the outcome could easily have included many fatalities.

> "The Lord gives strength to his people; the LORD blesses his people with peace." (Psalms 29:11)

Prayer:
I thank you, God, for your help and for our safety. Thank you for peace you give me as I continue to do the best job I can in difficult situations.

JANUARY 14

Frank C. Schaper, Deputy Fire Chief (Retired) –
St. Louis Fire Department; Chief (Retired) – St. Charles, MO;
Training Officer – Smeal Fire Apparatus

COME TO THE LIGHT
He's waiting

DIRTY AND tired from a first-alarm house fire, our busy hook-and-ladder company's return to quarters was postponed by a second alarm. In short order, we were in front of a boarded up two-story flat. The fire appeared to be on the first floor. We had no water, so decided to keep the building tight until an engine company arrived. A lady's screaming quickly changed that plan: "Someone's trapped in the building."

My captain ordered a ladder to the second-floor window. One crew member climbed to the window and pried off the plywood. My partner and I climbed the ladder and made our way over the windowsill. Fire reached from the baseboard to the ceiling. After finding the first room empty of furniture and victims, we made our way to a hall to check the rest of the second floor. As we worked our way down the hot, black hallway, we heard the trapped man yelling. My partner turned to check a room on the right. I moved farther down the hall. The yelling got louder. "Oh, God help me," the man yelled.

I felt along the wall, crawling low until I located a door opening and heard the distraught man. Kneeling at the door with my large hand light, I yelled, "Come to my light. Come to my light."

18

From out of the darkness, the man leaped on me, knocking off my helmet and sending my ax flying. I held tightly to my light, pulled the man to the floor hoping for air, and dragged him down the hall. Our low-air alarms were ringing loudly as we found the stairs and made our exit. The man suffered burns and smoke inhalation, but we saved his life.

Like that man, I was once lost in the darkness. Career, marriage, and even church didn't fill my void until I came "to the light." Since coming to the light my life has not been the same. I'm not perfect. I still sin. But now I have Christ in my heart, and I know my salvation is secured through him. I know what my life was like before I asked Christ into my heart, and I am not going back there. I know when I fall short, he is there to drag me down the hall to the light.

> "Here I am! I stand at the door and knock." (Revelation 3:20)

Prayer:

Christ, thank you for standing at the door of my heart.
I hear you knocking and my heart is open to you. When I fall short,
thank you for your steady light guiding me back to you.

J A N U A R Y   1 5

Craig Duck, Lieutenant, Engine Co. 11 – Washington, DC, Fire Department; Fellowship of Christian Firefighters International Atlantic States Regional Director / International Board Member

WHO IS YOUR NEIGHBOR?

Treating all firefighters with respect and dignity—
Willing to give honor to who honor is due

THE FIRE service has our legends, great companies, and favored departments, but to say we've treated all people equally and with dignity and respect, unfortunately, isn't true.

Martin Luther King Jr. said, "I have a dream that one day this nation will rise up and live out the true meaning of its creed: 'We hold these truths to be self-evident: that all men are created equal,' . . . I have a dream that one day every valley shall be exalted . . . the rough places will be made plain . . . and the glory of the Lord shall be revealed, and all flesh shall see it together." I wonder if he realized the struggles of black firefighters in the very city he was making the speech in, Washington, DC. At the time King made his speech, black firefighters worked in segregated firehouses with outdated or no equipment at all. When detailed to white firehouses, they were limited to certain areas of the firehouse, and their plates were thrown away after they were used.

As a rookie in 1986, I still felt the tension among different groups at various firehouses. This treatment, however, was not limited to the District of Columbia.

Segregated and unequal treatment practices have been changing. The fire service has become better at treating everyone equally. The Bible addresses treating everyone without partiality. In Leviticus we learn, "Do not . . . bear a grudge against one of your people, but love your neighbor as yourself" (Leviticus 19:18). Making the concerns of others our own is what this verse is calling us to do. Our neighbor isn't just the person next door, but all people. To truly love our neighbor, we are to make the persecutions, sufferings, and injustices of others our own and treat every person we come in contact with as we would treat ourselves. As Christians, it's our duty.

> "Do not seek revenge or bear a grudge against one of your people, but love your neighbor as yourself. I am the Lord." (Leviticus 19:18)

Can you imagine what the fire service would look like if we all treated everyone the way Jesus instructed us to? Then Martin Luther King's dream would truly become a reality, and every fire department would be treating everyone with love and compassion.

On this, Martin Luther King's birthday, let us resolve to treat our neighbors the way Jesus wants us to.

Prayer:
Help me, Lord, to consider all firefighters my neighbor and treat them the way that you would have me treat them.

Susan Ortega, Widow of Fallen Firefighter Robert M. Ortega, Los Angeles City Fire Department

MEASURE OF A REAL HERO
How you live

APRIL 8TH ordinarily would have stood out as a spectacular day under any other circumstances. It was bright with the sun and its accompanying cotton clouds and the scent of that springtime hope we all love. My best friend, Carla, and one of her sons joined my kids and me for the day. We were on our way to the funeral home to take care of those details that need to be taken care of after someone dies. It was my husband, Bob. He had died the day before—when it wasn't so sunny.

On the way, I told my kids that on the day Dad died an American flag was lowered to half-staff at his last station to honor him. On the way home, my youngest son, Ben, age thirteen, asked me, "Momma, how many people know about Dad?"

"Well," I said, "a lot of people, why?"

"Because all the flags I see are at half-staff."

It dawned on me that the Pope recently passed away and it was true—all flags had been lowered. It made perfect sense to my son, as it did to us all, that every flag on the planet should bow in honor of Bob Ortega.

> "I THEREFORE, the prisoner for the Lord, appeal to and beg you to walk (lead a life) worthy of the [divine] calling to which you have been called [with behavior that is a credit to the summons to God's service]." (Ephesians 4:1 AMP)

We all felt that way. Not just because one is automatically a hero if he's a firefighter, or because his death was duty-related and considered heroic, but because of how he lived.

My husband walked steadfastly and imperfectly every day with his Lord. He was kind and gracious at the station, in our community, at church, and at home. He was meek and unassuming, and he put us first. He refused to be promoted because the copious amounts of studying required would have taken him away from home more than he wanted to be during those critical, irretrievable years of child-rearing.

In hindsight, what a legacy! How my kids and I are treated now in many ways is a direct result of how Bob lived his life, because that is the measure of a real hero—how he lived.

Prayer:
May I be a real hero in the eyes of those you place in my life,
Lord, not because of my career but due to the way I lead my life.

JANUARY 17

Reverend Wayne Detzler, PhD, Chaplain (Retired) –
Charlotte, NC, Fire Department; Fellowship of
Christian Firefighters Regional Director

WE ARE THE CHURCH
When the building burned

"LAWYERS ROAD Baptist Church is on fire." The dispatcher got my attention. "Respond immediately, chaplain. We may have firefighters down!" I was immediately in the car on my way to the fire scene.

"Chaplain, it's serious," the battalion chief greeted me. "I almost lost my whole crew." He explained that his crew had been caught in a back-draft, and it almost incinerated the firefighters inside the church. The chief was still visibly shaken by this near miss.

"Look at that front window," the chief continued. "It looks like a massive cannon ball shot right through it. That's the result of the backdraft. He led me back into the smoldering fire scene. My heart was wrenched as I surveyed the once-lovely worship center, now just a pile of smoking rubble. The pulpit was gone. The choir loft stood in charred silence—no music in this one. Pews where people worshipped the Lord were now just stinking coals.

> "You yourselves are God's temple, and . . . God's Spirit lives in you."
> (1 Corinthians 3:16)

"How are you doing, Chief?" I sought to assess his mental state.

"I'm stunned," the chief replied. "As a Christian, this one has really hit me hard. It could have been my home church." Then he added, "There's a little cluster of church members outside. Please go and see how they are."

Praying as I went, I crossed the little lawn to speak with my shocked brothers and sisters. "Have you reached the pastor?" I asked them. They replied that he was on his way, returning from a conference in a distant city.

"But how are you all doing?" I asked the patient, strangely calm Christians as they stared at the burned-out shell of their beloved church. Their worship would never be the same again.

"Oh, we're fine, Chaplain," they amazed me. They pointed to the fire scene. "You see, that's not our church. *We* are the church!"

With tears in my eyes I prayed with them and thanked the Lord for their safety.

Less than a year later we gathered for a Sunday morning service. It was a celebration of the new church, raised from the ashes. It reminds me of the powerful assertion by Jesus, "I will build my church, and the gates of Hades will not overcome it" (Matthew 16:18). Ours is a sinful and a dangerous world, and Satan strikes repeatedly at the church, but victory is assured by the very words of our Lord Jesus Christ.

Prayer:
Lord, thank you for making people your
living church, priests of our God.

Craig Duck, Lieutenant, Engine Co. 11 – Washington, DC, Fire Department; Fellowship of Christian Firefighters International Atlantic States Regional Director / International Board Member

FIREFIGHTER REVIEW
"Well done," not "You're done"

FOR MOST fire departments, January is that time of year when officers fill out evaluations for the firefighters who serve under them. For firefighters, evaluations can be a stressful time. *What does my officer think of me? What are my shortcomings? Have I done anything wrong this year?* These are all common thoughts that go through firefighters' minds when they see the officer typing the evaluation forms. No matter what firefighters tell you, evaluations are important to them. For some fire departments, evaluations are used for promotions, pay raises, and even terminations. In addition those evaluated want to know that their officer appreciates them and thinks they're doing a good job. Everyone wants to know they're considered worthy or valued. All firefighters want to hear, "Well done," not "You're done!"

As important as these evaluations are to the success of fire departments, the Bible speaks of another, far more important evaluation that is

23

coming. At the end of our lives, we will be evaluated. This evaluation will take place when we all must stand before the Lord. This led Paul to write, "For we must all appear before the judgment seat of Christ, that each one may receive the things done in the body, according to what he has done, whether good or bad" (2 Corinthians 5:10). As Christian firefighters, believers in Jesus Christ, we will not have to approach this evaluation fearfully or with a sense of the possibility of losing our salvation. Instead we will be eager to stand before our Lord and hear "Well done, good and faithful servant . . . Enter into the joy of the lord" (Matthew 25:21 NKJV).

> "For we must all appear before the judgment seat of Christ, that each one may receive the things *done* in the body, according to what he has done, whether good or bad."
> (2 Corinthians 5:10 NKJV)

The challenge for Christians is to live our lives in service to Jesus with excellence and for his glory. We should not be tempted to be dragged down into the miry pit of backtalking, filthy language, drunkenness, laziness, or any other habit that causes us to fall short of the glory of God. Our role should be to point others to God. We need to be an example of what followers of Jesus should be according to the Bible. If we are faithful to God, then our evaluations will not only change with our work supervisors, but more importantly with our Lord.

Prayer:
Help me, Lord, to understand that as a Christian firefighter I need to live my life in light of eternity. When my life is over and I stand before our Judge, God's Son, I want to hear, "Well done, my child, well done."

JANUARY 19

Gabe Heatherly, EMT Monticello Volunteer Fire Department, KY; Teacher State Fire Marshal Office; President Lake Cumberland Chapter Fellowship of Christian Firefighters International

NOT A LOT OF PIZZAZZ

But zealous about bringing Christ to the lost

MY STORY isn't one with a lot of pizzazz, yet I praise God. Through his grace he allowed me to stay in this world long enough to return to him. He didn't have to, but he did.

In Acts, chapter 5, Ananias and Sapphira were struck dead for deceitfully keeping money they claimed they were giving to the Lord. How many times did I neglect to give God what was his? In 2 Samuel 6:3–8, Uzzah had the best intentions when he touched the Ark of the Covenant to prevent it from falling, but God had commanded that only the Levites touch the Ark. Consequently, Uzzah was struck dead. How many times did I fail in following God's commandments?

> "Like Moses, let us proclaim our Lord." (Deuteronomy 32:3–4)

I grew up believing there was a God and knowing about Jesus, but I wasn't a Christian. When nineteen, I saw smoke blowing across a rural Alabama road, stopped, assisted, and was asked by the attending firefighter if I was interested in volunteering. I was unaware God was putting me on the path of a true calling for him and service to my community.

God used the fire service to bring me to him by placing me with a Christian firefighter not afraid to share his faith. Through him, I came to understand that while I'm not worthy of God's love and salvation, it's a free gift through faith and a personal relationship with him. Previously, I wanted to use my good deeds to take the place of submission and discipleship to God. Over time, God transformed me inside and out. I learned that even though I followed the rules, helped when I could, and treated others how I wanted to be treated, by God's standards I was unclean and repulsive. It's only by his grace, redeeming love, and sacrifice of his Son on the cross that I've been made clean.

Sharing my faith was terrifying at first, even though I'd formerly spoken in front of thousands. As a Christian firefighter I'm aware of the awesome avenue first responders have for taking God's Word to the lost and dying. With God's grace and Holy Spirit we can all be as zealous about bringing the lost to him as we are about saving someone's child from a burning house. We're all God's children and at risk of dying in the eternal flames. Like Moses, let us proclaim our Lord.

"I will proclaim the name of the LORD. Oh, praise the greatness of our God! He is the Rock, his works are perfect, and all his ways are just. A faithful God who does no wrong, upright and just is he" (Deuteronomy 32:3, 4).

Prayer:
Thank you for the awesome avenue to share your greatness with all those you bring my way. I praise you, Lord, for you are faithful, upright, and just.

Rick Barton, Fire Safety Officer; Rick Barton Ministries,
Gunnison, CO; Fellowship of Christian Firefighters
International Ambassador-at-Large

BUT I DON'T WANT TO . . . LORD

Isn't it contradictory to say, "No, Lord"?

I NOTICED HIS shirt as we waited for the plane to load. It was the T-shirt of a fire department in Colorado. I said "Hi" as we sought our seats, and then it was off to Nashville. I wondered if I should offer him

> "If you love me, you will obey what I command."
> (John 14:15)

an *Answering the Call New Testament*. And then I dismissed the thought as I took my seat and settled in for the flight.

As we deplaned, I once again saw the fireman. He was apparently on vacation; his wife and kids were with him. I wondered again, should I offer him the Bible? The answer seemed to be yes, but I was in a hurry and he seemed busy. Once again I returned to my own agenda. But I guess God had other plans because after getting about fifty feet down the concourse, the prodding came again to share the Word with him. "But Lord, I've already left him, but he'll think I'm strange, but, but, but . . ." I was becoming a "motor boat Christian."

I turned around and went back; he looked surprised and then pleased as I offered him the *Answering the Call*. His young son grabbed it and excitedly began scanning the pages. "Thank you!" the firefighter said as I headed for the baggage claim and rental car.

I'm not sure how God will use his Word in this fireman's family. I do know he said his Word will not come back void. I also know he used the whole situation to teach me obedience.

Sometimes God speaks in a loud and clear voice. Other times it may be a gentle whisper. Maybe it's just an uneasy feeling you get when a thought crosses your mind: *Maybe I should share the Lord.* Then you ignore it because of *your* agenda. But, when you stop and think about it, and what his Word instructs us to do, isn't it contradictory to say, "No, Lord"?

God clearly instructs us to go and preach to all nations and to keep his commandments.

Prayer:
How blessed I am to have your Word and the freedom to share it freely!
As I listen to your prodding, be they gentle whispers or a loud, clear
command, may I be obedient and respond Code 3.

26

Aaron Johnson, Fire Inspector – Martin County, FL

FAN INTO FLAME
Applying the oxygen of God's Word

OXYGEN, COMBINED with heat and fuel, is one of the main requirements for fire. If a small fire begins to smolder in an enclosed space (a closed-up room, aircraft cockpit, etc.) it will smolder for a while and then, when all the oxygen is burned up, the fire will be extinguished. However, if, during the smoldering phase, additional oxygen is introduced to the fire, for instance if a door or window is opened, the fire grows rapidly.

A danger for firefighters that immediately confronts us when we arrive on scene is lack of knowledge about the fire in front of us. We often don't know how long a fire has been burning. Consequently, as we make our initial entry we must be careful. If oxygen is introduced to an almost oxygen-depleted fire, an explosive backdraft could

> "Therefore, I remind you to keep ablaze the gift of God that is in you through the laying on of my hands."
> (2 Timothy 1:6 HCSB)

result (as demonstrated in the movie of the same name). For a firefighter entering a burning structure, oxygen can be a negative and dangerous additive.

But what about the Christian's walk with God? How are we to introduce "oxygen" to the fire that God has placed within us?

We all have God-given abilities and purpose. However, if we do not work on these, enhancing our gifts, skills, and aptitude, and furthering God's purpose in our lives, the smoldering fire within us will die, and we'll live a non-fruit-bearing life.

If God gave you a musical talent, you must use it. Study music, listen to music, read about music, play music, sing music—do music. If you don't, the music God placed within you will die.

If God gave you the gift of preaching and/or teaching, you must utilize it. Preach, teach, learn the art of public speaking, read about preaching and teaching, and increase your knowledge of the material to be preached (God's Word).

Oftentimes people come to Christ, but there is no growth or consistent walk with the Lord. What all too frequently happens is they have insufficient amounts of oxygen to fan their flame of salvation. New Christians need to be surrounded with other Christians, they need to be led to

Christian resources, and they need to spend considerable amounts of time with God in his Word, in prayer, and in Christian fellowship.

Prayer:

Dear God, may I constantly be applying the oxygen of your Word to the flame of salvation within me. May I be a godly oxygen supply for those who need encouragement in their walk with you.

J A N U A R Y   2 2

Chaplain Russell Stammer, Firefighter — Oakland, NJ, Fire Department; Fellowship of Christian Firefighters International Regional Director / International Board Member

ANSWERING THE CALL

As firefighters, we answer the call every day without a second thought

SEVERAL YEARS ago there was a recruitment campaign designed to recruit volunteer firefighters. The campaign used the slogan, "What if no one answered the call?" This campaign was designed to get people to volunteer their time by joining their local volunteer fire department, not leave it up to someone else.

I've been a volunteer firefighter for many years now and I've seen towns with full rosters of firefighters and other towns who can't get anyone to sign up.

As a child, my parents had a house fire and we were all amazed at how professional the volunteer firefighters were and how they took care of the situation quickly with little damage to our house. That experience stayed with me through the years. I couldn't imagine what would have happened had no one answered that call for help and we lost our home because of it.

In Matthew 28 we see that there is another call for help, a call repeated in Mark 16:15. This call comes from Jesus and he is telling us what we need to do. As Christians it's our responsibility to serve our Lord and Savior because of all he's done for us. It's not a deed to earn salvation, but one to bear fruit. Just like in the recruitment campaign, we need to be concerned about, "What if no one answers this call?" What if no one goes out to make disciples of all nations? We need to look at our fire-

28

house and those we serve as the nations mentioned in Matthew. In our service we should be the light in our firehouses and an example of the love Jesus has shown us.

> "He said to them, 'Go into all the world and preach the good news to all creation.
> (Mark 16:15)

Too many people believe that missions require us to go overseas, but that is not true. We have a great mission field right here. Will you answer the call to serve your community? Will you answer the call to serve our Lord as diligently as you serve others?

Prayer:
Lord, please make me a light to our fellow firefighters.
May I be an example of your love and may I boldly share
my faith with those in the firefighting family, those I serve
in my community, and most of all you, Lord.

JANUARY 23

Steve Kidd, Firefighter, Orange County Fire Rescue, Florida; Central Florida Chapter of the Fellowship of Christian Firefighters; Author of the Carbusters video series

NO MATTER WHAT— GOD CAN RESCUE US!

This is not an old-fashioned belief that died with the Israelites in exile

LOST IN THE desert, hungry and thirsty, lives ebbing away, sitting in darkness, the deepest of gloom, suffering in iron chains, rebellion, afflictions; all these perils are addressed in Psalm 107. The good news is— God stepped in to help. No matter what it is that distressed God's people then or distresses them now, with God's help you can get through it. It can be hard to remember God's love and compassion when being tested by fire, but his Word assures, "He delivered them from their distress" (Psalm 107:6) and he will do the same for you.

First responders understand perils; many have been on a call where they witnessed devastation similar to that described in Psalm 107, or know someone who has.

29

No matter what emergency situation we face, with lights flashing and sirens blaring, we rush to the scene. As firefighters, we step into harm's way frequently, taking calculated risks that test the limits of our training and

> "And he delivered them from their distress." (Psalm 107:6)

endurance so we can save lives and protect property from harm.

But who is looking after the firefighter, whose private life may be full of concerns and burdens as well, all that time? The sickness of a family member, children who are running down the wrong path in life, money problems, marital disharmony, and even simple problems such as heavy traffic and busy work schedules. These type of burdens heap large amounts of stress on one's heart and mind.

The fact that the Lord lifted the Israelites from their distress is not an old-fashioned belief that died with the Israelites in exile. The description of lost and downtrodden people symbolizes those who have not found the satisfaction that comes from knowing God and inviting Christ into their daily life. Once you recognize how lost you are or were without Jesus, you can receive his offer to satisfy your needs.

The answer to "Who is looking after us?" is clearly answered in the Bible over and over. God, of course! He is with us always.

Is something troubling you today? If so, pray "A Firefighter's Prayer for Intervention" below and insert what is burdening you in the blank space.

A Firefighter's Prayer for Intervention
O heavenly and gracious God, I'm thankful for your presence.
The things that burden my heart today are
_____. I turn these problems
over to you, O Lord, and accept your will, because I know
it comes from your love. For with you, all is possible, and with
you, I can handle anything that comes my way.

Stepping Into Harms Way (Courtesy of Robert M. Winston, Boston, MA)

Doug Carbol Jr., Air Sea Rescue Member, 26 years; Deputy District Chief Aide / Firefighter – Chicago Fire Department

WE'RE THERE WHEN YOU NEED US!

When we think we are alone, God is there

ALONE, ENTANGLED, low on air, and lost in a trench with zero visibility while doing a dive in the flooded lower level of the Chicago Filtration Plant, I wondered if I'd come out alive. Another time, I was a crew member of a helicopter that spiraled into Lake Michigan during a heavy windstorm. On a different dive, I pulled a fellow diver from the bottom of the lake. Then there was the time I responded to a crash that took the life of one from my firehouse. Each time, close to death, my life was spared.

> "A man of many companions may come to ruin, but there is a friend who sticks closer than a brother." (Proverbs 18:24)

It was my desire to work in this profession long before I entered the department officially. In my teens, I helped recover three drowning victims with my dad, a member of the Chicago Fire Department's Scuba Team. I watched my Dad and other firefighters help others, be it at a fire or a drowning in Lake Michigan. I wanted to be a rescuer, a helper, a Chicago firefighter.

I'm blessed to be among a group of first responders willing to help, whether it's shoveling the snow for a fallen friend's widow, freely opening their wallets for worthy causes, sharing holiday meals with soldiers, or the ultimate sacrifice of risking, and some giving, their life for a stranger. That's our motto: "We're there when you need us."

You, too, have no doubt faced a time when you had to stand alone. It may have been during sickness, marital problems, the death of a child, financial troubles, or facing retirement. During these times you may have a tendency to shut others out or keep issues hidden deep in your soul. "What would people think if they knew I was dealing with this or had allowed myself to get into this mess?"

There is Someone who knows these things and still is closer than a brother. He promises to never leave or abandon you. That person is Jesus Christ. He desires a personal relationship with you. He doesn't promise you'll never have problems, but he does promise to stick closer than a brother and walk with you through them.

Being better leaders, employees, spouses, and parents, are admirable goals, but you will still face hard times. Unless you have a personal relationship with Jesus Christ, you'll feel as if you're standing alone. With Christ you can be assured he is at your side.

Prayer:
Friends—they are a special gift from you, God. Bless my friends and thank you for being a friend who is closer than a brother.

JANUARY 25

Battalion Chief Keith Helms, Charlotte, NC, Fire Department; President Charlotte / Mecklinburg Chapter Fellowship of Christian Firefighters

A TEMPORARY ASSIGNMENT
We are not home

THE INITIAL excitement of being promoted from firefighter to captain in our Charlotte, North Carolina, department is buffered by the reality of not having a permanent assignment. For three to four years, new captains serve in a relief capacity, covering vacancies for officers on leave. They rarely work at the same station for more than four days, often working at two different stations in a twenty-four-hour tour. New captains learn they can't get too comfortable. They arrive with athletic bags filled with turnout gear, bedding items, clean uniforms, workout gear, etc. They unpack, arrange their office and bedroom, and the next morning repack everything and prepare to travel to a different station on the next scheduled day.

No matter how effective relief captains are at making a station comfortable, they're never at home. Although they have all the authority and responsibility of a permanently assigned captain, they're just there on a temporary basis. All they can do is serve in the best manner possible, knowing they'll have a home in the future.

The life of a Christian is similar. After believing in Christ as their Savior, the realization this world is still imperfect sets in. We can and should do all we can to improve this world. We should pray for the sick, help the needy, encourage others, and more. However, no matter how hard we try, we'll never be able to recreate Eden or create heaven on Earth.

Some become discouraged and take the wrong path. They place their primary focus on trying to make this world comfortable. Their prayers reflect this as they ask God to cooperate with their plans for a comfortable life now.

Others understand that true blessings and rewards, whether on Earth or in heaven, result from focusing on glorifying the Lord and increasing our intimacy with him.

The Bible refers to believers as "aliens and strangers in the world" (1 Peter 2:11; Hebrews 11:13). Like the relief captain, we're not home. This life is just a temporary assignment. But don't lose hope. Our home is in heaven. Take a look at Hebrews 11:13–16; 1 John 2:15–17; and Colossians 3:1–25 for more of what God says about our role and status here on Earth.

> "But as for me, it is good to be near God. I have made the Sovereign LORD my refuge; I will tell of all your deeds."
> (Psalm 73:28)

In Psalm 73 the psalmist acknowledges the difficulties of this world and ends with the pronouncement it's good to be near God.

Prayer:
May all I do be a reflection of my nearness to you. You are my refuge and I will tell others of all your deeds and goodness.

JANUARY 26

Captain Trevor Nelson, Safety Officer Jacksonville Fire Rescue, FL; President Jacksonville Chapter Fellowship of Christian Firefighters

GOD-GIVEN CATCH PHRASES
"HELL . . . There is a fire you cannot put out!"

I'M ASTOUNDED when people take an ordinary phrase and turn it around to help people remember something about their business, phone number, e-mail address, or themselves. I even have my own catchphrase with my phone number.

I believe some catchphrases can be God-inspired, such as those on T-shirts that say "GAP = God Answers Prayer."

While showing the movie *Fireproof* at a national fire conference, I asked God, "How do I impact people in the future when the excitement of the release of *Fireproof* is gone?" I believe he spoke to my heart, saying, "The firefighters we're trying to reach at these conferences have to realize that 'There is a fire that you cannot put out—HELL.' But they can become fireproof."

Just as in the movie, the fires of hell will always be there, but we have to be able to withstand them when they occur. The only way humans can withstand these fires is by covering ourselves with the "fire-resistant coating" provided when we become a child of God and co-heir with the King, Jesus Christ, the first and greatest "fire rescuer."

A friend reminded me when we were "God-storming" in the book of Daniel how Jesus performed the first "fire rescue" when He was walking around in the fiery furnace with the three Hebrew men who wouldn't bow to the king!

We reach out to those who are not yet "fireproof." We reach out to those who keep getting burned by those "fiery darts" because they haven't put on the whole armor of God to protect their heart from Satan's' temptations. I have come up with this catch-phrase: "HELL . . . There is a fire you cannot put out!"

> He [the king] said, "Look! I see four men walking around in the fire, unbound and unharmed, and the fourth looks like a son of the gods."
> (Daniel 3:25)

You cannot put out the fires of hell, but you can become fireproof. Not by completing the latest and greatest training, not by the protective clothes you wear, not by the number of bugles on your collar, not by your level of education . . . but only by accepting Jesus as your eternal Rescuer from the fire.

He, Jesus, did the first "fire rescue." He walked around in the fire and wasn't burned.

Prayer:
There is a fire I can't put out—the fires of hell. But I can
share with others who the first Fire Rescuer is and that you are
there for all. As I share with others about you, may
hearts be open and receptive to your truth.

Chief Lee Callahan, Burlington, MA; Fellowship of Christian Firefighters International Regional Director / International Board Member

JOURNEY OR FINAL DESTINATION

Does Miley get it right?

MANY FIREFIGHTERS desire to add more than required to their department or community, such as extra enthusiasm for the job, extra training, additional formal college education for promotion, or becoming an EMT, paramedic, or officer. Perhaps they encourage others to become firefighters, volunteer at fire department activities, or teach fire safety to children. The bottom line is that many first responders, whether paid or volunteer, are involved in a lengthy journey throughout their fire service careers.

Whatever journey you personally embark on to make yourself more valuable, it takes commitment, effort, and time.

A song, "The Climb," by teen recording star Miley Cyrus addresses challenges in life's climb, such as uphill battles, moving mountains, voices in the head, and never reaching your dream. The song lists things that metaphorically make going through life hard. After noting difficulties of life, Miley sings that it "Ain't about what's waitin' on the other side. It's about the climb."

Does Miley get it right? It's a question worth pondering. The climb, our daily Christian life, is certainly important. Local church participation and stewardship of spiritual gifts are truly important parts of our daily climb through life. Using our physical and mental abilities for God counts for something as others witness our lives. Prayer is essential to keep us from falling during the climb. Bible study, worship of our Lord, and regular sharing of our faith are other components that need to be included in our daily climb.

> "And this is the testimony: God has given us eternal life, and this life is in his Son."
> (1 John 5:11)

Again I ask, "Does Miley have it right?"

What about what's "waitin' on the other side"? For those who have put their faith in the work of Jesus Christ and have a personal relationship with him, I suggest it's *all* about what's "waitin' on the other side":

eternal life! All aspects of your daily walk mean nothing if not guaranteed by an eternity with Christ.

God's Word is clear about what's "waitin on the other side" of the mountain of life when the Christian's journey is over. There is redemption (Hebrews 9:12), salvation (Hebrews 5:9), inheritance (Hebrews. 9:15), reward (John 4:36), purpose (Ephesians 3:11), joy (Isaiah 51:11), and glory (1 Peter 5:10; 2 Timothy 2:10) . . .

Yes, the journey is important, but the destination is the most important part of the journey of life. I trust that you agree.

Prayer:
*Lord, may my journey be honoring to you. Thank you that
my destination—heaven—is "waitin'." I know it is the
most important part of the journey of life.*

JANUARY 28

*Lieutenant Danny Legge, Paramedic/Chaplain—
Clay County Fire Rescue*

START CPR
Take a daily dose of aspirin

IN OUR PROFESSION most are well aware that a physical heart attack or cardiac arrest is caused by blood clots that in turn are caused by such things as a poor diet, lack of exercise, or perhaps an inherited tendency. To decrease the chances of having a physical heart attack we can maintain a proper diet, exercise, and take an aspirin a day. If a heart attack does occur, and we have determined there is no pulse, we administer CPR.

But what can we do for a spiritual heart attack? What can be done to prevent one from occurring? For a physical heart attack everyone knows diet is a factor. It's no different for your spiritual heart condition. What are you ingesting? Is it spiritually "heart healthy"? Some people indulge on the "sweets" of salary, status, and sinful desires.

> "But the Lamb will overcome them because he is Lord of lords and King of kings—and with him will be his called, chosen and faithful followers." (Revelation 17:14)

Others gorge themselves on TV, computer addictions, and other unhealthy media input that leads to a buildup inside your spiritual heart. This buildup, or clot, decreases your heart's ability to perform, eventually blocking major areas as it becomes cold and dead.

Another factor common to both types of heart attack is lack of exercise—being a pew warmer and spectator, not a participator! Staying active in your role as a true follower of Jesus Christ will prevent your heart from drying up and becoming brittle. To prevent a spiritual clot, try aspirin:

A Acknowledge: "In all your ways acknowledge him, and he will make your paths straight" (Proverbs 3:6).

S Submit: "Submit yourselves, then, to God. Resist the devil, and he will flee from you" (James 4:7).

P Pray: "Pray continually" (1 Thessalonians 5:17).

I Investigate (Seek): "Seek first his kingdom" (Matthew 6:33), and be the kind of person the Lord is seeking. "For they are the kind of worshipers the Father seeks" (John 4:23).

R Repent: "There will be more rejoicing in heaven over one sinner who repents" (Luke 15:7).

I Integrity: "I know, my God, that you test the heart and are pleased with integrity" (1 Chronicles 29:17).

N Never give up—endure! "If we endure, we will also reign with him" (2 Timothy 2:12).

Prayer:
Lord, I seek to be called one of your followers with a healthy heart as I ingest your A-S-P-I-R-I-N and rely on you; obey, study, and practice what I learn from your Word; love others as you love us; and resist Satan.

JANUARY 29

Chaplain Gilbert Gaddie, Captain – Indianapolis Fire Department; President Indianapolis Chapter Fellowship of Christian Firefighters

POLITICAL CORRECTNESS
Or misconstrue the truth

EVER WALKED past folks at the firehouse tuned into the television and decided to stop to see what they're watching?

I confess, the majority of my "idle," or undirected, TV-watching at the firehouse occurs between runs, after the daily requirements of equipment inspection, housework, and training are complete. It may not be my intended pastime, but I end up finding something interesting and I'm trapped.

Recently, while so enticed, my curiosity gave way to anger. The program's portrayal of right and wrong for a Christian misconstrued God's truth as a cleverly written lie. Sin was disguised as tolerance. Accepting these misconceptions on TV is no different from being persuaded by a cult. Any form of misrepresentation of God's Word and truths, such as depicting false philosophies, is wrong. "No matter how you live or what you put your faith in, you will all end up the same place anyway" may seem peaceful and politically correct, but it's not biblically correct. It's an abomination to God.

Political correctness pleases people. Biblical correctness pleases God. Man's correctness changes. God's correctness never changes.

Jesus, full of grace and mercy, dealt with all kinds of people and "correctness" (sin). But he didn't tell them to go on and keep doing what is wrong. Jesus said, "Go, and sin no more" (John 8:11 KJV). This was not an impossible task by any means. When Christ ascended to heaven, he sent the Holy Spirit to guide and strengthen us. The very Spirit that raised Jesus from the grave quickens (revives, resuscitates, makes alive) our mortal bodies and gives us the power to overcome sin and temptation.

> "Your throne was established long ago; you are from all eternity." (Psalm 93:2)

Jesus awaits all his sheep, all those who confess and believe he is Lord. They will not end up in the same place as those who reject or misconstrue the truth for political correctness.

When that TV blares at the firehouse, pray for an opportunity to counter its negative influence with a godly one. God's throne was established long before television. Heaven is not a figment of someone's imagination. It's your eternal home if you so choose.

Prayer:
Lord, as a believer, I'm not without hope, as are those who have fallen prey to the belief that whatever they believe in, all people end up in the same place. Thank you that you are in heaven waiting with open arms.

Gus Bomgardner, Firefighter/Paramedic, Callahan, FL

THE LOSS OF A FRIEND
God's grace was right there to help me

NOW LISTEN, you who say, 'Today or tomorrow we will go to this or that city, spend a year there, carry on business and make money.' Why, you do not even know what will happen tomorrow. What is your life? You are a mist that appears for a little while and then vanishes." In these words from James 4:13, 14, God doesn't leave much to the imagination. Our life on Earth is like a mist.

This Scripture passage became a reality for Henry Hobbs on his seven-year anniversary as a ranger with the Florida Department of Forestry. When he came home from work and retreated to his backyard to visit with a neighbor, Henry unexpectedly collapsed from a heart attack.

I was on duty when the Nassau County Fire Rescue was called out. I'd worked with Henry on brush fires and other fire-related incidents in our county. It's an emotional time working a cardiac arrest when it's someone you don't know. That feeling is multiplied many times over when it's someone you *do* know. Thankfully, God's grace was there to help me.

Always smiling, Henry and his joy had brightened everyone's day no matter how grumpy they were. He loved fishing, and his job, coworkers, family, and multitude of friends. Henry was only thirty-eight years old when he went home to be with the Lord—too young according to our standards, but not God's.

> "Why, you do not even know what will happen tomorrow. What is your life? You are a mist that appears for a little while and then vanishes." (James 4:14)

According to God's timetable, Henry's work here was complete. Does this make it any easier to say good-bye to a friend? No. But remember—what we are really saying is, "See you later."

Henry will be greatly missed, but not forgotten. I am sure that if he were able to tell us anything, he would say to "make the days count." His life was evidence of that.

We are only given a short time on Earth to serve God. Many of us become so consumed with the job, status, and love for all the worldly possessions and power Satan flaunts in our face we cannot be used by

God. But remember—none of us is assured of our tomorrows here on Earth.

Prayer:
I know I can't change the past, but as I look over what I have done so far, I can change any of my ungodly priorities to honor the things that really matter to you. I don't know what tomorrow holds, Lord, but I know all my tomorrows belong to you.

JANUARY 31

Reverend Wayne Detzler, PhD, Chaplain (Retired) – Charlotte, NC, Fire Department; Fellowship of Christian Firefighters Regional Director

WHERE'S MY BARNEY DOLL?

When mercy became my priority

WORKING FIRE," the dispatcher said. "Respond immediately, Chaplain, there's a family involved." When I arrived on scene the house was a smoldering scene of destruction. Much of the second floor was damaged by fire or smoke; the downstairs was soaked, with water dripping.

Sitting along the street was a small family, including one little girl. She'd lost her home. She was frightened and weeping. Because of the chill in the air, EMTs invited the family to sit in a warm ambulance. No injuries were apparent, but the gloom of the huddled group matched the gray skies of the Connecticut winter.

Sometimes pain is much deeper than tears. For the little one, life would never again be the same. Although her parents were safe and were uninjured physically, she ached down deep. The very few playthings she had were gone. Her meager supply of clothes was destroyed. So, she wept with soft sobs.

"I lost it," the little girl began to cry. "I lost my Barney doll."

"Honey," I began softly, thinking of our own children, "do you remember where it was?"

"It's on my bed, upstairs," she sniffed out between tears.

When a firefighter came by I grabbed his arm and asked, "Is the children's room safe?" He assured me it was. "Can you possibly go up and try to find the little girl's stuffed toy?"

40

A few minutes later the burly firefighter emerged carrying the purple dinosaur as if it were a trophy. He pressed it into my hands before going back into the ruined house. "Thank you!" I shouted after him.

Then I opened the ambulance door and handed the toy to our new little friend. She shrieked with joy as she hugged Barney tight to her body. From that day onward we carried a teddy bear on each piece of equipment, so that we could give it to children on the worst day of their lives.

Comforting words would never stop the sobs. Even a warm blanket and a caring EMT couldn't take the chill off her heart. Nor could the hopeful promises of parents assuage the grief. She wanted her little stuffed animal back.

In times of inexpressible grief I turn to the Psalms, and each time the assurance comes that God is with me. It is he who has "collected my tears in his bottle. He has recorded each tear in his book" (Psalm 56:8, author's paraphrase).

Prayer:
*Lord, help me to love the little ones, whom you
invited specially to come to you.*

Smoldering Scene of Destruction (Courtesy of Hugo Ferchau,
Gunnison County Fire Protection District)

Captain Raul A. Angulo, Seattle Fire Department;
Fellowship of Christian Firefighters Regional
Director / International Board Member

FIREPROOF

It doesn't mean the heat won't come

"FIREPROOF doesn't mean the heat won't come; it means we will be able to withstand the heat."

That was one of my favorite lines in the movie *Fireproof*. In our business, the buildings that are "fireproof" are Type I high-rise construction. However, we don't use the term "fireproof," but "fire-resistive." What makes those buildings fire-resistive is a spray-on coating of "fireproof" material that protects the steel from flames and heat. This is the highest-rated material for fire protection in building construction. Type I construction has fire-resistive ratings from two to four hours depending on the components. That means (in theory) we have anywhere from two to four hours to fight this fire before the building starts to fail and collapse.

However, the fireproofing material has to be maintained. Exposed steel will react like Type II construction, which doesn't have a time rating. Unprotected steel will lose its strength at approximately 1,000 to 1,100 degrees (temperatures easily reached in even a well-involved house fire), fail, and collapse under its own weight!

During a preview showing of *Fireproof*, with about two hundred people in attendance, there was barely a dry eye in the house. Most of the people crying were enginemen, but there were a few truckmen holding back the tears—so I was told (I couldn't see through all *my* tears). It's a very emotional movie, pertinent to all marriages,

> "Finally, brothers, whatever is true, whatever is noble, whatever is right, whatever is pure, whatever is lovely, whatever is admirable—if anything is excellent or praiseworthy—think about such things." (Philippians 4:8)

but especially so to first responders. One veteran firefighter said, "This was my marriage. Maybe if I'd seen this earlier, I could have saved my marriage." The unique challenges presented in the movie, when met with God's love and promises, can change the weakest of marriages into the strongest.

So, is your marriage fireproof? Have you been maintaining the fire-resistive coating of your marriage? Or do you have some exposed areas making your relationship vulnerable to the heat and flames? Is your marriage on the verge of failure and collapse?

Or have you set your mind on things that are praiseworthy about your spouse? Have you turned your life and marriage over to God, communicated your concerns with your spouse, pastor, or confidant, and then taken the necessary steps to apply a "fire-resistive coating"? If not, there is no better time than now!

Prayer:

Lord, I know that every time I say unkind words, act disrespectfully, take my spouse for granted, and behave selfishly, I'm implying I don't cherish my spouse and am therefore deliberately chipping away at the fire-resistive coating that protects the strength of our marriage. Help me preserve the fire-resistive coating, not destroy it.

FEBRUARY 2

Chaplain Gaius Reynolds, President – Fellowship of Christian Firefighters International; Volunteer Firefighter – Livermore, CO, Fire Protection District

COMFORTER

He is only a whisper away

IT WAS A dark, snowy evening; you know, the kind where you like to stay home, watch the fire in the fireplace, appreciate its warmth, and have a good book in hand. It was the kind of evening when you want to stay in, not go out. However, when the pager went off, I went out! Yes, someone needed my help. As I left my home to respond, my mind started reviewing the potential scene: *How many vehicles, how many patients, what will we find on arrival? Are they young, are they old, will they be viable or will it be a "code black" response?*

This night, it was a single-vehicle MVA (motor vehicle accident): two adults and two infants in a car that rolled over and landed on its wheels (a much easier extrication than one that lands on its roof). The adults had multiple broken bones and lacerations, the infants' injuries were much more serious. When an infant is not crying, you know it's serious! And these two were quiet!

Both were breathing, but not crying, moving, or responsive to our voices. As we began the task of getting them out, concern for their survival was evident on all the responders' faces. Carefully, oh, so carefully, still strapped in their car seats, we carried them out of the vehicle. As we placed them in our med unit, they began to whimper. A good sign! How can we comfort them? What can we do to help them relax?

The firehouse quilts we carry in our unit flashed across our minds. Reaching into our cabinet we pulled out one for each infant. Something must have "clicked" with them because they hung on tightly! They were comforted, they allowed us to assess their injuries, and they responded to our voices! As we transferred them to the hospital med unit, they were sure to hold on to their quilts. Hugging tightly, they allowed the transfer and new personnel to treat them and transport them to the hospital.

> "And I will pray the Father, and he shall give you another Comforter, that he may abide with you for ever."
> (John 14:16 KJV)

The adult victims were so thankful their children were cared for that their own injuries became secondary. When they contacted the department weeks later, they thanked us for the quilts and shared that the kids treasure them and keep them with them all the time!

While a quilt can comfort a child, we as Christians can call on our own personal Comforter. He is only a whisper away.

Prayer:
Thank you, Lord, that you are only a whisper away.

*Reverend Wayne Detzler, PhD, Chaplain (Retired) –
Charlotte, NC, Fire Department; Fellowship of
Christian Firefighters Regional Director*

HANGING OUT THE WINDOW
Who left her behind?

"RESCUE." The dispatcher used a key word. "People are inside and the house is fully involved." I sped to the other side of town, and the smell of smoke and sight of fire guided my way.

"Look, Chaplain," a firefighter pointed. "Look at the second floor. A woman's legs are hanging out the window." Her husband had jumped, but his wife was pregnant. She couldn't take the risk of a two-story leap.

45

So, she sat on the window sill with her legs hanging down as she yelled for help.

"Get the ladder," the incident commander shouted into his radio. "Put it up to the window and help her down." Immediately the firefighters placed a ladder and helped the woman step out. Slowly, surely, they guided her down to safety on the ground, where her family waited to receive her.

Medics loaded our lady into an ambulance and took her to the emergency room to be checked for smoke inhalation. Her husband joined her, because he, too, had been caught in the early flames.

Once the woman was safe, our attention turned to the fire. Hoses were trained on the structure as it crackled. It took a long time to extinguish the blaze, but time flew by. The rescue of our young friend overshadowed the fire-fighting task.

> "Call upon me in the day of trouble; I will deliver you, and you will honor me." (Psalm 50:15)

Finally the black plume of smoke turned white. We knew the fire was out. Now it only remained to find hot spots and hit them with a hose. As the incident ended, we picked up the equipment and returned to an interrupted night of sleep.

When I prayed with the firefighters we had a lot to be thankful for. Both (actually, all three) members of the little family had been rescued, and were relatively uninjured. None of our fellow firefighters had been injured in the attempt. It was a good end to a bad night for one family. As I drove home through the night, thanksgiving welled up in my heart. I thanked the Lord for sure-footed fire rescuers who are in the business of delivering people from peril, and those they saved that night.

Always remember—there is One who is waiting for you to call him, not just when in physical peril, but in times of emotional and spiritual distress.

Prayer:
*Thank you, O Lord, for the sure-footed firefighters
who lead so many to safety.*

Marybeth Farrell, Wife of Firefighter Ryan Farrell, Fellowship of Christian Firefighters International Central Alabama Chapter

A FIREFIGHTER'S WIFE

Include me, don't exclude me

WHEN RYAN was hired by Vestavia Hills Fire Department in Alabama, the childhood dream of a four-year-old boy came true and I became a firefighter's wife. Like many others I know, and ones I don't know, firefighter spouses differ in many ways, yet we have one commonality; we all play the special and unique role of being married to a first responder. Do I wish he were home every night? No, I wouldn't change a thing. I'm proud of the career he chose. I know he's exactly where God called him to be and doing the work God called him to do.

Frequently I'm asked, "Do you feel afraid and worry about him?" I've met other firefighter wives whose lives are plagued with worries about the dangers their husbands face. But, the truth is I don't have to be afraid. Together, Ryan and I serve an awesome and faithful God who loves us both. King David said, "My times are in your hands . . ." (Psalm 31:15), and I've made the same choice. I choose not to worry, because Ryan is in the hands of our loving heavenly Father, who created him!

I get discouraged at times with Ryan's schedule, but I know I can't allow discouragement to gain a foothold and rob me of my joy. I need to "Stay alert! Watch out for your great enemy, the devil. He prowls around like a roaring lion, looking for someone to devour." (1 Peter 5:8 NLT). Selfish thoughts will not only rob me of joy, they'll lead to resentment toward Ryan and the work he loves. When these thoughts of discouragement and self-pity start to creep in, it's important for me to be suited up and ready to fight—attired with God's armor, in his Word, and in fellowship with others. My friendship with other firefighter spouses, who understand and experience the same emotions I face, is a huge comfort to me.

> "My times are in your hands; deliver me from my enemies and from those who pursue me." (Psalm 31:15)

I challenge all first responders—include your spouses in fire-related extracurricular activities. Encourage them to find a support group such as a Bible study or dinner with friends. Ask them how they feel about your career, hours, and the danger you face. Include them; don't exclude them from the life you lead when you're apart for long periods of time. Doing

47

this is just as important for you as an individual as it is for you and your spouse as a couple.

Prayer:
Thank you for my spouse. Guide me as I seek to more completely understand my loved one's feelings toward his career.

*Captain Raul A. Angulo – Seattle Fire Department;
Fellowship of Christian Firefighters Regional
Director / International Board Member*

ARE YOU A WARRIOR OR SIMPLY A TARGET?

I ended up being a target, not a warrior!

ON A SUNNY day in Seattle I joined a group of firefighters for a friendly competition of paintball. When I arrived, I found the guys dressed for battle. I, on the other hand, wearing a T-shirt, quickly realized I'd underestimated the danger and pain associated with this sport! As one guy shared his war stories and others chimed in with their equally daunting tales, I said, "That's it!" and walked to my rig. The teasing immediately started. They thought I was quitting. Instead, I donned my bunker gear that was conveniently waiting in my car.

I was humbled in the first game when the first two shots splattered paint all over my face shield. I never saw them coming. If these were real bullets, I'd have been killed in action! By the third game, I started thinking about our servicemen. There would have been no Bronze or Silver Star medals for me, no Medal of Honor; only Purple Hearts and a body bag. Had this been real combat, I'd have been taken out in the first few minutes of battle. In these games, I ended up being a target, not a warrior!

The day was peppered with sobering analogies of how we're attacked by the Enemy. Obviously, I wasn't alert enough. It impressed me how fast those paintballs came at me. Attacks from the Enemy can come just as fast, especially in areas where we're vulnerable to sin.

Enemies, like lions, attack the herd. They wait for an injured or weak animal that has fallen behind. They look for the naive animal who wan-

48

ders away from the protection of the herd. When they are separated, they're isolated and vulnerable to attack. Lions hunt in teams and can easily surround a lonely prey. Doesn't this sound like a key strategy of Satan's?

> "Be self-controlled and alert. Your enemy the devil prowls around like a roaring lion looking for someone to devour."
> (1 Peter 5:8)

When we're engaged in secret sins like drugs, alcohol, pornography, gambling, sexual sin, cheating, or stealing, we tend to do them in private, when we think no one is watching, including God. And our vulnerability becomes obvious.

Let's be clear. God does see sin and it grieves him to see his children wander away from him. It's like the coal away from the fire; it's impossible for it to retain its glow and heat on its own. Slowly, the ember cools and the glow fades until it is extinguished.

Prayer:
When you see my behavior, hear my thoughts, may they be pleasing to you and not cause you grief.

FEBRUARY 6

Captain Raul A. Angulo – Seattle Fire Department; Fellowship of Christian Firefighters Regional Director / International Board Member

FULLY PREPARED OR A LIABILITY?

Are you prepared for battle?

HOW ARE people to take on the devil's schemes if not fully protected? Note, we're talking of the devil's *schemes* (plural); there's more than one attack scheme. Ephesians 6:12 explains that our struggle is not against flesh and blood. It's against powers of the dark world and spiritual forces of evil. These are powerful forces greater than any knuckle-dragging, chainsaw-blade-flossing truckman, greater than the meanest, strongest warrior who ever existed. These demons exist in another dimension, but they can attack us in our dimension.

Paul says in Ephesians 6:13 that to be strong in the Lord and mighty in his power (to stand against the devil's many and varied tactics) we need to "put on the full armor of God." A close parallel to a firefighter's personal protective gear can be made here.

Firefighters must be fully armored. They're continually instructed to wear all their personal protective gear. Unfortunately, many take shortcuts. Sometimes equipment gets left behind. Firefighters start entering a building without their SCBA (self-contained breathing apparatus), or maybe the high-rise bundle stays on the rig so it doesn't have to be repacked. When the threat isn't recognized, firefighters sometimes become complacent. The firefighter who enters with only some protective gear and equipment is looked at as "experienced." The firefighter who's all snapped up with the neck collar firmly secured and pulling off the hose for the fourth time is viewed as "inexperienced." But, when the battle breaks loose, which firefighter is prepared for it?

> "But your servants, every man armed for battle, will cross over to fight before the LORD, just as our lord says."
> (Numbers 32:27)

Without the full armor of God, you're not operating with optimum efficiency. When you go into battle, you want be victorious, not marginal. If you can't attack, resist, or defend against the Enemy, then you're ineffective and a liability. You can't provide guidance, encouragement, or assistance to others in the spiritual battle because you're not prepared yourself against enemy fire.

Picture a fire crew ready to enter a burning house with a known rescue and the officer notices a member without his fire helmet and the member on the nozzle without gloves. Those firefighters just rendered that attack team useless to the rescue. Now they have to fall back to a safe defensive position and fight the fire from the exterior. In fact, they cannot rejoin the battle until every member has their "full armor," or protective ensemble.

As a Christian, do *you* put on *your* full armor?

Prayer:
Lord, may I have my PPE (personal protective equipment) on for battle both spiritually and physically, just as Moses commanded his warriors.

Craig Duck, Lieutenant, Engine Co. 11 – Washington, DC, Fire Department; Fellowship of Christian Firefighters International Atlantic States Regional Director / International Board Member

ARMOR OF GOD

Christian firefighters come in the strength of the Lord

GOD'S INSPIRED Word is as relevant today as when written. It was written to draw people closer to God. Ephesians 6 addresses the armor of God. When it was written, Roman soldiers were everywhere and their armor was always visible.

Today, firefighting gear is also easily recognized. It serves as a sign that help is on the way. Christian firefighters come in their own strength and in that of the Lord. When "bunkering up," think about the similarity of your gear to God's added protection, which enables you to stand against the devil's wiles.

"Therefore put on the full armor of God, so that when the day of evil comes, you may be able to stand your ground . . . Stand firm then, with the belt of truth buckled around your waist, with the breastplate of righteousness in place, and with your feet fitted with the readiness that comes from the gospel of peace. In addition to all this, take up the shield of faith, with which you can extinguish all the flaming arrows of the evil one. Take the helmet of salvation and the sword of the Spirit, which is the word of God" (Ephesians 6:13–17).

> "Put on the full armor of God so that you can take your stand against the devil's schemes." (Ephesians 6:11)

The main part of a Roman soldier's armor was his breastplate. For the firefighter it's the coat. For the Christian it's God's righteousness. When we walk in him we're truly protected. Roman soldiers traveled extensively on foot, requiring good foot protection. Firefighters need protective boots when entering a fire. The Christian's feet are covered with the readiness that comes from the gospel of peace.

The Roman soldier's shield was his last line of defense. Firefighters can't get close to fire without their SCBA (air tank). When the evil one's fiery darts and flaming arrows add to the assault, the Christian uses the shield of faith.

The helmet of salvation protects the most important part of the body. As did Roman soldiers, firefighters wear helmets; Christians put on the

51

helmet of salvation. Roman soldiers had the sword. Firefighters use hose to put out fires. Christians use the the sword of the Spirit, God's Word, to attack their enemies.

Preparation is essential. Roman troops trained continually. Firefighters train to acquire needed skills. Christians read their Bibles and pray for protection in spiritual battles. The only way to be prepared is to daily put on the whole armor of God.

Prayer:

*Thank you for your Word, which provides the full armor
needed when facing the battles with the devil. As I "bunker up"
I rely on you for my ultimate protection.*

FEBRUARY 8

*Scott Pruiksma, President – Interlockingarms.net; Firefighter –
Borough of Midland Park, NJ; FCFI North Jersey Chapter*

EYES

What are your eyes are focused on?

THE ARMOR of God described in Ephesians 6:10–18 refers to protecting ourselves from the flaming darts of the evil one. As we read these verses, it's easy to equate God's armor with our personal protective equipment. Our helmets, turnout gear, gloves, boots, and SCBA (self-contained breathing apparatus) can all be pictured in relation to the helmet, breastplate, belt, and shield these verses speak of. But I've noticed the one part of the body not mentioned as being protected with all our firefighting equipment is our eyes.

Eyes are essential to what firefighters do. They're needed to see smoke, burning embers, flames, and a full-fledged fire. They're vital for the work we perform on the fire ground. Imagine if we put all our gear on and then closed our eyes and went to work. What a disaster that would be! True, when we go into a smoke-filled room we can't see and, if not trained, a chaotic experience awaits us. Thank God for training and training instructors!

The eye is the lamp of the body according to Matthew 6:22, 23, and if our eyes are good, our whole body will be full of light. Conversely, Matthew continues by saying we will be full of darkness if our eyes are bad. This became evident while working a house fire with a rookie. This was his first experience inside a burning structure. When we departed the scene he mentioned the overwhelming heat, darkness, and smoke he encountered. "I couldn't see my hand in front of my face!" he exclaimed.

"Welcome to the world of firefighting," I responded.

Like this rookie, many of us experience darkness. I know I was trapped in darkness until I opened my eyes to God's saving light.

What are your eyes focused on? If your attention is on inappropriate things, those images become tattooed on or embedded in your minds. Those "dark" imbedded images do not lead to good. Lives become chaotic when people walk around in such darkness.

> "The eye is the lamp of the body. If your eyes are good, your whole body will be full of light. But if your eyes are bad, your whole body will be full of darkness. If then the light within you is darkness, how great is that darkness!"
> (Matthew 6:22, 23)

Thank God for his Son, Jesus, the Light of the world! With proper training over time, and with the help of God and his children, everyone can overcome the desire to look at darkness.

Are you keeping your eyes on the Light? Are you looking up? God is waiting to illuminate any darkness your eyes are focused on.

Prayer:
Thank you, Lord, for being my Light when darkness threatens to overcome my vision.

FEBRUARY 9

Dwayne Clemmons, Adjunct Instructor – Virginia Department of Fire Programs; Founder – DMC Ministries; Author of Exploits, Jesus Rides in an Ambulance, and Utterances from the Throne Room; Volunteer in Fire and EMS for forty years in Virginia

WALK IN THE SPIRIT
People will notice you're special

HE WALKED into the station with an aura of confidence and experience about him. All eyes focused on his presence. A rookie whispered, "Who is that man?" Another responded, "He's our previous chief, a true legend in our department."

When you enter a room, is there an aura about you that causes people to stop and look up? Do you enter a room with God's radiance? Do you walk in the Spirit?

The book of Genesis says you were made in the image and likeness of the Father, Son, and Holy Spirit. This means you're a mirror image of the Trinity. When people look at you they should not see you—they should see God. Mirroring God is an ongoing process that requires a willing spirit and knowledge of God and his truth.

You are a spirit being with a soul that lives in the flesh. Before salvation your life was controlled by the soul, which is the mind, will, and emotions. Life operated on the world's wisdom and knowledge. You did whatever you wanted, said whatever came to mind, and acted without regard to what others thought. All that changed when you were saved.

> "So I say, live by the Spirit, and you will not gratify the desires of the sinful nature. For the sinful nature desires what is contrary to the Spirit, and the Spirit what is contrary to the sinful nature. They are in conflict with each other, so that you do not do what you want. But if you are led by the Spirit, you are not under law."
> (Galatians 5:16–18)

The Bible says that when you were saved, old things passed away and all things became brand new. Yet we still seem to struggle with our old nature and habits. Why is this? Aren't old things gone and all things new?

The answer is yes. However, this takes time. Your mind has to be renewed daily. You do this through the Word. The Word says God wants you to prosper as your soul prospers. That is your mind, will, and emotions.

You need to learn the ways of God. As you do, you enable the Spirit to lead and guide you into all truth. You relinquish more and more control of your life. Your life is not your own, it is God's. When you walk in the Spirit, God's aura surrounds you. People may not stop and look up, but they will notice you're special. You're a reflection of God's love.

Prayer:
As I go through this and every day, Lord, enable me to focus on you in all I do. Create in me a passion to seek your face, your fellowship, your counsel, your purpose, and your direction for each day. Then, empower me to be bold and confident in what you have directed me to do. Transform me into your image so others will see you through me in all that I do.

54

*Reverend Wayne Detzler, PhD, Chaplain (Retired) –
Charlotte, NC, Fire Department; Fellowship of
Christian Firefighters Regional Director*

FAITH IS A MARATHON

Let us "run with patience"

SOON AFTER joining a Connecticut fire department I encountered the Fellowship of Christian Firefighters. Slowly, cautiously, we launched a very small branch in our town. It linked us with a larger circle of fellow believers in the Lord and gave courage to believers in their witness for the Lord.

When I was appointed to the Charlotte Fire Department I met two heroes, brave men of God in the fire service. The first is Donny, who had served in the high pressure world of Washington, DC. There he held the torch of faith high and others gathered around him. Together they built a powerful witness among the responders in our nation's capital. Upon retirement Donny moved to Charlotte, but he didn't lose his vision. His calm confidence in the Lord led many firefighters to stand up for Jesus. Soon he was helping the Charlotte Fire Department launch a branch of the Fellowship of Christian Firefighters. He gathered around him committed firefighters and officers, most of whom were significantly younger than Donny.

Not only did Donny organize a fellowship, he also invested in the lives of these young men and women, especially one young officer named Keith. When Donny and I first met Keith, he was a newly minted captain. Keith grasped the leadership in Charlotte and began to surround himself with a cadre of Christians.

Under the Fellowship of Christian Firefighters banner, Keith organized three early-morning prayer breakfasts—one for each of the department's three shifts. Out of this fellowship came the appointment of the first fire chaplain for the Charlotte Fire Department. This role multiplied into a firefighter support team, a group available to strengthen their comrades in good times and bad.

Donny and Keith are true heroes of the faith. Despite retirement, Donny still leads the charge in praying and participating with the Fellowship of Christian Firefighters. Keith is now a battalion chief and has a tight network of believers throughout the ever-growing department. Donny and Keith are faithful men. Around them are dozens of others who have learned from their example.

From the vision and faithfulness of these two "heroes," many in the fire service have learned of God's love and truth and in turn shared it with others. God wants to use each and every one of us, and as we respond, he will be there to keep us strong.

> "He [the Lord Jesus Christ] will keep you strong to the end." (1 Corinthians 1:8)

Prayer:
Looking to Jesus, Lord, help me to be faithful and to finish well in my life of faith.

F E B R U A R Y   1 1

Tommy Neiman, Author of Sirens for the Cross; EMS Training Officer – St. Lucie County, FL; Fellowship of Christian Firefighters International Regional Director / International Board Member

A MISSED OPPORTUNITY

Balking at an opportunity to share the love of our wonderful Savior

THE APOSTLE PAUL while in prison encouraged everyone to be bold and share the truth in all situations. This admonition became embedded in my heart when I responded to a call for "a person experiencing back pains."

The call sounded simple, maybe even a little boring. Not expecting anything too critical, I grabbed our basic jumpbag and headed in to find our patient, Rick, lying flat across the bed. "Sorry about all the fuss," he said. "I was fine when I woke up, but all day I've experienced increasingly heavy pain in the middle of my back."

We asked more questions and took vitals. His skin was sweaty and pale and he looked "shocky." His blood pressure was alarmingly low. Further examination revealed a hardened area in his upper abdomen, gently pulsating. Most likely, he was bleeding to death on the inside.

Aggressive treatment was needed. We placed him on high-flow oxygen, had a quick-look EKG, and a large-bore-needle IV was established and was running wide open as we transported him.

A full complement of ER nurses, a portable X-ray crew, and two physicians were standing by in expectation of our arrival.

As I headed over to the report table, knowing Rick's chances weren't good, I wondered where Rick stood with the Lord. Then my focus shifted to producing an impressive narrative for my run report rather than dwelling on a potential spiritual need. I could go to his side and talk to him, but, cowardly, I thought, *There are too many people; maybe I'll just wait.*

Down the hallway, grave concern covered the family's faces. I felt another tug at my heart to go to Rick and share God's salvation message, but instead I made more evasive excuses and lost my opportunity to share with a man facing eternity. Rick's time had come. My chance to share Christ died at that report table.

> "Because of my chains, most of the brothers in the Lord have been encouraged to speak the word of God more courageously and fearlessly."
> (Philippians 1:14)

Writing about this call, while painful, reminds me to never again let an opportunity to share the Lord slip needlessly away.

How about you? As a child of God, have you been prompted by the Holy Spirit to share the love of our wonderful Savior, and yet balked at the calling?

Prayer:
Lord, may I never miss an opportunity to share your salvation message. May Satan never keep me quiet when prodded by the Holy Spirit to share your testimony with someone. May I always be true and obedient to the Spirit's calling, for it may be the only opportunity I have to share Christ before a person goes unexpectedly to eternity.

FEBRUARY 12

Chaplain Marc Santorella, Firefighter Danvers Fire Department, MA; Public Fire and Life Safety Educator and Certified Fire Instructor Level 1

A SIMPLE REMINDER
Christianity does not put God in a box

DAD, HOW can God hate religion?" my daughter asked after we'd watched a movie depicting Jesus' displeasure with what religion has become in our society. As I got ready to launch into a theological explanation, backed by the Old Testament, I stopped dead in my tracks. I was

57

talking to a ten-year-old who only two weeks earlier had asked about the reality of Santa Claus. How do I explain religion to one so young? Is it different from explaining it to a newly born-again adult, such as a first responder?

Not really, I deduced as I explained that religion puts God in a box, but God wants people to be free to worship him. I picked up a book. "Let's pretend this book contains more than six hundred house rules I've decided you must follow. If you follow every one of them, I'll love you. But, if you mess up on even one, you're not worthy of being my daughter, and I won't accept you." I paused to observe her smile, indicating she understood I love her unconditionally, then continued.

> "Jesus said, 'Let the little children come to me, and do not hinder them, for the kingdom of heaven belongs to such as these.'" (Matthew 19:14)

"Religion says we have to live up to a specific set of rules to 'qualify' for God's love." I went on to explain that such beliefs are just not true. God provided Moses an extensive list of requirements that describes what a perfect walk looks like, but God also knew we'd never be able to meet those requirements by ourselves. That's why he sent Jesus, who lived up to every rule, suffered on the cross for our sins, rose from the grave, and is now with God in heaven.

Christianity, unlike "religion," doesn't put God in a box. In Jesus, we not only have an example to live by, we have a friend who stands by our Father in heaven and speaks on our behalf.

My daughter smiled with understanding and headed for school. My thoughts shifted to the firehouse and other new believers who express confusion regarding religion. Regardless of chronological age, the truth is the same.

The chief at the station surely expects you to follow the rules. Your job or rank may be in jeopardy when they're broken.

God also provides a rule book, but failure to follow the book doesn't threaten a loss of position or status. Seek his forgiveness, repent, and remember—when you fail, Jesus is able to say to God, "Forgive."

Prayer:
God, thank you that I'm your precious child and you love me with an unconditional love. Thank you for always receiving me with open arms.

Tommy Neiman, Author of Sirens for the Cross;
EMS Training Officer – St. Lucie County, FL;
Fellowship of Christian Firefighters International
Regional Director / International Board Member

AN UNGRATEFUL CHOKER
Oh, that people would praise God

FIRST RESPONDERS answer calls ranging from false alarms to life-threatening emergencies. Some are those rare emergencies in which life and death are split seconds apart and only an immediate action performed on scene saves a life.

I praise God for using me on several of these calls, but I'm humbled by the realization a physical life saved is only temporary. A far more important life saved is a spiritual life. If a nonbelieving person is snatched from death only to live out the remainder of life without accepting Christ, the life saved doesn't mean much from an eternal perspective. But on these rarest of calls, like the one that follows, my heart cries out as King David's did: "Oh that men would praise the LORD for his goodness" (Psalm 107:8 KJV).

The call was for an unresponsive choking victim at a mental health facility. Her face was an eerie ashen blue; her body pale and lifeless. I grabbed the laryngoscope and forceps, inserted the laryngoscope blade and exposed her trachea. Beyond her vocal cords was an object that completely obstructed her air passage. When I removed the mass, the patient made no personal effort to breathe so I continued to try other lifesaving measures. Then, between two ventilations, I noticed a small chest rise. "She's trying to breathe," I excitedly said, continuing to assist with her still-inadequate attempts at ventilation.

> "Let them give thanks to the LORD for his unfailing love and his wonderful deeds for men, for he satisfies the thirsty and fills the hungry with good things." (Psalm 107:8, 9)

During transport she began showing good chest rise with increased respiration. Her eyes began flickering. Despite her amazing recovery, she only complained and grumbled, "Why is my throat hurting? Why didn't you do a better job? I think you loosened one of my teeth!"

I never expected such an ungrateful response. Then a thought crossed my mind. Isn't this how we, as children of God, sometimes respond to him? God sent his only Son, Jesus Christ, to save our lives not only temporarily, but forever, and yet, like that ungrateful choker, groaning and whining about minor and temporary inconveniences of the flesh, we cease to praise Christ and all he has done and continues to do for us.

Have you ever been like the ungrateful choker? If so, focus on Christ and praise him! As you do, fewer complaints will come to mind.

Prayer:
*Lord, help me remember to praise you for your goodness,
to focus on you, and to not allow the little inconveniences
of life to distract me from all you do.*

Dwayne Clemmons, Adjunct Instructor – Virginia Department of Fire Programs; Founder – DMC Ministries; Author of Exploits, Jesus Rides in an Ambulance, and Utterances from the Throne Room; Volunteer in Fire and EMS for forty years in Virginia

THE CONDITION OF YOUR HEART

What's the real point of Valentine's Day?

THE FORTY-FIVE-YEAR-OLD man, awakened from sleep by a severe pain in his chest and sweating profusely, dialed 9-1-1.

Medics arrived momentarily, took his vital signs, obtained a twelve-lead EKG, administered oxygen, and advised transport. While in transit an IV was administered, nitroglycerin was placed under his tongue, and two milligrams of morphine eased his pain. He was having a heart attack. He needed immediate surgery; three stents were installed to open the arteries and restore blood flow to the heart. The surgery was a complete success.

The events that precipitated this attack included bad habits regarding diet and exercise. He was informed that if he wanted to live a long life then these issues would have to be addressed. His reply was an emphatic "Yes!"

This is Valentine's month and I've often wondered the real point of this holiday. It seems strange to truly recognize those close to you only one day a year. What about the rest of the year? Was the attention and emotion real or just another case of tradition?

On Valentine's Day, I encourage you to express your love for your dear ones, and then go a step further. Evaluate the condition of your heart. Not from a physical or relationship standpoint, but from a spiritual one. Are you walking around like the gentleman above with symptoms that could lead to eternal death? Are you steeped in tradition oblivious to your need to get your spiritual health in order?

> "The goal of this command is love, which comes from a pure heart and a good conscience and a sincere faith."
> (1 Timothy 1:5)

The Bible plainly states there is only one God, one faith, and one way to salvation. The only way to guarantee eternal life in heaven is by believing in God, acknowledging that Jesus came and died for your sins, and then asking Jesus to be the Lord of your life.

That's the easy part. The challenge is living your life in a way that honors God. The Word says you're not to be deceived, God will not be mocked, we will reap exactly what we sow.

God will do spiritual surgery on you if you consent. I guarantee the surgery will be a success and you'll live for eternity. Then, celebrate his love and the love you have for others this Valentine's Day—and every day.

Prayer:
*Create in me a pure heart, Lord, and help me to share
your love each and every day of my life.*

FEBRUARY 15

Craig Duck, Lieutenant, Engine Co. 11 – Washington, DC, Fire Department; Fellowship of Christian Firefighters International Atlantic States Regional Director / International Board Member

MARRIAGE—GOD'S PLAN
Living a godly marriage within the fire service

FIREFIGHTING is a dangerous job. Every day in America firefighters put their lives on the line in order to save lives and protect property. We are able to do this because our equipment has been designed to withstand the punishment of the fire ground. Today's firefighters are able to go deeper into the fire and withstand more heat because of their "state-of-the-art" equipment. Behind each piece of equipment there is a mastermind who designed it for a specific job. Whether it's a ladder, hose, or apparatus or even your marriage there is a mastermind behind each masterpiece. God, the mastermind of marriage, has designed marriage and he has a plan for marriage and instructions on how it works best.

Understanding God's plan for marriage can be very confusing in today's world. Television, the Internet, movies, and magazines distort what love is and how a husband and wife should interact with each other. Couples easily fall into traps, going to everyone for help with their marriages—except to the One who *created* marriage. "Has not [the LORD] made them one? In flesh and spirit they are his. And why one? Because he was seeking godly offspring" (Malachi 2:15).

> "For this reason a man will leave his father and mother and be united to his wife, and they will become one flesh." (Genesis 2:24)

With help, couples can tap into God's plan for marriage and begin to learn how to have a love that will last a lifetime. The Bible is full of passages that will help you understand how to work through life's challenges and, as a couple, draw closer to our loving God. And then, as you grow closer to God, you will draw closer to each other. When God's love enters the equation, the blessings multiply.

I encourage you to seek godly couples who can lead you to biblical passages that will help you develop a marriage that will last a lifetime. I urge you to consider attending a couples' conference. Whether your marriage is strong or struggling, a Christian marriage conference will bless and strengthen your relationship. And while you're at it, be sure to watch the movie *Fireproof*, and dare to love your spouse as God desires.

Prayer:
*Help me, Lord, to love my spouse with an
everlasting love, just as Jesus loves the church.*

Rick Barton, Fire Safety Officer; Rick Barton Ministries, Gunnison, CO; Fellowship of Christian Firefighters International Ambassador-at-Large

WAIT—COME BACK!

I had missed the most important point of all!

SUDDENLY IT hit me—I had missed the most important point of all!

Recently, I was assigned to a wildland fire in northern California. Shortly after arriving in camp a man noticed my Fellowship of Christian Firefighters' T-shirt and asked what being a Christian firefighter meant. As I answered, he began sharing that

"I do not set aside the grace of God, for if righteousness could be gained through the law, Christ died for nothing!" (Galatians 2:21)

even though he'd been raised in a Christian home, he now felt that all religions were equal and our job was to simply pick one and we'd be fine, as long as we were sincere.

Firefighters on the Front Line (Internet Resource)

We talked at length: I shared with him the uniqueness of Jesus, his claims, and his offer of salvation. I urged the other firefighter to realize that Jesus was either a liar, if he said he was God and knew he really wasn't; a lunatic, if he thought he was God but wasn't; or Lord, because he in fact is all he claimed to be. Jesus couldn't be just a good teacher or prophet because of who he said he was—the only Son of God and the only way to heaven.

Our conversation was cordial and ended with no apparent progress made on my part. The next morning he was gone, and suddenly it hit me. I'd missed the most important point.

If any religion were sufficient to get us to heaven, if doing our best would suffice, then why did Jesus have to come and die? There were plenty of religions at the time, lots of folks doing their best, but only Jesus' death to pay for our sins could restore us to fellowship with God. As Galatians 2:21 says, "I do not set aside the grace of God, for if righteousness could be gained through the law, Christ died for nothing!" I wished I could have had another chance.

As I shared my failure with a brother in Christ on the fire line, he reminded me that the Holy Spirit gives us the words to share at the time, and that we can pray and trust that he will bring someone else along to finish what I began. I know my brother was right, but I pray that next time I won't forget this basic truth. There is no other way to come to God except through the shed blood of his Son, Jesus!

Prayer:
*Lord, give me the words you would have me share
with those you bring in my path.*

FEBRUARY 17

*Robert Curnow, RN/Certified Flight Nurse; Medical Base
Supervisor, MEC; UCSD Resident Training Coordinator –
Mercy Air Base 5, Carlsbad, California with the assistance of
Kelly Forman, RN Flight Nurse – Mercy Air, California*

MERCIFUL FATHER
To comfort those who are alone at their last moments

EACH AND every day when our shift begins, there's an excitement about what the day holds in store. While flight crews do not wish tragedy on anyone, they are proficiently trained to handle that "big one," that provides a chance to perform advanced skills, glean a few seconds of TV time, and if lucky, yield a gallon of ice cream. It is those calls that seem to put our lives into perspective.

It was a beautiful sunny day when both Mercy Air 5 and Mercy Air 6 were launched on a flight to Pauma Valley, a remote area in northern San Diego County, California, for a motor vehicle accident with extrication in progress.

"Some trust in chariots and some in horses, but we trust in the name of the LORD our God. They are brought to their knees and fall, but we rise up and stand firm. O Lord, save the king! Answer us when we call!." (Psalms 20:7–9)

I'm not sure when I (Robert) was most challenged. I don't think it was the critical condition of either of my two young patients, who were both broken, but stable. Perhaps it was witnessing the horrific magnitude of the crash with two young mothers, draped in yellow blankets, lifeless in the front seats. Or, it could have been the sobbing requests of little ones confused by no response to their cries of "Mommy."

My commitment to the Lord is deep. I'm grateful for a tremendous job, truly a mixed blessing of sorts: the beauty of his worldly creations—gorgeous sunrises and sunsets, the vast Pacific Ocean, and so many more vivid images of beauty and grace—contrasted with catastrophic crashes and heart-wrenching suffering by his children . . . all of us.

Extrication (Courtesy of Robert Curnow and Kelly Forman, Mercy Air, CA)

Preparing to Transport (Courtesy of Robert Curnow and Kelly Forman, Mercy Air, CA)

As we removed the two surviving children and turned them over to Mercy Air 6 we thought it was over. I then discovered another child, still alive, crushed beneath her two dead brothers. It took another hour to cut the minivan apart and pull the eighty-thousand-pound truck off. I remember moments of waiting while the work went on. I had to stay focused, but I was also praying to our Father to spare this one child and give me a chance to bring one more family member home.

I think I'm in a unique position to help the sick and injured with my medical training, and that's what I signed up to do. It's clear to me our Lord has a plan and brought me to this field to comfort those who suffer, such as these children, as well as to comfort those on other calls who are alone at their last moments on Earth.

Prayer:
Thank you, Lord, for this tremendous job filled with mixed blessings, and for using me when tragedy strikes. Help me bring comfort to those you place in my path. My trust is in you. Thank you for the beauty of your creation and the hope I have in you.

Reverend Wayne Detzler, PhD, Chaplain (Retired) –
Charlotte, NC, Fire Department; Fellowship of
Christian Firefighters Regional Director

BLUE HELMET ON
A SLIPPERY NIGHT

Assurance on a scary night

SNOW AND ice are always treacherous, but they're especially danger-ous when one fights a fire. When runoff water hits the ground it freezes. Working on the roof is like working on an icy ski jump. For fire-fighters in the north, this is a common occurrence. It rolls around every winter.

It was one of those nights when an old house burst into flame. The outside temperature was frigid, and the house was blazing away when first responders rolled up on scene. Quickly they checked for victims and found none. Hoses were stretched and almost immediately water flowed to the fire.

But the blaze persisted. "We've got to open up that roof." The incident comman-der saw it clearly. "Throw up a ladder and cut a hole." Firefighters immediately climbed to the roof, but it was slick with ice. They had to crawl their way to find the right spot to cut their ventilation hole.

"Glad you're here, Chaplain," greeted the captain. "This is really a messy one. It's dangerous up there on the roof." Then he added something I never expected to hear: "I was so glad to see your blue helmet. When I did, I knew God wouldn't let me fall off the roof tonight."

> "We are therefore Christ's ambassadors, as though God were making his appeal through us. We implore you on Christ's behalf: Be recon-ciled to God."
> (2 Corinthians 5:20)

For my friend the blue helmet was sort of a "lucky charm." He thought there was some sort of mystical power in the chaplain's presence. It was my job to teach him about the power of prayer, about the saving presence of the Lord. The power is not in a distinctive blue helmet or in the presence of a chaplain. No, the power rests solely, completely, in the hands of the eternal God.

It is so easy to depend on something or someone. In reality it's only the Lord who can save us on a slippery roof, and it's only the eternal God who can save us for all eternity. We as chaplains and as Christian fire-fighters are simply messengers bringing the Gospel news. As for the blue helmet, just like a Christian lapel pin, cross, decal, or shirt with a Christian message, it serves as a sign you're one of God's children, there to share his love and truth.

Prayer:
Help me today, O Lord, to be an ambassador for you in a lost world.

Sue Reynolds, Missionary – Fellowship of Christian Firefighters International (FCFI), and Chaplain Gaius Reynolds, President – FCFI; Volunteer Firefighter – Livermore, CO, Fire Protection District

GOD'S MAGNET
A person after God's own heart

MEN WERE drawn to David like a magnet in the years preceding his coronation as king of Israel. Literally thousands of warriors, officers, and men who were drawn to and loyal to David and his cause are documented in 1 Chronicles 12:23–40. During David's rigorous years of refinement and maturity before becoming king, his armies and followers continued to multiply. When people heard the news of his victories and understood the heart of David, the man God had anointed as future king, because he was a man after his (God's) own heart, they rallied to David's side.

As the news media shares the heroic deeds of first responders, as people personally witness the results of their heroic tasks, as documentaries share the life-ending valor of those who responded to the Attack on America, and as movies depict the challenges of first responders, many are drawn to emergency service careers. These careers are like a magnet is to iron to those who desire to serve.

David was fighting for God's cause. First responders are serving their communities. Is it any wonder people were, and are, drawn to these worthy causes?

Many firefighters have mentioned how thankful they are when they learn of others in their departments or the fire service in general who are after God's own heart—men and women who bring not only their train-

68

ing and skill on a call but also bring Christ with them.

The worldly nature and atmosphere of many departments has hindered Christians from stepping forward, proclaiming their faith, and bravely sharing the greatest cause of all—salvation of mankind. It's essential to others' eternal destiny that believers step forward steadfastly. It is through faithful, brave, and determined followers of Christ, sharing the greatest cause ever, that others will be drawn to you, and therefore to Christ, as a magnet is attracted to iron.

Salvation is the greatest cause of all. What good is it if you save a physical life only for the person to face eternal death? Likewise how foolish to serve and save those you don't know, and fail to share your saving knowledge with those you work with! Are you a person after God's own heart?

Prayer:
Lord, may my walk with you be one that draws others to you.

FEBRUARY 20

Reverend Wayne Detzler, PhD, Chaplain (Retired) –
Charlotte, NC, Fire Department; Fellowship of
Christian Firefighters Regional Director

TRAINING DAY
Out the window

HAVE YOU ever been in a working fire?" the chief in charge asked me.

"No," I responded and then added, "I've responded to fires and even manned the hoses, but I've never been inside."

"Today's your 'lucky' day," the chief informed me. "You're going inside this training fire." It was a flaming house on the outskirts of Charlotte. "Get your gear on, Chaplain," he ordered. "If it goes bad," the chief yelled, "throw the chaplain out the window." Then someone handed me an air pack and I followed a firefighter inside the burning structure.

"Hit your knees, Chaplain," the firefighter told me. So I knelt down. This is not a bad position for a chaplain, I thought. "Follow me," she shouted over the din of the fire, and I crawled behind her into the kitchen, where fire danced along the walls and ceiling. "It's more than 1,100 degrees," the young firefighter reminded me as I stared at the fire, mesmerized by its power, its fury.

The chief came on our radio. It was time to go back outside. Even now my smoke-scarred helmet hangs on the wall in front of my desk. It's a constant reminder of that training fire. Never will I forget the courage of the firefighters and the skill with which they knocked the fire down.

Training is a way of life for all of us in the fire service. We train as medics so we can help those who cannot help themselves. We train as firefighters, so we can win the war against the raging inferno. As chaplains, we train as counselors, so we can ease the burdens of our brother and sister firefighters. Training never stops.

> "But grow in grace and in the knowledge of our Lord and Savior Jesus Christ." (2 Peter 3:18)

This is like the Christian life. We never stop learning. From the day of our conversion to the day of our promotion to glory, we are constantly learning, ever embracing new truths from the Word of God. In his final instructions to young Timothy, the apostle Paul urged him to continue to grow in his knowledge and practice of Scripture. This should also be *our* motto, goal, and desire.

Prayer:
Lord, keep my heart and mind open to the truth of your Word.

Lieutenant (Retired) Lou Dattolo,
Tallahassee, FL, Fire Department

STRONG MAN'S HOUSE
"Firefighter up" and do what you need to do

IN ORDER to be a combat firefighter, a person must be in excellent physical condition. Working out in the weight or conditioning room can greatly increase strength, reduce stress and injuries, and help keep that expanding midsection at bay.

All firefighters have no doubt witnessed or heard of feats of strength and endurance in their department. My department has its own legends to remember. One involved a retired officer who, back in his prime, raised the formidable "Bangor" ladder single-handedly. More recent was the outstanding achievement of the firefighter who brought home a gold medal in the bench press from the State Firefighter Olympics. Admirable achievements for sure.

Unfortunately, physical strength is not the main component for holding our families together. I suspect statistics will back up the belief that firefighter families are under more stress than the average American household. The shift work requiring us to be away from home so much, the manifold pressures of the job, and the added general stress and temptations in our society, can cause serious problems in our homes.

> "How can anyone enter a strong man's house and carry off his possessions unless he first ties up the strong man? Then he can rob his house."
> (Matthew 12:29)

Though I'm taking Matthew 12:29 out of its main context, the stand-alone truth of this verse applies to our thoughts and lives today: "How can anyone enter a strong man's house and carry off his possessions unless he first ties up the strong man?" Our family is to be cherished above all our possessions. Unless we tie up the things of the world that weaken our homes (instead of them tying *us* up), our family unity is at risk.

It is your responsibility to resist at all costs being bound by sin, even "the sin that so easily entangles" (Hebrews 12:1). No excuses! The welfare of your family is at stake. Too many firefighters' homes have been "spoiled" in the past. It can happen to your home if you are not diligent.

The Lord stands ready and willing to help you overcome anything that binds you. Seek today to clearly see the things that are weakening your home and then enter the "conditioning room"—be it counseling, family conferences, or personal study. Be strong, "firefighter up," and do what you need to do today.

Prayer:
Lord, help me not to go another day bound by sin. Forgive me for putting my family in jeopardy by doing things that are not pleasing in your sight. Thank you for helping me overcome.

*Rick Barton, Fire Safety Officer; Rick Barton Ministries,
Gunnison, CO; Fellowship of Christian Firefighters
International Ambassador-at-Large*

FALLEN HEROES
Sin will be exposed

"GUYS," HE SAID, "I'm hurting. One of my heroes in the faith has just fallen, and I had to be the one who exposed his sin."

I'd just reported for a seminar along with six other men. One of the guys seemed pretty distraught. As he shared his story, our hearts broke with him. His former youth pastor, who had been his mentor, the one who had discipled his wife and him, had become entangled in sin. This man resisted accountability and eventually slipped into an immoral relationship with a teenage girl. My friend, now a pastor on the same church staff, received a tip. Along with the senior pastor they discovered them in a motel room.

The youth pastor had been a legend in the community. For thirty years he'd served in the church. When rumors began to surface of improper conduct, they were brushed off. After all, he was "the Man." The other pastors asked him to follow a set of common

> "Do not be deceived: God cannot be mocked. A man reaps what he sows." (Galatians 6:7)

sense safeguards: don't counsel girls alone, don't give them rides home without someone else in the car, etc.

He ignored the rules. Eventually, the other pastors laid the law down. No more improper meetings or you're fired. He announced he was leaving; a huge retirement party was planned for this much-loved friend. Then the "tip" came and the discovery was made, followed by public disgrace.

He was immediately terminated. His family and many others were deeply hurt. His legacy of almost three decades was destroyed.

Why is it that we think God doesn't care about sin in our lives? Why do we fail to understand that God meant what he said for us not to be deceived, to understand that God cannot be mocked, and understand that we will reap what we sow (Galatians 6:7).

Please remember two things: First, God is not mocked. Our sin will be exposed and we will suffer punishment for it. Second, our sin never affects only us. It hurts our families, friends, and co-workers, as well as untold numbers of folks who look up to us. As firefighters, husbands or wives, parents, and Christians, remember—folks we don't even know are watching us. Let's set up good safeguards for our conduct. Let's seek and welcome accountability, and when we begin to stray, let's seek his face and ask our fellow Christians to help us "fly straight."

Prayer:
God, I know you can't be mocked. If I stray, please bring fellow Christians to guide my path so I will "fly straight."

Reverend Wayne Detzler, PhD, Chaplain (Retired) – Charlotte, NC, Fire Department; Fellowship of Christian Firefighters Regional Director

I HAVE NO ONE LIKE HIM
Faithful men who are qualified

WHEN WE met for the first time, he was beginning his career. At the same time, I was a new chaplain to the department. Soon we found each other as friends and I gained enormous respect and appreciation for Bill's physical strength (in the community he served as a high school wrestling coach).

At the same time, I learned to respect Bill's unwavering commitment to the Lord. It matched his physical strength, and more. To enhance his ability, he enrolled in a local seminary and started to take courses. He was preparing for more ministry; more service for the Lord.

At the invitation of the seminary, I became his mentor. Together we walked through several years of study. He never gave up. He never wavered in his devotion to the Lord and his service. At the same time Bill became a valued friend and a right-hand man in the chaplaincy ministry. He was always available, always there to lift the burden.

Someone has said true disciples of Jesus are "F-A-T" people. They are Faithful, Available, and Teachable. This sounds basic, almost simplistic. But Bill certainly fits this picture. He graduated from his seminary program and is a valued part of the chaplaincy team. However, this is not the main reason I remember him.

One summer Bill and his wife, Holly, accompanied us on an evangelistic mission trip to Vienna, Austria. It became obvious to all of us Bill was a very gifted evangelistic preacher—speaking nightly on the streets of the Austrian capital. His messages were winsome, attractive to listeners from various cultures.

> "... reliable men who will also be qualified to teach others."
> (2 Timothy 2:2)

Late one night my wife suffered from a severe weakness. She could hardly walk. Without a moment's hesitancy, Bill came alongside and helped her home. His training as an EMT became a lifeline for us as a family.

When retirement time came for me, Bill stepped up again. He became a valuable part of the team who assumed the chaplaincy of the fire department. I felt like the apostle Paul in his estimation of Timothy: "I have no one else like him" (Philippians 2:20).

Prayer:
Lord, bless those faithful men and women who never give up. Help me to be counted among the faithful.

FEBRUARY 24

Chaplain Gilbert Gaddie, Captain – Indianapolis Fire Department; President Indianapolis Chapter Fellowship of Christian Firefighters

I HAVE NON-CHRISTIAN FRIENDS
Being good isn't what it is all about

YES, I'M a firefighter and I do have friends. And for that, I'm blessed. Among my friends are people I feel a burden to share Christ's love and truth with. Unfortunately, it seems many are not ready to accept God's gift.

I understand where these folks stand. There was a time when I was not a true believer in Christ—a time I was open to any and all theologies. I knew God existed, but felt there was an understanding between us: if God wouldn't get in my business, I wouldn't get in his. Arrogant and stupid, yes, but it seemed logical and fair at the time.

Are there people like that in your life, in or out of the workplace, with a similar philosophy? Your knowledge of God's Word may be what they need to hear. Do you have an influence on them? If so, may God lead you to help them understand his truth, even if their measuring stick convinces them they're good according to the Ten Commandments. They may justify their rejection of Christ by saying, "I never killed or seriously hurt anyone," or something similar. But—being good isn't enough.

Regardless of someone's "goodness" the Bible says our decency and righteousness are insufficient. Furthermore, religion, denomination, church, or someone else's relationship with Christ won't save anyone. Only a personal relationship with Christ can do that.

There are religions that tell of being good, and good coming to you, but none, other than Christianity, provides a way to be sinless righteous in God's eyes. None other offers everlasting life through Christ's sacri-

> "Then he [Christ] opened their minds so they could understand the Scriptures. He told them, 'This is what is written: The Christ will suffer and rise from the dead on the third day, and repentance and forgiveness of sins will be preached in his name to all nations, beginning at Jerusalem. You are witnesses of these things.'"
> (Luke 24:45–48)

fice. God's salvation is available to all who confess with their mouth and believe in their heart that Christ is Lord. God raised Christ from his grave, and before his ascension, Christ was a witness and testimony to God, assuring that all who believe on him shall be saved.

With your friends and co-workers, do you feel the same burden I feel? If so, I urge you to be bold. Share the Scriptures, and pray that their eyes will be opened to understanding God's eternal and unfailing truths.

Prayer:

Lord, after you rose from the grave, you witnessed God's love to many, creating an example for me to be the witness you've commanded me to be. Give me the words and help me see the opportunities you've given me to share your truth. Help me be the kind of friend who is not afraid to boldly share your love.

Bob Crum, Co-founder – Fellowship of Christian Firefighters
International (Retired) – Denver Fire Department

SPUR ONE ANOTHER
God's Word directs us to what he holds in high priority

A ND LET us consider how we may spur one another on toward love and good deeds. Let us not give up meeting together, as some are in the habit of doing, but let us encourage one another" (Hebrews 10:24, 25). This foundational verse for the Fellowship of Christian Firefighters International, when expanded to all Christian firefighters, serves as an inspiring and life-changing goal. When bogged down with the details of careers, home, church, community, and ministry responsibilities, God's Word directs us to what he holds in high priority.

Take a close look at Hebrews 10:24, 25. It doesn't speak about ministries. It addresses personal relationships. Is it possible to "spur one another" if we've failed to establish meaningful personal relationships? Sharing a family meal, engaging in conversation in which we truly listen and invest in the other person, and regularly gathering for fellowship, praying, and sharing are all ways to establish trustworthy relationships.

> "So we all agreed to choose some men and send them to you."
> (Acts 15:25)

A new chaplain shared how he enthusiastically started visiting firehouses and, at the first one, headed for the kitchen. He noticed the conversation took a turn from the personal to a stilted, formal exchange of words. He asked the chief about it. The chief explained, "This is the second home to these crew members. Would you walk into a friend's kitchen without being asked?"

Relationships take time to develop. You can't force them into existence. Failure to make the effort results in missed opportunities to share God's truth and love. Busy lives require you to make a concerted effort to support and encourage one another. That can be over coffee, at family meals or activities, via telephone calls or conversations at work. Select a means that fits you, but do not give up meeting together.

Pray about who needs your fellowship. As you do, remember that meeting together as Christians for encouragement is a command of Scripture that needs to be diligently obeyed. Someone's life could depend on it—eternally.

Relationships with other Christians may be the strongest witness you make that Jesus is your Lord and Savior. You are for Christ and you need to conduct yourself in such a manner. Is God speaking to you? Is he saying, "I have chosen you to go and fellowship and speak with others in your workplace, family, community, church . . . ?"

Prayer:
Lord, I say yes, I will go fellowship, encourage,
and share your Word and love.

Captain Raul A. Angulo – Seattle Fire Department;
Fellowship of Christian Firefighters Regional
Director / International Board Member

WELL-GROOMED, OR NOT?

What are you like deep down inside?

ONE SUNDAY, after following my normal Sunday morning routine of an extra-long shower followed by careful grooming—cologne and all—I headed for God's house and wanted to show my respect. I was seated next to a man dressed in clothes he probably hadn't changed in weeks. His dirty hair was matted. He wore old, scuffed dress shoes without socks.

Firefighters are well-acquainted with the dress—and smell—of America's homeless. When the pastor said to turn to the person next to you and say, "I'm glad you're here today!" I wanted to say, "I get enough of this smell at work." But, my wife noticed the man crying and extended her hand in welcome.

Normally, I'm pretty good with the homeless. In our line of work we handle many different smells. Everything smells: fires, burnt food, CPR, vomit . . . and street people. But I wrestled with the thought of that guy all week—I should have shaken his hand. I had let my personal bias and judgmental attitude—my selfish, sinful nature—control my behavior. I realized that when I look at people in church who are well-dressed, I automatically assume they're nice. Talk about judgmental!

Jesus directly addresses this attitude. He clearly says not to judge or we'll be judged—not by human standards, but by God's.

As firefighters we work hard to keep our outward appearance healthy and attractive, but what is in our hearts is more important. The way we are deep down, where others can't see, is what matters most to God.

77

What are you like inside? When you became a Christian, God made you different on the inside. He will continue the process if you ask. God wants you to seek healthy thoughts and motives, not just healthy food and exercise. All your good works are just filthy rags. He wants your heart. But so does the devil and he's not going to let go of you without a fight, an inner spiritual battle that never stops. That's why you must be vigilant against temptation.

> "Do not judge, or you too will be judged. For in the same way you judge others, you will be judged, and with the measure you use, it will be measured to you."
> (Matthew 7:1, 2)

If I spent as much time examining my conscience and preparing my heart as I do preparing my body, I'd be better off. How about you?

Prayer:
Lord, I know that no matter how many times I shower and perfume myself, I can never remove the smell of sin. That stench is only removed with the blood of Jesus Christ. Thank you for removing my smells (sins) and that through your grace, mercy, and love you accept me just as I am.

FEBRUARY 27

Steve Kidd, Firefighter Orange County Fire and Rescue, Florida; Central Florida Chapter of the Fellowship; Author of the Carbusters video series

RIT TO RESPOND
Why would anyone reject rapid intervention and a free rescue?

COMMAND TO dispatch, requesting RIT to respond!"
Rapid Intervention Team—the phrase conjures thoughts of working in a dangerous area while our brothers and sisters are standing by, well-equipped, and ready to save a firefighter in danger. All first responders hope and pray that the day never comes when the Rapid Intervention Team are called upon to save them. To prevent that situation, they train extensively on survival techniques, tactics, and fire ground safety rules.

Jesus Christ had the best idea for rapid intervention. More than two thousand years before any of us was born, Christ intervened on our behalf. He didn't wait for the distress call, because he already knew we were in trouble. He didn't wait to be dispatched; he stepped right in to save us. Christ died so all sinners could live a life everlasting. His intervention was costly to him—rejection, suffering, and an agonizing death. To us, *his rapid intervention* was a free gift. But like any free gift

> "For God so loved the world that he gave his one and only Son, that whoever believes in him shall not perish but have eternal life." (John 3:16)

it does require a simple choice: acceptance or rejection.

Can you imagine a dangerous situation where a life is at stake, the RIT shows up ready to rescue, and then they are turned away? Seems incomprehensible! Makes one wonder why anyone would reject Jesus' rapid intervention and free rescue. But many do.

We would never throw caution to the wind and depend solely on an RIT. That would be truly foolish. Just as foolish would be living a life of sin—irresponsibly depending on the ultimate gift from Christ to save our souls at the very last moment of our mortal walk on Earth.

Christians and many non-Christians are familiar with John 3:16. It is a foundational verse of our faith. If you have accepted Christ, may your foundation be strengthened as you learn more of his truths each day. If you haven't made the choice for acceptance, may his truths become real to you and lead you to eternal life.

Prayer:
Lord, may I never take the greatest of all blessings, your rapid intervention, for granted. Thank you for your gift of eternal life and forgiveness of sins.

Rick Barton, Fire Safety Officer; Rick Barton Ministries, Gunnison, CO; Fellowship of Christian Firefighters International Ambassador-at-Large

OOPS!
Ever feel like a "Class A" dummy?

MY SHIFT was over. I'd drained and parked the engine, and was enjoying a good home-cooked meal when the phone rang. "Barton; go to the garage, get your engine, and head toward Lake City for a smoke report. We want to hit it tonight while it's still small."

It was the middle of fire season and the H's and O's (hazard pay and overtime) would be a blessing. I threw on my Nomex (flame-resistant) clothes, headed to the forest service garage, loaded my gear, picked up my co-worker, and off we went. Adrenaline kicking in, we planned our strategy.

Before long the boss called with directions. As we jostled up a rugged four-wheel-drive road I was impressed how well the engine was doing. It was almost as if it wasn't loaded with 250 gallons of water—oops!

Ever feel like a real "Class A" dummy? Here I am responding to a wildfire with a type 6 brush engine and suddenly realizing I'd forgotten to refill the water tank. Being young, dumb, and scared to death of my fire management officer (FMO), I didn't say anything and started looking for a stream to draft water from. Nothing!

When we arrived on scene, the boss said, "It's up a nasty hillside and we can't safely get to it tonight. Besides, it's in the rocks and not going anywhere. You guys head back to town."

Jesus tells us, "Be dressed ready for service and keep your lamps burning" (Luke 12:35). The apostle Paul admonishes us to "be prepared in season and out of season" (2 Timothy 4:2) to share the truth of Jesus and his salvation. I don't know about you, but I don't want to let my Savior down by showing up with an "empty tank" and not being ready to serve and share the Gospel. I want to refill daily by reading his Word, being in prayer, and yielding to the Holy Spirit's control.

What's that you ask? Did I ever tell my FMO about the empty tank? I can't exactly remember. It's been thirty years or so, and maybe he's reading this . . .

> "In the presence of God and of Christ Jesus . . . I give you this charge: Preach the Word; be prepared in season and out of season; correct, rebuke and encourage—with great patience and careful instruction."
> (2 Timothy 4:1, 2)

Prayer:

Lord, help me be truly prepared in the things that matter most: knowing, showing, and reflecting your Word and truth in all I do. When "Oops!" describes a situation, may I humbly turn to you and learn from the experience what you have to teach me.

Tommy Neiman, Author of Sirens for the Cross;
EMS Training Officer – St. Lucie County, FL;
Fellowship of Christian Firefighters International
Regional Director / International Board Member

GOD'S WAYS

Placing everything in God's hands

MOVIES AND television shows about fire responders appear to have an endless appeal to viewers. *Emergency* was my favorite TV program as a child, one I missed only if forced to. I couldn't get enough of the drama: speeding fire trucks, ambulances, action, quick responses, and realistic heroes in uniform. The intrigue continued into my teenage years. Eventually, armed with a driver's license, I was always on the lookout for the flashing lights of emergency vehicles. But, my first passion in life was sports—in particular, baseball. I loved the game, and from childhood through college, baseball was a central part of my life.

When I turned nine, I experienced God's wonderful saving grace and trusted Christ as my Savior and Master. I sincerely prayed that God's will for my life was professional baseball. And, indeed, throughout high school and college it appeared that baseball was the direction God planned for me. My skill continued to grow until my second year of college, when an awkward fall produced a partial dislocation of my shoulder. As the effects of my injury lingered, doubts filled my mind in regard to a baseball career. All I could do was place everything in God's hands.

> "For my thoughts are not your thoughts, neither are your ways my ways," declares the LORD." (Isaiah 55:8)

As I prayed for direction, my interest in emergency work, especially fire-rescue, heightened. With continued prayer, God's plan began to further unfold. After working in autopsy and several other areas, I felt God ultimately leading me in the direction of the fire academy and paramedic school. I started a career as a full-time firefighter, paramedic, and EMS training officer with the Fort Pierce/Saint Lucie County Fire District in Florida. I also have had opportunities as an ordained pastor to share God's amazing love, provision, and how he best knows his plans for my life and yours.

Discouragement, frustration, doubts, and even anger are common emotions when the plans we have for our lives seem to go awry. I've personally experienced the truth that God's ways, while not always how we would want things to be, are always the best for his glory and our life.

Prayer:
Lord, I know that my thoughts and ways are not always yours.
I also know I can trust in you because your plans are for
me to prosper. Moreover, they are for your ultimate glory.

M A R C H 2

Chaplain Marc Santorella, Firefighter Danvers Fire
Department, MA; Public Fire and Life Safety
Educator and Certified Fire Instructor Level 1

MY HARD HEART
God's grace goes beyond understanding

WHEN A Samaritan woman came to draw water, Jesus said to her, 'Will you give me a drink?' . . . The Samaritan woman said to him, 'You are a Jew and I am a Samaritan woman. How can you ask me for a drink?' (For Jews do not associate with Samaritans.) Jesus answered her, 'If you knew the gift of God and who it is that asks you for a drink, you would have asked him and he would have given you living water'" (John 4:7, 9, 10).

> "Jesus answered, 'Everyone who drinks this water will be thirsty again, but whoever drinks the water I give him will never thirst. Indeed, the water I give him will become in him a spring of water welling up to eternal life.'"
> (John 4:13, 14)

The Samaritan woman must have thought she needed to explain to Jesus who she was (just in case he didn't know).

We do that. We come to God in earnest seeking blessings, but we start by clarifying how undeserving we are (as if God doesn't know). It's like a disclaimer just in case our prayer isn't answered. We give God an out first by praying something like, "Dear God, I know how awesome and perfect you are and how imperfect I am."

God doesn't need a reminder of our imperfections. He already knows. We do, however, have to constantly remind ourselves of God's grace. It's easy to rake ourselves over the coals, while it's difficult to accept the grace of God. We know we're forgiven. God made it clear that his grace goes

82

beyond our understanding, yet we behave as if we still have to earn God's love. We say, "If only I had the same understanding of Scripture as that preacher or behaved as that person . . ." But we should never compare ourselves with others. It's our personal relationship that counts! God is going to meet us where we are now and today: "For the Son of Man came to seek and to save what was lost" (Luke 19:10). He seeks, we respond.

Firefighters are people of action and accomplishment, but think they're the exception to God's grace. This is not so! The cross is for everyone who calls on the name of Jesus. We know there is no sin that can separate us from the love of the Father. So why would we think we are the exception to God's grace?

Prayer:

Soften my heart so I can allow your present Spirit to overcome my fears, my doubts, and restore me to a right relationship with you. I know I'm not the exception to the rule; I'm loved enough to be the recipient of the grace you offer me and I accept that grace today.

MARCH 3

Captain Raul A. Angulo – Seattle Fire Department; Fellowship of Christian Firefighters Regional Director / International Board Member

KEYS TO COMMUNICATION
Applying the fruit of the Spirit

ONE OF THE five leading causes of line-of-duty deaths in the fire service, according to NIOSH (National Institute for Occupational Safety and Health) reports, is a lack of effective fire ground communications. I'd bet that the lack of effective communications also ranks in the top five causes of divorce. Part of the problem firefighters have in communicating with our spouses is the way we're trained.

When we are first married, we're in what is commonly referred to as "the honeymoon period," when problems are amicably resolved. The relationship is pretty fireproof. But we all know from building construction, fireproof material has to be inspected and maintained for its shielding integrity. Steel is probably the strongest material known to man. If we want something to be strong and withstand all kinds of abuse and pressure forces, we build it out of steel. Yet, this strong element has one vulnerable weakness: fire. So we fireproof the steel. It's ironic that this insulating material that protects the great strength of steel can be chipped away with a spatula!

Marriage is no different. The insulating factors that protect a marriage are fragile and can easily be neglected and chipped away.

From Day 1 in fire training, we're trained to be rescuers who respond to emergencies and then fix them! Every emergency starts with a size-up of the problem. We have to quickly identify the problem. What's going on here? Who's in danger? We have to figure this out, come up with solutions, pick the best one, and execute it; and all in a matter of minutes—sometimes even in a matter of seconds! If that solution doesn't provide the desired results, we quickly select another alternative (Plan B) and try that one. Once the problem's solved, we pick up and go on to the next crisis.

> "But the fruit of the Spirit is love, joy, peace, patience, kindness, goodness, faithfulness, gentleness and self-control." (Galatians 5:22, 23)

Sizing up and identifying a problem in a marriage is an important first step in avoiding or "fixing" a crisis, but it's only a first step. Sometimes fixing isn't the issue. Listening attentively with the heart (and patiently with eye contact) to the feeling behind the words is essential in effective communication. It's two-way; it's relational. Fixing and moving on isn't the issue. Incorporating the fruit of the Spirit as listed in Galatians 5:22, 23 is the issue.

Prayer:

Help me communicate my love through my words and actions with patience. Impatience will lead to a breakdown in communication and ultimately a breakdown in the relationship. May the fruit of our love be joy, peace, kindness, goodness, faithfulness, gentleness, and self-control.

M A R C H 4

Rick Barton, Fire Safety Officer; Rick Barton Ministries, Gunnison, CO; Fellowship of Christian Firefighters International Ambassador-at-Large

OFF THE BRIDGE

Rethinking our approach

ARE THE "bridges" you're depending on strong enough to carry you? It was springtime and fires were escalating. Tragically, the spring of 2008 saw the deaths of four wildland firefighters in Colorado. A SEAT (single-engine air tanker) pilot, a water tender driver, and two firemen driving through dense smoke all perished. Each tragic death meant wives, children, and other loved ones left behind.

The two men driving through the smoke were experienced fire personnel attempting to save the lives and property of their friends and neighbors. They had probably driven the road numerous times. But this time, as they crossed a flame-weakened bridge, it suddenly collapsed beneath them, hurling them to their death.

This tragedy should cause all of us to rethink our approach when driving through smoke, fog, or other poor-visibility settings.

What about during the "smoky" times of our lives? When our marriage, finances, or career seems to be going up in smoke, what's going to hold us up? Are the "bridges" we're depending on strong enough to carry us through?

> "He is like a man building a house, who dug down deep and laid the foundation on rock. When a flood came, the torrent struck that house but could not shake it, because it was well built." (Luke 6:48)

As much as they love us, family and friends alone aren't always enough. Fortunately, there is a God who loves us and wants to bring us safely over these burning bridges of life. First Corinthians 10:4 explains how our forefathers "drank from the spiritual rock that accompanied them, and that rock was Christ." A chorus, familiar to many, sings of that truth: "On Christ the solid rock I stand . . ."

What do you rely on? Who is your foundation to bring you safely over the burning bridges of life? If you want a strong foundation, then turn to Christ, the spiritual Rock. He is only a prayer away. Jesus calls out to each of us, "Come to me, all you who are weary and burdened, and I will give you rest" (Matthew 11:28). In other words, he really is our "bridge over troubled waters."

Prayer:
Lord, I turn to you today and every day. Thank you for your Word to guide my way safely over each bridge in my life. Bless and bring your peace to the families and loved ones of those who have lost their lives serving others.

Reverend Wayne Detzler, PhD, Chaplain (Retired) –
Charlotte, NC, Fire Department; Fellowship of
Christian Firefighters Regional Director

LIVING FOR OTHERS
How to give your life away

WHEN WE were missionaries we translated into German Dawson Trotman's little book *Born to Reproduce*. The German title *Fuer Andere Leben,* was so fitting, as it is translated into English, *Living for Others*. Over the years I've met several who understood this, but none did it better than my friend Charlie. We met at our local Fellowship of Christian Firefighters group.

This story goes back to a strange fellow who hung around our church. Each day, during the midday, he came and shot baskets. He never seemed to play basketball with anyone; he just shot baskets on his own. We nodded and said, "Hello," but we knew nothing about him.

One day I came back to the church from a funeral to find him sitting on my steps. "Have you got time for me?" he asked. I ushered him into my office and made him comfortable. Then his story spilled out.

"My name is John. I just feel peace when I'm here at the church," he said. Although he was Jewish, he somehow sensed the church might have answers for him. The day before, he had lost his job at a local hotel, and when he returned home his wife threw him out. Now he was ready to listen.

> "Finally, brothers, pray for us that the message of the Lord may spread rapidly and be honored, just as it was with you."
> (2 Thessalonians 3:1)

Quietly, I explained that the Lord loved him and cared about him. He was more than ready to hear the Gospel, and he was also ready to receive Jesus Christ. I realized he needed someone to disciple him. I prayed for help.

My friend Charlie, the big burly firefighter, came through the door at that very moment. I introduced Charlie to our new brother. The two of them went off for the day. Actually, they spent two days together. Charlie poured his life into the new believer.

What's next? This question dogged our new friend. So, he telephoned his brother in Florida. John's brother was thrilled. He'd come to Christ some time before and had been praying for John. Several weeks later John telephoned from Florida. He had found a large, thriving community of Messianic Jews. He was sitting under the tree teaching Scripture and growing in his newfound faith. It all began because Charlie knew how to give away his life to a new believer.

Prayer:
Help me to multiply my life in the lives of others as I make disciples.

Tommy Neiman, Author of Sirens for the Cross;
EMS Training Officer – St. Lucie County, FL;
Fellowship of Christian Firefighters International
Regional Director / International Board Member

A CALL FOR SPIRITUAL WARFARE
A heated battle between spiritual rulers

I NEVER CONTEMPLATED the great extent to which Paul was cautioning believers regarding spiritual warfare in Ephesians 6:12 until I answered an unusual rescue call for a "sick person." Our suspicions that the caller used a pay phone outside a convenience store were confirmed when we found an older, heavily clothed man crouched near the phone wearing tattered tennis shoes and clutching a plastic bag of odds and ends. The musty smell of moldy clothes was mingled with the smell of stale alcohol on his perspiration-soaked clothes. His eyes reflected frustration and anger.

Experience taught me most vagrants only want a good meal and a place to sleep. I assumed this would be no exception as I spoke to the man. He responded by turning his back toward me and blatantly avoiding me.

When one of my attendants questioned him, he responded without hesitation. I watched closely to see if the man would make eye contact with me. He never did. This was now obvious to everyone.

"I don't feel well. I want to go to the hospital," he insisted, ignoring me and speaking only to my attendant.

As we loaded him into the ambulance, I looked him square in the eye and asked, "Why don't you tell me why you're not feeling well? It seems as if you don't want to talk to me."

He momentarily glared into my eyes. His blurry eyes reflected hate and bitterness. Sadistically, with an evil glare, he said, "Christians will burn in hell!"

I was stunned. He didn't know I was a Christian, yet he attacked me as one. His further actions made it obvious that the power of darkness existed in his speech and actions.

I prayed that God would show me how to respond. When we arrived at the hospital, I looked at him and said, "Hell is a place where demons and people of Satan, not Christians, will burn forever!" As he looked away, I felt assured that the Lord gave me that simple reply. I guess this vagrant needed a little clarification of hell's inhabitants—or at least the evil ruler in this man's dark spiritual world did.

> "For our struggle is not against flesh and blood, but against the rulers, against the authorities, against the powers of this dark world and against the spiritual forces of evil in the heavenly realms." (Ephesians 6:12).

There must have been a heated battle between our spiritual rulers on that day when Ephesians 6:12 took on a very real meaning for this Christian paramedic.

Prayer:
Lord, I thank you for all your protection, be it physical
or against the rulers and powers of darkness.

Dessa Patton, Paramedic Olive Branch, MS and Horn Lake Fire Departments, MS; North Mississippi Medical Center-Fulton Ambulance Service in conjunction with all Itawamba County, MS fire departments

LIFE IS TOO SHORT
So, I kiss my kids more, hug my hubby,
and call my parents frequently

LIFE IS too short to leave things unfinished. Today, when I returned from my twenty-four-hour shift, I kissed my kids each time they came near, hugged my hubby more often, and called my parents just to say, "Hi!" (and I didn't even ask for money).

My entire family was involved in the fire service, and I felt certain I'd join the ranks as well; and eventually I did. Then, when our fire department responded to a tragic wreck, something stirred within me. My admiration for firefighters didn't diminish, but my heart was touched. I felt a distinct calling to the Emergency Medical Service (EMS).

Paramedic courses, a job, marriage, family, and long shifts followed. Planning presented a challenge, especially when the holidays approached. Donning a smile after a tragedy posed an even greater challenge. Sometimes sleep was interrupted, filled with visions of destruction and loss. But, I love what I do.

The first responders I work with make a difference. We perform services that are difficult to describe and sometimes to understand. Daily we face the unusual, causing me to realize second chances are rare. Never was that lesson more vivid than the day I worked back-to-back wrecks that involved children. In the first, a car had been hit broadside. A child died on impact. Until then, I'd felt secure that if my daughter were in her car seat she would be safe. My security blanket was ripped away, my outlook altered. I began to more fully realize the only safe place is in God's hands. Never once have I heard a dying patient say, "I wish I'd spent more hours working."

> "...to bestow on them a crown of beauty instead of ashes, the oil of gladness instead of mourning, and a garment of praise instead of a spirit of despair." (Isaiah 61:3)

Being in emergency services is a constant reminder that no one is guaranteed their next breath—a fact that can cause a jaded outlook. The trick is not to let it. To realize it's okay for your heart to break from time to time, that it's normal to be upset, and that you're not alone. Nurturing your walk with the Lord, getting your priorities in order, and loving and spending time with the important people in your life—those are what's important.

So, I kiss my kids more. I hug my hubby often. I call my parents frequently and don't even ask for money.

Prayer:
Lord, life is too short to leave the important things unfinished.
Bring to my mind the things you would have me do each day
and help me develop relationships built on your love.
Bestow upon me the oil of gladness.

Rick Barton, Fire Safety Officer; Rick Barton Ministries, Gunnison, CO; Fellowship of Christian Firefighters International Ambassador-at-Large

DEAD ON THE MOUNTAIN
Caught in the "blowups"

WHILE I was driving through Tennessee, the radio news announcer broke in: Fourteen firefighters had died on a mountainside in my home state of Colorado. And not just any firefighters, these were hot shots, smokejumpers, and helitack. Fourteen of our strongest, most highly trained men and women perished hours from my home.

I knew Rich, one of the helitack crew, but even those I didn't know personally were part of our fire "family." What had gone wrong? I could have been on that fire, but the Lord had redirected my steps. What unexpected event had occurred? How were they caught off guard? And most of all, why didn't they go into a safety zone?

Every spring, wildland firefighters are required to attend a fire safety refresher to review basic rules and especially the importance of establishing Lookouts, Communications, Escape Routes, and Safety Zones (LCES).

> "I have hidden your word in my heart that I might not sin against you." (Psalm 119:11)

As the details of the South Canyon / Storm King tragedy unfolded, one thing became apparent. Even though these were some of the finest wildland firefighters in the United States, they laid aside the basics of LCES: No lookouts were posted, communication with dispatchers concerning the upcoming high winds was absent, their escape route was up a steep slope, and no adequate safety zones were identified.

When the fifty-mile-per-hour winds aligned with the steep slopes and narrow canyons, disaster was imminent. Looking over all the reports, my heart cringed. Over and over again I heard the expression, "We didn't feel right about it, but . . ."

How many times has the same thing happened to us? Do we ever wonder, "Am I missing something?" Does that little voice inside ever say, "Are you sure about this approach?" As firefighters we know we'd better listen and reevaluate our actions!

How about in other areas of our lives? The Bible tells us we're to hide God's Word in our hearts. This will help us not get caught in the "blowups" of sin (Psalm 119:11). When we have a regular regimen of reading, meditating on, and memorizing Scripture, we're equipping the "little voice" inside us, our conscience, to sound an alarm and warn us away from the death sin brings. And, when the alarm goes off, it's essential to heed it and rethink our direction.

Prayer:
Lord, I don't want to find myself, or my friends, in a funeral procession for fallen servants of Christ, dead on the mountain. May I listen to my fire training and to my training in your will and Word with equal intensity, and then carry out what I learn.

MARCH 9

Lieutenant Danny Legge, Paramedic/Chaplain – Clay County, FL, Fire Rescue

TEFLON PEOPLE
Nothing sticks to them

EVER WISH God would give you his judgmental powers for a few minutes so you could clean up some of the mess this world is in? I've thought about that on more than one occasion, and I'd venture to guess so have you. Having the occasional thought of vengeance isn't going to erase your salvation—nothing can do that! But dwelling on the judgment of others could cause you to be dehydrated and fill your once-overflowing heart with anger—anger toward those "Teflon people" who seem to get away with "murder" and nothing sticks to them. They do what they want. However, if you dwell on such thoughts—it'll drive you insane.

It's good to know God's Word contains such questions and cries for help. Asaph writes in Psalm 73 about God's goodness to Israel and the pure of heart, but Asaph himself almost slipped because of envy for the arrogance and prosperity of the wicked. He views them as free of struggles and burdens, healthy, prideful. He also sees them as violent, callous of heart, and evil-minded people who mock, speak maliciously, set their mouths against heaven, and question God's knowledge. He wonders why they always appear at ease and increase in wealth.

Then personal questions crossed Asaph's mind and he wondered if all his upright and innocent deeds were in vain.

Despair and hopelessness set in as Asaph tried to understand. Then the light shone on the destiny of the wicked and he understood that their destiny was one of destruction, being swept away by terror.

We may never see the wicked among us fall, and I'm not so sure that should be our goal. Our goal should be for the wicked to be saved.

> "But as for me, it is good to be near God. I have made the Sovereign LORD my refuge; I will tell of all your deeds."
> (Psalm 73:28)

I don't pretend to understand why they do what they do or why those who have been placed in charge of them allow them to continue on their path of destruction. I've learned not everybody has been to the "foot of the cross." Jesus prayed to his Father, while on the cross, "Father, forgive them, for they do not know what they are doing" (Luke 23:34). We have to allow these words to enter our hearts and flow from our lips. I no longer pray for the power to "Smite them!" I pray they will meet the One who can guide their next step toward paradise.

Prayer:
I pray not for revenge but for all to meet you. You are my sovereign Lord, my refuge. It is good to be near you as I tell of your deeds.

MARCH 10

Aaron Johnson, Fire Inspector – Martin County, FL

MUCK MOUTH

If you had to eat your words, how would they taste?

THE THIRD chapter of James compares the tongue to a forest fire. A small ember can ignite a huge forest fire. This analogy is pertinent for many reasons. Forest fires can burn quickly, they can cause extensive damage, and they often quickly grow out of control. The forest fire can, and generally does, have far-reaching consequences including the loss of lives, homes, property, new vegetation growth, and the wildlife population.

An amazing thing about forest fires is the creation of "muck fires." When a forest fire occurs, there are often, in areas of extremely heavy brush or swamp, soft areas that cannot be fully extinguished. As a result of this type of terrain, despite firefighting efforts to fully extinguish them, muck fires occur. A muck fire is when this mud or thick growth continues to burn. It can smolder for days, weeks, or even months before finally extinguishing itself.

So it is with the tongue. Whether the tongue is used for good or evil, your words can smolder on forever in your mind and in the minds of those you've offended or hurt.

> "Consider what a great forest is set on fire by a small spark. The tongue also is a fire."
> (James 3:5, 6)

Words are a powerful tool. If you make a joking, flippant, negative comment, it may not mean much to you, but those words you spoke can simmer and smolder inside the hearer indefinitely. As they simmer, friendships can be destroyed, fully or partially extinguished, and people often become hurt, insulted, angry, or even vengeful.

On the other end of the continuum, if you give a quick word of encouragement, or a positive statement, though it may not mean that much to you, the effect of that good word can stay with a person forever.

As you speak, you should remember that the things you say may be no big deal to you, but to the listener they often have a lasting impact. The cliché "You can't eat your words" is more than a saying. If you had to eat them, how would they taste? I encourage you,

Don't be a "muck mouth"!

Prayer:
*Lord, remind me to think before I speak. Give me
control over my mouth and the things I say.*

*Reverend Wayne Detzler, PhD, Chaplain (Retired) –
Charlotte, NC, Fire Department; Fellowship of
Christian Firefighters Regional Director*

THE WORST POSSIBLE NEWS
When it only gets worse

BELIEVERS GATHERED in our family room for a weekly prayer time. These evenings were very precious to us as we shared our lives and our burdens with the Lord. In many ways this was the core of our pastoral ministry to a lovely little congregation in mid-Connecticut.

The ever-present fire department pager interrupted our prayer. I stepped into another room to return the call to our dispatcher. "Chaplain, it's a bad scene." He gave me more information. "There is a fatal accident, and it's at the corner of your street."

Seconds later I was on scene. The accident looked deceptively benign. A small car and a pickup truck sat in the middle of the intersection. The captain met me and briefed me as we walked toward the wreck.

"We've transported the driver, a young woman," the captain began. "She died on the way to the hospital." Her passenger is still in the car. He encouraged me to get into the car, knowing prayer for the victim's family would provide comfort. I sat next to a body covered in a blanket.

"Lord, help us to care for this sad family tonight," I prayed. Then I asked the captain, "What's that white fluffy thing next to my leg?"

"It's her head," the captain replied. "The accident decapitated the passenger." It turned out the passenger, an older woman, was the mother of the driver. Two generations of mothers were gone.

> "Cast your cares on the Lord and he will sustain you." (Psalm 55:22)

I took a police officer and went to the house. A young man was there. We told him the horrible news: His mother and his grandmother were gone. "No, that can't be," he said in shock. "They went to pick up my sister." We took him with us as we went to pick up his younger sister.

Late that night I reached their father at his workplace. When he arrived at the hospital it was my task to tell him that both his wife and his mother-in-law were gone. We helped him identify the bodies.

Only the Lord can give peace at a time like this. We were able to comfort this dear family, because the Lord is our shelter and strength. Only by casting our cares on God can we find peace amid such an incomprehensible and tragic loss.

Prayer:

Thank you, Lord, because no burden is too big to roll over onto you.

Rick Barton, Fire Safety Officer; Rick Barton Ministries, Gunnison, CO; Fellowship of Christian Firefighters International Ambassador-at-Large

PRESCRIBED FIRE OR WILDFIRE

I'd lit off too much at once

BARTON, IS everything okay up there? The Buena Vista District called and reported a lot of smoke coming from your location."

"Affirmative, everything's fine," I answered as I scrambled to hold a section of line the rapidly moving fire was threatening. And, the problem was, I'd lit the fire!

One of the more enjoyable tasks of wildland firefighters is conducting prescribed burns. Under the right conditions, we mark off a section of ground that would benefit from fire. Then, we set a fire under controlled circumstances. This benefits the ecosystem and is much cheaper for the taxpayer than mechanical thinning. The downside is that prescribed burning is as much an art as it is a science—it's just not precise. Just a slight miscalculation in fuel moistures, a change in wind speed or direction, or an unexpected weather system, and things go crazy. Even the best fire managers have been caught off guard. And I wasn't one of the best. I was a green forest service employee entrusted to burn off a small corner of land on Waunita Pass. I'd lit off too much at once—it seemed like the whole world was on fire, and I was sweating bullets!

> "And this is my prayer: that your love may abound more and more in knowledge and depth of insight, so that you may be able to discern what is best and may be pure and blameless until the day of Christ."
> (Philippians 1:9, 10)

Isn't life like that sometimes? Aren't there some pretty good things in our lives that, if left unmonitored, can become destructive? Maybe it's being a hard worker. Obviously that's a good thing! But what happens when we spend so much time and energy at work that we begin to neglect our family and church? Perhaps it's a hobby, sporting activity, or even video games. Not necessarily bad in themselves, but bad when we lose control and they consume us. I've found that the simplest acts, with just a few miscalculations and lack of oversight, can turn a beneficial, productive "prescribed fire" into a tragic, destructive "wildfire" in our lives. I can even spend so much time doing ministry that I don't have time for the One I'm ministering for.

What happened on Waunita Pass that day? Well, the Lord gave me grace. When the fire hit my control line, it stopped. I learned a lesson. Don't light off more than you can manage, and keep watch all the time. Not a bad lesson for life, is it?

Prayer:
Give me godly discernment, Lord, so I am careful about the activities, even "good" ones, in my life, so they remain beneficial for my family, God's kingdom, and me.

Jeff Turkel, Firefighter/Dispatcher – North Pole, Alaska; Fellowship of Christian Firefighters Regional Director

AFTER THE ADRENALINE
It was a different story

WHILE STATIONED at Eglin Air Force Base in Florida, I awoke to lights and bells as the dispatcher's not-so-soothing voice ordered us to a mutual aid call for a vehicle accident.

We found a Volkswagen Beetle, with the headlights almost pointing at the taillights and the hood wrapped around a power pole that had been split in two. A sixteen-year-old girl's ejected body was removed from the scene when the first ambulance arrived. Crews waited almost an hour before starting extrication while the power company shut down the power. I assisted the paramedics with primary and secondary surveys for this second sixteen-year-old girl.

To this day I can tell you how she looked, dressed, and how her voice sounded. She was alert and oriented to time and place

> "We wait in hope for the Lord; he is our help and our shield. In him our hearts rejoice, for we trust in his holy name."
> (Psalm 33:20, 21)

as I asked all the standard questions. She didn't appear to be in much physical distress other than being agitated about her boyfriend's condition; he was also still trapped in the car. As I laid the stretcher strap across her stomach, she let out a scream; I feared she was suffering from severe internal injuries. However, a look of peace I'll always remember came over her when I told her she was being taken care of by the best paramedics in the world and that we would soon have her at the hospital. Then I broke the cardinal rule—I told her, "You'll be okay."

Her boyfriend suffered from a doorpost embedded in his skull. He was seventeen, alive, but brain dead. The last body extricated was that of a sixteen-year-old boy.

Back at the station afterward, unable to sleep, I drank cup after cup after cup of coffee. On scene, I was okay, concentrating on the task at hand. However, I found that when the adrenaline left, it was a different story. Soon we learned disheartening news: The second girl had been pregnant. She and the baby had died at the hospital.

Three teens tragically lost their lives. One precious unborn baby died. One boy was left brain dead, the tragic result of drinking and driving.

No, I don't think I'll ever forget this one.

Prayer:
When images of the calls that are hard to forget haunt my mind,
help me remember you are my Rock and my Fortress, and that
I must dwell in your shelter and peace, not in memories
of things over which I have no control.

MARCH 14

Rev. Joe Smaha, Chaplain/Fire Inspector/Firefighter/EMT/
Hazmat Specialist – Paramus, NJ, Fire Department;
Fire Instructor – Bergen County, NJ, Fire Academy;
Pastor – Community Church of Paramus

ROUTINE

On a seemingly routine call,
I learned to "be prepared for the worst"

TIME SPENT at the firehouse waiting for calls can be monotonous, especially since many are routine calls jokingly referred to as "smells and bells" calls. "Smells" come from individuals who smell, or feel certain they smell, smoke, natural gas, or other unfamiliar odors. "Bells" refers to fire alarms caused by unattended cooking, burnt toast, or dust from cleaning or construction projects, alarm malfunctions, and malicious intentional false alarms. Other routine calls are good-intent calls from a passerby unable to discern a real fire from the smoke of a backyard grill or steam from an overheated automobile. All these result in a large percentage of our daily responses being false alarms.

I admit I've wrongly assumed a call was another of those false alarms. Such was the case when my Paramus, New Jersey, fire department was dispatched to a residential fire alarm. Ninety percent of our residential fire alarm calls range from alarm system malfunctions to unattended cooking, so I assumed this was another of "those calls." As we approached this "routine call," our ears perked up, our attitude changed, and adrenaline flowed at the sight of the smoldering inferno before us.

As part of the first line in, I descended the stairs into the smoke-filled basement, staying low until finding the seat of the fire a burner on a stovetop that ignited the surrounding contents, walls, and ceiling. As we extinguished the source of the fire, we discovered the flames extended into an adjacent walk-in closet and laundry room. Grabbing the pike pole, we opened up the walls and ceilings and extinguished the fires.

> "Preach the Word; be prepared in season and out of season; correct, rebuke and encourage— with great patience and careful instruction."
> (2 Timothy 4:2)

From a firefighting standpoint this was a "routine" fire. But it was not the 90 percent variety we have come to expect. Other, not-so-routine, calls followed and unfortunately, with our preconceived belief that they were "smells or bells" calls, we sometimes ignored proper firefighting procedure.

God was looking out for us. In addition, I learned not to be lulled into a false sense of security by thinking a call is just "routine." My new motto is "Be prepared for the worst." It's better to be safe than sorry.

Prayer:
*Lord, I pray that when a call appears to be a "smell or bells"
call I won't assume it is a "routine" call but will view it as I should
any other call and be prepared. When opportunities to share
your love present themselves, may I be equally prepared.*

Dr. Jonathan Newell, Missionary Malawi, Africa

WOUNDS THAT SPEAK OF THE GREATEST LOVE

His wounds were not something to be ashamed of!

AFTER AN extremely serious fire in a warehouse in the town of Limbe, Malawi, Africa, acting in my role of chaplain on behalf of the brave men I work with, I met with an insurance company to discuss possible financial assistance for the Malawian firemen. One fireman had risked his life to save two of

> "Then I saw a Lamb, looking as if it had been slain, standing in the center of the throne." (Revelation 5:6)

his colleagues from certain death in that burning warehouse. Since the fire had been extensively covered in the national papers, I asked this fireman to accompany me to the arranged meeting. When I met him, he still had the wounds and scars on his hands and face caused by the burns he received.

As he talked to the insurance company representative, I noticed she was very much aware of his wounds from the fire. My mind then drifted to the importance of our faith and the reality of it.

This man risked his life to save two colleagues. He entered into the dangerous flames to save his friends and in so doing he was burnt himself. Did he think about it first? I doubt it. His selfless actions are living outward proof of his love for his colleagues and it was there for all to see. His wounds were not something to be ashamed of!

There was another man, who entered into the fires of sin for us. He gave up his life for us so we might not be burnt by those flames. It was terribly costly for him to do this. So costly, in fact, that the wounds he suffered in sacrificing his life for us will be there for all to see in heaven forever. He did this willingly, even though he knew in advance what he would suffer.

Why should we ever doubt the love of our God when we think of our Lord Jesus Christ and those wounds he bears today on his hands and feet and in his side because of that love? Are you aware of those wounds? Do they reaffirm your faith in times of peril (and in times of safety)?

Prayer:
Our Father, thank you for sending your Son to die for me. Whenever I start to doubt your great love for me, help me remember the wounds your Son bears today as he stands in Glory at your right hand.

Captain Ed Godoy Jr., Firefighter – Monroe, NY;
FDNY Auxiliary Corps

GOD HAS A PURPOSE FOR YOU: THE SIGNS ARE THERE
Nothing is too small for God

WHILE SEARCHING eBay for fire memorabilia, I came across a die-cast kit-bash model of my old fire company's truck, Engine 54. I bid on it for my extensive collection until I won.

The seller asked if I was a New York City fireman. I explained I was a retired auxiliary firefighter from Engine 54 and spent most of my life around fire engines. I shared Engine 54's history, and pictures of Engine 54 and Ladder 4 apparatus. The seller gave me the e-mail address for John, the gentleman who lost the bid. John's father, Edward Fitzgerald, was assigned to Engine 54 in the 1950s and 1960s. I knew his father but lost track of him when he transferred to Ladder 35. I learned he had passed away from a brain tumor in1983.

John asked if I had a picture of his dad and the fire company. Regrettably, I didn't but was inspired to locate one. Meanwhile, John met Mike Myles, a former member of Engine 40 who worked with Ed for fifteen years. I told John I had a company photo taken in 1968 and Mike was in the picture. I forwarded it to John, who in turn showed it to Mike.

> "The Lord will fulfill [his purpose] for me; your love, O Lord, endures forever—do not abandon the works of your hands." (Psalm 138:8)

A month later, I received a call from Pete, one of the Engine 54 guys who looked after me when I was growing up around the firehouse. He'd talked to Mike Myles and thus the surprise call after ten years of no contact.

I know God had his hand in this. Still I was disappointed I couldn't provide John with pictures of his dad. But God wasn't done. I awoke early one morning, felt prompted to search eBay, and discovered four 1960 photographs of old Engine 54; to my amazement a young Ed Fitzgerald stood in two photos. John and my prayers were answered. I made a winning bid and e-mailed John the photos.

God works in mysterious ways. Nothing is too small for God. He guided me to the truck on ebay, which opened the door to help one man obtain information and history of his father's past and see him as a young

New York City firefighter. This experience reminded me God does have a purpose for everyone. He is with me, guiding me in all things.

Prayer:
Thank you for always being there and caring about all things, whether major or minor. Help me to never ignore your promptings even if I need to step out of my normal routine or comfort zone. Thank you that your love endures forever.

M A R C H   1 7

Reverend Wayne Detzler, PhD, Chaplain (Retired) – Charlotte, NC, Fire Department; Fellowship of Christian Firefighters Regional Director

A WORLD BETWEEN
Life and death in the urban jungle

IT'S A STRANGE strip of territory. Our small town had several conflicted areas and this was the most pathetic. On one side of the street children played. Some of them were even the children of a young mother from our church. On the other side, drug deals went down in plain sight. Nothing seemed to stop the drug business, and we prayed daily for the safety of the dear little ones.

"Working fire" was the alert I received from our dispatcher. The address was familiar, right in the middle of the drug district. Quickly, I made my way to the scene. The flames had been knocked down by the time I arrived. I reported in to the incident commander, and he instructed me to proceed to the second floor of the burnt building.

"Over here," a firefighter shouted. "Chaplain, come over here." Laid out in the long hallway was a human form, a man. His face was ashen; it really looked like white ash. Out of his jeans came little tongues of fire. He'd obviously burned to death in the blaze.

"Hit it with the hose," the officer instructed. A firefighter focused the whole stream on the dead body, instantly extinguishing the little flames. "Now, pray with us, Chaplain," instructed the officer, asking me to kneel and pray.

Seeking words of hope, I paused briefly as I went to my knees. Then I prayed for the family of this man. His identity was not yet known, so

101

we'd not been able to track down a next of kin. All I knew was that he died a terrible death in the midst of an out-of-control fire.

Then I prayed for the firefighters. I thanked the Lord they were there. I asked the Lord to wipe from their memories the scene before us. After we prayed, I waited

> "I am the resurrection and the life. He who believes in me will live, even though he dies." (John 11:25)

with them for the medical examiner to come. As I waited, we thanked the Lord for his presence in this dark scene of death. We don't know if the man knew the Lord, but we do know that if he did, *he will live again* with the Lord.

Calls like this bring to the forefront of our minds how quickly a person can leave this earth for eternity. Jesus is the resurrection and the life, he is the eternal hope we pray for and seek to share by our words and actions.

Prayer:
*For this eternal hope even in the face of tragic death,
I thank you, Lord of Life.*

MARCH 18

Tommy Neiman, Author of Sirens for the Cross; EMS Training Officer – St. Lucie County, FL; Fellowship of Christian Firefighters International Regional Director / International Board Member

JUST BEAT IT!

He couldn't understand the meaning of the words "Beat it"

RICO OFTEN staggered around the higher-crime area of our district hoping for a handout. Such was the case when we responded to a call for "a possible stroke" victim at an elderly lady's house in a high-crime area. When we arrived on scene, there was Rico in his usual intoxicated state, hanging around the house and blocking our way. No doubt, when he heard the sirens, he anticipated his golden opportunity for a handout from the fire-rescue guys. He probably thought he was lucky because he didn't even have to flag us down in traffic—we'd already

102

stopped and were easily accessible. He persisted in his begging. We ignored him as much as possible, rushed past him, proceeded to the front porch, and headed toward our patient. She appeared conscious and alert. We began to assess her condition and gather medical information. Rico, refusing to be ignored, boldly walked up to the front porch. Disgusted, my partner ordered Rico to go away.

Did Rico listen? Of course not. Not only did he not leave, he then decided to open the porch door and walk in.

"You got a dollar?" Rico asked in response to being told to leave.

The more my partner tried to get Rico to leave, the more persistent Rico became. The clincher came when I heard my partner say, "Rico, just beat it!"

So what did Rico do? He started dancing around in his intoxicated state singing the words to the then-popular Michael Jackson song "Beat It."

I couldn't hold back my laughter despite my compassion for this poor lady. We knew further on-scene assessment was out of the question. We loaded her quickly into the unit. As we headed for the hospital, we dodged a dancing Rico at the end of the driveway. He just couldn't understand the meaning of the words "Beat it."

> "Here I am! I stand at the door and knock. If anyone hears my voice and opens the door, I will come in and eat with him, and he with me." (Revelation 3:20)

Laughter is a great way to relieve stress and frustration, but there is an even better way. We have an Advocate who is standing on "our porch," but he won't come in uninvited. We must open the door and ask him in. When we do, he willingly comes in. What a joy to eat with Christ and share personal fellowship with him!

Prayer:
I thank you, Lord, for the gift of laughter, but those thanks are multiplied beyond mention for when you stood at my door and entered into my life when I uttered the simple words, "Yes, Lord, come into my life."

Ken Cofiell, Dispatcher/Firefighter/EMT (Deceased) –
Anne Arundel County, MD, Fire Department

EVERY CALL

"I sit beside my lonely fire
And pray for wisdom yet.
For calmness to remember,
Or courage to forget."

CHARLES HAMILTON AIDE

EVERY CALL a firefighter goes out on leaves a lasting impression. Sometimes the memory is permanently imprinted in the recesses of the mind, occasionally returning to haunt one's consciousness. I've had several of these as I'm sure others have as well.

When I began this job everything was red lights, sirens, fighting fires, and trying to save lives. With time the gravity of the job surfaced. One call that caused this was for a fifteen-year-old girl lying across the bed with an elderly man supporting her head. With tears, he said, "She's dying, she took something."

> "God is our refuge and strength, an ever-present help in trouble. Therefore we will not fear, though the earth give way and the mountains fall into the heart of the sea." (Psalm 46:1, 2)

When she gasped for air and whispered, "Please don't let me die!" I mentally promised her I wouldn't let her die. As I administered CPR, I felt her pulse rapidly slowing. "We need to get her to the hospital. NOW!" I called to the other medics.

The crew worked feverishly as we transported her. When we arrived at the hospital, the back of the unit was covered with empty supplies and debris from the valiant attempt at lifesaving. She was in full arrest. The drugs failed; the defibrillator was exhausted of power. The hospital staff wanted to take over CPR, but we wouldn't quit. A promise, though never verbalized, had been made.

As continuous drugs and shocks had a diminishing effect, her frantic words, "Please don't let me die!" ran through my head. I refused to give up. One doctor said, "There's one more thing we can try," and an external defibrillator was wired to her heart. CPR continued while the device was installed, but her heart didn't react. There was nothing more to do.

All we had done was to no avail. Even though she lay lifeless, I continued to hear her voice: "Please don't let me die."

What would make a fifteen-year-old girl do this? How could one so young experience such complete despair?

Informing the family was heart-rending.

"She took a whole bottle of her grandfather's heart pills," the mother sobbed. "She's been depressed because she thought she wasn't pretty or popular. Now she's dead."

As the girl's plea for life continued to ring in my ears, I turned to my source of strength, my heavenly Father. Then I wept that this child who chose death instead of God's strength and promise of eternal life. Bowing my head, I praised God for first responders and medical personnel who refuse to give up and prayed that they, too, seek God's refuge and draw their strength from him in times of trouble!

Prayer:
Lord, I thank you that I am a part of this profession filled with men and women who do not give up and are dedicated to serving others even though we take a little bit of every call with us. I turn to you when calls discourage my heart and haunt my thoughts.

MARCH 20

Sue Reynolds, Missionary – Fellowship of Christian Firefighters International (FCFI), and Chaplain Gaius Reynolds, President – FCFI; Volunteer Firefighter – Livermore, CO, Fire Protection District

WHAT HAPPENED
A brother in need is a brother indeed

I DON'T UNDERSTAND what happened! He's a pillar in our department and our church, and active in the ministry to the firefighters and their families in his area. If anyone needed anything, he was there or made sure someone else was. He seemed to have it all together—a loving wife, two kids—and now this?" As I listened to him pour out his concern for a friend stepping outside God's will, I understood why God recently directed me to a study of King David.

David advanced through the ranks, so to speak, from shepherd to hero when he slew Goliath, then to military prowess, and then to the role of anointed king. Unlike most kings before him, he was highly honored and respected by both God and man. He wrote many psalms expressing to God his anguish, and his adoration of God. He was God's anointed king who brought victory and security to Israel. With his position came recognition, many luxuries, and, unfortunately, leisure time. As he idly wandered about at night on his rooftop, while his men were fighting for Israel, he looked, paused, and failed to heed God's command, acting on temptation. His consequent sins brought continued strife to his family.

> "... for though a righteous man falls seven times, he rises again, but the wicked are brought down by calamity. Do not gloat when your enemy falls; when he stumbles, do not let your heart rejoice."
> (Proverbs 24:16, 17)

David would have been much better off if he had understood what God later wrote through Paul in 1 Corinthians 10:12: "So, if you think you are standing firm, be careful that you don't fall!"

Isn't it just like that old crafty tempter to attack people when they're down, in need, or feeling as if they are so strong in their ministry and personal relationship with God they let their defenses down? Be it idleness, absorption in good works, or false assurance leading to the belief, "Not me. I'd never do that!" Satan knows our weaknesses and is out to destroy people's ministries.

Are you feeling blessed? Used of God? Secure in your walk with him? If so, praise God, enjoy your blessings, but stay alert to the continual necessity of avoiding sin.

If a friend is succumbing to temptation, help him rise again, and don't gloat. Pray, be there, and pray some more.

Prayer:
Let me always act on the principle that "a brother in need is a brother indeed." When I see a brother or sister falling, use me, Lord, to lift them up and not gloat. Likewise, help me never feel I'm "standing so firm" that I'm above temptation. May I continue to let your Word be a light for my path.

Steve Kidd, Firefighter Orange County Fire and Rescue, Florida; Central Florida Chapter of the Fellowship of Christian Firefighters; Author of the Carbusters video series

THE FIRE THAT SHOULD NEVER BE EXTINGUISHED

Seems contrary to what most firefighters dedicate their life to

"THE FIRE on the altar must be kept burning; it must not go out." This passage from Leviticus 6 seems contrary to what most firefighters dedicate their life to—putting out fires. And putting out fires is good; firefighters are trained to put out fires with skill and precision. Add to that the spiritual application for the Christian firefighter of extinguishing the flames of hell. We know that is eternally good. But keeping a fire burning? How can that be good? What does God mean by that? How does that apply to you today?

The fire referred to in Leviticus speaks of an Old Testament law that the fire on the altar that must not go out because it was a sacrificial fire where burnt offerings were made to God as a sweet and pleasant aroma.

We no longer are required to use burnt offerings as part of our worship, thanks to the ultimate offering Jesus gave on the cross in our behalf. However, the flame mentioned here is symbolic of the eternal flame that burns within all of us that was lighted by the Holy Spirit when Christ entered our lives. Notice that each morning the priest was to do his part to keep that flame burning. That application is important to us as well. We must do our part to keep the flame burning— be it prayer, study, fellowship with other Christians, service, tithing, or listening to Christian radio, television, or CDs. We must do something every day that keeps the flames of the Spirit burning within us. A growing relationship with God depends on it.

As firefighters continue to answer calls for help, fight fires, and save lives, if we've accepted God as our Lord and Savior, we

> "The fire on the altar must be kept burning; it must not go out. Every morning the priest is to add firewood and arrange the burnt offering on the fire and burn the fat of the fellowship offerings on it. The fire must be kept burning on the altar continuously; it must not go out."
> (Leviticus 6:12, 13)

can know without a doubt he lives within and is tending the fire within us as we do his work. God's love for us is a forgiving love and his Spirit is brightened each time we serve him by serving others.

Are you taking Jesus with you? Are you sharing that eternal flame with those God brings in your path each day?

Prayer:
Thank you, Lord, for the lessons from the Old Testament that remind me of the importance of keeping the flames of my faith burning. Thank you for living within me and tending the fire within me as I do your work.

MARCH 22

Dwayne Clemmons, Adjunct Instructor – Virginia Department of Fire Programs; Founder – DMC Ministries; Author of Exploits, Jesus Rides in an Ambulance, and Utterances from the Throne Room; Volunteer in Fire and EMS for forty years in Virginia

WHY DO WE NEED TO FELLOWSHIP?

Synergy: The parts together are greater than the sum of the individual parts

FIRST RESPONDERS are, by nature, social people. Most like to engage in communication, develop relationships, and participate in a variety of activities. In the fire service you won't last long if you don't like to be together with people. In fact, it's essential for survival that we get along.

What is the true benefit of fellowship? Hebrews makes it clear we are to provoke one another to love and good works. Fellowship leads to friendship. Friends are powerful allies who enable us to accomplish more together than if we remain isolated. There's a word, *synergy,* that means that the parts together are greater than the sum of the individual parts.

The nature of our business is teamwork. We have RIT teams, HTR teams, hazmat teams, hose teams, search-and-rescue teams, and EMS crews. We have companies, districts, battalions, and divisions. All are collections of people and resources designed to accomplish specific tasks.

The Fellowship of Christian Firefighters is a support organization with the mission of encouraging and bringing hope and unity to fire service workers. It has an international board subdivided into regions and chapters to afford people the opportunity to achieve the greatest result from their efforts.

Now, let's get personal. Are you deliberate and intentional in your desire to spend time and fellowship with your spouse and children? We see, and have experienced, the results one's occupation can have on the family. However, I'm convinced we often use our profession as an excuse for an escape from family problems.

> "And let us consider how we may spur one another on toward love and good deeds. Let us not give up meeting together, as some are in the habit of doing, but let us encourage one another—and all the more as you see the Day approaching."
> (Hebrews 10:24, 25)

I challenge you as a Christian to purpose in your heart to be deliberate in your actions, and to commit to God to not forsake spending time with your family. To fellowship with them, encourage them, exhort and edify them, and be the glue that binds them together. To provoke them to love, love them to life, and lead them to God.

If you do this at home, then it will be an easy transition at work, in your church, and everywhere else you go. It's all about relationship. This begins with your relationship with God.

Prayer:
Lord, help me be a team player at work, at church, and most of all at home. Show me how to be a better encourager and how to create synergy in all I do.

MARCH 23

Daniel A. Clegg, Rural-Metro EMT; Engineer/EMT–Indianapolis Fire Department (Retired); Fellowship of Christian Firefighters Regional Director / International Board Member

ENJOY LIFE
Take time to "smell the flowers"

LET ME encourage you to slow down, enjoy life, and be content. Everything that needs to be done will be, and if not, was it more important than taking time to enjoy life? Have you stopped to just take time to enjoy your family, to read a good book, to just stroll through the park with your wife or children, and to talk to and praise God?

Because of the nature of our job, firefighters seem to live on the edge of instant activity and yes, there is a time and need for that. But there is also a need to take time to relax and enjoy the gifts God has given you. Are you too busy to be content? Do you feel as if there are too many achievements to reach, too many dollars to be earned, too many promotions to be sought? Have you ever thought that if you were content, someone might think you've lost your ambition?

Jesus encourages you to rest in him because he is humble and gentle (Matthew 11:28–30). The only true rest from hectic lives comes from God and resting in his love, which endures forever. Staying on that fast track—when it's a pattern of life—can cause you to lose your ability to be content with

> "I will praise you, O LORD, with all my heart; I will tell of all your wonders. I will be glad and rejoice in you; I will sing praise to your name, O Most High." (Psalm 9:1, 2)

what you have. It hinders your appreciation for the family God has given you. Isn't that exactly what Satan wants to do? And he is definitely on the fast track. He is here to steal, to kill, and to destroy. We know this because Jesus told us so in his own words: "The thief comes only to steal and kill and destroy . . ." Then came the most important part: Jesus came so we can live a full and abundant life (John 10:10).

Are you taking time to enjoy God's gifts? Is your life abundant? Are you taking time to smell the flowers? Are you taking time to enjoy your family? And are you praising God for all the gifts he has provided for you?

The Psalms contain numerous verses of praise to the Lord. Praise is a reflection of our heart condition—a heart that rests in God and takes time to enjoy the abundance he has bestowed upon you.

Prayer:

I praise you, Lord, for all you have done for and given me. I rejoice in you and yes, Lord, I will take time to "smell the flowers."

Chief Lee Callahan, Burlington, MA; Fellowship of Christian Firefighters International Regional Director / International Board Member

TIME TO HEAL
God's Word says so

MORNING equipment check is complete, so you stop for that first cup of coffee around the station's kitchen table. Conversation turns to what's happening in everyone's families, sports teams, current news events, and quite often politics.

Politics seems to bring out the best, or should I say "beast," in people. Everyone seems to have an opinion on almost every issue. During election years, we're fed a constant buffet of fifteen-second sound bites about why we should vote for a particular candidate. After a long primary season, political parties select their final candidates, who try to persuade voters they're the best choice. Finally comes the opportunity—no, the obligation—to vote. At the end of the day new leaders are elected.

Political discussions (and hopefully not-too-heated debates) may be supplemented by a bumper sticker or a yard sign in support of your candidate, or you may even have contributed to a campaign financially. Maybe you're among those who quietly watch the process and pray you'll make a wise decision when you vote.

No matter how you handle elections, there's no question that they tend to polarize people. Many people love their candidates and can't stand their opponents. Feelings

> "A soft answer turns away wrath, but a harsh word stirs up anger."
> (Proverbs 15:1)

become extremely strong, and the firehouse is not immune to those strong feelings. Many things are often said in the heat of debate that would never otherwise be said. Feelings are often hurt and wounds opened that may take a long time to heal. It seems that happens all over the country as people line up on candidates' sides.

Due to the huge effort to get voters to participate in the process of electing our leaders, the animosity that grows for the other party's candidate can transfer to our personal and firehouse relationships.

Many feelings are hurt because of politics. The workplace is no different than anywhere else such discussions take place. But now is the time for healing, to reach out to those you disagree with, seek forgiveness, and start new with those you work with. Speak with great anticipation regarding the future. And if you think arguing about your differing opinions is better than seeking reconciliation, think again. God's Word says otherwise.

Prayer:
*May my words be pleasing to you, Lord. May they
be spoken in love and forgiveness, not anger.*

M A R C H   2 5

*Reverend Wayne Detzler, PhD, Chaplain (Retired) –
Charlotte, NC, Fire Department; Fellowship of
Christian Firefighters Regional Director*

RAIN, WIND, AND WEDDING
What God has joined together

THE HAPPIEST task a fire chaplain has is bringing firefighters together in marriage with their loved ones. Over the years I have married people in every imaginable situation. Sometimes it was in a quaint little Southern chapel, but most times it was in an unusual place.

A few months after my appointment in Charlotte, I joined a happy wedding party on a lovely cruise boat. As we glided across a picturesque lake, the arson investigator and his fire captain fiancée stood on the upper deck. There I joined them to one another.

As the bride progressed to the position of battalion chief our friendship grew deeper. None of us would ever forget the lake cruise wedding and the good old Southern "pig picking" that served as the reception.

One of the investigator's colleagues caught the idea. He asked me to meet him and his fiancée at a nearby lakeside park. The Saturday afternoon was picture perfect, but it was also windy. As I shouted the wedding words over the noise of the wind, the investigator and his love said their "I do's." Decorations flew around the site in a wild twist on wedding scenery.

Jeff was a long-time firefighter, and he and his fiancée invited me to perform their wedding behind their home. It looked like a simple garden wedding. North Carolina weather virtually guaranteed an ideal setting. So, at the agreed time we showed up and surveyed the scene, beautifully adorned for the big event. As the bride and groom had arrived before me, the ceremony started. So did the thunder. Scarcely had I uttered my "Amen" when the rain pelted down.

I love weddings. They are a perfect opportunity to retell the story of God's love for us.
The picture from Scripture is a bridal picture,
because the believers are collectively the bride
of Christ. The Gospel assures us that Jesus
loves us with the purest and most powerful
love possible.

> "What God has joined
> together, let man
> not separate."
> (Matthew 19:6)

Furthermore, the wedding takes us all the way back to the Garden of
Eden. There the bride and groom were the first ever, and the Lord himself married them. Together they became "one flesh" (Genesis 2:24).

Rain and wind, the storms of life come and go, but when God has
joined two, who are then one flesh, that strong unity can weather the
worst of storms. With God, nothing is impossible.

Prayer:
*Loving Father, I do thank you for giving me the
great example of a Christian marriage.*

*Daniel A. Clegg, Rural-Metro EMT; Engineer/EMT–Indianapolis
Fire Department (Retired); Fellowship of Christian Firefighters
Regional Director / International Board Member*

MY MENTOR

*Alzheimer's robbed her of her speech, memory, and balance,
but not her love of Jesus*

MARY WINGLER was a vibrant lady, full of vigor, love, and concern. She always had time for others and always took time to pray.
For six years she was my Sunday school teacher. She taught me how to
read, cross-reference, and trust the Bible, and find God's promises for
myself. I'll never forget my first prayer vigil. Mary was my prayer partner. We were supposed to pray thirty minutes straight. I was sure that was
impossible. We began to pray. Two hours later I got up to leave for work.
Mary was still on her knees praying.

Then Mary was afflicted with the dreaded disease of Alzheimer's. For
nearly seven years she was confined in the Brownsburg Health Care Facility west of Indianapolis. My job as a care-a-van driver for Rural-Metro
Indianapolis led me to that nursing home on several occasions. Whenever
there, I visited Mary. I struggled within to walk down the hall to her

room. I'd have rather remembered her the way she was, but I always made that journey. As I did, I asked God, "Why did you bring this disease on a faithful servant like Mary? Why, God, did you strike her down with such a dreaded, debilitating affliction?"

When I attended Mary's homegoing, a ray of understanding penetrated my heart. I listened to her three children, Shirley, Mark, and Barbara, talk about their love for their mom. They talked about a woman who never lost her smile and never lost her sweet disposition. She was a witness to those who lived in the nursing home, those who worked there and those who visited. Alzheimer's robbed her of her speech, her memory, and her balance, but not her love of Jesus. Nothing could destroy that precious woman's love, integrity, gentle disposition, or kindness.

> "Let your conversation be always full of grace, seasoned with salt, so that you may know how to answer everyone."
> (Colossians 4:6)

Jesus said he would never leave us or forsake us. He never left Mary nor did he forsake her.

I thank God I made the right choice to visit Mary up until the end of her earthly life. I'll always remember this special mentor whom God brought into my life and I'll always remember the beauty of Jesus that always shone through her every action

Prayer:
Thank you, Lord, for the special people you bring into my life to teach me and remind me you are an ever-present God and will never leave or forsake me. Let my actions and conversations glorify you alone.

MARCH 27

Sue Reynolds, Missionary – Fellowship of Christian Firefighters International (FCFI), and Chaplain Gaius Reynolds, President – FCFI; Volunteer Firefighter – Livermore, CO, Fire Protection District

AN ECHOING
He is risen!

"HE IS RISEN!" Each spring there's an echoing of these words reminding people that Resurrection Day, commonly known as Easter, is here.

When you hear "He is risen," what crosses your mind? Are you thankful for a special Sunday service, maybe an extra day off work, or a day to have a special meal and family gathering? These are special events to be thankful for, but the fact that "He is risen indeed!" is the crux of God's promised resurrection for all believers. That is the core of God's plan, that whoever has accepted Christ as their personal Savior will never, ever be separated from him. These words mean that the crucified Jesus Christ, whose side was pierced with a spear to assure his mortal death before being removed from the cross, is not dead at all, but alive! They attest to the fact that what God says, happens. Many of God's prophecies are yet to happen; others, like those in Isaiah 53, have already come to fruition. Isaiah prophesied the life and death of Christ, from his beginnings as a tender shoot, to rejection by men, suffering, carrying of our sorrows and infirmities, slaughter, and then the good news.

"He is risen"—three words that sum up the love of God. Without the Resurrection, the celebration of his birth at Christmas and death at Easter would just be another day. Jesus—the Son of man, the Son of God— was fully man and fully God. He came, shared, demonstrated God's love and power of healing, died, and he lives forever.

> "After the suffering of his soul, he will see the light [of life] and be satisfied; by his knowledge my righteous servant will justify many, and he will bear their iniquities." (Isaiah 53:11)

Jesus is the fulfillment of Isaiah 7:14: "Therefore the LORD himself will give you a sign: The virgin will be with child and will give birth to a son, and will call him Immanuel [God is with us]."

Jesus' resurrection is our assurance of eternal life with God the Father, the Son, and the Holy Spirit if we take action, and accept and love Christ with our heart, soul, and mind.

A popular Christmas saying is, "Jesus is the reason for the season." This Easter let's remember: "He is risen—our insurance that heaven waits." To have this assurance, you must receive the reason. You must receive Jesus.

Prayer:
You are risen and therefore, heaven waits; what a blessing! Thank you, Jesus, for coming, sharing, suffering, bearing my sins, and becoming my life insurance policy for eternity. You have risen. Praise God!

*Reverend Wayne Detzler, PhD, Chaplain (Retired) –
Charlotte, NC, Fire Department; Fellowship of
Christian Firefighters Regional Director*

NO SHOES, NO HOPE

Handing hope to hopeless kids

IT WAS ANOTHER bitter cold day. Fire swept through the apartment,
sending the little family out into the cold. Next door a neighborhood
shopkeeper took them in, sheltering them
from the cold.

Finally the fire was knocked down. The
crews were making a second pass in search
of hot spots, looking for smoldering clothing. They came out having found no further
flames.

> "Whatever you did not
> do for one of the least of
> these, you did not do for
> me." (Matthew 25:45)

My heart went out to the victims, and as chaplain that was my main
task at a fire scene. I noticed the mother and her little children, who
looked to be about six or seven years old. Then I noticed that the little
guy had no shoes. On a chilling cold day he was shoeless.

"Are there any shoes up there?" I asked a firefighter. "One of the kids
is barefoot; he couldn't find his shoes in his haste to escape." The firefighters checked and found none. Again they went through the kids'
rooms and found nothing.

Not only had they lost their home, their clothes, and their toys, they'd
lost their shoes. It was a picture of hopelessness one never forgets, one
etched on the mind.

I found a phone and called the women's center—a crisis pregnancy
center led by my wife in a nearby town. She provided clothes for kids
and for their mothers. I told her about the little boy and gave her a
specific shoe size. Working together we were able to find the needed
footwear.

Sometimes needs are basic, so basic we might miss them. Jesus
reminded his disciples of this basic principle of caring: "I needed clothes
and you clothed me, I was sick and you looked after me, I was in prison
and you came to visit me" (Matthew 25:36).

Caring is the core of Christian living. When we reach out to people
in need, the Lord is glorified and his love is communicated. This is espe-

cially true when we care for kids. The Lord loves the little and the least among us, and so must we.

Prayer:
*Open my eyes to see the little ones who are
in such deep need, loving Lord.*

M A R C H   2 9

Chaplain Robert Osbourn, Sylacauaga, AL, Fire Department

WHAT ARE YOU LOOKING FOR?

Gazing at the great events ahead

HAVE YOU ever gone down the road in the fire truck or been looking out the bay door and it looked as if everyone was staring into the sky and you wondered what they were looking for? While fighting a fire, have you noticed enthralled spectators that appear unable to take their gaze off the flames?

At Jesus' ascension, he gave his disciples their commission to share the truth and his promise to return. Then the disciples just stood there staring up into the sky.

I wonder how many people today claim to be Christ's disciples, then stand staring into the sky doing nothing.

Looking for something from God isn't a fault. As a matter of fact, there are some great events you should all be looking for with eager anticipation.

> "So then, dear friends, since you are looking forward to this, make every effort to be found spotless, blameless and at peace with him."
> (2 Peter 3:14)

You should be looking for Christ's return. Scripture makes it clear: He will return (Matthew 24:42, 43; Matthew 25:13).

When Christ *does* return, there will be glorious changes. All the redeemed will experience a great bodily change. I'm looking forward to those changes—how about you? You can read about them in 1 Corinthians 15:51, 52; 1 Thessalonians 4:13–18; 2 Corinthians 5:1–8; and John 3:1–3).

You should also be looking for that city that is your inheritance. In Hebrews 11:10, Moses "was looking forward to the city with foundations, whose architect and builder is God." John was privileged to see that city (Revelation 21:1, 2), a city that will be your home forever. And there won't be a mortgage.

What about the coming of the Day of God, the day God keeps his pledge? Here's what Scripture guarantees: "But in keeping with his promise we are looking forward to a new heaven and a new earth, the home of righteousness" (2 Peter 3:13).

Where are you gazing? The Bible says, "Let us fix our eyes on Jesus, the author and perfecter of our faith" (Hebrews 12:2).

No doubt, all these things will be wonderful to experience. Meanwhile, as you run your present earthly race, be sure to spend your days looking to Jesus for his help and leadership and then lovingly serving him.

Prayer:
Jesus, you are the sum total of all things. I thank you for your promises and look forward to your glorious reappearing. Meanwhile, may each day be lived according to your will and for your glory.

MARCH 30

Rick Barton, Fire Safety Officer; Rick Barton Ministries, Gunnison, CO; Fellowship of Christian Firefighters International Ambassador-at-Large

I DON'T NEED A MARRIAGE CONFERENCE
I wondered if people would think we were having problems

I DON'T REALLY think we need to attend a marriage conference, do you?" I asked my wife after she mentioned the upcoming conference. Hey, after all, I'm a Christian man! I treat my wife well, and I know the magic words: "You're right honey, I was wrong." For more than twenty years I had truly proven to be the "perfect husband," or so I rationalized as I sought to follow God's principles for marriage.

My loving wife pointed out that as a wildland firefighter I attend safety refreshers every year. Wouldn't a marriage "refresher" be just as important? Catching her tone of voice, I began to rethink my objections. *Sure*, I thought, *it couldn't hurt*. Of course it didn't hurt. In fact, just as

118

fire refreshers help me refocus on the basics of fireline safety and keeping out of harm's way, the marriage refresher reminded my wife and me of some biblical basics to build and protect our marriage. Plus, it gave us a good excuse to have a weekend away in a nice setting.

We are told, "Submit to one another out of reverence for Christ" (Ephesians 5:21) and, "Love your wives, just as Christ loved the church and gave himself up for her . . . In this same way, husbands ought to love their wives as their own bodies. He who loves his wife loves himself" (Ephesians 5:25, 28).

> "For this reason a man will leave his father and mother and be united to his wife, and they will become one flesh." (Genesis 2:24)

Yes, initially, when my wife suggested we look into the marriage refresher, I resisted. I do love her with all my heart, but I had other plans for the weekend. Plus, being human and subject to what others think, I wondered if people would think we were having problems. But I quickly learned that by going to the conference, I was saying to my wife that our marriage is a priority and that I want to keep it strong.

That's not a bad thing, is it?

Prayer:
Lord, I thank you for my spouse and that when we married, with you as our witness, we became one flesh. Help me to love my spouse with reverence and respect and to be a good listener. When we need a refresher course help me not to resist.

MARCH 31

Reverend Wayne Detzler, PhD, Chaplain (Retired) – Charlotte, NC, Fire Department; Fellowship of Christian Firefighters Regional Director

SMOKY MIX-UP
When mistakes go up in smoke

AT LAST we had a weekend away. We'd been stretched to the limit in a new pastoral ministry and finally had a weekend in my home town of Detroit. I was scheduled to preach at an exciting missionary conference, and we couldn't wait.

119

In the Lord's plan, our friends from Wales came to visit. The husband is an excellent preacher and was willing to fill in for me in my home pulpit. The couple savored a quiet weekend in our lovely parsonage in the hills of central Connecticut.

"Let's have a fire in the fireplace," he suggested to his wife, who warmly welcomed the idea. He dashed out to the woodpile and brought back an armful of damp but usable wood. Carefully, he stacked it in the fireplace and added kindling and a little paper.

When he lit the match it caught immediately. So, they sat back and waited to enjoy the fire. At first there was a little smoke, no more than one would expect. Then the smoke thickened. Soon it filled the family room and seeped into the kitchen and living room nearby.

"Call 9-9-9 (the English emergency number)," he shouted to his wife. Then she remembered that in America it was 9-1-1. She quickly dialed for help, and the dispatcher sent a fire engine. After all, they feared the worst. Perhaps the parsonage was on fire.

> "The LORD is gracious and righteous; our God is full of compassion. The Lord protects the simple-hearted; when I was in great need, he saved me." (Psalm 116:5, 6)

When the crew came they quickly extinguished the blaze and blew the smoke out of the house. Then they checked the fireplace for safety. It was the flue. My Welsh friend had forgotten to open the flue, so all the smoke simply came back into the room.

On Monday we returned to a red-faced friend. He explained what had happened. Needless to say, the firefighters never let me forget it. They always asked about my friend with the closed flue.

Thanks to an alert fire service, no harm was done.

We can thank the Lord. He is gracious, righteous, and full of compassion. He saves us from naive actions and he saves us in times of our great need.

Prayer:
Thank You, Lord, for saving me from my foolish and sinful actions.

Rick Barton, Fire Safety Officer; Rick Barton Ministries, Gunnison, CO; Fellowship of Christian Firefighters International Ambassador-at-Large

SECOND-HAND SMOKE

Pretend Christian lives

HERE IT IS April 1 and I feel I have to make a confession. After writing about wildland fire experiences for several years, I have to admit, I've never actually been on a fire. I know that sounds crazy, but I've been able to pick up the language and some great stories from friends of mine who actually fight fires. There are times I feel like I've actually been with them. I can almost smell the smoke, hear the helicopters, and feel the awe they experience when the fire "blows up." However, it finally dawned on me. It's not honest for me to say, "I'm a firefighter," when all I've had is "second-hand smoke."

Okay, read the date at the top of the page again. But it hit me tonight; isn't that a little like what Jesus meant when he said that some folks would use his name, and even do miracles, but never really know him (Matthew 7:21–23)? Thom Rainer, a top Christian scholar, said he's convinced that almost one-half of the members of his

> "If you confess with your mouth, 'Jesus is Lord,' and believe in your heart that God raised him from the dead, you will be saved." (Romans 10:9)

denomination aren't born again! He came to that conclusion by asking two simple questions: "If you died today, would you go to heaven?" and, "If you died today and went to heaven, why would God let you in?" The answers were very revealing: "I go to church," "I've done my best," and a variety of other "good works" responses poured out from these regular church attendees.

What would you answer?

The only answer that works is, "I've confessed my sin to Jesus Christ, placed my faith and trust in him to forgive me, and turned my life over to him to be my Lord and Master." Nothing else will do! God's Word makes that clear in Ephesians 2:8, 9 when he says it's through faith and grace (God's undeserved love) that you're saved. Anything else is just "playing church"! Unless we turn away from our rebellion against God and the sinful deeds that result, we can't come to know him. He won't place his Holy

121

Spirit in us. We are destined to live "pretend Christian lives" and doomed to a godless hell for eternity.

Prayer:
I know, Lord, that bearing fruit is an indication I am alive in you.
I do confess with my mouth and I do believe in my heart that
you raised your Son, Jesus, from the dead. Now I
want to grow as a member of your family.

APRIL 2

Tommy Neiman, Author of Sirens for the Cross; EMS
Training Officer – St. Lucie County, FL; Fellowship of
Christian Firefighters International Regional
Director / International Board Member

JOHNNY'S GOING NOWHERE
God has a sense of humor—no doubt about it

I'M SURE you've had some of those days, weeks, and perhaps even months where the volume and intensity of calls cause you to wonder, *Can I possibly handle another tragedy?* I know I have, and it's at those times a call seems to come in that tickles the funny bone and in the process eases the tension. No doubt, God has a sense of humor and awesome timing.

One day, feeling the weight of my job and silently hoping the tones wouldn't ring, the tones rang anyway. But, instead of a life threat or worse, the dispatcher called out, "A child stuck in a chair."

Combine an overactive five-year-old boy, a chair, and a cool, calm, and collected mother and you have the makings of an amusing and tension-relieving call.

We arrived to find the child, Johnny, with his head wedged between two rungs on the backrest of a dining room chair. He wasn't crying, and his mom didn't seem unusually upset. In fact, from the time we entered the house until we left, the mom merely related one incident after another about Johnny's mischievousness.

Johnny finally met his match when he started playing with that dining room chair that left him bending over with his head sticking out between the two rungs. Looking like a prisoner behind bars, Johnny was going nowhere. He looked puzzled, as if thinking, *Are you going to free me from this cell or not?*

122

Meanwhile, his mother looked at us and said, "Wow, you were fast getting here!" She appeared to be enjoying her son's quietude and captivity as she spelled out reports of his behavior.

> "Praise be to the Lord, to God our Savior, who daily bears our burdens." (Psalm 68:19)

When she halted her friendly discourse, we coated the sides of his head with K-Y Jelly, pulled on the rungs, and rather easily freed Johnny from his temporary prison. Without a word, he immediately left us and went to taunt his brothers and sisters in the front yard.

As we walked out to the truck, his mother yelled, "Do you think he might do that again?"

Wishful thinking, Mom!

Life is full of wishful thinking, stressful situations, and resulting disappointments. But God is just a prayer away, and he must have a great sense of humor.

Prayer:

When the heartbreak and burdens of my career, relationships, or life in general appear insurmountable, I turn to you, Lord, the One who has promised to help me bear all my burdens. I thank you for bringing calls or situations that lighten my spirit when I most need them.

APRIL 3

Chaplain Gerald E. Brock, Darlington County, SC, Fire District Station 8; "Fear Not," the Fire Dog

CHRIST'S AMBASSADORS TO THE FIRE SERVICE

Saved! Now it is God's desire that we grow, serve, and bear fruit

WHEN YOU became a Christian, you received the free gift of salvation through Jesus Christ. You were presented with the Gospel message of Jesus Christ and believed. Therefore you've been freed from sin and death and know without a doubt you will have an abundant eternal life with God. When you face trials, you have the comfort that God will walk through them with you.

123

While salvation stands alone and is not obtained by works, it is God's desire that you grow, serve, and bear fruit. This makes you one of God's missionaries commissioned to go into all parts of the world to tell others about Jesus Christ, so they will also believe and have an abundant, eternal life.

It was God's plan that someone shared the Gospel with you, so that you, in turn, could present his message to others. God "wants all men to be saved and to come to a knowledge of the truth" (1 Timothy 2:4). This is why Jesus commanded us, "Go into all the world and preach the good news to all creation" (Mark 16:15).

Are you necessarily commanded to go internationally? No. You are just told to go. The fire/EMS service is a mission field in your own backyard filled with many who don't know our Lord and are suffering from the aftermath of tragedy. To bring the Good News of Jesus Christ to the world is a privilege that has been given to every Christian. For Christian firefighters, that privilege has a new, special dimension because we work with many who have a giving, compassionate heart. Why else would they willingly put their lives on the line for others? Yet many still don't have the peace and comfort that comes only from God.

> "We are therefore Christ's ambassadors, as though God were making his appeal through us."
> (2 Corinthians 5:20)

You can help fulfill the Great Commission by sharing God's love and truth by your words, actions, and attitudes. Supplement that with your prayers and you can be confident the seeds you plant will produce fruit for God's kingdom.

Prayer:
Dear God, thank you for all my blessings. Thank you, Lord, for enabling me to be a missionary right where I am and to be of service to others. Thank you for saving me. Please help me to do your will each day. I pray for other missionaries. In the name of Jesus Christ, amen.

Rick Barton, Fire Safety Officer; Rick Barton Ministries, Gunnison, CO; Fellowship of Christian Firefighters International Ambassador-at-Large

THE CASE OF THE BROKEN COMPASS

He roves afar,
Past compass, chart and calendar.

WALTER DE LA MARE

IT WAS another busy forest fire season. This time the fire was up Crystal Creek and it was a stubborn one. The steep hillsides were heavily timbered. Evidence of elk dotted the landscape, but if we shot one here, due to the precipitous terrain and heat, we'd better have a frying pan and utensils because we'd have to eat it right on the spot.

We'd attacked this fire with hot shots, the forest crew, and my contract crew. Only a few of us now remained to make sure the fire was dead out.

As crew boss, I climbed high on the hillside opposite the area we were working in order to direct crew members staged at the bottom of the canyon to the various smokes as they began to show. Because I was so far from the crew's location, I took a different route in. Every morning and evening I followed a flagged path from an established trail. The crew used the main trail that followed the creek. In the evening we'd meet at the trucks.

> "There is a way *that seems* right to a man, But its end *is* the way of death."
> (Proverbs 14:12 NKJV)

After a week of this routine, I was tired of the same flag line that seemingly wandered about. I was sure I could take a shorter route out. Before too long, I reached the main trail. Congratulating myself, I headed toward the trucks. Soon, however, I began to notice something strange. The trail had been clear of trees when I went in that morning. Now there were a number of trees across it. Puzzled, I pressed on.

Within a half hour, I knew something was definitely wrong. Pulling out my compass for the first time, I discovered another problem—my compass was malfunctioning! It had to be, because it said I was headed in the wrong direction! According to the compass, I was headed deeper into the woods and farther from my truck. My mind said to head one way, the compass said the other. It was one of the toughest decisions I've ever made in the woods, but I turned around, trusting the compass. Soon, familiar territory appeared.

Later, after joining my crew, I reflected on the day's experience. Sometimes what feels right isn't right. Once again, I learned to trust my compass, not my feelings.

Likewise in life, God's Word is a compass I can always rely on, regardless of circumstances, temptations to do it my own way, or opinions from others.

Prayer:
When tempted to go my own way, whether on a fire or in life, may your Word remind me that your way is not only the right way, but it is always the best way.

Reverend Wayne Detzler, PhD, Chaplain (Retired) – Charlotte, NC, Fire Department; Fellowship of Christian Firefighters Regional Director

WELCOME TO GOD'S HOUSE
How to help God's people

CHAPLAIN, CAN you help us?" An administrative pastor sounded desperate. "We need a liaison with the fire department to help us open our new church." He explained that supplementary sprinklers were needed for our new building, and only the fire department could help.

"Let's go see our fire marshal," I suggested. The marshal was a strong Christian and he might be able to advise us. Thankfully he was in the fire prevention office when we arrived.

We explained that the work was underway, but would take a few days to finish. We had long planned to open the building the next Sunday. The marshal suggested we bring in a fire officer for fire watch. This would enable us to open the church on time.

My first call was directed to our local Fellowship of Christian Firefighters. I explained our need and they set to work seeking possible fire watch volunteers. The church was more than happy to reimburse them for the off-duty service. As opening day drew near we contacted a willing

126

fire captain. He agreed to come to the opening services as a fire watch officer.

On a glorious Sunday in May, worshippers swarmed into the new worship center. None was aware of the fire prevention measures as the captain moved quietly through the building. He just seemed to be part of the praise and worship.

> "I rejoiced with those who said to me, "Let us go to the house of the LORD." (Psalm 122:1)

The worship was glorious! The preaching of God's Word was powerful. It seemed as if a bit of heaven descended on the scene. The glory of the Lord almost overwhelmed us all as we sang great worship songs.

Afterward, I sat down with the fire captain to chat. He was moved by the sincerity and the fervor of God's people. He'd come to protect us and ended up sharing in the blessing. For the remaining weeks of fire watch we were able to welcome other firefighters into our services.

It's truly a time to rejoice when worshippers gather together to share, learn from, and reflect God's love. When the serendipity is obvious, and those extra blessings flow as those who join in worship share in the blessings, God is surely looking down and rejoicing with his people. Whether guests are there to serve, like this fire captain, or to feel God's love, it's good to be in God's house. Let us not forsake fellowshipping with one another.

Prayer:
*Lord, we do thank you for the privilege of worship
with God's people each Lord's Day.*

*Joel Kelm, Firefighter/EMT – Gallatin Gateway, MT; President –
Big Sky Chapter of Fellowship of Christian Firefighters*

CALLED BUT DISCOURAGED BY THE RESPONSE!

Who better than a Christian firefighter to reach out to first responders?

EVER FELT as if God called you to serve in a specific way but those you reached out to didn't respond? Yes, serving God can be discouraging. I encourage you to persevere, hang in there. God moves at his speed, not ours. We may never see the fruits of the seeds we plant in this life. Yet, we are commanded to keep planting them.

God tells us the harvest is ripe and, while the seeds we plant may not be recognizable, we must still keep on keeping on. Building credibility doesn't come instantaneously. Developing relationships and trust takes time, and yes, that word we are told not to pray for, *patience*, is essential. Who better than a Christian firefighter to reach out to those first responders who don't know our Lord and his grace, mercy, and love?

God took my desire to share God's love from an interest to a burning passion for the fire service. I desire greatly to help churches realize how "ready" first responders are for the hope Christ offers. Emergency service personnel face death every day. Unlike civilians, first responders are forced to not just think about their eternal destinies, but to come to grips with what they truly believe. Those grounded in God's truth, encounter endless opportunities to be God's tools for reaching first responders with God's hope and truth.

> "You must serve faithfully and wholeheartedly in the fear of the LORD. In every case that comes before you from your fellow countrymen who live in the cities—whether bloodshed or other concerns of the law, commands, decrees or ordinances—you are to warn them not to sin against the Lord; otherwise his wrath will come on you and your brothers."
> (2 Chronicles 19:9,10)

As discouragement knocks on my door, I'm thankful for people who are willing to heed what God says about encouragement: "Now go out and encourage your men" (2 Samuel 19:7). We need to overcome discouragement and all obstacles and serve faithfully and wholeheartedly.

Prayer:
Lord, when the human side of me becomes discouraged, I turn to you and my Christian friends for encouragement so I can serve faithfully and wholeheartedly.

Chief Steve Parsons, St. Albans, WV, Fire Department

ARE YOU IN GOD'S SERVICE?

For me it was no sacrifice at all

WHEN I departed for a mission trip to Africa in 2007 many Christian friends asked, "Why are you doing this?"

When I was reading of the many needs, especially the need for training firefighters in Malawi, Africa, my heart was touched. When many of these challenging questions came from friends, I was somewhat dismayed. Doubts began to surface. *Is it too much to put myself at risk? Was the expense too much? Where would the funds come from? Was it unfair to ask my family to help pay the expenses* and *do all the chores for a month?*

As I prayed, my faith was strengthened. I realized that, for me, it was no sacrifice at all. God brought to mind that if his Son, the Lord Jesus Christ, can give up his life for me, then why can I not do what is required of me and serve others?

> "My sheep hear my voice, and I know them, and they follow me."
> (John 10:27 KJV)

"What good is it, my brothers, if a man claims to have faith but has no deeds?" (James 2:14). If we are to have faith—true faith—we will want to add action to our belief and do good deeds for our brothers and sisters—if not for all humanity. If we love those who need love and provide for those without, is this not the example Christ would want us to set if we are his followers?

James uses the example of Abraham and his sacrifice of Isaac. Abraham's actions and faith were working together and his faith was made complete by what he did. Matthew 25:35–40 lists things that, when you do them for the least in society, you do them for Jesus. It is our Christian duty to help those who need help.

I am so glad I made the trip! Not only was I able to give valuable training, help provide much-needed equipment, and later host Malawian firefighters in my hometown. Most important, I was able to share God's Word with people in many villages.

Listen to God's voice through the Holy Spirit. I'm sure thankful I did, for by going and giving of my time and training, I received so much more.

Prayer:
Father God, help me to die unto myself and learn to serve you. Help me hear your voice through the Holy Spirit and move into action with the

deeds you would have me do. Move me, Lord, from my comfort zone, and place me where the talents you have blessed me with can be used to bring glory to you. In the precious name of Jesus, amen.

Reverend Wayne Detzler, PhD, Chaplain (Retired) – Charlotte, NC, Fire Department; Fellowship of Christian Firefighters Regional Director

SHADOW OF THE ALMIGHTY
Dark days do not dim his presence

A DEBRIEFING TOOK me to a small town outside Charlotte. When I entered the volunteer fire station, the room was filled. As we introduced ourselves, I realized police, fire, and medics were all there. The occasion was an arson fire that covered a more serious crime, the murder/suicide deaths of five people from one family.

"When we arrived the mobile home was fully involved," a fire officer started out. "As we tried to break into the house to check for victims, our way was blocked." It was the body of a man rolled against the door. Further investigation discovered the murdered and charred body of his wife. And there was knocking, a loud knocking sound heard over the fire.

The police officer in charge had suggested checking another house. "It seems to me that there are relatives in another nearby town." When the local police entered that house, they found three more bodies stacked in a bathroom.

The sadness snowballed. Even the most hard-bitten emergency workers and police officers now had tears in their eyes. We, too, as CISM team members had never heard such a saga of sorrow.

"Back at the original scene the knocking continued," the fire chief explained. "Firefighters had brought the blaze under control, but they still heard the knocking." So, they checked nearby buildings. In a garden shed they found three frightened children, locked away to protect them from the grisly scene in their home. Their father had locked the children away before shooting their mother and taking his own life.

Social workers were summoned to the scene. They knew the family well. For several years they'd been tracking the little ones, protecting them and caring for them at school. In fact, social services had hired trained

130

counselors to help the children each day at school. One of those counselors was a very compassionate Christian man. He combined good care and Christian love as he daily devoted himself to helping his little charges through schoolwork.

> "For in the day of trouble he will keep me safe in his dwelling; he will hide me in the shelter of his tabernacle and set me high upon a rock."
> (Psalm 27:5)

The children faced problems much too immense for adult minds, let alone children's, to understand. Yet, through it all, God provided his shelter through the misled father, giving social workers, and dedicated firefighters.

Prayer:
*Lord, thank you for providing protection for the most
vulnerable in our midst, for our children. And, Lord,
I thank you for protecting and watching over me.*

APRIL 9

*Ann Christmas, Fellowship of Christian Firefighters, St. Louis
Chapter; American Red Cross, North County Citizen Corps*

THE PUMPER WITHIN
How's Your Heart?

LOVING ONE another—what a concept! Most find it easy to love family members, many find it simple to love friends, but the majority find it is challenging to love complete strangers.

Where are our hearts? What is in there? What makes us who we are? How come it is so hard to just love everyone?

There is something unique about the heart of a firefighter. Some may say it's their warped brains (who runs into a burning building, anyway?). From what I've seen, it is the love, the continual concern for others, the desire to make a difference in a bad situation that fuels their spirits. Everyday they put their own lives at risk to save the lives of others.

Firefighters are my worldly example of what Paul speaks of in Romans 12:10. The New Life Version of the Bible shares this verse in such beautiful words: "Love each other with genuine affection, and take delight in honoring each other." In John 13:34, 35, Jesus Christ orders us to love one another. God's Word is just filled with love—his love for us and how we are to honor him by following the example he gave us through his Son.

Paul continues in verse 13 by stating, "When God's people are in need, be ready to help them." Not everyone is called to run into a burning building, but we all are called to assist each other. The key to working together effectively is a lot of training and practice. The same can be said about our hearts. How do we get ourselves to the place of loving everyone? The answer—a lot of practice and training!

> "Teacher, which is the greatest commandment in the Law?" Jesus replied: "'Love the Lord your God with all your heart and with all your soul and with all your mind.' This is the first and greatest commandment. And the second is like it: 'Love your neighbor as yourself'."
> (Matthew 22:37–39)

Take a chance today to put a smile on your face and say hello to five complete strangers who walk by you. Let that pumper within show God's love.

Prayer:
Lord, I thank you for guiding me into being the person you desire me to be. Teach me to be more affectionate to those whom others do not love. Lord, you love the unlovable; I wish to do the same. Thank you for opening up my eyes to what is in my heart. I yearn for more of you and less of me, Lord. Thank you for giving me the ability to help others. In Jesus' name, amen.

APRIL 10

Reverend Wayne Detzler, PhD, Chaplain (Retired) – Charlotte, NC, Fire Department; Fellowship of Christian Firefighters Regional Director

UP THE LADDER
Learning to trust

WE JUST took delivery on a new ladder truck," the chief said as he asked me to report for orientation. "This is the state of the art in firefighting," he added proudly. He'd worked for months with the city council and with the manufacturer to get us exactly what we needed.

It was dazzling. The beauty and sophistication of the new truck really surprised me. As we watched, the crew put the ladder through its paces. A huge basket atop the ladder gave firefighters plenty of safe room to maneuver, and a powerful hose was poised on top of the ladder to pour a high volume of water on any fire.

"How about you, Chaplain?" the chief asked. "Do you want to try it out?" He invited me to get into the basket with him and ride the ladder to its top, nearly a hundred feet off the ground. I thanked the Lord for my experience climbing telephone poles in my younger days in Michigan.

"Spin it around," he shouted down the order to the firefighter manning the ladder. The basket began to circle, as we surveyed the town from our perch. "Now lower the basket," the chief ordered. "We want to step out of the basket onto the roof." Slowly the basket was lowered into position, and the chief led me out onto the roof of our fire station. We walked around on the rain-slicked roof for a few minutes.

> "We live by faith, not by sight." (2 Corinthians 5:7)

"You pass the test, Chaplain," my friend the chief approved. "You can go up in the ladder any time you need to." He obviously foresaw a time when I might need to assist firefighters as they fought blazes.

Riding the ladder was purely a matter of trust. I had confidence in the equipment, and I trusted that the chief knew what he was doing. So, I put my life in their hands and soared nearly a hundred feet.

It seems as I get older the Lord has one plan for my life. He is trying to teach me how to live by faith and not by sight. Just as I was saved by faith, now he wants me to live by faith.

Prayer:
Help me to trust you more as I walk through this day, O Lord.

A Matter of Trust (Courtesy of Robert M. Winston, Boston, MA)

*Tommy Neiman, Author of Sirens for the Cross; EMS
Training Officer – St. Lucie County, FL; Fellowship of
Christian Firefighters International Regional
Director / International Board Member*

I'M ALIVE

*Without God's hand of protection my life
would have drastically changed*

THE SOUTH Florida coast, known for its concrete cities and beaches, has hundreds of square miles of inland residential wooded areas that are of particular concern during the brush fire season. Dry weather, combined with strong winds, frequently leads to fast-spreading, unpredictable, and treacherous fires.

One spring day a man traveling the interstate intentionally and successfully started fires in several counties along his route. As a paramedic, I didn't expect to be called out, but the immensity of the situation required all trained hands.

Hot airborne embers, carried by the increasing winds, ignited additional fires wherever they landed. The day's challenges just kept coming. Once one fire was under control, the wind shifts sent fire heads in numerous other directions. My responsibility was to ride on the back of our brush truck with the nozzle to locate and hit the spotovers. Our feelings fluctuated from discouragement and frustration to the excitement of meeting the continual challenges. Many times after locating a spotover, we'd hurry to it only to see it escalate into a large, unmanageable head.

> "Because he loves me," says the LORD, "I will rescue him; I will protect him, for he acknowledges my name."
> (Psalm 91:14)

Near the end of the day, we drove through a fifty-foot strip of high brush to get in a position to hit burning grass. As we got into the midst of that volatile brush, a sudden strong wind shift ignited heavy brush all around us. I knew I was a goner! I was going to roast—truck and all! With flaming orange all around me, I slammed myself against the back windshield in a fetal position. "Oooooh," I yelled as I heard the truck rev hard and make full power. My lieutenant made a wise and fast decision. Instead of a right or left turn, which could have left us moving with and staying in that head of fire, he gunned us straight through to the previously burned spotover area.

134

When he stopped, I opened my eyes. "Praise God! I'm alive!" I shouted. The Lord, whom I love and worship, had pulled us through. I know that without God's hand of protection my life on Earth would have been drastically changed or even ended.

Prayer:
*May I never cease to love you, Lord, and to share that
love and the power of your protective hand.*

APRIL 12

*Fire Chaplain John Kalashian, Caledonia, Wisconsin;
Founder/Director – Men with a Burden, a ministry
to the homeless men at the Milwaukee Rescue Mission;
Founder/President – Corvettes for Christ*

A BRIDGE OF RESCUE
*Like a first responder, Christ
rescues us from life's perils*

I WAS RECENTLY privileged to observe three days of rope training for Caledonia Fire & Rescue personnel. Have you heard the common expression, "So easy a child could do it"? Well, I'll tell you what—it's not true when applied to rope rescue!

I gained a deeper knowledge that rescuers have to be trained and skilled in the masterful use of equipment, techniques, and tricks of the trade. Their gear must become a reliable bridge of rescue bringing the victim out of harm's way. Carabineers, prusiks, anchor plates, bar racks, pulleys, 4-to-1 systems, z-rigs, tag lines, rescue centers, stokes, the list goes on and on.

Rescuers are faced with making quick lifesaving decisions, while choosing the best rescue system and its components. Wide chasms and various situations confronting rescuers come in unpredictable assortments and circumstances while the health of the victim and the geographical setting further test the firefighters' response and resolve. Their duties involve providing a successful rescue in a victim's critical situation, which could have been caused by mistakes, deliberate harmful behaviors, or unfortunate daily occurrences.

In like fashion, Jesus Christ has the duty of rescuing each of us from life's perils—perils created by incorrect decisions, bad habits, mistakes, and just plain old sin. Like firefighters and their rescue gear, which become a bridge to safety, Jesus Christ can be our "Bridge of Rescue," spanning the gap from a life of despair and destruction to a life full of peace, safety, and eternal hope with God. We find this referenced in Hebrews 7:25: "Therefore he is able to save completely those who come to God through him." In other words, he can go anywhere and any distance—Christ has no limitations!

> "Therefore he is able to save completely those who come to God through him." (Hebrews 7:25)

Miraculously the love of Christ and his cross become the rope and tackle necessary for our successful rescue. The Bible further tells us "neither height nor depth, nor anything else in all creation, will be able to separate us from the love of God that is in Christ Jesus our Lord" (Romans 8:39). No matter the height of our circumstances or the depth of our problems, it's comforting to know we can call upon Christ as our one and only First Responder. God wants us to know we can faithfully and personally call upon him to be our Deliverer and Savior.

Prayer:
*Thank you that I can faithfully and personally
call upon you as my Deliverer and Savior.*

APRIL 13

*Chaplain Gaius Reynolds, President – Fellowship of
Christian Firefighters International; Volunteer
Firefighter – Livermore, CO, Fire Protection District*

GOD'S NOT IN A HURRY
In his time, not yours

WHEN THE tones sound, manned fire departments become a scene of efficiency and expedience as crews hurry to bunker up, man their apparatus, and respond to the call. Volunteers' homes often reflect that same urgency when their beepers sound. Whatever "honey do" is in progress is dropped; meals and family-and-friend gatherings come to an abrupt halt. Volunteers hurry to their personal vehicles to report directly on scene or to the unmanned stations and their waiting emergency vehicles. Whether paid or volunteer, the urgency is just the same.

Our God, however, is a God of patience, and, according to Hebrews, he isn't in a hurry. After listing in Hebrews 11 those who lived by faith, God's Word explains in verse 13 that while these people were living by faith when they died, they were only allowed to see from a distance the things God had promised. They didn't receive the things promised during their earthly abode. They had to wait until they were with God, face to face, for the things promised.

At times, especially for first responders, saving a life or a structure can depend on how much you hurry. In many of life's situations, it just isn't so. Like those "heroes of the faith," God wants you to be patient. Most of you have been warned not to pray for patience, for in doing so, trying times to help you develop that patience are sure to follow. But just as God is patient, you, too, will benefit from that trait.

> "These were all commended for their faith, yet none of them received what had been promised. God had planned something better for us so that only together with us would they be made perfect."
> (Hebrews 11:39, 40)

God's promises will all come to completion. Literally hundreds of his prophecies have already come to fruition. A study of just those that Christ himself fulfilled verifies this truth. But many other of his promises we will not see during our earthly sojourn.

A conglomerate of emotions—from anger, frustration, and rebellion to doubt—plague lives when promises are seemingly broken. But God does keep his promises; not in your time but in his time. What's more, he has planned far better things than your human mind can fathom.

Prayer:
Thank you, Lord, that many of your promises have come to completion already and that in your time the others will all be fulfilled.

*Rick Barton, Fire Safety Officer; Rick Barton Ministries,
Gunnison, CO; Fellowship of Christian Firefighters
International Ambassador-at-Large*

A NEW LCES!

*Does "Locate Cooler, Establish Shade" translate
to "Lazy Christians Elude Service"?*

AS I CIRCLED the fire near Norwood, Colorado, trying to ensure that our forces were being kept safe, I made a stop at our heli-base. There on a wall I saw a new definition of our tried and true "LCES."

As every wildland firefighter knows, LCES stands for "Lookouts, Communications, Escape Routes, and Safety Zones." All should be in place before we engage a wildland fire. Doing so has saved thousands of lives over the years. This four-letter acronym was developed

> "They devoted themselves to the apostles' teaching and to the fellowship, to the breaking of bread and to prayer."
> (Acts 2:42)

Rat Creek Fire, outside of Wisdom, Montana, 2007 (Courtesy of Rick Barton)

by the late Paul Gleason, an ex-hotshot superintendent who knew that in the heat of battle, we sometimes forget the "Ten Standard Fire Orders," the "Eighteen Situations That Shout Watch Out," and the "Common Denominators." Gleason boiled everything down into an easy-to-remember foursome: Lookouts, Communication, Escape Routes, and Safety Zones.

But on the wall at the heli-base there was a new LCES: "Locate Cooler, Establish Shade." Funny, yes—but is it really? As we look at the fatalities, serious injuries, and near misses on incidents, isn't the main cause a lack of following our basic protocols? Do we get distracted from our mission and focus on our comfort?

How about in our daily Christian life? Most of us started off strong when we received Jesus as Savior and Lord. We knew we were in a battle for our eternal souls and those of the folks around us. We put on the "whole armor of God" (Ephesians 6:10–18). Our big four was found in Acts 2:42: We devoted ourselves continually to reading and studying the Bible, staying in fellowship, renewing our vows to God and each other in Communion, and talking to God continually in prayer.

Have we slipped into a new big four? "Lazy Christians Elude Service"? Just wondering . . .

Prayer:
How easy it is to slip into the "Lazy Christians Elude Service" mode! I know that you and your Word help me to be on the lookout for temptations that keep me from communicating with you and realizing that you have provided the escape route from sins. In you, Lord, I am safe. Help me, Lord, to continue to put on the full armor of God by devoting time to studying your Word, staying in fellowship, and keeping my vows to you.

APRIL 15

*Holly Duck, Wife of Craig Duck, Lieutenant –
Washington, DC, Fire Department*

WE ARE ONE

Communicate, date, and remember
that God is in control

SCRIPTURE CLEARLY states that when a man and woman marry, they become one flesh. To me this means as one we serve the Lord.

My husband, Craig, is a lieutenant with the Washington, DC, Fire Department, where he's served for more than two decades. When we married, I knew his career aspirations. To this day I'm thankful Craig has a job he enjoys so much where he serves his community, helps those in need, and also has the opportunity to witness to those around him. We both know God put him in the fire service for this special reason.

Craig was a first responder at the Pentagon on 9/11. Friends and family came to the forefront of our minds when we didn't know what was going on with Craig. It was a blessing to know we could pray for Craig with the assurance God heard our prayers. Was I concerned? Yes! Was I worried? No! I know the Lord is with my husband. That promise gives me peace and a freedom from fear that could easily plague the spouse of a firefighter.

God has given us four teenage boys. I've been asked how they feel about their dad's job, the danger he faces, and his unique schedule. Praise God, they, too, encourage and support their father in the fire department. We all make an effort to work and plan around Craig's schedule.

> "For this reason a man will leave his father and mother and be united to his wife, and they will become one flesh."
> (Genesis 2:24)

Is this a one-way support and praise effort? No! Again, I praise the Lord because Craig supports and edifies us as well. He invests his time in our activities and interests, and when off duty he sincerely asks about our activities and how we felt while he was at the station. As a family we take God's Word to heart. We are one; as one we do as God desires: love of God first, followed by our obligations to family, then work, followed by our service to our Lord.

I highly recommend that you communicate with your spouse; go on dates; find time to be alone even if that means turning the TV off and talking; never go to bed mad at each other; and remember—God is in control. He has everything planned in our lives and he will not give us anything we cannot handle.

Prayer:
Communication and edification of our loved ones is important to you, God, and to those I love. May I remember to humble myself, put aside selfish desires, and love others as you love me.

Reverend Wayne Detzler, PhD, Chaplain (Retired) –
Charlotte, NC, Fire Department; Fellowship of
Christian Firefighters Regional Director

THE MIRACLE BABY

An amazing highway rescue

THE SUN had not yet risen. It was a pitch-black Saturday morning and I hoped to sleep in. But the persistent pager changed all that. Flipping on the light, I reached for the bedside phone and dialed dispatch.

"It's a fatal accident on the interstate, Chaplain." He had few details. In fact, it was less than a mile from our house. When I rolled up on the scene it was eerie, silent. A crumpled car was nosed into the bridge pylon. The passenger compartment looked relatively untouched. Still the dispatcher's identification of a fatal accident lingered in my mind.

Behind the wheel was a motionless figure shrouded in a tarp. She was dead. She'd died instantly when her car crunched against the concrete. Firefighters briefed me quickly on this bizarre one-car crash.

Nothing could be done for the driver, but there was a passenger. In the back, a toddler sat safely in his car seat. He was so shocked and extremely scared that hardly a cry came from the poor little one's lips. A burly firefighter sat next to the little one whispering calmly into his ear.

The incident commander sent me to the hospital with the little boy. He had no idea that his mother was dead, and we had no idea what propelled her into the pylon of the bridge. The reality would dawn on him later, very much later. For now, the urgency was medical.

> Jesus said, "Their [children's] angels in heaven always see the face of my Father in heaven" (Matthew 18:10).

At the hospital, doctors discovered that the little one had a broken femur. This was quickly set and a cast applied. A phone number found at the scene connected social workers to the little lad's family. This enabled us to hand over our little friend to his grandparents, even as they were informed of their daughter's death.

Somehow this amazed me. Like most emergency workers, I'd seen death and destruction. However, young victims still tug at my heart. Perhaps it is because Jesus showed us how to love and care for children. He picked them up and blessed them. Their helplessness called forth the protection of God's Son.

Prayer:
Lord, help me to care lovingly for the little ones in my life
and in my communities. As the pain transfers to
my heart, I seek your comfort and peace.

A P R I L   1 7

Captain Raul A. Angulo – Seattle Fire Department;
Fellowship of Christian Firefighters Regional
Director / International Board Member

THE BROTHERHOOD

It is lacking when compared
with "Till death do us part"

IT'S EASY to get sucked into "The Brotherhood." It's enticing because it's all about the battle, bravery, and heroics. Most take this oath seriously, as they should. It's much easier to keep this oath when you're single, but you take different oaths when you get married; oaths of "for richer, for poorer, in sickness and in health" and they end with "What God has joined, let no man separate"! That's a pretty heavy-duty oath—but it's not heroic!

> "A man of many companions may come to ruin, but there is a friend who sticks closer than a brother."
> (Proverbs 18:24)

Allegiance to the first oath at the expense of the second oath is in essence like having another spouse, but it's disguised as The Brotherhood. We can devote so much of our time and energy to the fire department that it actually becomes a mistress and sometimes even our god. The love and devotion that's reserved for God and our spouses gets devoured by worthy causes, union meetings, committee meetings, special projects, charitable events, political action, overtime, deployments . . .

Why are we willing to lay down our lives for complete strangers, but we're not willing to live out our lives with sacrifice for the ones we love the most? Why do we love to use slogans like "strength and honor" and "never leave your partner behind" with each other, but not with our spouses? These are great words to live by and die by—if you say them to your family. Hanging tough in marriage and weathering the storms of raising kids take sacrifice.

Let me tell you something about The Brotherhood—it is found lacking when compared with "'Til death do us part." When you're sick or disabled, who, this side of heaven, is going to be there for you? When you're lonely, depressed, or scared, who will comfort you? Who will have patience for you? Who is it that vowed, "In sickness and health"?

Marriage, family, and friendships rooted in Christ are not based on battle, bravery, and heroics—they're based on love.

Prayer:
Thank you, Lord, for The Brotherhood represented by the camaraderie we share as first responders. May I honor that brotherhood but not at the expense of my marriage and family.

APRIL 18

Tommy Neiman, Author of Sirens for the Cross; EMS Training Officer – St. Lucie County, FL; Fellowship of Christian Firefighters International Regional Director / International Board Member

LET THE BLOOD FLOW
Because he loves you

"LET THE blood flow!" Does it trigger thoughts of an impending gory rescue call?

The details of the following, while unfortunately horrific, serve as a reminder of God's unfathomable love.

The call came from a phone booth for a bleeding woman in the worst part of town. When we arrived, we found the bleeding woman cradled in the arms of a huge man. At first, it appeared the man was holding her until help arrived. With a closer look, I realized the giant of a man, who was obviously mentally disabled, was restraining the semiconscious woman. Knife slashes covered her body. The man's words were slow and deliberate. His movements were sluggish and uncoordinated. While he appeared content to bear-hug this woman, something was amiss. This gentle giant protectively held the woman and chanted, "Let the blood flow."

We immediately called for police backup as we helplessly watched her lose more blood from the deep incisions that covered her face, arms, and upper torso. A crowd of bystanders joined our plea for the misguided protector to let go of her. He just continued to chant, "Let the blood flow." One bystander unsuccessfully attempted to separate him from the woman causing him to cry louder, "Let the blood flow, it's comin' from her heart, the blood has to flow, just let it flow . . ."

> "He was oppressed and afflicted, yet he did not open his mouth; he was led like a lamb to the slaughter." (Isaiah 53:7)

When the police arrived they freed the woman and we quickly went into action. At the hospital hundreds of stitches and extensive treatment followed. Through the mighty hand of God, this woman survived.

In the aftermath, we discovered she'd been knifed by another man, not the giant who clung to her at the scene. Still I wondered how a person, sane or not, could let another person bleed like that. Then I remembered the story of Jesus' death on the cross.

God, Jesus' own Father, forsook his Son on the cross. Jesus' Father let the blood of his own Son flow. And he did it because of his love for us and desire not to be separated from those he created for all eternity.

As Christ's precious blood flowed from his maimed body, his Father refused to stop it because he loves you.

Prayer:

May my eyes and heart never take lightly the blood that flowed from Calvary that day two thousand years ago when God said, "Let the blood flow"! May I always remember that God loved me so much that he sent Jesus to die on the cross so I can spend eternity with him in heaven.

Dwayne Clemmons, Adjunct Instructor – Virginia Department of Fire Programs; Founder – DMC Ministries; Author of Exploits, Jesus Rides in an Ambulance, and Utterances from the Throne Room; Volunteer in Fire and EMS for forty years in Virginia

PRAY CONTINUALLY

Spending time with the Creator of the universe

HAVE YOU prayed today? First Thessalonians 5:17 says, "Pray continually."

Praying continually is an act of communicating with God. Our God deeply desires to communicate with, fellowship with, and disseminate his love and wishes to, for, and with us. We have an awesome opportunity to spend time with the Creator of the universe if we are saved, born again, and filled with the Spirit of God. The problem is that many first responders have serious issues when it comes to relationships, and I really don't fully understand why. Aren't we a brotherhood? Don't we have to depend on each other? Isn't it essential that we work with each other and seek to provide a united front on scene? Why do we, in spite of the very nature of what we do, have difficulty developing, maintaining, and enhancing relationships? Is it because we fail to communicate? Sure, we talk, but do we *communicate?* And if not, does that inability transfer to our prayer life?

> "Be joyful always; pray continually; give thanks in all circumstances, for this is God's will for you in Christ Jesus." (1 Thessalonians 5:16–18)

If we will humble ourselves and acknowledge that we must submit ourselves to God, fulfill the call he has on our life, and accept that the Word says we were created by him for him, we will develop a hunger for praying to and communicating with God.

We do the things in our life that are a priority. Our priorities tend to consume and occupy our mind and time, and then develop into our passion. Whatever we are passionate about we talk about, think about, and focus on. Our passions lead to what we perpetuate or reproduce.

God wants our walk with him to be our top priority. He wants us to pray without ceasing and have intimate, focused, and deliberate communication with him. Prayer is not random, abstract, or erroneous. God hears everything we say, think, and do. Do you take time to listen to God? Remember, prayer is not one-way communication.

God desires to have an intimate, passionate, and productive relationship with you—and that happens through prayer. Prayer is essential to your life.

Prayer:
Lord, how thankful I am that I can come directly to you in prayer and that you want to be involved in every area of my life. Help me perpetuate (reproduce) your life, God, for all to see. Open my eyes and help me see the signs. When I come to you in prayer, God, may I receive your divine download and then go forth and do what you have called me to do.

APRIL 20

Reverend Wayne Detzler, PhD, Chaplain (Retired) – Charlotte, NC, Fire Department; Fellowship of Christian Firefighters Regional Director

FIND THE ARM
God gave him a hand

HE'S LOST his arm." The radio caught my attention. "We're heading for the emergency room." Immediately I responded hoping to help this man in need. When I rolled up to the hospital the medics and the firefighters were there in force.

"Find the arm." The dispatcher ordered a ladder truck to head for the site of the accident. The crew responded to the grisly scene. The question remained: Could they find the severed limb in time to reattach it?

As I strode into the emergency room, a familiar face greeted me. It was a young woman, a member of our church fellowship. "Is it your dad?" I guessed.

"Yes, it's Dad." She was desperate. "His arm was ripped off in the gravel machine at work."

"The firefighters are trying to find the severed arm, but there is no response yet." I assured her that we were working to help them. Soon it became clear that it was too late and too serious to reattach the arm.

As the hospital team hustled him into a helicopter, I loaded his daughter into my car and headed for the trauma center in nearby Hartford, Connecticut. When we arrived the helicopter was just landing, and they were bringing her dad down to the emergency room.

146

Soon they stabilized him. The good news was that his life had been saved. The bad news was that his arm was gone, brutally amputated by a gravel machine. By late in the afternoon the victim was settled in his hospital room and we were allowed to visit.

Shock was his first response, as it was ours. We couldn't believe that this hard-working father from our church had lost his arm so tragically. His daughter and I comforted him as we prayed with and for him. His life and his work would be transformed forever.

At times like this it's good to know that the Lord is with us—he never leaves us. Human support and family love are great sources of comfort, but the best comfort of all comes from the Lord.

Prayer:
Lord, may I be that human support when tragedy strikes. Thank you, Lord, for being the best and closest comfort I can ever know.

A P R I L   2 1

Captain Raul A. Angulo – Seattle Fire Department; Fellowship of Christian Firefighters Regional Director / International Board Member

TOBACCO WARNING LABELS
Why is the struggle so hard?

OOOH, GET that STINKY cigar out of here," my cousin's wife exclaimed as she explained her effort to have another baby and her awareness of the hazards of tobacco smoke.

I looked at the warning label. It read: *Cigars are not a safe alternative to cigarettes. Cigar smoking can cause cancers . . . even if you do not inhale.*

Substitute the word *sinning* for *Cigar smoking* and you'll see the foolishness illustrated in the stubbornness, rebellion, and hardness of heart in man. Many ignore the warnings of sin the same way they ignore the tobacco smoke warnings, because the consequences are accumulative and not immediate. They erroneously rationalize they're escaping internal damage.

It's the same reason many firefighters don't wear SCBA in post-fire situations, even though they're aware of the colorless and odorless characteristics of carbon monoxide. They ignore the danger because they can't

147

readily see it. Many seasoned firefighters take dangerous risks because they feel they have the knowledge and experience to survive.

Many Christians feel the same way about sin. If devastating consequences aren't immediate, they tend to feel they can dabble close to the edge. The longer the consequences aren't evident, the safer such playing at the edge appears. Desensitization builds and the warnings from their consciences aren't detected. Sin, like an internal cancer, can't readily be seen, but the result is evident—death, whether mortal or eternal. It takes an X-ray to see the presence and extent of lung cancer. Unfortunately, there's no such X-ray machine to view the condition of the soul. However, the effects of a sinful soul are seen through loss of integrity, position, influence, marriage and family, vitality . . .

> "If you live according to the sinful nature, you will die; but if by the Spirit you put to death the misdeeds of the body, you will live." (Romans 8:13)

Nothing of value is gained by living a sinful lifestyle. It always costs, because, "The wages of sin is death" (Romans 6:23).

The Bible contains many warnings more ominous than those on the cigar box. I urge you to pay serious attention to God's warnings.

Why is the struggle so hard? Perhaps because even though we've been saved by the blood of Jesus and are in a "redeemed" state, we still bear the mark of Adam. Be aware, this is not a license to keep sinning. Don't become desensitized, for the results are clearly stated by the apostle Paul: "If you live according to the sinful nature you will die." (Romans 8:13)

Prayer:
*Lord, I know you abhor sin. Help me, through the power
of your Spirit, to put to death the misdeeds of my body.*

APRIL 22

*Craig Duck, Lieutenant, Engine Co. 11 – Washington, DC, Fire
Department; Fellowship of Christian Firefighters International
Atlantic States Regional Director / International Board Member*

WHAT'S IN A NAME?
Willing to hear, obey, and change

THROUGHOUT American fire service history, various names have become famous. As a youngster, I read history books about the fire service and heroes like George Washington, Thomas Jefferson, and "Leather Lungs" Dougherty of San Francisco. When I became a District of Columbia firefighter, I was introduced to new legends: firefighters like the Tippet brothers, Bill Mould, Chief Breen, and Donald Edwards. As I became involved

in the Fellowship of Christian Firefighters International, I heard of others in service for Christ within the fire service: people like Bob Crum, Gay and Sue Reynolds, Dan Clegg, Tommy Neiman, and Chief Lee Callahan.

I also noticed that nicknames are commonly assigned. In the Washington, DC, Fire Department, there were Bucket Head, Fishy, Gordo, Scooter, and Ling-Ling. All received their names because of things they did on the fire ground or because of their personalities.

Peter provides the best answer to the question, "What's in a name?" The Greek meaning of *Petros*, or *Peter*, is "Rock" or "Stone." Peter's original name was Simon bar-Jonah (son of Jonah), but Jesus changed Simon's name to Peter in Matthew 16:18: "And I tell you that you are Peter . . ." Peter, mentioned frequently in the Gospels, holds nothing back. He's impetuous, brash, impulsive, loud, outspoken, self-confident, and even arrogant. So, why did Jesus choose such a man for his ministry?

For the same reason he picked us: to share Christ in the fire service. Jesus wants to transform—or better stated, to *conform*—us into his image, and to use us in his service. Paul best describes this when he writes in Romans, "Do not conform any longer to the pattern of this world, but be transformed by the renewing of your mind. Then you will be able to test and approve what God's will is—his good, pleasing and perfect will" (Romans 12:2).

One of Peter's best qualities didn't come from the list above—it came from Peter's willingness to change those things in his life that were not pleasing to the Lord.

What are you willing to do for God? Peter was willing to change his character in order to better serve God.

It doesn't matter what we're called around the firehouse, what matters is that we are willing to hear, obey, and change when God calls us.

Prayer:
Help me, Lord, to daily read your Word, the Bible, and be willing to change those areas in my life that are not pleasing to you.

Rick Barton, Fire Safety Officer; Rick Barton Ministries, Gunnison, CO; Fellowship of Christian Firefighters International Ambassador-at-Large

FROM THE HEART OF A CHILD

A young child showed us what it means to truly give

IT WAS A hectic scene on the outskirts of Tucson, Arizona, in 2003. A wildfire, started by a careless hiker, suddenly raced up Mt. Lemon and destroyed more than three hundred homes and businesses. Firefighters and rescue workers from around the country were arriving by the hour. Helicopters and air tankers were hammering the hillsides with water and fire retardant, hoping to slow the dragon of fire that seemed insatiable in its desire to destroy all before it.

Hundreds of residents were suddenly homeless, many awakened by rescue workers and often escaping with only the clothes on their backs. Family members were desperately trying to reach one another. Tears and disbelief showed on their faces. It was a time of despair, hopelessness, irreplaceable losses, and anguish for many.

In the midst of this mayhem, a woman and young child showed up at our incident command post. At first we thought they needed shelter and we were prepared to direct them to the Salvation Army or Red Cross. But no, they had an entirely different mission.

> "In everything I did, I showed you that by this kind of hard work we must help the weak, remembering the words the Lord Jesus himself said: 'It is more blessed to give than to receive.'"
> (Acts 20:35)

The youngster had taken the money she'd been saving for a special toy and put it in a jar. Then she went door-to-door in her neighborhood and collected additional money for the children who had lost their toys in the fire. With her mother proudly looking on, the little girl meekly approached and gave us the jar.

"Please use this to help the boys and girls in the fire," she said. And with that she and her mother humbly disappeared into the crowd of humanity surrounding us. I've never seen the child since, and I don't know

150

who she was, but I know God does. This small child put God's Word into action.

As we looked at one another in awe, Jesus' words came to mind: "It is more blessed to give than receive." (Acts 20:35)

Prayer:

I know that giving from my abundance, Lord, can bless, but
may I remember that giving from the heart, as this child gave,
is where my real abundance comes from. Thank you
for the signs of your love when situations are bleak.

APRIL 24

Reverend Wayne Detzler, PhD, Chaplain (Retired) –
Charlotte, NC, Fire Department; Fellowship of
Christian Firefighters Regional Director

COMFORTING THE COMFORTER
The God of all comfort

IN THOSE days she was an extremely effective company captain. In fact, her engine company covered the church I served. Frequently we saw her in action as the team handled medical calls at our church with great skill and compassion. The hundreds of children in our preschool loved the firefighters and their wonderful captain.

So I was amazed when the dispatcher paged me to meet our captain friend at the emergency room. She'd been injured in an off-duty accident. I raced to the hospital not knowing exactly what to expect. When I arrived she was lying on a gurney, her hand bandaged.

She'd been working her part-time job, her own lawn care business. In an effort to repair a lawnmower, she reached up under the skirt of the machine. The blade clipped off the tips of her fingers. While it was neither a life-threatening nor a career-threatening injury, it was an extremely painful injury. The most sensitive part of her fingers had been amputated. A doctor administered a pain block, a merciful relief. I prayed with my friend before she went into surgery for repair of the finger tips. Impulsively, I kissed her on the forehead. She was like a daughter to me.

She returned to duty almost immediately, and her skill and commitment were rewarded with promotion. She became our first female battalion

chief. Her promotion was welcomed by our
department. Secretly, I harbored hopes she
might even progress to deputy chief.

> "Blessed are those
> who mourn, for they
> will be comforted."
> (Matthew 5:4)

Years later I tasted grief in a deep way—
my father died. It was he who had led me to
faith in the Lord and modeled the Christian
life. My grief was deep when we gathered to give thanks for his life. As I
looked across the small crowd, I spotted a woman in a fire uniform. It
was my friend, the chief. She was there for me when I needed comfort the
most. My role is that of comforter, and the Lord remarkably rewards my
efforts by giving me comfort when I need it most.

Prayer:

*Lord, thank you for pouring the oil of comfort
into my life when I most need it.*

*Steve Kidd, Firefighter Orange County Fire and Rescue,
Florida; Central Florida Chapter of the Fellowship of Christian
Firefighters; Author of the Carbusters video series*

NEVER UNDERESTIMATE HIS POWER TO HELP YOU SURVIVE THE STORM

*There is no denying the pain
we feel when we see others suffer*

FIREFIGHTERS, first responders, and emergency workers see a myriad of examples of human suffering and loss of property, life-changing injuries, and painful death. There is no denying the pain we feel when
we see others suffer. Sure, we may try to hide behind translucent veils of
callousness, and we try our best not to show others we aren't all that sensitive or vulnerable.

To a certain extent we do develop resistance to what a layperson
would find truly horrific. However, at one time or another, it is normal to
question our beliefs or ability to experience one more tragedy. We may
wonder why, if Jesus could calm the storm and walk on water, why did

he have to let a terrible accident happen? If God can hide us from harm in the shadow of his wings, then why did an innocent child die in a random drive-by shooting?

We all have our problems: money worries, deteriorating family relationships, sickness, and even the death of a loved one can test our faith.

Does suffering life's disappointments mean God has abandoned us? No! God protects us in many ways. Pain tests us. Troubles teach us lessons that can only be learned from experience. Experience gives us wisdom. Wisdom allows us to help others.

God's protection comes from his guidance through our troubles. When we're faced with adversity, God is there to guide those who believe in God. And when we are called to help those who suffer, God gives us the strength and courage to help them through their troubles. But we must put our faith and trust in him.

> "Keep me as the apple of your eye; hide me in the shadow of your wings from the wicked who assail me, from my mortal enemies who surround me." (Psalm 17:8, 9)

Anyone who has raised a child knows the power of reverse psychology. Suggest one direction and the child will certainly take the other path.

Consider using some reverse psychology on yourself the next time you face a problem. Instead of cursing the problem, stop to thank God for the challenge. Ask for his guidance, and work through the problem with faith in him.

Prayer:
I give you praise for all things, Lord, and I ask you for guidance and help through each day. Hide me in the shadow of your wings.

APRIL 26

Bob Crum, Co-founder – Fellowship of Christian Firefighters International (Retired) – Denver Fire Department

EXCUSES

Our love, concern, and caring for one another will be the greatest influence

LONG SHIFTS at the firehouse, working as a team to extinguish a fire, assisting at an accident, or assessing someone's needs as a result of a

9-1-1 call creates a special type of fellowship common among first responders. Friendships are elevated to a new level as we share our interests, passions and dreams, goals, needs. Consequently a unique and special bond develops with our crew members.

Christian firefighters have more in common for we have a shared bond in Christ; we're one in the Spirit and we have a oneness with Christ and each other. Fellowship becomes more than work or a social gathering. Does that mean everything Christians do must be spiritual in nature?

Not necessarily, but whatever we do, or wherever we go, we need to have that unity that comes from our love and our commitment to the Lord and to each other. First John 1:3 says, "We proclaim to you what we have seen and heard, so that you also may have fellowship with us. And our fellowship is with the Father and with his Son, Jesus Christ."

> "If you have any encouragement from being united with Christ, if any comfort from his love, if any fellowship with the Spirit, if any tenderness and compassion, then make my joy complete by being like-minded, having the same love, being one in spirit and purpose." (Philippians 2:1, 2)

It has been said there is a natural tendency within people to shrink away from fellowship. This seems to be especially true for many who resist Christian fellowship. Ever wondered why?

Perhaps a person has come from a home devoid of love and family unity. It doesn't take long to understand the influence and distraction caused by sports, hobbies, TV. And what about the "Lone Ranger" syndrome, the "I can do it myself!" attitude? Maybe people feel they don't fit in. Past hurts or feelings of being let down can cause a distrust and a fear of being hurt again. Then there is the commonly heard phrase, "I've met too many Christians who are hypocrites. I don't need that in my life."

There are no easy answers to overcoming excuses, but we do need to keep reaching out in Christian love. Those who are completely outside Christian fellowship will eventually wither and dry up spiritually. Our love, concern, and caring for one another will be the greatest influence in helping them make a decision for Christ and bloom and grow, not wither away to eternal death.

Prayer:
Lord, through tenderness, compassion, and my joy from knowing and loving you, may I reach out in Christian fellowship with others. Many times you speak of the need for fellowship. Help me turn my excuses into achievements for your kingdom.

Chaplain Gilbert Gaddie, Captain – Indianapolis Fire Department; President Indianapolis Chapter Fellowship of Christian Firefighters

STRIVING FOR PERFECTION— NOT JUST A CUTE SAYING

Developing a daily relationship with God

"STRIVING FOR perfection" is not just a cute saying, the name of a church in Ft. Walton Beach, Florida, or efficiently fighting a fire without error. It's a state of being. It is also an instruction in the Bible telling you how to live. Not only are you told repeatedly throughout Scripture to strive for perfection, but you're told the Holy Spirit will lead and give you the power to overcome temptation. Striving for perfection helps you continue renewing your mind, which in turn will control your body. This allows your strengthened spirit to control your actions in a way pleasing to God.

Often when Jesus healed people, he told them to go and sin no more. At his ascension, he said he was going back to the Father and would send a Comforter, the Spirit of Truth, to indwell your body. The only requirement was that you make that choice and accept Jesus as Lord of your life. When you do, your body becomes the temple of God: "For we are the temple of the living God" (2 Corinthians 6:16).

> "Do not conform any longer to the pattern of this world, but be transformed by the renewing of your mind. Then you will be able to test and approve what God's will is—His good, pleasing and perfect will."
> (Romans 12:2)

Do you live as though you believe that? If you don't, you're not living up to your potential in the Spirit of God. Living a life of righteousness is similar to experiencing deliverance, since there can be a change in lifestyle. This change is usually a process that requires commitment, prayer, study, conscious effort, and diligence. Deliverance from the things that give the flesh control over the spirit gives the spirit the ability to take control only if you willingly give it that authority.

The more worldly things you're willing to give up, the more room you give spiritual things to grow. The more you grow, the more you're perfected in righteousness. This righteousness comes through God with the daily renewing of your mind through prayer and allowing yourself to become God's vessel. Without a daily relationship with God, you'll find yourself losing authority and power in God's glory.

Are you striving for perfection? If so, let the Holy Spirit guide you as you refuse to conform to the patterns of the world, and as you pray, read God's Word, and grow in righteousness.

Prayer:
Renew my mind daily, indwell me with your Spirit, show me what you want me to do, and help me make room for spiritual things to grow.

APRIL 28

Reverend Wayne Detzler, PhD, Chaplain (Retired) –
Charlotte, NC, Fire Department; Fellowship of
Christian Firefighters Regional Director

HURRICANE-SCRAMBLED WORLD
Helping sort it all out

ISABEL'S COMING! A massive hurricane took aim at the Outer Banks of North Carolina. It was like watching a car wreck in slow motion. We were glued to the television as the spinning storm crept up the coast from Florida.

Then the pager went off. It was our Critical Incident Stress Management team. "Can you give us a hand?" the team leader asked. "We need someone to work at the Emergency Operations Center in Raleigh (the state capital)."

We left immediately, trying to beat the storm. And we almost made it. On the way across our state the edge of the hurricane caught us as we drove through blinding rain and bone-shaking wind. After it passed, I stepped out to take a look at our car. It was plastered with little bits of leaves stripped from the trees by the storm.

When we reached the state capitol building it was eerily silent. Almost no one was on the streets of Raleigh. We easily found room in the parking garage. The wind was gone, but broken trees littered the streets.

Security quickly cleared us and issued a state identification. As I checked into the bunker below, the building was bustling with activity. FEMA representatives were there. The Red Cross was everywhere providing food and hot coffee. National Guard officers kept tabs on troops across our state.

"Can you help our governor?" Someone grabbed Margaret, my wife. She was pressed into service manning a phone bank in the governor's office upstairs. She fielded calls from concerned relatives around the country.

> "Blessed are the peace-makers, for they will be called the sons of God." (Matthew 5:9)

My job was to support the emergency workers. Each day I patrolled the secure site chatting with everyone from National Guard troops to FEMA workers, giving them support. At the same time, I manned a phone line where emergency workers could reach me in case critical incident stress debriefing was needed.

When Israel experienced chaos, God sent the prophets to show the way to peace. Jeremiah guided Israel when the Babylonians stripped Jerusalem. Daniel held the hands of his confused and shocked people. God's people are ambassadors of peace in tough times.

Remember you are being used of God to assist those in need. In the process, be sure to share God's peace and love—be it by your actions, words, or a combination thereof.

Prayer:
Prince of Peace, help me spread peace in a chaotic world.
Allow me to reflect the "Rock of Our Salvation."

APRIL 29

Daniel A. Clegg, Rural-Metro EMT; Engineer/EMT–Indianapolis Fire Department (Retired); Fellowship of Christian Firefighters Regional Director / International Board Member

OUT OF THE MOUTHS OF BABES

Harms of the world have come unto us,
Cups of sorrow we yet shall drain;
But we have a secret that doth show us
Wonderful rainbows in the rain.

RICHARD REALF

TORNADO ALLEY, Indiana, where I live and work, once again lived up to its reputation as storms plowed through, turning my day into one of challenges and discouragement, followed by a reminder of hope expressed through the wisdom of my three-year-old granddaughter.

157

Working tornadoes was not foreign. I felt confident when an onslaught of twisters and tornadoes suddenly descended on Tornado Alley. Our crew was notified we were needed in the Homecroft area of southwest Marion County.

My partner and I were aware this area had sustained widespread damage as twisters swept through, with approximately nineteen touchdowns. On arrival, we found things worse than expected. We crawled over poles, cars, broken homes, and damaged trees to reach victims. Each step of the way we encountered teary-eyed faces that reflected disbelief, loss, and fear.

The rain was relentless, fiercely pelting the ground. My cold, blistered, wet feet ached. I wished I was home or anywhere but in the midst of such destruction, sorrow, and piercing rains. Basically, I was having a pity party. I wanted to be out of there, but the job wouldn't allow it and neither would my heart. I had a job to do and people to help. My partner and I must have traversed five or six miles as we assisted and examined people.

Why does something like this have to happen? I wondered.

People treated us like heroes, but we didn't *feel* like heroes. We felt helpless and insignificant. Heartache surrounded us, and all we could do was listen, thankful no one was seriously hurt.

> "I have set my rainbow in the clouds . . . Whenever I bring clouds over the earth and the rainbow appears in the clouds, I will remember my covenant between me and you and all living creatures of every kind." (Genesis 9:13-15)

Nine hours later, I walked through the doors of my home. My three-year-old granddaughter, Mia, met me at the door with a gigantic smile on her face. "Grandpa, I saw God's promise today—I saw a beautiful rainbow in the sky."

I needed a rainbow—a reminder that after every storm there is hope of a new tomorrow filled with rainbows. I saw the awe in my three-year-old granddaughter's eyes and knew that "out of the mouth of babes" come words of wisdom and hope, and the promise of rainbows after a storm.

Prayer:
*As I walk through the storms, may my eyes
stay on you and the rainbows ahead.*

Chief Lee Callahan, Burlington, MA; Fellowship of
Christian Firefighters International Regional
Director / International Board Member

WHAT IS YOUR BENCHMARK?

A standard-setter to be compared to

DON'T YOU love a good healthy firehouse kitchen table debate? Sports fans debate who is the best player. Name a position and the debate rages about who stacks up as the best now or in the past. Civil War buffs will compare General Robert E. Lee to General Ulysses S. Grant, who both set standards in warfare due to their ability to win battles.

A recurrent biblical theme in regard to the kings of Israel's northern kingdom is how they lived and how they ruled. Repeatedly it is stated, "He did evil in the eyes of the LORD, walking in the ways of his father and in his sin" (1 Kings 15:26). When talking about Nadab, Jeroboam's son, Scripture speaks of the standard set by Jeroboam because of his failure to walk in a way pleasing to God. Jeroboam led Israel away from God by worshipping idols—an astounding benchmark nobody could be proud of.

The fire service is all about meeting standards. The National Fire Protection Association (NFPA) is chock full of standards that most strive to meet because they're established to protect against unsafe practices, manufacturing, processes and procedures . . .

> "... we have confidence before God and receive from him anything we ask, because we obey his commands and do what pleases him."
> (1 John 3:21, 22).

At home and in the workplace, what standard do you meet? Are you a mature Christian who exemplifies Christ? Are you a testimony to the goodness and love of Christ? Do your co-workers and your loved ones know which benchmarks are important to you?

Although not a lot of description is given us, we have some New Testament examples of those who meet that Christ-like benchmark, such as Phoebe (Romans 16:1) and Priscilla and Aquila (vv. 3, 4). And what about Melchizedek, who a couple of thousand years after his death is seen as a benchmark-setter by the writer of Hebrews (7:1–3, 21)? According to Scripture, all the saints meet those standards set by Melchizedek. Do those standards apply to you?

You have a choice. You can establish standards such as those set by Jeroboam (or some modern likeness of him known for his sinful ways). Or you can strive to set godly standards that will witness to others and be pleasing to God. Choose the latter and you gain the confidence to receive what you ask for if it is truly in obedience to, and pleasing to, God.

Prayer:
I seek to be a benchmark, a standard-setter, whom you, Lord, will be well-pleased with and others will want to be compared to.

*Rick Barton, Fire Safety Officer; Rick Barton Ministries,
Gunnison, CO; Fellowship of Christian Firefighters
International Ambassador-at-Large*

DON'T YOU DARE LAUGH

Or maybe you should *laugh,*
but with a humble heart

Have you ever tried really hard to be serious and failed miserably? I was the crew boss in charge of mopping up a one-hundred-acre forest fire. My position was above the crew on the adjoining hillside, from where I could direct them to spot fires. At the end of my shift I began heading cross-country to the main trail back to the vehicles. Instead of following the flagging, I took a "shortcut." I soon reached the main trail and started hiking out.

The problem was, I kept coming across fallen trees across the trail—trees that weren't there that morning. After a half-hour of struggling over the downfall, I pulled out my compass. It, too, was messed up. It said I was headed away from the vehicles and directly into the wilderness area.

What about the time we were in the midst of the Colorado Wildfire Academy? .The lead information officer for our incident management team was teaching a classroom full of eager trainees. Suddenly, one of the

> "A cheerful heart is good medicine, but a crushed spirit dries up the bones." (Proverbs 17:22)

students noticed that the sign on the door read, "Infoamation Officer." The instructor had goofed up her own title.

Or the time on fire patrol when I got turned around in "Lost Canyon" and called in a smoke that turned out to be the cement factory *south* of town? (A fact I discovered after I'd already sent everybody *north* of town to find the "fire.")

What do we do? How should we react in those moments? I think the only thing appropriate is to humble ourselves and laugh! We're human and we goofed. No one was hurt, only our egos. I think the Lord may allow us to "discover" that no matter how much of a legend we are in our own minds, we really are fallible. And realizing our weaknesses is a good thing. It reminds us we are still learning. It also demonstrates our need to show grace toward others when they make mistakes. Proverbs 17:22 addresses this: "A cheerful heart is good medicine"—better than any doctor can prescribe, if you ask me. What better way to achieve a merry heart than to laugh at ourselves?

Of course, I confessed my mistakes to my co-workers . . . six or seven years later.

Prayer:
Infoamation or information, Lord, you know my heart and intentions. May my actions always be with you foremost in my heart. That way I can approach everything with a cheerful heart.

MAY 2

Slade McLendon, Vice President – Sunbelt Fire Inc.

FOR SURVIVAL OR GOD'S GLORY?!

Make sure you attack the problem and not the person

DO YOU ever feel as if you're just surviving? When *I* do, the Lord gently reminds me of his promises in Matthew 6:31–34. God doesn't want us to worry about what we will eat, drink, or wear. He explains that the pagans run after these things but God knows what we need. He urges us to seek his kingdom and his righteousness and when we do, "all these things will be given to [us] as well. Therefore do not worry about tomorrow, for tomorrow will worry about itself. Each day has enough trouble of its own."

If you're like me, you forget this sometimes. When I do, worry creeps in. How about you? Are you ever overcome with worry?

At times when worry threatens to control my thoughts and actions, I'm thankful that God continually sends me reminders of the fact that I'm not in control on this journey of life—he is!

"As for man, his days are like grass, he flourishes like a flower of the field; the wind blows over it and it is gone, and its place remembers it no more. But from everlasting to everlasting the LORD's love is with those who fear him, and his righteousness with their children's children—with those who keep his covenant and remember to obey his precepts. The LORD has established his throne in heaven, and his kingdom rules over all." (Psalm 103:15–19)

I love my family and we believe that our Father is sovereign and always in control. Even when it doesn't feel like it, we know he has a plan at all times. Early in our marriage my wife was diagnosed with cystic fibrosis (lung disease). We realized at that point how truly not in control of our lives we really are. Our first response was anxiety and fear of the unknown. In and of ourselves we couldn't take the disease and knock it out. To date there is no cure, but we're learning that this is the exact plan God has for our family.

I had a man give me some counsel years ago: "As you travel through life make sure you attack the problem and not the person." I get this mixed up and have to stop at times and remember how valuable people are in my life. We need to not let the issues in life become the relationship. I'm learning this daily and sometimes not fast enough.

God's plan doesn't make sense to us at times, but his Scripture reminds us about his love for us.

Prayer:
Lord, as I journey through this life, may I make the most of each day, whatever I'm doing. May I do it all, as the apostle Paul said in 1 Corinthians 10:31, for "the glory of God."

MAY 3

Duncan M. Wilkie (Retired) – Denver Fire Department; Co-founder – Fellowship of Christian Firefighters International

ABUNDANT LIFE
Overcoming fear of rejection was tough

ABUNDANT life! Praise God it's mine, but my journey was filled with obstacles, poor decisions, and selfish priorities.

When I became a firefighter, the fire department and related activities became my focal point. A sixty-four-hour work week, department activities, and owning a construction company left no time for my family. I thought things were great; after all, my family had all the luxuries money could buy. Then all was wiped out in a moment by divorce.

For two years, I traveled abroad, sitting in bars, trying to fill the void. I watched guys being offered another drink—if they had the money (if they didn't, they weren't welcome). I concluded no one cared about me. Life was like a beautiful soap bubble with all the colors of the rainbow— you reach out for it and POP, it's gone! I found no reason for living. Suicide didn't look too bad. Compounding my dismal outlook were health

163

issues caused by two years of abusing myself. After surgery, I met and asked out my therapist. She consented to have coffee with me if I'd attend church with her.

I went. The preaching tore me up. I heard, "What good is it for a man to gain the whole world, yet forfeit his soul?" (Mark 8:36). That was me! I tried to gain everything and had nothing, not even a purpose for living. The preacher shared Jesus' words: "I have come that [you] might have life, and have *it* abundantly" (John 10:10 NASB). Soon I realized I couldn't buy what those people had. God's gift of Jesus and the forgiveness of my sins were free!

> "I have come that they may have life, and have it to the full." (John 10:10)

I wanted to do something to earn this acceptance. Growing up in a broken home, being left by my wife, and shallow friendships made it difficult to believe someone loved me! Overcoming fear of rejection was tough. Could I chance being left again?

Still, I wanted what Jesus had to offer and asked Christ for forgiveness and to come into my life. Then I headed for the bar. Soon I realized I needed to give Christ a chance. Drinking caused me to do things I was ashamed of. I left.

By his grace, that was the end of my drinking and the start of my abundant life. Easy? No! Tests? Yes! Yet, with every test, blessings come and my trust in God grows.

Prayer:
As I walk closer to you each day, may my blessings increase and my trust grow so I can share the truth of your abundant and full life with others.

Dessa Patton, Paramedic, Olive Branch, MS and Horn
Lake Fire Departments, MS; North Mississippi Medical
Center- Fulton Ambulance Service in conjunction with
all Itawamba County, MS fire departments;

ABOVE AND BEYOND

From duty's path, however steep, we ask . . .
Only for strength to finish well our task.

EDWARD A. CHURCH

"ABOVE AND beyond the call of duty" is a phrase often heard in reference to emergency personnel. Many describe "above and beyond" as doing something heroic or lifesaving by putting one's own life in peril. Each year hundreds of heroic people lose or endanger their lives by doing just that. But such heroic acts don't encompass the entire picture. The fire service is full of "unsung heroes."

There is no question a firefighter who goes into a flaming structure to drag an anonymous and unconscious man out is a hero. He deserves the tearful hugs of the man's wife, intent look of awe from the man's children, and oftentimes media coverage. But what about the same first responder who when off-duty raises money for charities or spends Christmas Day delivering packages to needy children? What about the little girl with happy tears streaming down her cheeks when her puppy is rescued? She knows who the real heroes in her life are.

The medics who let the dog out, take the cat in, retrieve the keys and purse, compassionately call a victim's family, and still manage to take superior care of their patients are heroes as well. Not only do they crawl into crushed vehicles to assess a patient who is clinging to life, they also comfort the grieving family of a patient with incurable cancer. On the trip to the hospital they give that same terminally ill patient a few last laughs. When the family sees the smile on the face of their loved one, they know EMS workers are heroes.

> "The report I heard in my own country about your achievements and your wisdom is true. But I did not believe what they said until I came and saw with my own eyes. Indeed, not even half the greatness of your wisdom was told me; you have far exceeded the report I heard."
> (2 Chronicles 9:5, 6)

Dispatchers do their best to alleviate panic in crisis situations by answering phones, running tags, and coordinating police, fire, and EMS all for the same emergency. When 9-1-1 callers get directions for CPR while waiting to hear the sirens, they know who the hero is.

These are just a few of the public servants who serve in every capacity and by every means imaginable. They, too, go "above and beyond the call of duty."

Prayer:

Lord, when someone calls me a hero, it is humbling. Let me remain humble in your sight and always remember that you, too, went above and beyond when you gave your life for me. May others say of me, "You have far exceeded the report I heard."

M A Y 5

Tommy Neiman, Author of Sirens for the Cross; EMS Training Officer – St. Lucie County, FL; Fellowship of Christian Firefighters International Regional Director / International Board Member

HOME WITH THE LORD
Don't even think about bringing me back

THE DEVELOPMENT of new and advanced equipment and technology is ongoing. Each facilitates our jobs as first responders. The expense can be mind-boggling. But this "life at all cost and effort" mindset took a back seat to God's perfect timing one Sunday morning when a call came about "an unresponsive person."

A young lady met us at the door. "My aunt isn't responding," she said as she led us down the dimly lit hallway. Our only light was the beacon light of our truck flashing against the walls of her living room.

"Find a light," I told my partner as I went to the woman's bedside. As he headed for a small lamp on the dresser, I touched the woman's wrist. "Never mind that light," I said. "We aren't gonna be working her. She's gone." Turning to the niece I said with compassion, "I'm afraid we weren't in time!"

We returned to the living room. Sobbing quietly, she said, "My aunt was ill for some time. And . . . she was a woman of great faith."

We spoke of the peace her aunt was now experiencing. Before I headed back to the bedroom, I explained what would happen next. I was stunned when I entered the room. Daybreak illuminated the room as if to purposely highlight the decor of this recently departed soul's bedroom. The niece's words, "a woman of great faith," rang in my mind

> "We are of good courage, I say, and prefer rather to be absent from the body and to be at home with the Lord." (2 Corinthians 5:8 NASB).

as I looked about the room and saw abundant evidence of a Lord and Savior she loved. Her wall was covered with plaques exclaiming Bible verses. On her nightstand was a large-print Bible opened to the Twenty-Third Psalm. *God surely gave her insight to this psalm on this, her final reading of the Bible*, I thought as I stood in awe.

Then it occurred to me: We had come with an abundance of modern technical equipment, all in the name of saving a physical life, but today all human effort was mocked by the wonderful plan of a loving Father calling a precious child home.

If this lady could have spoken, I'm sure she would have said, "Don't even think about bringing me back." The apostle Paul said, "To be absent from the body [is] to be at home with the Lord"—just like that! No waiting! An instantly fulfilled promise of God!

Prayer:
Thank you, Lord, for the assurance that someday I'll be home with you. Meanwhile, may I perform with compassion the responsibilities of my life as a child of God and first responder.

M A Y   6

Lieutenant Danny Legge, Paramedic/Chaplain –
Clay County, FL, Fire Rescue

DO NOT RESUSCITATE
Have you received Christ's DNR?

FIRST RESPONDERS are well aware that a Do Not Resuscitate, or DNR, order is a written order from a doctor that resuscitation should not be attempted if a person suffers cardiac or respiratory arrest. In some areas, the order may be instituted on the basis of an advance directive from a person or from someone entitled to make decisions on their behalf, such as a health care proxy. In some jurisdictions such orders can be instituted on the basis of a physician's own initiative, designed to prevent unnecessary suffering—usually when resuscitation won't alter the ultimate outcome of a disease.

Any person who doesn't wish to undergo lifesaving treatment in the event of cardiac or respiratory arrest can get a DNR order, although DNR is more commonly used when a person who has an inevitably fatal illness wishes to have a more natural death without painful or invasive medical procedures.

The world is full of people who are in possession of such orders. They have given in to the fact that they have a terminal illness and have given up all hope for a cure. The terminal illness I'm referring to is sin! This sickness is fatal if left untreated, but what many fail to realize is that sin is a terminal illness with a miraculous cure, a cure available to all of us. And it's free!

> "As far as the east is from the west, so far has he removed our transgressions from us."
> (Psalm 103:12)

Jesus has the best DNR offer yet. His DNR stands for "Does Not Remember." Once you confess your sins and repent, you are spared sin's fatality. You will still see the scars, but Jesus won't. He has thrown your sins away as far as the east is from the west.

What a blessing that you can be resuscitated and made alive again! Ephesians 2:1 makes it clear that at one time you were dead in your sins, but as a believer Christ has made you alive. Ephesians 1:7 puts it this way: "In him [you] have redemption through his blood, the forgiveness of sins, in accordance with the riches of God's grace."

I hope and pray you've received Christ's DNR. If not, talk to God today. Then, all your sins will be forgiven and forgotten.

Prayer:
Lord, thank you for your special DNR. May I,
too, forgive and forget as you do.

Aaron Johnson, Fire Inspector – Martin County, FL

RIT

Extend the hand of Christian friendship

RAPID INTERVENTION TEAMS—these are the firefighter's firefighters. When firefighters are in trouble or need help, whom do they call? They call in the Rapid Intervention Team (RIT).

RIT members are trained and have all the tools to rescue firefighters that become trapped, run out of air, or are disoriented. By some they are labeled "the superheroes" of emergency services. They can create an opening where one does not exist. They can get an emergency air supply to the trapped firefighter, or they can get him enough air to make it out of the situation. RIT is who the firefighter calls when facing an emergency.

For us Christians, our church family becomes a sort of Rapid Intervention Team . In times of need we can turn to our church family to "intervene" (intercede) on our behalf. When we have burdens too heavy to bear alone, we can call for others to rescue us and help us bear these burdens. When we have nowhere to turn, don't know what to do, feel the need for nonjudgmental input, or need assistance with family, financial problems, or even sinful thoughts and actions, the RIT team can support us.

> "Two are better than one, because they have a good return for their work: If one falls down, his friend can help him up. But pity the man who falls and has no one to help him up! Also, if two lie down together, they will keep warm. But how can one keep warm alone? Though one may be overpowered, two can defend themselves. A cord of three strands is not quickly broken."
> (Ecclesiastes 4:9–12)

Christian Rapid Intervention Teams; these are the Christian's Christians. They fulfill the purpose of the church—the body of Christ—to rescue those who are perishing.

Activating the RIT is one way in which this can be accomplished. Does your church have an RIT? Whether a formal team or not, God clearly wants his church to extend the hand of friendship, and if one falls down, to activate God's RIT.

What about at your workplace? Do your co-workers know that if they are spiritually or emotionally trapped, you are a member of God's RIT?

Prayer:
Father, thank you for the RIT you have surrounded me with.
Help me to be the RIT to those around me.

Reverend Wayne Detzler, PhD, Chaplain (Retired) –
Charlotte, NC, Fire Department; Fellowship of
Christian Firefighters Regional Director

WHEN PRESENCE SAYS IT ALL
When words are not enough

FROM THE outside, the high-rise apartment building looked deceptively calm. The casual observer saw no sign of smoke, no telltale black streaks rising from the windows. No one could have imagined the grisly scene inside.

On the ground floor one door stood wide open. Firefighters came in and out and the acrid smell of smoke filled the air. It was the scene of a particularly hot fire. And it was the scene of a particularly pathetic fatality.

"Come on inside." The chief ushered me into the fire scene. "There's something I want to show you." Sitting still in an electric wheelchair was the form of a man. The lack of light and the smoky air obscured the image.

"Come around to the front," the chief asked me. "I want to show you this guy. He was in my high school class." Then I realized the form in the wheelchair was dead, and the body was charred almost beyond recognition. We stood silent as the chief explained the perfect circle of blackened carpet. Something had ignited the electric wheelchair and the man burned to death. He was unable to escape.

We prayed, more for our crews than for anything else. I led the chief in a quiet moment of prayer, as we asked the Lord to calm our hearts and help us take care of the family of this poor victim. After the chief took me to view the body, I went back outside and found the lieutenant sitting up against a tree, propped up with his helmet off and his bunker coat unzipped. He was obviously finished with his task inside. Now he was

170

just sitting there trying to make sense of the evening.

"Is it okay if I sit down?" I asked my friend, the lieutenant. He nodded his agreement and I sat down next to him. Then I noticed he was weeping, caught up in the sheer sadness of the scene. I put my arm around his shoulders, and we just sat there comforting each other. As the stench of burnt flesh lingered in our noses, we realized words would never do. Tears flooded our beings as we were silently united in our grief at the alarming, bizarre loss of a friend. As I comforted my friend, the chief, I thanked God that when tears flood my being, he is always with me (Matthew 28:20).

Prayer:
Present Savior, help me to know when to speak and when not to speak. Thank you for being my strength when the sadness on scene is more than my mind can comprehend.

MAY 9

Captain Jim Herrington, Firefighter/Paramedic –
Poudre Fire Authority, Fort Collins, CO

FIVE-GENERATION REUNION
Love the baby

MY PARTNER and I, assigned to the "first call" ambulance, made endless runs to and from nursing homes or hospitals. No one becomes a paramedic to do transfers—but they come with the territory when you work for a small ambulance service. Near shift-end a woman approached. "Excuse me. We want to take our mother to the community hospital."

What's wrong with this hospital? I thought while responding politely. "You'll need to have a nurse call dispatch with transport authorization."

I edged toward the elevator knowing by having the nurse call, we'd have time to leave and let the new crew handle the transport.

"We have the doctor's permission. We just need her taken there."

Smiling, trying to hide my true feelings, I kindly responded, "When the nurse calls, it'll be no problem to have a crew take her over."

"My mother is comatose and dying of cancer. Her great-granddaughter just gave birth to her great-great-grandson. The family is over

171

there now. My granddaughter and her baby can't come here. We want to have all five generations together."

"Okay," I sighed.

When we entered the elderly woman's room, her body was thin and light. As I rode in back with her, my mind swirled: *What if she goes into cardiac arrest?* While touched by the sincerity of the request, I wondered,

> "Both low and high, rich and poor alike: My mouth will speak words of wisdom; the utterance from my heart will give understanding."
> (Psalm 49:2, 3).

Will she remember this visit? Won't this just make everyone feel sad when they should be focusing on the new birth?

When we arrived, the new mom's small room was crowded. "Mother," our patient's daughter said, "here's your great-great-grandson." Amazingly the elderly woman opened her eyes as they laid the baby in her arms. That limp body we'd picked up so easily was holding a new infant. She looked comfortable and at peace as she spoke words that will echo across the generations! "Love the baby."

I consider myself to be a pretty tough guy. To maintain my professional image, I hide my emotions as deep as possible. I've seen vignettes from almost every kind of nightmare that EMS has to offer, but this one touched a soft spot deep within. Transfer has never been the same since this call. And best of all, I have the memory of this special Five-Generation Family Reunion with me forever.

Prayer:
When the demands of this career begin to turn my heart to selfish thoughts of my own comforts, may I turn to you for your strength. Fill my heart with compassion and understanding.

M A Y   1 0

Reverend Wayne Detzler, PhD, Chaplain (Retired) – Charlotte, NC, Fire Department; Fellowship of Christian Firefighters Regional Director

MOTHER OF HEROES

Till the end they were close

FAMILIES ARE close in Connecticut, where my wife and I live. It's not unusual for grown children and their parents to live near each other

172

and to keep in close contact. The bond between parents and their children is often intimate and warm.

Flo is a heroic woman in anyone's books. She had eight children and impacted our fire department in a remarkable way. One of her daughters married a firefighter, and this attached her to our department in an inseparable way.

She shaped the lives of her children by example. Her life was a constant round of service for the Lord, service that was only exceeded by her loving devotion to her eight children and their families.

When the call came for short-term missionaries in Haiti, Flo was the first to respond. They needed someone to give immunizations, so Flo learned how to give shots. There was a further need for personal hygiene supplies. You guessed it, Flo gathered soap, washrags, toothbrushes, and toothpaste. She made dozens of little kits to take along on her missions trip.

> "I have been reminded of your sincere faith, which first lived in your grandmother Lois and in your mother Eunice."
> (2 Timothy 1:5)

Each year people opened their home for prayer week. Every night we went to a different home for prayer. Flo and her husband never missed. Each year they opened their home for the prayer-and-fellowship gathering.

Our church needed a preschool director. This time it was Flo's daughter who stepped up to impact our kids for the Lord. She'd learned this ready response from her mother, a model of Christian commitment and Christ-like service.

When it came time to launch our first Fellowship of Christian Firefighters chapter, a firefighter named Mark was ready to lead. His godliness was exceeded only by his willingness to lead our little fellowship. He learned this by watching his mother-in-law, Flo. Like her, he was committed to Christ and to the network of believers within the fire service.

It's amazing how wide the network of blessing spreads when a Christian mother like Flo leads the charge. Only eternity will tell the full extent of her influence.

Prayer:
Father of godly mothers, we thank you for
placing them in our lives and our world.

Jeff Turkel, Firefighter/Dispatcher – North Pole, Alaska;
Fellowship of Christian Firefighters Regional Director

IT HAPPENED TO ME
Asking for help is a sign of strength

SAFETY WAS the key subject I preached when challenged to share my experience with volunteer firefighters. After weeks of safety instruction, I thought they were ready for a training fire. I prepared a large brush pile, methodically ensured everyone was properly equipped, and instructed crews to lay two attack lines and one safety backup line.

Then I made a stupid decision. I used half a cup of gasoline to light the brush pile. Instantly I experienced a blast that knocked me to my knees, bunkers smoking, terrified to move. When I came to my senses I felt fine, so continued the training before heading to the hospital for cream for my burnt lips. Within minutes the ER had multiple IV lines in my arms, hooked me to an EKG, and began breathing treatments. The whole time I argued, "I'm fine."

> "And when we cried unto the LORD, he heard our voice, and sent an angel" (Numbers 20:16 KJV).

Ignoring me, they wheeled me into the critical trauma area. My blood pressure, pulse, and EKG were abnormal. Still, I continued to argue with the doctor, "I'm fine."

The truth: I wasn't okay. I'd been caught in the gasoline vapor explosion. The flames burnt the inside of my bronchial tubes.

Three days later I was back at work; no light duty or convalescent leave. Soon I started to have problems. I suffered from insomnia, lost appetite, headaches, and realistic accident flashbacks where I actually felt the heat. Fear of freezing on the fire ground overcame me. I didn't share these fears for two sleepless weeks. Then I apprehensively took advantage of a one-on-one critical incident stress debriefing. When asked to describe exactly what transpired, shaking uncontrollably, I obliged in painstaking detail.

"Jeff, after lighting the fire, what did you think the moment you realized something was wrong?" I was asked.

"I don't know."

The counselor was persistent. The more he asked the angrier I shouted, "I don't know!"

After forty-five minutes of "badgering," I screamed, "I thought I deserved to die because I was so stupid."

174

Instantly the floodgates of tears started to flow. The healing began.

Critical incident stress debriefings *do* work. Being the Lone Ranger doesn't. If you need help, please get it. Asking for help is not a sign of weakness. It is a sign of strength.

Prayer:
When I feel as though I'm in slavery to sin or in pain, I ask you to send an angel. Give me wisdom to seek the help you provide through so many gifted and trained counselors, be they friends or professional. Most of all, I seek your comfort and peace.

M A Y   1 2

Rev. Joe Smaha, Chaplain/Fire Inspector/Firefighter/EMT/ Hazmat Specialist – Paramus, NJ, Fire Department; Fire Instructor – Bergen County, NJ, Fire Academy; Pastor – Community Church of Paramus

THE FIRST LODD
The ultimate sacrificial expression of love

INJURIES AND death are common features of emergency services; each year we typically lose one hundred or more firefighters in the United States. Whenever a firefighter, police officer, emergency medical technician, or other emergency responder loses his or her life on the job, it's considered a line-of-duty death (LODD). They have laid down their lives while performing their duty to serve and protect others.

Jesus came into this world in human form, God in the flesh, to perform the will of his Father, to live a life of service, and to give his life as a ransom for many (Matthew 20:28). He appeared as a man and then humbled himself and obediently gave his life on the cross (Philippians 2:8). He clearly states there is no greater love than when someone lays down his life for his friends (John 15:13). Jesus came to save, and he willingly became the first LODD. He laid down his life for everyone in the world—even those who hated him. He did this out of love. Paul tells us in Romans 5:8, "God demonstrates his own love for us in this: While we were still sinners, Christ died for us." That is an ultimate sacrificial expression of love!

Firefighters run into burning buildings everyday, risking their lives for people they don't even know regardless of who they are. Every day as we

175

do our jobs as firefighters, we know it may be our last day on Earth. I've personally been in situations as a firefighter when I was unsure I would make it out alive to go home and see my family again. As emergency responders we learn to live with this uncertainty. It's part of the job. None of us knows

> "But God demonstrates his own love for us in this: While we were still sinners, Christ died for us." (Romans 5:8)

for certain we will lose our lives in the line of duty, but we realize it's a possibility. There is one thing we do know for sure—eternity with God is assured for all who know Jesus as their Lord and Savior.

Jesus knew not only that he would die while performing his duty, but also how he would lose his life. These are all reasons why I consider Jesus to be the first LODD! And he did it so whoever believes in him "shall not perish but have everlasting life" (John 3:16 KJV).

Prayer:
Thank You, Lord, for willingly being the first LODD. I pray for your protection for me as I perform my duties. Thank you that through my belief and faith in you, I will not perish eternally.

M A Y   1 3

Dr. Jonathan Newell, Missionary Malawi, Africa

PEOPLE, NOT PROJECTS; RELATIONSHIPS, NOT RIVALRY
Loving as Christ would want us to

EFFICIENCY, time management, training, and good stewardship of equipment are all vital to the effective running of fire services. Without these fundamentals lives would be lost, more properties would be destroyed, and firefighters' safety would be jeopardized. However, there is something missing from this list of principles—the most important thing: people.

Sometimes in our western culture that emphasizes achievement and projects before relationships, it's easy to forget that everything we do we should be doing for people. Let me give you an example of what I mean. Some years ago I arrived in the African country of Malawi to teach at the university there. After a few months one of my Malawian colleagues came to me and asked if we could have a chat. I agreed and we started to talk. Eventually he said, "Jonathan, the way you behave is offending people."

I was horrified, clueless, and unaware of anything offensive I was doing. I sincerely asked, "What is it I am doing? I'd never deliberately try to offend others."

"Well," he continued, "you need to understand that in our culture a person and their family are more important than the work they do. So, if you just go up to the secretary and ask her to do some work for you without first greeting her and asking about her family and relatives, then you've offended her."

I have never forgotten this lesson in loving as Christ wants us to love, which I was taught through my exposure to another culture.

We must be careful to avoid destroying others through a relentless drive to achieve, produce, compete, and succeed. People matter and so do our relationships with them. It might even be the case that uncontrolled personal competition, jealousy, and rivalry could do more harm in a fire station than professional inefficiency.

> "Therefore, if you are offering your gift at the altar and there remember that your brother has something against you ... First go and be reconciled to your brother; then come and offer your gift." (Matthew 5:23, 24)

In truth we must look to both professional efficiency *and* relationships if we wish to succeed. Let us give more time and prayer to our personal and professional relationships.

Prayer:
Our loving God and heavenly Father, I confess that sometimes
I forget about others and only concentrate on what I must achieve.
Help me to remember to build healthy relationships with
those around me both at home and at work.

Reverend Wayne Detzler, PhD, Chaplain (Retired) –
Charlotte, NC, Fire Department; Fellowship of
Christian Firefighters Regional Director

WHEN THE FAST
AND FAMOUS DIE

Death comes to all, rich and poor

IN THIS WORLD nothing is certain but death and taxes," wrote
Benjamin Franklin, stating the obvious. Our experience confirms it,
even when we don't want to think about it. Death often comes as a
cruel surprise.

This was certainly true when Dale Earnhardt, the NASCAR star, died
on the Daytona track in 2001. The crash seemed simple, but Dale Earnhardt died. Car #3 became an instant shrine. Shock surged through the
racing world. Nowhere was this more obvious than in Charlotte, North
Carolina, the home of stock car racing.

"Can you handle the memorial for Dale Earnhardt?" The phone call
shocked our lead pastor. It was assumed that our church alone could hold
the crowd. As care pastor, it became my task to organize the funeral and
handle the media.

Race fans showed up at the church. They wanted to take a brief time
to remember the champion, known on the track as "The Intimidator."
Day after day, people came through our doors asking for nothing more
than a few quiet moments at the flower-flooded front of the sanctuary.

Early in the week, I had a conference call with NASCAR leaders as
well as members of the Earnhardt team. We juggled the need for privacy
with the clamor of fans. My job was simple:
Keep media personnel at a respectful distance, while giving them the information
they needed.

> "You are my God. My
> times are in your hands."
> (Psalm 31:14, 15)

So, I called for help from my colleagues
at the Charlotte Fire Department. They
kindly came to our aid. They provided the family of Dale Earnhardt and
the racing fraternity a dignified, quiet service. Many of the firefighters
were members of our Fellowship of Christian Firefighters, and they saw
their service as an expression of the Lord's love.

One thing we all learned is this: Rich or poor, famous or forgotten—
everyone dies. For some, death is a high-speed crash and a blaze of glory.

For others, it's a silent room in a home for the elderly. The result is the same. To use a Bible word, this is an appointment none can avoid. Every person will die, unless the Lord returns for his own during their lifetime.

Prayer:
Lord, help me to remember my mortality
as I serve the world in our generation.

Ann Christmas, Fellowship of Christian Firefighters, St. Louis
Chapter; American Red Cross, North County Citizen Corps

A FORGIVING HEART
What if life is lost?

FORGIVENESS is shown and written about throughout the Bible. There are many examples how a Christian is supposed to act when wronged. One of the best examples, in my opinion, is Joseph in the Old Testament book of Genesis, chapters 37 through 50. Because of jealousy, his brothers conspired, sold him into slavery, ripped his coat and covered it with animal blood, making it look as if he had been killed by an animal, and took it to their father, Jacob. Jacob mourned the loss of his son until they were reunited years later. Joseph forgave his brothers and made the most of every bad situation he was handed.

What if the wrong is more extreme? What if life is lost? Such was the case in the book of Job, which relates a life filled with faith and forgiveness through many losses.

Emergency workers, especially police officers, sometimes deal with the deaths of colleagues. As they seek to keep order and safety while also providing protection, they're often placed in extreme danger. In the process, some sacrifice their own lives.

In February 2008, my city changed forever. Kirkwood, Missouri, mourned the loss of some amazing people, including two police officers, William Biggs and Thomas Ballman. Months later, my father's mourning deepened when his friend Mayor Mike Swoboda died from complications resulting from that same shooting.

Many lives were affected by this senseless act of violence. Likewise, anger manifested itself from many different angles. In contrast, abundant love also overflowed in our city in response to this tragedy.

How do you forgive someone who takes away the life of a servant? God is quite clear on how we are to forgive. The fact is—we're told to forgive. We're commanded by Jesus to forgive others, no exceptions. This isn't easy. Sometimes it might take a day, weeks, months, in some cases even years to forgive those who hurt you or someone you know. In Matthew, Jesus shares that we need to love our enemies and pray for them.

> "But I tell you: Love your enemies and pray for those who persecute you." (Matthew 5:44)

How do we move on? It can only be accomplished by following God's command to forgive, love, and pray. It's the peace we find in knowing Jesus that gets us through the pain of losing someone we love. It's this same peace that will help us forgive.

Prayer:

Lord, thank you for showing me how to forgive those who have hurt me and hurt those I love. I am called to love everyone just as you do. I want to be forgiven, Lord, so teach me to forgive in all circumstances.

MAY 16

Rob Hitt, Firefighter/EMT-I – Greenville/Spartanburg International Airport Fire Department; South Carolina Fellowship of Christian Firefighters International Regional Director

THEY WOULDN'T BEND
They wouldn't bend, they wouldn't bow, and they wouldn't burn!

FIRST RESPONDERS know about fire, challenges, and trials. Most of us are familiar with the biblical account of Shadrach, Meshach, and Abednego in the fiery furnace (Daniel 3). As these wise men stood before a pagan king, they were given the choice to renounce the Lord God or face immediate death. They chose to refuse to kneel to a lifeless idol or to participate in the Babylonian fads of the day.

Being one of three men against the entire Babylonian population would frighten and intimidate anyone. However, amid the pressure and stress of the moment, these men chose not to bow to, worship, or acknowledge the idol or the king's decree even if the Lord God chose not

180

to deliver them. These three stated, "O Nebuchadnezzar, we do not need to defend ourselves before you in this matter" (Daniel 3:16). This indicates they didn't have to think about their answer or its implications. It was automatic, deliberate, concrete, unmoving, and based on their faith that whether or not God delivered them, they would remain faithful to him—even at the threshold of their own death.

It's easy to say, "I stand for the Lord"! However, the big test comes when we are faced with adversities. Daniel 3:20, 21 states that Nebuchadnezzar appointed his mightiest men to bind the three Hebrew men, signifying they could not move and had to be physically thrown into the furnace. As the king stood and expressed his approval of their attempted execution, he saw four men loose and walking around in the furnace. In verse 25 he shouted, "Look! I see four men walking around in the fire, unbound and unharmed, and the fourth looks like a son of the gods." The Lord God had delivered them physically by removing the bonds. They escaped unharmed without any sign of fire or smell of smoke or ashes on them!

> "The Lord knows how to rescue godly men from trials." (2 Peter 2:9)

Are you bound by a fiery trial in your life? Does it seem as if there is no escape, even though you stand for the Lord and try to live for him? This is the same Lord that will deliver you and be with you in your "fiery furnace." Not only that, he will break those bonds that are holding you and preventing you from moving closer to him.

Prayer:
"Lord, I am bound by _____ and I'm facing this fiery furnace in my life. Please release me from this bondage and allow me to experience freedom only you can give. In Jesus name, amen."

*Chaplain Gerald E. Brock, Darlington County, SC,
Fire District Station 8; "Fear Not," the Fire Dog*

DEPRESSION VERSUS SERVICE
The most effective way to overcome depression

HAVE YOUR ever felt gloom? Sadness? Melancholy? Or maybe dejection? These are all words used by the American Dictionary to

181

describe *depression*. In cases of extreme depression, it's always wise to seek professional counseling. But, what about those times you just feel down or despondent, and lack motivation?

One great way to fight this type of depression is to become a firefighter. Firefighters are looked upon as people who go out and extinguish fires. To do this they serve others in many and varied ways. Most people I encounter, firefighters or not, realize that when they serve others—reach out and help those around them—they feel better than if they sit around and "feel sorry for themselves" about life's challenges and direction.

But is serving others by fighting fires, rescuing people, and attending to their medical needs enough to help a person overcome times of gloom that seem to plague most people? Think about that. Now think about the added blessing of being a serving and giving child of God.

> "... and whoever wants to be first must be slave of all. For even the Son of Man did not come to be served, but to serve, and to give his life as a ransom for many." (Mark 10:44, 45)

The death of a person who doesn't know the Lord will be one of eternal doom. So of what benefit is it to save that person's mortal life? Imagine the "antidepressant" Christians receive every time they go out and set hearts on fire (as opposed to putting out fires) for the Lord Jesus Christ. Is there anything greater than saving a life from Satan's pit and knowing you'll now see that person throughout eternity in heaven?

Training and knowledge are needed for success in every task you undertake. The more education and hands-on experience you have, the more effectively you can serve. This is even more applicable to you as a Christian. What do we need to know? Let's begin by counting a few of the things: prayer, Bible study, fellowship with other Christians . . . Keep on counting, listing, and applying these things so you'll be able to help others in eternal need.

Serving the Lord with knowledge of his Word and communication with him is no doubt the most effective way to overcome depression.

Prayer:
Dear God, Thank you for allowing us to be of service to others. Please help me handle the frustrations I deal with each day. Please help me comfort others who have lost property and other things due to fires and disasters. Please allow me to have the courage and strength that comes from you. In the name of Jesus Christ, I pray, amen.

Sue Reynolds, Missionary – Fellowship of Christian Firefighters International (FCFI), and Chaplain Gaius Reynolds, President – FCFI; Volunteer Firefighter – Livermore, CO, Fire Protection District

FAITH, MERCY, AND GRACE
The muscle power to be an effective witness

EXERCISING one's faith in order to be the witness God desires is just as important as exercising one's muscles to have the strength to survive the emergencies encountered by first responders. The apostle Paul also experienced numerous trials in which both his physical and spiritual power were tested. Through God's mercy and grace, Paul had the strength to survive those tests and exercise his faith.

By God's mercy, Paul received eternal life rather than the condemnation he deserved as a result of his ungodly actions and beliefs prior to his conversion. His change from enemy to friend of God on the road to Damascus was by God's grace. It was through God's grace Paul had the muscle power to persevere and exercise his faith.

The apostle Paul experienced many hardships in his ministry. Even though he was born into an elite family and blessed with exceptional skills, he eventually realized that without God's grace, he was nothing and lacked the ability to be an effective witness of his faith. Paul called God the "God of Grace," describing grace as "the free gift of God." Paul closed each of his twelve epistles with a prayer for grace.

In contrast to mercy, where you don't receive what you deserve (eternal death), God's grace is receiving something you don't deserve (eternal life with Jesus for all who accept him as their Lord and Savior). Grace includes God's complete and unconditional kindness, love, and favor. D. L. Moody said that grace comes from the very heart of God.

> "The Spirit and the bride say, 'Come!' And let him who hears say, 'Come!' Whoever is thirsty, let him come; and whoever wishes, let him take the free gift of the water of life." (Revelation 22:17)

Hardships weren't Paul's exclusively. They seem to go hand-in-hand with the lives of first responders, either firsthand or as they respond to others' emergencies. If one acknowledges rebellion or self-centered independence, and is willing to accept God's mercy and grace, they are available in an abundant, never-ending supply. Now *that's* muscle power.

God showed his mercy when he forgave his followers' sins instead of condemning them for those sins. God extended his grace (our undeserved gift) by sending his only Son to die for all sins. God's grace and mercy, as reiterated throughout his Word, are ongoing and continuous and available for all. Grace and mercy are the muscle power needed to exercise your faith.

Prayer:

Thank you, my "God of Grace," that by your mercy you don't give me what I deserve, and you do give me what I don't deserve— your grace. Thank you for the muscle power to exercise my faith.

MAY 19

Tommy Neiman, Author of Sirens for the Cross; EMS Training Officer – St. Lucie County, FL; Fellowship of Christian Firefighters International Regional Director / International Board Member

ROOKIE INITIATION
The target of a myriad of pranks

EVERY FIREFIGHTER'S been there. Regardless of rank, at one time every firefighter was a rookie and therefore the target of a myriad of pranks created in the highly imaginative minds of veteran firefighters.

On my memorable first day as a rookie, I found guys jumping out of the trash dumpster late at night, and that was just the beginning. Later, when I jumped in the shower the tones went off. Not about to miss my first call, I jumped out, threw on my jumpsuit, and ran to the pole. Still dripping, I literally flew down the pole. As I hit the bottom padding on the truck room floor, loud laughter accompanied my bump: "False alarm, Tommy!"

Things chilled out until I was informed I'd missed washing a dish. The information was stated so matter-of-factly, I believed them. When I turned the water on, I was hit with a hard stream of water from the side sprayer. They'd rubber-banded it wide open.

One by one, everyone headed to bed. I gullibly reasoned they'd had their fun and followed suit. I encountered a deathly quiet and pitch black dorm. I slowly crept in the general direction of my bed, not wanting to tap the wrong one. I felt confident as I neared my bed. *Home free,* I thought, just as a scary animal roar rang out. I was pushed onto my bunk. Not only was I startled to death, but I landed on a hard humanlike figure buried under-

> "The Lord has done great things for us, and we are filled with joy." (Psalm 126:3)

neath my cover. I jumped off to the sounds of massive laughter. I hit the bed light and pulled off the covers to unveil the rescue mannequin.

The rest of the night was call-free, and more importantly, practical-joke-free—except for the gentle coating of flour under the covers that added one more round of laughter in the morning before shift change.

When I remember that shift, it's with a joyful heart. Their joking in a spirit of camaraderie began a bonding that strengthened with each subsequent joke as well as with each tension-filled call. Laughter in the right spirit is truly a gift from the Lord. In the Psalms we are told to be joyful because of all the Lord has done for us.

Prayer:
Lord, you have done great things for me. May I never lose sight of that joy regardless of the situations I face. I thank you for being with me at all times whether during idle moments at the station when joking prevails or on tense and demanding calls that require discipline, expertise, and concentration.

M A Y   2 0

Steve Kidd, Firefighter Orange County Fire and Rescue, Florida; Central Florida Chapter of the Fellowship of Christian Firefighters; Author of the Carbusters video series

CHANGE IS INEVITABLE
When we face change, it's natural to experience fear and uncertainty

A WISE OLD fire chief once said that until everything is perfect, we should continue to train and improve the way we fight fires and save

185

lives. "After all," he continued while clenching a cigar in his teeth, "when playing golf, I always try out new golf balls to see which one flies the farthest!" It was impressive to see the silver-haired man outgolf all the younger players. This man was not afraid of change. And he was not afraid to demand more training from his crew.

However, if you ever want to start a lively discussion in a firehouse, just suggest a change in the routine, or training done differently from what was done in the past. Change is not often received positively. It doesn't matter if you're suggesting a change in the way you attack a fire, or an increase in the donation to the coffee fund; inevitably an argument will ensue.

Why do people resist change? Is it because of fear, or insecurity? Do we resist change because we are lazy, or locked into a stubborn mindset? Or do we simply have faith in the way things are, not in what others suggest they should be?

> "'I am God, the God of your father,' he said. 'Do not be afraid to go.'" (Genesis 46:3)

In Genesis 12:1, "The Lord had said to Abram, 'Leave your country, your people, and your father's household and go to the land I will show you.'" I have heard change referred to as taking your "Abraham Walk."

I wonder what Moses thought when God told him to make such a complete change. And can you imagine the thoughts that ran through Jacob's mind when God suggested he, too, leave his home and travel to a strange land? Both men were probably hesitant, even afraid, but they trusted and were obedient to the Lord.

When we face change, it's natural to experience some fear of the uncertainty that lies ahead. However, we should never let that fear paralyze us, consume our thoughts, or cause us to act without hope. Doing so would indicate we question God's willingness to take care of us.

Prayer:
May I view change as a challenge, examine the pros and cons, pray for direction, and then proceed without fear.

186

Dwayne Clemmons, Adjunct Instructor – Virginia Department of Fire Programs; Founder – DMC Ministries; Author of Exploits, Jesus Rides in an Ambulance, and Utterances from the Throne Room; Volunteer in Fire and EMS for forty years in Virginia

ARE YOU SUITABLE FOR THE KING?

Don't be afraid to change

WE ARE THE bride of Christ and must spend sufficient time preparing for the wedding. One way to prepare is to turn from wickedness. If God's people humble themselves, pray, seek him, and turn from wickedness, God promises he "will hear from heaven and will forgive their sin and will heal their land" (2 Chronicles 7:14).

Turning from wicked ways can be a controversial issue that causes great difficulty, especially to those entrenched in habits, traditions, and routines they feel unable to change. This is a common result of our flesh rebelling against our spirit. Couple that with "macho" firehouse behavior that tends to include language, movies, and other activities that don't always honor God, and the difficulty increases.

It's been said that anything you do three times a day for twenty-one days becomes a habit. If you smoke, drink, or cuss three times a day you will develop a habit. Also, the things you read and the people you associate with can influence you to take part in an activity you may not have previously considered. If this works for bad things, shouldn't it work for good things?

> "Repent of this wickedness and pray to the Lord." (Acts 8:22)

The answer is that it does. If you find yourself involved in destructive habits, attitudes, or associations, then you need to confess and submit them to God. Then stop doing them. It won't be easy, but God promises you victory. The more you allow him to shine his light on your iniquity the more he'll free you from these bondages.

Think about it! Are your friends really your friends? Do they edify, uplift, and exhort you? Or, do they use, abuse, and tear you down? If you're in fire/EMS, why do you need to smoke or drink? You know the devastating effects these activities have on people. Why do you allow the

Enemy to destroy your mind with pornography? Go to God and repent, turn away from these things, and watch God change your life.

If your friends leave, God will replace them with people who want to have a relationship—not a *re-leech-ionship*. If you get rid of bad habits, God will show you how to pray, praise, and worship. If your attitude changes he will enhance your mind, which can be that of Christ. Don't be afraid to change. You will be impressed by what God will do for you and to you.

Prayer:
Thank you, Lord, that through you I can put
away bad habits and be pleasing to you.

MAY 22

Reverend Wayne Detzler, PhD, Chaplain (Retired) –
Charlotte, NC, Fire Department; Fellowship of
Christian Firefighters Regional Director

CRASH MEETING
When the Lord alone is our safety

CITY TRAFFIC is hectic. Every day the rush hour crams the street with traffic jams. Weaving through the streets is a daily challenge for the engineer-firefighter behind the wheel of a massive truck.

Split-second decisions are the name of the game. Usually there's no time to think, only to react. The lives of the firefighters in the back depend on it, as does the well-being of the folks in our city. Their safety hangs on the engineer's skill.

The engineer saw the intersection ahead. His mind and eyes went on alert. He scanned the scene looking for cars, and it looked as if the intersection was clear. So, he leaned on the siren, blasted the horn, and headed into the intersection.

Out of nowhere came a car. It was directly in front of the truck—there was no room to swerve and no time to stop. He hit the brakes. It was too late. The massive fire truck almost ran over the car.

The car was a brand-new Cadillac. The owners were heading home from the showroom. Hanging in the shiny back window was the dealer's information sheet. The car had less than twenty miles on the odometer. But it was the driver who caused the firefighters real concern.

188

"Is she dead?" the engineer shouted. He waited for an answer from the firefighters who had jumped out of the truck to aid the driver. "Is the driver dead?" he asked again urgently.

> "Many are the plans in a man's heart, but it is the LORD's purpose that prevails." (Proverbs 19:21)

"No, there's a pulse." The firefighters shouted back to the engineer, "Let's get an ambulance." The engineer had already made the call. An ambulance was on its way. In the meantime the firefighters held the hand of the driver, while trying desperately to bring her back to consciousness.

Gently they loaded the driver into an ambulance. The trauma center was only minutes away and the firefighters helped the medics care for their patient. As the day wore on, they waited to see what would happen. To their amazement and great relief the driver made it—despite the badly crashed Cadillac.

We never know what the day has in store, but there is one thing we can be certain of: God's purpose *will* prevail.

Prayer:
I am so thankful, Lord, you are there even when things go wrong.

M A Y   2 3

Daniel A. Clegg, Rural-Metro EMT; Engineer/EMT–Indianapolis Fire Department (Retired); Fellowship of Christian Firefighters Regional Director / International Board Member

ONE OF US

What if God was sitting next to you right now?

A ONCE-POPULAR song on the radio asked, "What if God was one of us?" When I heard this song, I thought, *What if God was one of us; just a stranger on a bus, trying to get home?*

Here's a chilling addition to that thought. What if God really was one of us ignorant, shortsighted, fallible, easily influenced, trying to fit in and be "one of the guys," and compromising his principles in the process?

Or, on a more personal level, what if God was sitting next to you right now? Would that change anything in your life?

An even more unnerving question is, what if no one was in control, and no one could see the events of history from an eternal perspective?

189

Frightening thought, isn't it? No all-loving, all-powerful Being with a master plan? Fortunately the Bible has many reassuring things to say about God that dispel such false notions. Psalm 66:5–7 lists some of our Creator's amazing feats, reminding us he does indeed rule forever by his power. As you head to the New Testament, you'll read that nothing is hidden from God—he sees everything (Hebrews 4:13). Are you behaving as you would if God was physically sitting right next to you?

> "Love the Lord your God with all your heart and with all your soul and with all your mind and with all your strength." (Mark 12:30)

That verse goes on to say you will have to make an account for everything you do. God may not be visible, but he does see and hear your every action and word. And he cares.

There is no doubt God is all-knowing, all-powerful, and all-loving. He has never seen a person he did not love, and that includes you.

Are you reciprocating with love? Do you love him with all your heart, soul, mind, and strength (actions)? That's not an option, it's a command.

Prayer:
I love you, Lord, and I thank you that you are all-powerful, all-loving, all-knowing, and infallible. When I come before you each day, may it be in obedience to your commands.

MAY 24

*Lieutenant (Retired) Lou Dattolo,
Tallahassee, FL, Fire Department*

CHRISTIANITY IN CRISIS
Many "isms" contribute to this crisis

CHRISTIANITY is in crisis in America today. Various surveys reveal that, of some of the great truths of traditional, biblical Christianity, American Christians don't know what they believe and don't believe. Among those rejected truths are that Jesus is the only way to salvation and that the Bible is inspired communication between God and mankind. Some believe nothing exists after life on Earth and consequently they fail to understand they will spend eternity with either God or Satan.

How does this happen? How do lies replace God's truth, when it is clearly explained in his Word?

Many "isms" contribute to this crisis: relativism, evolutionism, humanism, and even egotism (believing in one's own inerrancy). The main contributor to errant beliefs is a lack of Bible knowledge. Many individuals, as well as churches, have dropped the ball in this respect. If Christians don't know what they stand for, they'll surely fall for anything.

The solution is simple: one praying born-again Christian, one open Bible, and one Holy Spirit to lead you into all truth, as Jesus promised in John 16:13. You can never go wrong if you pray first. Then, as you read God's Word, follow this prescription provided by a wise elder: "When the plain sense of Scripture makes common sense, seek no other sense; therefore take every word at its primary, ordinary, usual, literal meaning unless the facts of the immediate context—studied in the light of related passages and axiomatic and fundamental truths—clearly indicate otherwise." Pay special notice to the words *pray* and *studied*.

> "But when he, the Spirit of truth, comes, he will guide you into all truth. He will not speak on his own; he will speak only what he hears, and he will tell you what is yet to come." (John 16:13)

As a Christian, find some time at work (if possible) and at home to get alone with your Bible and do what 2 Timothy 2:15 instructs you to do: "Study to shew thyself approved unto God" (KJV). Then, as the Lord leads, pray, and even start a group Bible study (perhaps using the excellent materials provided by FCFI).

Most people probably won't be able to influence thousands on a Christian network, but I'll bet you're able to "feed" one, two, ten, fifty, or more of the Lord's beloved sheep if you're faithful in your own study and then willing to share the truth you find in the Bible.

Prayer:

Please, Lord, help me to make time to study your Word. Open my understanding of your truth as I study. Help me to grow and be able to accurately teach others. May I be approved by you and not ashamed as I rightly divide the word of truth. Thank you.

*Rick Barton, Fire Safety Officer; Rick Barton
Ministries, Gunnison, CO; Fellowship of Christian
Firefighters International Ambassador-at-Large*

MASS MURDER

*We can come out of the
"valley of the shadow of death"*

A YOUNG ACQUAINTANCE killed someone, and as a result injured a large number of others! With one violent act he destroyed his family, closest friends, and himself. And, his example will cause others to do the same thing.

Was he a terrorist? A homicidal maniac? A drug-crazed gunman? No, he was simply a distraught husband going through a tough time who decided to commit suicide.

If you've been around such a tragedy, you know many others are killed through this ultimately selfish act. Many friends and loved ones are eaten away by guilt and anguish when someone they love rejects them and chooses to "bail out" of life. Adding to the tragedy, he set a self-destructive example for others when they encounter tough times.

This may appear harsh, but ultimately this is what he did. Instead of humbly seeking help, he listened to Satan's lies that suicide is "best for everyone." He forgot that the devil's primary purpose is to "steal and kill and destroy" (John 10:10). He laid aside Jesus' promise that all who are weary and burdened could come to him and find rest (Matthew 11:28). The answer is not the coward's way out—the "quick fix"—but to ask God and those around for help. We can come out of the "valley of the shadow of death" because God will walk through it with us.

An epidemic of suicide exists based on lies that this trial is too big, no one understands or cares, suicide is better for everyone, God doesn't care if we murder ourselves . . . These lies come straight from hell. Satan knows he can't hurt God so he tries to destroy those whom God loves.

> "I am the gate; whoever enters through me will be saved. He will come in and go out, and find pasture." (John 10:9)

We're all tempted at times to give up. We all face discouragement and depression, but God promises he won't allow us to be tempted beyond our ability to resist—he will provide a way of escape (1 Corinthians 10:13).

When you're struggling, call a pastor or other Christian friend, and most of all Jesus. God has awesome plans for you! With his help you will come through! Don't let the devil make a murderer out of you!

Prayer:
*Thank you for pastors, Christian friends, and most of all for you,
Father, whom I can call upon. I praise you that you have an
awesome plan for my life even if at times I fail to see that plan.
Help me to be that Christian friend when others need to
learn of your awesome love and your plans for them.*

MAY 26

*Craig Duck, Lieutenant, Engine Co. 11 – Washington, DC, Fire
Department; Fellowship of Christian Firefighters International
Atlantic States Regional Director / International Board Member*

BE ANGRY AND DO NOT SIN
Anger at the firehouse, left unchecked,
is not pleasing to God

FIREFIGHTERS have all been there—angry at someone, or something, while at the firehouse. I'll never forget the day my wagon driver did almost everything wrong while driving and operating our fire truck. We were dispatched first due for a reported fire with children trapped in a rowhouse just up the street from the firehouse. Those words, "children trapped," will make anyone excited, but this time they made our driver so excited he couldn't do anything right. He laid out our three-inch supply line from a hole in the ground instead of a hydrant, went past the address, and worst of all couldn't get the water needed to put the fire out. Three firefighters almost went to the hospital. As a result, I was exceptionally angry at my wagon driver.

After the fire was over, I brought the driver into the fire building and began to berate him on his poor performance during a crucial time. My purpose was to ensure every firefighter on the truck would be capable of doing the job when the time came. Anger is like that: It turns our peaceful, Spirit-filled life into one controlled by a disruptive force within us that often causes harm.

There is a difference between righteous anger and sinful anger. Consequently, many times firefighters get angry at other firefighters even though that anger is not justified. Sometimes the stress of the job can be so overwhelming we end up unjustly taking our anger out on others. If left unchecked sinful anger can turn into bitterness and hatred and then consume our very soul. Angry firefighters eventually become unforgiving, less compassionate, and have a tendency to become violent. Proverbs

> "'In your anger do not sin': Do not let the sun go down while you are still angry, and do not give the devil a foothold."
> (Ephesians 4:26, 27)

tells us, "A man's discretion makes him slow to anger, And it is his glory to overlook a transgression" (Proverbs 19:11 NASB).

God wants Christians to live and work in harmony, for the purpose of helping others. If you have a problem with anger, seek out a godly co-worker to help you come in line with what the Word of God says concerning anger.

Prayer:
Help me, Lord, to control my anger both at fires and around the firehouse, that I might not sin against you or destroy my testimony.

Trapped (Courtesy of Captain Eric Mitchell, St. Albans, WV, Fire Department)

Captain Raul A. Angulo – Seattle Fire Department;
Fellowship of Christian Firefighters Regional
Director / International Board Member

ILLUMINATION

There's no reason to work in the dark

AFTER A well-involved room fire is extinguished, the charred remains inside make it extremely dark and hazardous. Putting up portable lighting prior to overhaul is an important fireground task. There's no reason for firefighters to work in the dark when they have the ability not to. Yet, this important safety task is often overlooked.

Firefighters are often content with simply using flashlights and battle lanterns. Most departments have portable, heavy-duty, industrial string lights that provide excellent lighting. Why don't the firefighters use them? Some do, but haphazardly. I've seen lights strung out along the floor where they're subject to dirt and contamination or blocked by furniture. On the ground firefighters can kick, step on, trip over, or crush them, often breaking the bulbs. On the floor they do provide light, but to maximize illumination, the lights should be hung high with nails or hooks, or propped up with pike poles and baby ladders.

> "No one lights a lamp and hides it in a jar or puts it under a bed. Instead, he puts it on a stand, so that those who come in can see the light." (Luke 8:16)

The analogies between our Christian walk and post-fire lighting are obvious. "No one lights a lamp and hides it in a jar or puts it under a bed. Instead, he puts it on a stand, so that those who come in can see the light" (Luke 8:16).

What does it mean to be the light of the world? For bold and courageous believers, it may seem easy. For those who are anxious, fearful, and without hope, being the light of the world seems overwhelming, if not impossible.

In the book of John we learn that Jesus was the light of men (1:4) and that whoever follows him will never walk in darkness (8:12). As the moon reflects the light of the sun, we are to reflect the light of Jesus. But, how? Jesus shows us how to be the light.

When he shows compassion and tenderness to the needy, encourages and meets the needs of the poor, feeds the hungry, heals the sick, mingles with the lost, hurting, destitute, prostitutes, broken, and downtrodden, Jesus is showing us how to be light. Jesus invested his time (that's one way to spell love, by the way—T-I-M-E). He showed mercy and love. But the arrogant and proud he scolded; to the hypocrites, he showed his anger.

What an awesome example he gave us! As a follower of Jesus, be sure to let your light shine so others can see it.

Prayer:
Lord, help me not to be anxious, fearful, and without hope.
Help me be bold and be a bright light for you.

M A Y   2 8

Chaplain Marc Santorella, Firefighter Danvers Fire Department, MA; Public Fire and Life Safety Educator and Certified Fire Instructor Level 1

THE RENEWING OF THE MIND
A wonderful place to be

FIREFIGHTERS don't think or act like other people. Our jobs carry over into our everyday lives. It began the day we decided to become firefighters. We see dangers, take precautions, and are more safety-conscious than others of the world around us. This gives us the ability to act when needed in a manner necessary to preserve life and property. We should be grateful for this. It's what separates us from those we are called to serve and protect.

The same can be said for Christians. We certainly don't think or act like other people, and we shouldn't. The Bible says, "Do not conform any longer to the pattern of this world, but be transformed by the renewing of your mind" (Romans 12:2). We are to allow ourselves to become who we know we were meant to be. This began the day we came to the cross and accepted Jesus as our Lord and Savior. Again, not something that happens naturally. However, once we make that decision, it, too, carries over into our everyday lives.

Paul spoke of this transformation in 2 Corinthians 3:18. He said we believers, who with unveiled faces reflect the Lord's glory, are being transformed into Christ's likeness with ever-increasing glory that comes from him. When Christ takes his rightful place in our hearts we immediately begin to see, think, and feel differently.

196

Thoughts are the beginning of an action, so when our thoughts are on Jesus, our behaviors and our attitudes change. This is called *sanctification*. It happens continuously over time.

"And we, who with unveiled faces all reflect the Lord's glory, are being transformed into his likeness with ever-increasing glory, which comes from the Lord, who is the Spirit." (2 Corinthians 3:18)

God is calling us to a perfect place, but we haven't arrived yet. In fact, we will never know perfection until this world has passed away and we stand with him in Glory. For now, we need to take comfort in knowing we are continuously being transformed into the image of Christ. Now *that* is special!

Walk every day seeking and acknowledging the presence of God and you will soon see that this world can no longer hold you to its patterns or desires. Every passing trial will bring strength, and each victory will bring praise to God the Father.

You are continuously being transformed by the renewing of your mind and that is a wonderful place to be.

Prayer:
Father, I want to be like you. Change my heart and my desires to be the same as yours. Let me walk in your perfect will and see you at work in the world around me. Show me today how I can make a difference.

MAY 29

Rick Barton, Fire Safety Officer; Rick Barton Ministries, Gunnison, CO; Fellowship of Christian Firefighters International Ambassador-at-Large

WHAT NUMBER ARE YOU?
Whatever your number, the rewards are eternal

WE WERE standing on a fire line in northern California. The division supervisor noticed my Fellowship of Christian Firefighters patch and began the conversation. It continues to amaze to me how a pin or patch that lets others know I'm a child of God opens the door to many and varied conversations. Our conversation immediately focused on Christianity, as we discussed God, Jesus, and the Bible. He wondered if Jesus was really the only way to know God. A myriad of other sincere, searching questions followed. Soon, it was time to resume our duties. I asked if I could pray with him and he readily consented. Then he said, "You remind me of Fred, the hot shot superintendent, I met two years ago. He told me the same things you shared. Do you know Fred?"

I did know Fred from several fires we worked together, so my new friend and I talked about our mutual friend and even gave him a call. Then we prayed together. As the division supervisor and I parted company to resume our duties, I gave him a copy of *Answering the Call* with encouragement to read the inserted testimonies along with some of God's Word each day. I assured him God would answer his questions.

As I thought about it later, I realized this is what the apostle Paul was talking about in 1 Corinthians 3:5–9. One of us plants the seed of God's Word in someone's life. Another waters it, and yet another harvests. Then others begin the process of nurturing the new Christian.

Most folks don't accept Jesus the first time they hear the Gospel message. It may take four or five times before they make a commitment to the Savior. Our job is to be ready to share as he opens the door. We never know what number we are in that person's life; and we never know if God is using us to plant seeds, harvest, or nurture; but whatever the role, the rewards will be eternal.

> "I [Paul] planted the seed, Apollos watered it, but God made it grow. So neither he who plants nor he who waters is anything, but only God, who makes things grow. The man who plants and the man who waters have one purpose, and each will be rewarded according to his own labor. For we are God's fellow workers; you are God's field, God's building."
> (1 Corinthians 3:6–9)

Prayer:
Use me, Lord, to plant, to water, to nurture, to reflect your truth, and to be the fellow worker you have called me to be.

Craig Duck, Lieutenant, Engine Co. 11 – Washington, DC, Fire Department; Fellowship of Christian Firefighters International Atlantic States Regional Director / International Board Member

FIREFIGHTERS AND DEATH
Challenged to share Christ with the fire service

FIREFIGHTERS know all about death. We see it often when we go to work. We've seen death come to the very young as well as the old. We've seen death knock when people least expected it. Some firefighters remember the names or faces of those we were not able to rescue or help in time. Whether it was on medical calls, accidents scenes, or at fires, we have observed death firsthand. September 11, 2001, was a day we will all remember as a day our nation saw evil. The fire service saw 343 brave firefighters die that day, and many of us saw death firsthand in New York, Washington, DC, and Pennsylvania.

> "For it is by grace you have been saved, through faith—and this not from yourselves, it is the gift of God— not by works, so that no one can boast." (Ephesians 2:8–9)

With this constant reminder of just how fragile life can be, why do many firefighters have difficulty in talking about our eternal destiny? Typically firefighters change the subject when the topic of heaven or hell is brought up in the sitting room. Many times firefighters in Washington, DC, have told me, "Religion does not belong in the firehouse" as they got up and left the room. But death eventually will hit every firehouse, and typically when you least expect it.

I remember getting a tragic call one Memorial Day weekend. It was the type of call every officer in the fire service dreads. "There has been a bad fire," the firefighter on the other end relayed. I learned that two co-workers were dead, and a third was in critical condition. I was at Engine Co. 26 at the time, and fellow firefighters needed help and guidance during this difficult time—the kind of help that can only come from God.

Firefighters are familiar with "Greater love has no one than this, that he lay down his life for his friends" (John 15:13). But most firefighters are unfamiliar that this verse is talking about the work Jesus has done for our eternal life. Jesus paid the penalty for our sins; firefighters need to trust in him alone for salvation. We need to find ways to share Christ with the fire service—before it is too late. God has more in store than this earthly life and he commands us to share his plan with others.

Prayer:
Help me to be diligent, sensitive, timely, and faithful in sharing Jesus Christ with my fellow firefighters before it is too late.

MAY 31

Reverend Wayne Detzler, PhD, Chaplain (Retired) – Charlotte, NC, Fire Department; Fellowship of Christian Firefighters Regional Director

REMEMBERING FALLEN FIREFIGHTERS

From the grave to glory in our memory

ON THE LAST Monday of May the United States federal holiday called Memorial Day is observed. Formerly it was known as Decoration Day to honor Union soldiers of the American Civil War. After World War I it became an occasion to honor Americans who died in all wars. Change continued and by the early twentieth century it became a special day for people to visit the graves of their deceased loved ones, whether they had served in the military or not. September 11, 2001 further expanded who is honored on Memorial Day.

On that unforgettable September morning in 2001, my pager said, "Plane into the World Trade Center." A few minutes later there was a second plane. Then a third plane went into the Pentagon. Another one crashed into the Pennsylvania countryside.

By day's end we knew that our brothers and sisters, along with thousands of civilian victims, bore the brunt of that day. Many first responders became some of the first victims. A brave chaplain knelt to pray with one victim, and his life ended while he was on his knees in the collapsing World Trade tower. He joined the ranks of martyrs for freedom.

Now Memorial Day has a whole new meaning. Living here in Connecticut, we often look at the south end of Manhattan, an area still scarred by the torture of terrorism. The absence of the Twin Towers reminds us of all we hold dear, of our brothers and sisters whose lives ended that bright September morning.

200

As we remember those who perished that day or have gone before us, a flood of memories sweeps over us. Grief is often our first response, but it's not our best response. We need to focus beyond the sorrow on the abiding purpose and accept it as a challenge to

"Let us consider how we may spur one another on toward love and good deeds." (Hebrews 10:24)

carry the torch of freedom—freedom only God can give us. It is, furthermore, our solemn responsibility to remember with thankfulness those who have gone before as well as those, who have laid down their lives for us.

Prayer:
Thank you, O God our Savior, for those who have lived and died as heroes.

Scarred Cityscape of New York City after 9/11 Attack
(Courtesy of Sue Reynolds)

Tommy Neiman, Author of Sirens for the Cross; EMS
Training Officer – St. Lucie County, FL; Fellowship of
Christian Firefighters International Regional
Director / International Board Member

MISTAKEN IDENTITY

Do people wonder if you're a Christian?

MY BROTHER, Robbie, and I are "like two peas in a pod," as the saying goes. You see, we are identical twins and so closely identical most people can't tell us apart. At times this has led to some fun pranks; at other times it led to confusion and even problematic results.

One Sunday afternoon as Robbie transported the kids home on the church bus, one of the kids became suddenly ill, nearly passing out. One look at the pale, lethargic child prompted Robbie to stop at the nearby fire station to have the kid checked out by the paramedic on duty.

Robbie headed for the nearest fire station, not realizing it was a basic response station with emergency medical technicians and no paramedics. As he honked the horn, a firefighter/EMT came out and asked him what the problem was.

"One of my kids is sick," Robbie said. "He nearly passed out a little while ago."

Robbie and a couple more firefighter/EMTs walked to the back of the bus. The child was now resting and talking, but still looked pale and weak. Concerned, Robbie asked for a diagnosis. Instead of getting medical advice, his inquiry was met with a look of disbelief from the firefighters. Perhaps they figured I was pulling one of my frequent pranks. "Come on, man," one commented. "This is no time for pranks, Tommy, you're the paramedic. You're supposed to know what's wrong with him, so why are you asking us? Are you messing with our minds?"

> "As water reflects a face, so a man's heart reflects the man."
> (Proverbs 27:19)

Robbie broke out laughing. "I'm Tommy's twin brother."

The kid laughed, too, and immediately began to feel better.

Has anyone ever mistaken your identity? Have your attitude, actions, words (or perhaps the absence thereof) made people wonder if you were a Christian or not?

One of the best comments a person can make about you is, "There is a person who walks the talk—a person who always reflects God's love."

Prayer:
Lord, I pray no one ever mistakes my identity. I love you, Lord, and seek to be a reflection of you in all I say and do.

Chaplain Robert Osbourn, Sylacauaga, AL, Fire Department

SET OFF THE TONES, A DISASTER IS COMING
Have we tuned out God's alarm?

WE ARE living in days that remind me of the days of Noah, when sin ran rampant. The revenue of the U.S. pornography industry exceeds the combined revenues of ABC, CBS, and NBC. Child pornography revenues are in the billions-of-dollars range. Thousands of babies are murdered daily! Other sins are spiraling at equally alarming rates. It doesn't take a statistician to realize the staggering numbers of people affected by equally ungodly behaviors.

> "My prayer is not that you take them out of the world but that you protect them from the evil one. They are not of the world, even as I am not of it. Sanctify them by the truth; your word is truth." (John 17:15–17)

Are we really living in days like those of Noah? Have we tuned out God's alarm? Are we so dedicated to complacency, self-satisfaction, and personal gratification we fail to hear the tones of approaching disaster? Are we living for the moment, forgetting to look toward eternity? Have we allowed the media to desensitize us to rampant sins?

In Noah's day, "The Lord saw how great man's wickedness on the earth had become, and that every inclination of the thoughts of his heart was only evil all the time" (Genesis 6:5). I can only assume how the Lord views today's sins. I do know for certain the only way to avoid the disastrous personal and eternal consequences of evil is to place our faith in Jesus Christ for salvation.

The Bible tells us the tones will sound: "As it was in the days of Noah, so it will be at the coming of the Son of Man. For in the days before the flood, people were eating and drinking, marrying and giving in marriage, up to the day Noah entered the ark; and they knew nothing about what would happen until the flood came and took them all away. That is how it will be at the coming of the Son of Man" (Matthew 24:37–39).

Jesus is coming. He made it clear that "one shall be taken and the other left." What a glorious day that will be for the saved! What a disaster for the unsaved!

When you hear the tones of an imminent disaster ringing, turn to God's Word and be comforted, because our Lord Jesus is praying for us.

Prayer:
Thank you for praying for me. Protect me from the evil one. While I am living in the world, I am not of this world.

JUNE 3

Rick Barton, Fire Safety Officer; Rick Barton Ministries, Gunnison, CO; Fellowship of Christian Firefighters International Ambassador-at-Large

HOW FAST IS YOUR CAR?

God will do whatever it takes to give us a chance to respond

I NEED TO pray with you!" the firefighter said, with a real sense of urgency. I had just finished speaking at a chapel service for the Arizona Wildfire and Incident Management Academy. Fifty or so attended and the Lord did some neat things. The worship team did a wonderful job. The speakers before me got things going strong and prepared the way for my message. When my time came, I shared the Gospel—and God's presence was evident.

After I finished the message and gave those in attendance a chance to respond, the group began to break up. Some left for dinner, others were praying or enjoying fellowship, others headed home. Suddenly a young man approached me. "I need to pray with you," he said. Then he told me a remarkable story.

The Lord had touched him during the service but he'd decided to leave without making a commitment. As he started his car, a song came

205

on the radio. The words went something like, "You can get in your fast car and drive away, or you can come back and change your life forever!" He came back and yielded his life to Jesus.

Isn't it amazing that God loves us so much that he not only sent his Son to die for us, but that he will do whatever it takes to give us a chance to respond? Out of all the things he could be doing, he decided to play a love song for a child he wanted to come home.

> "Let us draw near to God with a sincere heart in full assurance of faith, having our hearts sprinkled to cleanse us from a guilty conscience and having our bodies washed with pure water." (Hebrews 10:22)

What about you? Are you driving away, or are you headed home to heaven?

Is there an area in your life that you need to yield to the Lord? Is there an area where you have pulled away from God? He wants us to draw near him with a sincere heart. Listen to him and you will be amazed at the changes in store for you.

Prayer:

Lord, I want to come home, rest in your presence, and draw nearer to you each day. With a sincere heart, I yield all to you. Make your presence foremost in my life.

JUNE 4

Reverend Wayne Detzler, PhD, Chaplain (Retired) – Charlotte, NC, Fire Department; Fellowship of Christian Firefighters Regional Director

CHOPPER DOWN

When rescuers need to be rescued

IT ALL STARTED when a motorcycle rider skidded, spun out, and crushed his leg. First responders sized up the situation and called for help. They summoned a LifeStar helicopter from the top trauma center in our state capital. Immediately the crew launched and headed south to our accident scene.

Hurriedly firefighters set up a landing zone, providing as much light as possible. Anxiously they waited to hear the familiar sound of the helicopter as they made the patient more comfortable and stabilized his leg.

"There it is," someone said, picking up the sound of the chopper, "it will soon be here." The pilot circled the site checking out his landing zone. Then he began a steep descent.

One thing escaped the flight crew's attention, and this was a major problem. They couldn't see the low-slung power wires crossing the road. They flew under the wires by mistake. The cables ripped the tail rotor off the helicopter, and the aircraft spun into a wooded grove nearby.

> "The name of the LORD is a strong tower; the righteous run to it and are safe." (Proverbs 18:10)

"Get to the accident site on the double, Chaplain." The dispatcher sent me to the main highway, not a mile from our house. As I arrived injured crew members were being loaded into an ambulance. Their destination was their own trauma unit.

"Hey, Chaplain," a lieutenant shouted, "over here! Give us a hand!" He was working to free the body of a dead crew member from the downed helicopter. As I backed him up, I prayed for the crew member's family and his crew. We stretched out on our bellies to crawl into the chopper's damaged cockpit.

Gently we lifted the pilot from his seat and handed the body over to the medical examiner. As I checked out of the accident site and headed home, my mind was filled with thanksgiving for those who had survived this unusual accident. At the same time I committed the family of that brave pilot to the Lord.

Prayer is the only answer to a chaotic scene like that helicopter wreck. Only as we flee to the Lord can we find peace and comfort.

Prayer:
Our strong Tower, I flee to you when the world around me is in confusion and chaos.

Daniel A. Clegg, Rural-Metro EMT; Engineer/EMT–Indianapolis Fire Department (Retired); Fellowship of Christian Firefighters Regional Director / International Board Member

RELAXING IN THE MIDST

An elderly woman, a fire, and a lesson on faith

PEACE IN the midst of smoke and fire from a burning room is a rarity. Couple that with a tinge of deceit, and you have one puzzled firefighter.

While assigned to Ladder Truck 27, I was dispatched to a residence fire with heavy smoke spiraling from one of the bedrooms.

"Everyone is out of the building," one man stated.

Nevertheless, we began our search-and-rescue operation. I crawled through the first room. No one there! I felt my way into the next room. The visibility was next to zero. I blindly felt my way around the room in search of civilians. Extending my arms, my hand landed on something that felt like a leg. I edged closer. Peering through the smoke, I discovered a lady in her sixties peacefully sitting in a wheelchair. She held a handkerchief over her mouth to filter out the dense smoke.

"I'm just fine," she calmly stated. "Go ahead and keep searching the rear of the house for the source of the fire," she continued, not the least bit alarmed.

"Ma'am, first I'm going to get you out of this smoke and into some fresh air," I told her as I got behind her chair and we waded our way through the smoke and to the door.

Reentering the house, I, along with others, found the source of the fire, extinguished it, and headed back to the station.

"I thought the crowd said everyone was out of the house," I said to the lieutenant.

> "And the peace of God, which transcends all understanding, will guard your hearts and your minds in Christ Jesus." (Philippians 4:7).

"You'll never guess who gave that erroneous information," he replied. "It was the woman's husband! What's more, when I was asked why he said that, he stammered, stuttered, and never offered an explanation."

The husband's response will be a puzzle to me for the rest of my life, but the more amazing part of the puzzle is remembering the elderly lady sitting back in her wheelchair, apparently relaxed and comfortable in her situation. With all the chaos around her and the knowledge of her husband's exit from the house, she just sat in her chair relaxing in the midst of turmoil. Faith like this is a rare commodity. Her faith was rewarded and she was saved from the fire. Though still puzzled, I'm thankful for the special lesson I received that day on the power of faith.

Prayer:
When the storm clouds of life roll in and I look to you,
please grant me that peace that only comes from you
and that transcends all understanding.

JUNE 6

Fire Chaplain John Kalashian, Caledonia, Wisconsin;
Founder/Director – Men with a Burden, a ministry to
the homeless men at the Milwaukee Rescue Mission;
Founder/President – Corvettes for Christ

BECOMING YOUR BEST
Calling on Christ, our ultimate First Responder

THREE DAYS of extrication training, while not a normal activity for a chaplain, was an incredibly worthwhile learning experience for me. With great admiration and respect, I was privileged to witness the skills, intuitive planning, and masterful use of emergency extrication tools and the techniques involved in this one aspect of firefighting. It was experientially evident that being a skilled firefighter and EMT involves studying and applying the tools of the trade.

It wouldn't do firefighters much good to have all the equipment and tools available to them, but to lack the needed knowledge about their proper use and operation. In a crisis, these tools are absolutely essential for a firefighter's safety and a successful rescue effort. Think of it for a moment—what kind of firefighter would respond to a call without being properly trained, prepared, equipped, and wearing protection? You might do more harm than good!

"Come to me, all you who are weary and burdened, and I will give you rest. Take my yoke upon you and learn from me, for I am gentle and humble in heart, and you will find rest for your souls. For my yoke is easy and my burden is light."
(Matthew 11:28–30)

I liken God's Word in our lives to the tools of the firefighter. In much the same way as the firefighter's tools and manuals, the Bible is our instruction manual for success in our daily life. The Bible is a lifesaving extrication tool when we find ourselves in the midst of a personal crisis. Living without Christ, his Holy Word, and his promised shield of protection is like a firefighter answering an alarm without bunker gear, tools, and the proper preparation. The Gospel protects, prepares, and it saves:

It protects by instructing us in the way we should live.
It prepares by giving us wise and godly counsel.
It saves by directing us to the Lord Jesus Christ, who is indeed the ultimate saving "Jaws of Life," for "everyone who calls on the name of the Lord will be saved" (Romans 10:13).

Prayer:
Thank you for always being with me, during training or on scene. At times, especially when extrication is involved, the tragedy before me causes my heart to be heavy-laden. Thank you for your Word, filled with godly instruction, rich counsel, encouragement, and comfort. Please bless my family as I serve the people who "call" upon me.

J U N E   7

Craig Duck, Lieutenant, Engine Co. 11 – Washington, DC, Fire Department; Fellowship of Christian Firefighters International Atlantic States Regional Director / International Board Member

CAST OFF THE WORKS OF DARKNESS
What does God say about alcohol and firefighting?

FIREHOUSE social events present wonderful opportunities to fellowship in an informal setting with those we work with regularly. I recently attended one of these events hosted by our firehouse. My purpose was to mingle with and be an encouragement to those I work with.

You've probably attended one or two of these types of parties, so you know what I mean when I say loud music and alcohol are often the two main ingredients. As the drinking progresses, the music gets louder. Eventually many say and do things they wouldn't normally say or do in their right and sober minds. Unfortunately, a lot of citizens think this is how all firefighters act, they think it is just "part of the job." This creates a poor example, or image, for emergency services.

I've even seen Christian firefighters get caught up in the frenzy or excitement of the moment and begin to drink alcohol. Some feel they need to show they are "cool." Perhaps they think they need to join in so they'll be accepted. Maybe they are truly addicted. Whatever the reason, here are two questions to ponder: Is drinking alcohol wrong? And, what is the difference between having a drink and becoming drunk?

> "The night is nearly over; the day is almost here. So let us put aside the deeds of darkness and put on the armor of light. Let us behave decently, as in the daytime, not in orgies and drunkenness, not in sexual immorality and debauchery, not in dissension and jealousy. Rather, clothe yourselves with the Lord Jesus Christ, and do not think about how to gratify the desires of the sinful nature."
> (Romans 13:12–14)

Firefighters (along with everyone else) are encouraged in Ephesians, "Do not get drunk on wine, which leads to debauchery. Instead, be filled with the Spirit" (5:18). The term "drunk" is a matter of control. When firefighters overindulge in alcohol, they lose control of what they say and how they act. When control is lost, the ability to think logically diminishes and normal behavior is changed; drunkenness results, and that is wrong.

If alcohol dominates your thoughts or dictates your schedule, then you have lost control and are under the power of alcohol. Firefighters, Christian or not, should seek help before their reputations, relationships, or safety are jeopardized. God promises that when we recognize our problems and turn them over to him, he'll give us strength and power to overcome addiction.

Maybe you struggle in this area. I encourage you to turn it over to God and seek godly counsel. Maybe you have friends or co-workers who allow alcohol to dominate their actions. You may be just the tool God has in mind to help them.

Prayer:
Help me, Lord, to understand that Christian firefighters have been called to a higher standard and need to be "salt and light" to those in the fire service. Help me to be that salt and light.

Rick Barton, Fire Safety Officer; Rick Barton Ministries, Gunnison, CO; Fellowship of Christian Firefighters International Ambassador-at-Large

YOU'RE THE MAN!

Are you the friend or the one on the edge?

THE MAN was a legend in the fire business. His expertise was respected far and wide. Only one thing was wrong, he was treading dangerously close to losing his marriage, family, and integrity through an inappropriate relationship. Sound familiar? You're his friend, not a close friend, but someone he may listen to. What should you do?

In the Bible a prophet named Nathan faced that dilemma (2 Samuel 12:1–14), except his stakes were much higher. If his friend, the king, didn't like to have his sin pointed out to him, then Nathan would die. Still, Nathan realized he had a duty, both to his friend and, more importantly, to God. So he went. After telling King David of a man who had betrayed his neighbor, David replied that the man was guilty and deserved to be put to death. Nathan then looked David in the eye and said, "You're the man."

Nathan had a choice: take the safe route and say nothing; or risk rejection, and even death, and speak God's Word.

> "I acknowledged my sin to you and did not cover up my iniquity. I said, 'I will confess my transgressions to the LORD'— and you forgave the guilt of my sin ... Therefore let everyone who is godly pray to you while you may be found; surely when the mighty waters rise, they will not reach him. You are my hiding place; you will protect me from trouble and surround me with songs of deliverance."
> (Psalm 32:5–7)

David also had a choice: humble himself, repent, and ask for forgiveness from God and man; or—the ungodly way—kill Nathan. Of course if he killed Nathan he still had God to worry about. David made the right choice. He repented. His testimony is in Psalm 32:1–7.

All of us are in that picture, one way or another. We're either the man who's on the edge of sin or the friend who needs to talk to him. God loves us and doesn't want us going down a road that will destroy us. So, he sends us a message. Usually it's through the counsel of another person, although it might be through a traffic stop, radio program, or other means. The point is, Will we listen, turn from sin, and return to God?

Prayer:
What an awesome God you are! Thank you for forgiving my sins,
for those you place in my life to help me make godly choices,
that I can pray to you, and that you may be found. You
are my hiding place and protection from trouble.

Joel Kelm, Firefighter/EMT – Gallatin Gateway, MT; President –
Big Sky Chapter of Fellowship of Christian Firefighters

RESPONSIBILITIES AND PRIORITIES
Especially for men, but not exclusively

GOD HAS done, and will continue to do, what some may think the impossible, if we but look to him and his Word, love, and example. As I mull over what God has done for my wife and me in our marriage, I'm amazed and thankful. You see, we were rapidly approaching divorce until God spoke to us through our home church. Throughout two painful years of weekly meetings, as Christ promised, the wounds began to close, the tears began to dry, and two broken hearts began to mend as we walked into the mercy of God's loving arms.

I don't know the future, but I know one thing: I can rest in the goodness and the promises of Jesus Christ. It is only through Christ we can truly be happy and content in our jobs and our marriages.

As the God-ordained leaders of our homes, we are not only responsible to pray for, support, and encourage our families' spiritual growth. We need to realize that, as Christians, we have added responsibility to those in our communities. We are the ambassadors of Christ, not just in our families but in the workplace. We are automatically a "chaplain" in the sense that if we are a "known" Christian, those around us are looking to us to see right attitudes, right decisions, and a love that only God gives.

If you fail in these areas, your marriage will fail, your spiritual growth will be stunted, your role as a positive father model will be lessened, and your testimony to those "looking for something" will be lost.

I encourage you to stand strong until the return of our Lord, make it known that you are a lover of God, your spouse, and your children. Then make sure your spouse and children feel that love each and every day. When you're at home, do something special for your spouse, then the two of you make a

> "Husbands, love your wives, just as Christ loved the church and gave himself up for her." (Ephesians 5:25)

pact with the one true God, that you intend to lead your family instead of taking a back seat. Start giving a little more and God will make it worth your while, either here or in the air.

Prayer:

God, because you are indeed faithful, I come to you in thankfulness for my wife and family. Please give me the right attitude and help me to make the right decisions in regard to loving you, caring for and edifying my wife and family, and then in service to you. May others know that I love and serve first you, then my wife.

JUNE 10

Karen Freshwater, Wife of Firefighter Captain Frank Freshwater

SO YOU'RE A FIREFIGHTER'S WIFE

React to each interruption with a heart filled with love

WE'D BEEN home from our honeymoon for one day and were snuggled under the warm covers when it happened—those horrible, high-pitched tones rang. Covers went flying, lights glared, and my husband pulled on his socks, boots, and turnouts. Clunk, clunk! His heavy boots headed out the door. I thought I was having a dream created by Alfred Hitchcock himself. This was my introduction to being a firefighter's wife.

Many similar scenarios followed, some funny, sad, frustrating, and some that made me downright mad! One time a young man shot himself. Another time an old man killed himself because he thought he was becoming a burden to his family. My role was to listen to my husband and be supportive.

The life of a firefighter's spouse is unique. In addition to the fire and first-aid runs, your spouse is often attending drills, ongoing training, and other requirements to be a well-trained firefighter. At times you'll feel the department is more important than you are. This is especially true when you have dinner guests. There must be a connection between the carving knife and the pager.

When it really gets to you is holidays. The family's over, you've cooked for two days, and everyone's at the table. Off goes the alarm and with it your spouse.

Whenever you have something special planned, there'll be a fire or first-aid run. But a firefighter's spouse needs to realize a fire won't wait, and a first-aid run can't be

> "Do everything in love."
> (1 Corinthians 16:14)

ignored. At times you'll hate the department and hope your spouse quits, or at least stops feeling irreplaceable at work.

You're not alone. There isn't a spouse who hasn't felt that same way. But when you stop to realize you're married to a person who cares enough about others to risk life and limb, you realize the sacrifice is worthwhile. When you encounter someone who is alive today because your spouse answered a call, the times of frustration, sadness, and anger dissolve into a smile and you realize how proud you are to be married to a firefighter. That love you felt when you were first married grows, and you're reminded to react to each interruption with a heart filled with love.

Prayer:
Lord, when the interruptions are more than an inconvenience, remind me to react with a heart filled with love. Help me understand my spouse and respond with that same love. When we married, we became one, so whether I'm the one responding, or left behind in wait, my trust is in you, Lord.

JUNE 11

Tommy Neiman, Author of Sirens for the Cross; EMS Training Officer – St. Lucie County, FL; Fellowship of Christian Firefighters International Regional Director / International Board Member

THE VOICE
"But it was so real and loud"

IS SATAN real? Ever been asked that question? Ever wondered yourself?

215

Seeing the suffering and violence that crack cocaine produces removed any doubts about the damage caused by drugs. While responding to a call for a twenty-five-year-old, the voice of Satan once again rang loud in my ears. We found the dirty, unkempt, roughed-up young man behind an old, abandoned building, crying. He grabbed my hand. "I need help. I can't go through what I just did." He shared how he tried cocaine for the first time the night before. "I've been on the streets for two weeks but never before touched drugs. I was planning to go back home and start over. But this morning something told me I had to have more of the stuff I tried last night. I saw a lady walking on the street and that same voice told me to take that lady's purse so I could get some more of that stuff. The voice kept yelling at me to go—'go take it now.'" He placed his head in his hands and said, "I just freaked—I can't live like this."

I clutched hold of his hand and shared how the Lord had kept him from assaulting that woman. I further told him the voice of temptation he heard was straight from the mouth of Satan himself.

> "The voice of the Lord is powerful; the voice of the Lord is majestic."
> (Psalm 29:4)

"But it was so real and loud."

I responded. "That drug makes Satan's voice come alive in your mind. I have no doubt you actually heard it. But the awesome power of God is far greater than anything Satan can say or do."

I looked him in the eye. "Are you a believer?"

"Yeah, but I've lived far apart from God."

"That's doesn't mean he's lived far apart from you. I'm sure he sent me here today."

The man consented to seek help from a health facility. As we parted, I reminded him that his greatest help, Christ, was already inside his heart.

Three days later he completed his treatment and returned home.

Satan is out to destroy both the body and the mind. The only hope of victory for the body and the mind is Christ in the heart. The only way to completely overcome Satan's attempt to defeat a person with any mind-deceiving, flesh-devouring, addictive drug is through Christ.

Have you tried Jesus? Are listening for his voice over that of his adversary?

Prayer:
Lord, it is your voice I seek to hear over any other.

*Reverend Wayne Detzler, PhD, Chaplain (Retired) –
Charlotte, NC, Fire Department; Fellowship of
Christian Firefighters Regional Director*

THE DAY THE EARTH SHOOK

A seismic shock breeds prayer

THE WHOLE neighborhood shook." A reporter had obviously been caught off balance by the explosion. It sucked windows right out of houses. Foundations cracked. A dozen miles away, Sunday morning was disturbed by the blast.

"I was awestruck by the magnitude of the devastation," a member of the town council admitted. Then she added, "I felt a sinking feeling of tragedy." The Sunday

> "When I am afraid, I will trust in you." (Psalm 56:3)

shock to a quiet Connecticut town came when workers were "purging gas lines" at a power plant under construction.

They knew it was dangerous work. So, they undertook the task when only a skeleton crew was on the site. But they couldn't have guessed just how dangerous it was. When the gas line exploded it threw some pipefitters fifty feet through the air. Survivors had broken bones and internal injuries—but not everyone survived.

Five of the workers were lost, unaccounted for, as emergency crews struggled to bring the flames under control. Desperation marked the first day as medics and firefighters carried out the injured and ferried them to nearby hospitals. Emergency rooms went on full alert as they enacted their mass-casualty plans.

Finally the flames were knocked down. Survivors had been rescued from the scene, and darkness fell on an eerie sight. The skeleton of a power plant with its skin hanging loosely from the frame was silhouetted against the evening sky. Fire marshals secured the plant. They suspected that negligence might be the cause of this holocaust.

At first light Monday morning, the recovery phase of the operation began. Members of the pipefitters' union stood vigil waiting for their comrades' bodies to be recovered. Silently, five covered forms were carried out of the blackened building. Everyone stood at attention in honor of these hardhat heroes.

"Just pray for us," a union member pleaded with the public. "Pray for their families, too." Then he added an amazing statement: "Prayer is the best thing you can do."

217

In this seemingly secular age it was very moving to hear this plea for prayer. It shook to the core the blasé viewers in these New York City suburbs.

Prayer:
*Thank you, O Lord, for the assurance that you
are in control when our world shakes.*

*Rick Barton, Fire Safety Officer; Rick Barton Ministries,
Gunnison, CO; Fellowship of Christian Firefighters
International Ambassador-at-Large*

CARELESSNESS CAUSES ALL KINDS OF PROBLEMS!

*Be not careless in deeds, nor confused
in words, nor rambling in thoughts.*

MARCUS AURELIUS

"FIRE BURNING up the Rainbow Lake Road," came the urgent call over the radio.

It was the summer of 2000. We'd had our hands full with forest fires throughout the region. Just the previous day I'd returned from a fire assignment in Wyoming. My crew and I were enjoying a much-needed day off after being out for twenty-one straight days. But, when the dispatcher calls, you go.

We were the second engine on scene, arriving after the fire management officer (FMO), who had already started suppression. A National Park Service engine and another forest service engine followed us.

The fire was burning in sagebrush and moving fast. After the initial size-up, the FMO deployed the various engines around the fire. For several hours we battled the blaze and then, as we began what would be several days of mopping up the remaining hot spots, a firefighter called out, "Take a look over here!"

We congregated around an abandoned campsite and the cause of this second fire became apparent. We'd risked life and limb because of someone's carelessness. Out of the ring of rocks came a small black line. At first it crept and then it expanded into an ever-increasing, fan-shaped flame

218

front. Pushed by the ridgetop winds, it quickly poured down the hillside destroying all in its path.

"What kind of person would do something like this in a drought year?" someone asked. It seemed incomprehensible that any rational human being wouldn't take the time to completely extinguish a fire. Warnings and cautions are issued in many and varied ways to help people realize the fire danger, especially in a drought year. Then I wondered, *How many times have I been careless—not necessarily with fire, but in my relationships—perhaps saying something that might leave a spark of anger or hurt in someone else? How often have my words been like a hurtful sword? How often have I failed to ask forgiveness for an unkind word or action?*

> "Let us therefore make every effort to do what leads to peace and to mutual edification."
> (Romans 14:19)

One look at that blackened hillside reminded me that carelessness causes all kinds of problems—in life as well as in the woods. It reminded me God's Word instructs us to edify, not criticize.

Prayer:
May my words and thoughts edify, not judge. Help me remember to ask forgiveness for any unkind word or action.

JUNE 14

Dwayne Clemmons, Adjunct Instructor – Virginia Department of Fire Programs; Founder – DMC Ministries; Author of Exploits, Jesus Rides in an Ambulance, and Utterances from the Throne Room; Volunteer in Fire and EMS for forty years in Virginia

RIGHTEOUSNESS AND HOLINESS
You are called, anointed, and appointed to model the life of Christ on this earth

HAS THE church today, as did the church in Ephesus, turned from its first love? As a Christian who is saved, born again, and filled with the Spirit of God, are you allowing yourself to be pulled backward and forward, tossed to and fro, going in and out of sin? Are you giving in to the pressures of the world? Have you wondered why you don't feel free, when you know the truth? Even though you have read the Word, do you feel empty?

Could it be, as part of God's church, you've abandoned your first love? Today is Flag Day, a day to remember all that the flag stands for: freedom based on our godly heritage.

God is calling like never before for his church, his bride, his beloved to sanctify, purify, and glorify themselves in and through the Word of God. He is summoning his people to return to their first love, to come back to him (Revelation 2:4, 19). This takes humbling yourself, seeking to know God intimately, repenting, and praying. If you want to walk in righteousness and holiness, and to have joy in the midst of trials and the peace that passes all understanding, you must first believe it is God's will for your life to reflect righteousness and holiness. Second, you have to purpose in your heart that he is able to do this through you. Third, you must commit to walking in righteousness and holiness every day. Next, you would benefit from documenting your daily walk so you can reflect on the victories and the defeats. Finally, you have to praise and worship him every day no matter what happens.

> "If my people, who are called by my name, will humble themselves and pray and seek my face and turn from their wicked ways, then will I hear from heaven and will forgive their sin and will heal their land."
> (2 Chronicles 7:14)

Is this easy in the workplace? Probably not! Is it easy at home? Not always! Does God desire you to? Absolutely! A pattern of praise, prayer, and worship will change your life. It will draw you closer to God and as it does it will change the lives of others you work with and are around each day. It will change your family. It will change your church.

You are called, anointed, and appointed to model the life of Christ on this earth.

Prayer:
Lord, help me to answer your call today, to humble myself, pray earnestly, seek you in all I do, and turn from any sin that plagues my life. I want your forgiveness, your healing, and most of all I want to hear your voice.

Sue Reynolds, Missionary – Fellowship of
Christian Firefighters International

ATTITUDE OF THE HEART
Where's your focus?

W E WERE just sitting down to our Father's Day dinner. Both the kids were with us, along with our five grandchildren, on this rare opportunity when schedules allowed us to all be together and express our love and thankfulness for the three dads present. Time was a factor. The kids needed to get home and had a distance to travel, but they had put aside other responsibilities to celebrate Father's Day.

Then, the pager went off. "Do you have to go?" one of the grandkids pleaded. "Can't you let the others go this time?" another asked. "You're a volunteer, you don't have to go," another added as my husband donned his bunker gear and headed out the door. Each child expressed what the adults were thinking to themselves, wondering why he chose to leave when everyone was here primarily for him. Some thoughts even wandered to why he chose someone he didn't know over family.

Then before eating they asked me, "Mom, since dad's gone will you give thanks?"

I wasn't feeling too thankful at that moment. But our actions and words shouldn't depend on momentary feelings. While putting out the last food items, I wondered what I should pray for. Then I realized attitude and perspective are the keys to thankfulness. There's a lot of power in the two words "Thank you," when spoken genuinely. They can change a gloomy atmosphere to a bright, merry one. Giving thanks is liberating and changes heart conditions such as negativism, pessimism, and cynicism to gratitude. It immunizes us from the disease of resentment. As I continued to prepare my heart for a sincere prayer, I remembered why we were gathering. We were here primarily to honor the elder of the dads, the patriarch of the clan so to speak, and to give thanks for this man who takes his responsibilities seriously as a husband, father, grandpa, and volunteer firefighter, and to God—a man who stands on his word. He volunteered to help those in need, when he was needed, not when convenient.

> "Sing and make music in your heart to the Lord, always giving thanks to God the Father for everything, in the name of our Lord Jesus Christ." (Ephesians 5:19, 20).

Without a doubt, God reminded me, thankfulness is an attitude of the heart.

Prayer:
Lord, may my focus always be on what I'm thankful for and not what I think I'm missing. Thank you for all first responders who seek to serve and help others in need. Give me a sincere "attitude of gratitude."

JUNE 16

Lieutenant Mike Gurr, Pompano Beach Fire Rescue,
Florida Instructors, Coral Springs Fire Academy;
Fellow of Christan Firefighters Area Director

WITNESSING AT THE FIREHOUSE
Stepping out of your comfort zone

HAVE YOU felt the Holy Spirit tug at you to share the Lord with someone, only to dismiss it, letting the opportunity pass, because you thought it wasn't the right time, place, or person? Why are Christians afraid to tell others about our Lord? Why do we run scared and let these God-given appointments slip through our hands?

Maybe we fear rejection. But who's really being rejected? You, or God? We know that it's God, not us, being rejected, yet many still stand silent while missing opportunities to do God's work!

Firefighters have many opportunities during a twenty-four-hour shift to share Jesus with co-workers. But, before we start telling others about the Good News, we should be demonstrating our love for Christ by being a model employee, tuning up on the latest knowledge and skills of our trade, giving the best patient care and treatment possible, displaying a positive attitude toward the job and life in general, refraining from gossip, and conducting ourselves as true professionals.

Yes, you must be careful how you present the Gospel at work, and you can't subject others to listening against their will. I've discovered one way to witness is by showing a genuine interest in others and asking how they "really" are. From there I lead into questions about their life and activities while seeking to understand the emotions behind the words. It's amazing what people share when you show an authentic interest. Many co-workers are hurting and facing difficult times. What an opportunity to share how God has sustained your family and you in tough times!

If and when the conversation turns to church and God, that's when Satan loves to interfere and destroy confidence with arrows of doubt and insecurity. He loves to tell you you're wasting time and that this co-worker will never accept Jesus as his Lord and Savior. Don't let him. That's where prayer comes in: prayer for God to soften hearts, open eyes, and give you the words God would want you to say. Having a copy of *Answering the Call*, another pocket New Testament, or this devotional book to give them is a plus.

> "Yet when I preach the gospel, I cannot boast, for I am compelled to preach. Woe to me if I do not preach the gospel!" (1 Corinthians 9:16)

Remember someone had to reach out and go out of their comfort zone to witness to you—shouldn't you do the same?

Everyday at the firehouse is a great day, especially if God opens doors to share with others.

Prayer:
Guide me as I step out of my comfort zone and share your love.

Loadius Sendaluzi, Chief Fire Officer –
Zomba, Malawi, Africa, with Jonathan Newell

GOD, PUT OUT MY FIRE OF JEALOUSY
A *letter written on the tablets of the human heart*

MY YEARS of experience, including fighting major factory fires, were insufficient to prepare me for the worst fire I'd ever face a fire that raged inside my heart because of jealousy. On my own, I couldn't put it out.

In spite of my professional success and being born into a Christian family, my jealousy led to telling lies against others, mostly high achievers. Because of this sin, I frequently avoided attending church. On one infrequent visit, the preacher read 1 Corinthians 16:15–20 and explained that true believers in the Lord Jesus are the temple of God. He said heaven has no room for jealousy, an emotion that leads to many other problems.

The message lingered in my heart. I was convicted, but uncertain of what to do. A visiting evangelist was another one of God's tools. He stressed the dangers of jealousy and the need to pray for protection, which I did. Though not fully delivered, I started to get away from the problem. To enrich my spiritual life, I joined groups in my local church, attended Bible studies, and began learning more about God's love, grace, and forgiveness.

Still burdened by jealousy and sin, I struggled for years until I attended another meeting. The topic was, "A Christian who is saved is a letter to the world," from 2 Corinthians 3:1–6. "This letter," the preacher explained, "is not written with ink, but with the Spirit of the living God, not on tablets of stone but on tablets of human hearts. . . . Jesus is the best letter you can read. He faced many trials but never gave up." As the preacher spoke of the sorrow caused by sin, including jealousy, and said people who are full of jealousy and lies are cheating themselves, my heart was touched. I stayed to tell the speaker about my sinful problems. He prayed for me. I confessed my sin before the Lord Jesus and accepted him as the Lord and Savior of my life.

The Lord continues to help me overcome my challenges and develop a new attitude as a father who seeks to love and teach my family members and share with them the love of God through our Saviour, Jesus Christ. I now participate in church programs with an open mind, without jealousy and lies.

> "You show that you are a letter from Christ, the result of our ministry, written not with ink but with the Spirit of the living God, not on tablets of stone but on tablets of human hearts."
> (2 Corinthians 3:3)

Prayer:
Lord, may my letter be a reflection of your love in my life. I thank you that you can rid me of the darkest sins, making them white as snow.

Chief Lee Callahan, Burlington, MA; Fellowship of Christian Firefighters International Regional Director / International Board Member

FIREFIGHTER HEALTH
Bought at a price

DO YOU ever wonder where the writers of articles get their material? Something or someone inspires them. It may be a life incident,

224

friend, or colleague. It may be an observation of a current event or the prospect of something happening in the days ahead. It may be the story of someone who overcame adversity. For those of us who claim Christ as Savior, the Holy Spirit may be our inspiration.

I recently read an article in a fire magazine about a firefighter safety authority who recounted his first colonoscopy procedure, designed for early detection of colorectal cancer. The writer's goal was to convince people of the importance of tests to screen for cancer and other firefighting-related diseases. Many cancers have been linked to firefighting. Lung cancer is one.

> "Therefore honor God with your body."
> (1 Corinthians 6:20)

First responders have an obligation to do everything in their power to decrease the risk they face for falling victim to diseases. Cancer and heart disease take their toll, not only on the victim, but on family and friends, too.

Proper and timely use of personal protective equipment at each and every fire is our first line of defense against firefighter cancers. Proper screening and healthy lifestyles help put up other barriers against the disease.

You may think, *God will take care of me and keep me from getting cancer or similar life-threatening illness.* And he may. God may also want to show or teach you something. He could use illness to reach, encourage, and embolden you, or he may use it to teach, reach, encourage, or embolden someone else.

You may wonder, since God is in complete control, *Why should I try to protect myself?* What does God say about this? The Bible tells us our bodies are a temple for the Holy Spirit. Paul admonished the Corinthians, and us, about this and he continued by mentioning we were bought at a price (the great price of Christ's life). He also tells us to honor God with our bodies (1 Corinthians 6:19, 20).

Prayer:
*Thank you for the reminders, Lord, to take care of my body,
a temple of the Holy Spirit. Thank you for the people
you use to perform your good works.*

225

Scott Pruiksma, President – Interlockingarms.net; Firefighter – Borough of Midland Park NJ; FCFI North Jersey Chapter

THE ABUNDANT WATER SUPPLY
Fully connected

THE SPARKLE in children's eyes is a special reward if you have the opportunity to share your career with them. When you show up with the big engine, they're eager to share what they know about firefighting. They're equally excited to learn and hop on board and sound those sirens.

If you've asked children what they think the most important thing on the engine is, you'll hear a variety of answers. If you proceed to questions about firefighters' main responsibility, they have no hesitation responding with something such as "get the wet stuff on the red stuff." This opens several doors. If you have the freedom to share God's truths, those doors can lead to more than saving a structure. I begin by explaining that to get the water on the fire we need to have a hydrant or good water source and we must be connected to it. While we carry water on our rigs, it's not enough for extended firefighting. We need an abundant, never-ending water supply to fully put the fire out.

> "If anyone is thirsty, let him come to me and drink. Whoever believes in me, as the Scripture has said, streams of living water will flow from within him."
> (John 7:37, 38)

This presents an opportunity to share the eternal supply of water Jesus mentions in John 7:37: "If anyone is thirsty, let him come to me and drink." When I tell them Jesus says that if they believe in him, "streams of living water will flow from within [them]" (John 7:38), I equate his eternal water supply in our lives to the never-ending supply of water needed to put out physical fires. Jesus supplies all we need, but we must be connected to him.

I then ask the challenging question that I will also put before you: "Whom or what are you connected to?"

The world offers many things to get plugged into: money, status, drugs, alcohol . . . If we're only plugged into worldly things, and not plugged into a never-ending resource, our water supply will run out. Being plugged in to God's abundant water supply by accepting him as our Lord, reading the Bible, praying, having Christian fellowship, and applying what we've learned is not just for children. It's essential for everyone. Furthermore, being plugged in and then not applying the resources God gives us

226

is fruitless. Imagine the futility of having all the water in the world to put out the fire and not opening the nozzle.

Prayer:
God, thank you that we have all the water in the world at our disposal if we are connected to you. Thank you for the Living Water! Thank you for your provision of Jesus, for he will not fail.

Chaplain Marc Santorella, Firefighter Danvers Fire Department, MA; Public Fire and Life Safety Educator and Certified Fire Instructor Level 1

PERSEVERING TOGETHER
The starting gun went off the day you gave your life to Christ

ONCE A fairly avid runner, I'm able to say with confidence that running can be a love-hate relationship. Whether you're an elite athlete or a novice runner at the back of the pack, running has its share of pains. But there are rewards associated with running, such as health benefits, seeing your name on a list of finishers, comradeship among runners, and your witness or example to others.

Running is physically and emotionally exhausting, and not easy to do alone for long periods of time. First responder training, or long hours on scene, can be equally exhausting. Regardless of the type of race, perseverance is the key to success. The writer of Hebrews addresses this: "Therefore, since we are surrounded by such a great cloud of witnesses, let us throw off everything that hinders and the sin that so easily entangles, and let us run with perseverance the race marked out for us" (Hebrews 12:1).

Some days, when you feel as though you're being carried on the wings of angels sent to minister to you, you'll find running is easy. Other days you may wonder why you

> "We ought always to thank God for you, brothers, and rightly so, because your faith is growing more and more, and the love every one of you has for each other is increasing. Therefore, among God's churches we boast about your perseverance and faith in all the persecutions and trials you are enduring."
> (2 Thessalonians 1:3, 4)

tried to run. Keep in mind, on both the good and bad days, even if you run slowly, you're making progress. This is the essence of perseverance. Remember—if you stop running, you'll never finish.

While you persevere, it should be a comfort to know you're not the only one running. God is always with you. In addition, you're surrounded by other runners (believers). You're not alone.

The starting gun went off the day you gave your life to Christ. The finish line is fast approaching. When you meet runners struggling or falling behind, be sure to offer a helping hand and word of encouragement.

Remember that God doesn't worry about how well you run. He only wants you to not give up. Keep your eyes focused on Jesus. Two things are certain: 1) Your perseverance will be a witness to others. 2) You will finish, and, when you do, Jesus will be there to say, "Well done, good and faithful servant" (Matthew 25:21, 23).

Prayer:

Father, I pray for perseverance so I may be an encouragement to those around me who need to know you. I pray for other believers I interact with today so we'll be a comfort to each other as a reminder we are not alone. I know you're with me and have set the path I'm asked to travel. I want to run the race in a manner that glorifies you today.

JUNE 21

Tommy Neiman, Author of Sirens for the Cross; EMS Training Officer – St. Lucie County, FL; Fellowship of Christian Firefighters International Regional Director / International Board Member

AN ENCOURAGING WORD
Mutually uplifted

MY MOTOR HOME'S on fire and it's close to my house," the man anxiously announced. The boredom of the previous hours' low volume of calls was replaced with anticipation, anxiety, and unanswered questions. Were people caught in the flames? Was anyone in the mobile home? What about the vehicle's fuel and propane tanks?! Would we be able to contain the flames and save the house?

The heavy surge of traffic near the fire area slowed us down. Numerous spectators, in car and on foot, also decided to respond. They were in a slow, deliberate mode as they neared the fire, determined not to miss one moment of action. Many chose to ignore our loud siren.

A police cruiser arrived before us and, to facilitate our approach, blocked off the street to traffic. There was no problem identifying the fire. Flames consumed the entire forward end of the motor home. The heavy, black smoke made it impossible to tell if the adjacent house was on fire.

We rolled to a stop and received our orders. I was directed to examine the owner, an older gentleman, who was standing in the front yard closely studying every detail of the effort to quench this fire and save his house. Evidently he'd tried to do a little garden hose firefighting before we arrived, for he had suffered minor burns. There was redness on the top of his hand and biceps. He was visibly shaken and mildly hyperventilating. I joined him in his studious gaze at the fire suppression effort and noticed the house was no longer in jeopardy.

> "May our Lord Jesus Christ himself and God our Father, who loved us and by his grace gave us eternal encouragement and good hope, encourage your hearts and strengthen you in every good deed and word."
> (2 Thessalonians 2:16, 17)

"I'm sorry about your motor home," I said after he mentioned his planned trip for the next day. "Maybe God didn't want you to take this particular motor home on that trip."

"Yes, I believe you're right," he said. As the conversation progressed, I learned he was a pastor who at this moment, instead of ministering to others, needed someone to encourage him by reminding him of God's love. As we conversed freely about Christ's love and how, in difficult times such as this, God is always there, we were mutually uplifted. God gave me an opportunity to encourage this brother in a time of need, and, in turn, his words were encouraging to me.

Prayer:
*In times of loss, even those most grounded in your love need
your eternal encouragement and strengthening.
Lord, use me as a vessel of your hope.*

Reverend Wayne Detzler, PhD, Chaplain (Retired) –
Charlotte, NC, Fire Department; Fellowship of
Christian Firefighters Regional Director

PERSISTENT PRAYER PAYS OFF

When prayer prompts service

PRAYER BREAKFASTS are a priority at the Charlotte Fire Department. From the first, the Fellowship of Christian Firefighters has hosted regular early morning prayer breakfasts. Each month there's a breakfast for each of three shifts.

Sometimes these breakfasts center on comfort. When a firefighter goes through a death in the family or the devastation of divorce, he or she can find comfort with others at the early morning prayer times.

At other times firefighters are committed to Christ for special assignments. Many members have gone on missions trips around the world. They know that their most faithful prayer partners come from the monthly prayer times.

Fellowship is also a key to these regular times. Driving through the silent streets in the early morning, brothers and sisters know they'll find understanding and encouragement at the prayer breakfast.

Each month a leader shares basic Bible teaching. This is especially important, because it's tailor-made for the busy bustle of life in the fire station. Relevance is as regular as the sunrise.

However, this is not just about encouraging one another. Out of these early morning Bible studies has come a strong support team for the firefighters in our department.

> "Surely it is you who love the people; all the holy ones are in your hand."
> (Deuteronomy 33:3)

When department members go through tough times, their first call is the firefighter support team. Within minutes, a team member will come to the hospital, or make a visit at the fire station.

Administrators also rely on the firefighter support team. They call on our team when sickness strikes a firefighter or his family. When death snatches a family member, administrators call on support team members to stand with the firefighter. Often, it's a team member who leads the funeral service.

Fellowship and service function like alternating current in the Christian life. We draw strength from fellowship. In prayer we seek the Lord's energizing power. Then we return to the world to serve. It's always a temptation to spend time in the warmth and comfort of a caring fellowship, but the Lord sends us to serve a lost and dying world. The "current" must flow both ways.

Prayer:
Help me to remember every day that I was saved to serve, O Lord.

Steve Kidd, Firefighter Orange County Fire and Rescue, Florida; Central Florida Chapter of the Fellowship of Christian Firefighters; Author of the Carbusters video series

THERE IS NO ROOM FOR EXCEPTIONS TO GOD'S SAFETY RULES

A well-balanced firefighter has both courage and wisdom

HEAVY FIRE burned through the attic of the large, open storefront, burning away the wooden trusses that supported the heavy roof. The first-due engine company, wanting to save the building and its contents, took an aggressive approach to the fire, hoping to make a difference in the fire before gravity took over and pulled the roof down.

All firefighters have been warned to stay out from underneath and off the top of burning wooden-truss roofs, yet this engine company thought they could get away with a quick dash in and out and cheat danger for just a moment. It's the old candle-and-moth theory being tested—but with the high price of human life up for grabs. To consider going inside on such a fire isn't against the rules of safe practice. We all consider the factors and after weighing the potential consequences, we make the decision to act. So the consideration of the act isn't the violation of safe practice. The violation came the minute the crew ignored the established safety rules, stepped over the threshold, and started to attack the fire from a dangerous position. The consequences were fatal.

After "In the beginning," people's second-most-familiar Old Testament passage is usually the story of Adam and Eve falling to the temptation of the serpent in the Garden of Eden. As we read this accounts closely, we learn it isn't a sin to be tempted. The sin is committed when we fail to resist the temptation and commit the act. James 1:12 tells us about the blessings and rewards we will receive if we don't give in to temptation.

> "Blessed is the man who perseveres under trial, because when he has stood the test, he will receive the crown of life that God has promised to those who love him." (James 1:12)

When you're tempted, it isn't God who tempts you. It is man's sin nature within you that causes the temptation. There's no excuse, no blaming others, and no room for exceptions. You solely are to blame.

A well-balanced firefighter has courage and wisdom when facing the fire. A well-balanced Christian has courage to fight temptation, but sometimes needs wisdom to flee temptation.

Prayer:
May I persevere, pass your test, and be wise as well as courageous as I carry out my duties on the job and as a Christian.

JUNE 24

Dwayne Clemmons, Adjunct Instructor – Virginia Department of Fire Programs; Founder – DMC Ministries; Author of Exploits, Jesus Rides in an Ambulance, and Utterances from the Throne Room; Volunteer in Fire and EMS for forty years in Virginia

SMALL BEGINNINGS

Doing something out of the norm at your workplace

FOLKS AT the station gave him a hard time: "Hey, guys, here he comes—better watch that language." The taunts were constant, but he just smiled and joked with the guys. He walked his walk without criticizing and judging, only sharing when the opportunity arose. Then it happened. One of their own perished in a fire. Guess who they all turned to.

Willingly he prayed with the rest of the crew, reached out to the family, and shared God's promises. He made himself available.

To be effective ministers we must be available to deliver the Good News wherever God places us—be it on scene, at home, or in our workplace. Is this easy? Not always! But remember, God has not given us a spirit of fear. Romans 8:15 says, "For you did not receive a spirit that makes you a slave again to fear, but you received the Spirit of sonship. And by him we cry, '*Abba*, Father.'"

Rather than being fearful or even hesitant to minister to those around us, we can rely on our personal Father, our "*Abba*, Father," who dwells within us. He enables us to go somewhere we might otherwise turn away from.

Ministering in a secular environment can be intimidating. But remember, God's hand is in whatever his children do. Scripture assures us that without a doubt God is for us. First John 4:4 says, "You, dear children, are from God and have overcome them, because the one [Christ] who is in you is greater than the one [Satan] who is in the world." James 1:22 says, "Do not merely listen to the word, and so deceive yourselves. Do what it says." In other words, be a doer of the Word. Don't just listen, and don't be deceived.

> "A man finds joy in giving an apt reply—and how good is a timely word!" (Proverbs 15:23)

Begin by being available. Then pray continually over your role in your workplace. You may have this "little" thought one day to do something somewhat out of the norm. Maybe there are one or two folks who would welcome you sharing a Scripture or prayer with them. Don't despise small beginnings. God will be blessed, his kingdom will grow with your timely words, and you will find joy.

Prayer:
When it comes to sharing your Word, love, and peace, I will be a doer of the Word of God. Thank you for blessing me as I seek to bless others. I pray, Lord, that daily you will reveal how you will use me in my workplace.

Tommy Neiman, Author of Sirens for the Cross; EMS
Training Officer – St. Lucie County, FL; Fellowship
of Christian Firefighters International Regional
Director / International Board Member

LEFT BEHIND

Will you make the most important call?

AN ODD feeling came over me as I walked through the vacant truck room when I arrived for my shift. Our full shift was ready for duty, but there were no trucks to respond in. In addition, the bay doors were open, indicating the previous shift had departed in a hurry.

I called dispatch for an update and found out I'd just missed an opportunity to assist in a major accident. I'd never wish misfortune on anyone, but when a need such as this arises, it is always disappointing to be left behind. With all the trucks gone, I knew I'd remain idle for a good part of the morning. When the guys returned I overheard one of them say, "You missed it!" as he continued to share the unfolding drama of the call.

The usual shift-change procedures followed. We signed off drug logs and restocked used supplies. About fifteen minutes later, the shift supervisor called. "Bring the spare rescue truck to the Central Fire Station. We're going to put a full inventory of equipment on it and return it to service at another station," he explained.

Boring, boring, boring, I thought as it dawned on me that should a call come in, another station would respond while we were assigned to Central, taking care of this tedious three-hour detail. "No doubt," I whined, "another major call will come in and we'll be doing mundane tasks and be left behind."

> "For the Lord himself will come down from heaven, with a loud command, with the voice of the archangel and with the trumpet call of God, and the dead in Christ will rise first. After that, we who are still alive and are left will be caught up together with them in the clouds to meet the Lord in the air. And so we will be with the Lord forever."
> (1 Thessalonians 4:16:17)

The popular book and movie series *Left Behind* came to mind, and to counter my temporary disappointment, I reminded myself that when the most important call of all comes in, I will not be left behind. When

Christ returns, because I have professed faith and love for him. a trumpet will sound and I will go to meet my Lord in the air.

I pray that all of you will answer that call as well. All it takes is your sincere faith and belief that Jesus Christ is the Son of God and the one and only Way to God.

Prayer:
When the call that eternally matters comes in, I thank you
that because of my faith and belief in you, Jesus, God's
Way to eternal glory, I will not be left behind.

Mike Moyer, Battalion Chief – Jackson Hole, WY, Fire/EMS

MENTORING

Our lives should say, "Join me as I follow Jesus"

HAVE YOU been fortunate to have a mentor during your career in emergency services? Your mentor may have been a captain or chief officer who "has seen it all." He or she has run thousands of the common calls, such as dumpster fires, altercations at a bar, and motor vehicle collisions. They have also run many of the more peculiar calls that leave rookie firefighters or EMTs frozen in their boots. These mentors inspire us to learn, grow, and step up when others step back.

Sometimes mentoring is an official affiliation set up within a department. However, often it is an informal relationship initiated by an old hand who is willing to invest in the career of a person coming up through the ranks. The best mentors recognize a person's strengths and weaknesses, point out where someone is off course, and then challenge them to improve. Often the mentors in my life have impacted me most not by what they said, but how they did their job when the pressure was on.

Are you a mentor? Any of us can be a model for others. It might be by how we react calmly in the face of a sudden change in fire conditions or how composed we are as we coordinate the resuscitation of a six-year-old drowning victim.

In the same way, we have the opportunity to be an example in day-to-day life by getting to know more about our co-workers' lives, their families, and their struggles. We can take time to listen when a spouse has left,

235

share a verse with someone struggling with the challenges of a wayward teen, or point someone to Jesus for the first time.

> "Reflect on what I am saying, for the Lord will give you insight into all this." (2 Timothy 2:7)

Be a mirror that reflects Jesus, not attracting our own followers, but drawing people to Him. Take some time to read Paul's encouragement to Timothy in 1 Timothy 1:18, 19 and 2 Timothy 2:1–7. Paul encourages Timothy to be strong in grace, teach others what he has learned from Paul [spread the truth of Christ], endure hardships like a good soldier, and compete according to God's rules. Like Timothy and Paul, our lives should say, "Join me as I follow Jesus."

Prayer:

Lord, may I not only learn from the mentors you place in my life, but may I be a mentor and true reflection of your Word and love. May I inspire those I meet and work with to learn, grow, and step up.

JUNE 27

Bob Crum, Co-founder – Fellowship of Christian Firefighters International (Retired) – Denver Fire Department

COMMITTED, CONVICTED, AND DIRECTED
Implementing God's plan

GOD HAS a purpose and a plan for you. That is a fact, not an opinion, that he clearly states in Psalm 32:8. No doubt about it, for God's Word clearly states, "I will instruct you and teach you in the way you should go; I will counsel you and watch over you." He reinforces this fact in Jeremiah 29:11: "For I know the plans I have for you," declares the LORD, "plans to prosper you and not to harm you, plans to give you hope and a future."

Individually, and as a group of Christian firefighters with a heart for the fire service, God has a plan for us. One doesn't have to stand in a pulpit or go overseas to do this. Prayer time or Bible study with even one other person in the workplace may be the missions work God has for you and with which you are most comfortable. His commandment requires you to reach out and share Christ where he has placed you in this world.

It involves encouraging our brothers and sisters to do the same while standing firm in the Lord. To be effective in implementing his plan, you must do your part. It won't just happen. You need to be committed, convicted, and directed. Committed to understanding God's Word so you know what that plan is. Convicted that his plan is best. And then comes direction.

Self-examination is a good start. Have you established your priorities? Do you have an attack plan? No trained firefighter enters a burning building without a strategy on how to best extinguish the flames. Should extinguishing the flames of sin take any less planning?

> "I will instruct you and teach you in the way you should go; I will counsel you and watch over you." (Psalm 32:8)

Do you use your time for self-gratification and worldly happiness, or for the joy found in your relationship with Christ? Have you met with others to collectively visualize the vastness of God's plan for you as a group? Do you have an attack plan to put out the fires set by the attacker (Satan)? If not, today is a good day to start planning.

Prayer:
I am committed and convicted, Lord, to share your love. As I read your Word may the plan you have for me become distinct and clear.

JUNE 28

*Chaplain Gilbert Gaddie, Captain – Indianapolis
Fire Department; President Indianapolis Chapter
Fellowship of Christian Firefighters*

VICTIM INSTEAD OF RESCUER
I learned to rely on God's never-ending grace

SINCE AUGUST 1997, my body has served as a constant reminder that it is only by grace I'm able to face each new day. It was then that, while responding to a call, I became the victim instead of the rescuer. To this day no one knows exactly what happened. What I do know is that I never made it to the call.

When I awoke in the hospital, I learned the ladder truck rolled over and I was the only one injured. I was covered with cuts and bruises, and I suffered multiple injuries including a crushed left leg, crushed pelvis, head trauma, and injuries to my right shoulder. I was told I'd never return to work. Since then, my body has been the unwilling recipient of many surgeries for my colon, shoulder, ankle, and pelvis. Many times, uncertainty regarding God's plan for my life has caused a restless spirit.

When confined to a wheelchair because my leg wouldn't move, I had to believe that God would heal me. I realized that sometimes God grants spiritual healing alone. Other times he grants physical *and* spiritual healing. I prayed for the latter.

Before the accident, I thought I was tuned in to not taking things for granted and resting in God's peace and grace. With my ongoing surgeries, I was continually reminded that relying on God's love and grace is a process, and not always an easy one. Trials and tribulations caused discouragement, and questions plagued my mind. I

> "He saved us, not because of righteous things we had done, but because of his mercy. He saved us through the washing of rebirth and renewal by the Holy Spirit, whom he poured out on us generously through Jesus Christ our Savior, so that, having been justified by his grace, we might become heirs having the hope of eternal life." (Titus 3:5–7)

wondered why, if I was serving God, my life was so full of pain and at times, yes, even torment? Then I remembered that God gets a lot of glory when he goes through the trials with us, instead of keeping us from having to go through them. Likewise, our value to God increases because of the knowledge we gain. We become more focused, we understand how fragile life is, we gain compassion and empathy, and we learn to rely on God's never-ending grace.

God saved me from my sins, not because of anything I did, but because of his mercy. By his grace, he also saved me from the accident and allowed me to go back to full-time work on the fire department when doctors had said I'd never walk—let alone work—again.

Am I fully healed physically? No. Am I growing in the knowledge of his faithfulness and goodness? Yes.

Prayer:
*When I face those challenges, whether physical or emotional,
I thank you I can rely on you, Lord, and your grace.*

Reverend Wayne Detzler, PhD, Chaplain (Retired) – Charlotte, NC, Fire Department; Fellowship of Christian Firefighters Regional Director

RAIDER, THE FIRE DOG
Lessons learned from a faithful dog

WHEN I joined the Charlotte Fire Department there was a new fire dog. He was Raider, the black Labrador Retriever. As Labs go, he was small—small, but packed with energy and always ready for action. Over the years, I learned a lot watching both Raider and his successor.

First, I learned that faithfulness is Number 1. He never strayed from the side of his handler. Neither the oppressive atmosphere of a smoke scene nor the challenges of rough footing could throw him off. He was always there for us.

Second, I learned from Raider the lesson of teamwork. He loved to work with the firefighters. He would persist in his task of sniffing out accelerants until he found the source of the blaze. He was a very valuable member of the team.

> "But the fruit of the Spirit is love, joy, peace, patience, kindness, goodness, faithfulness, gentleness and self-control."
> (Galatians 5:22, 23)

Third, I learned that kindness is paramount. No matter when we came into the Arson Investigation Task Force building, if Raider was there, he greeted us with a wagging tail and a welcoming bark.

Fourth, I learned patience by observing Raider, who was patient when he needed to be. After a long, hard night at a fire scene he seemed glad to get back into his kennel. He would wait there for the handler to come. He seemed to have patience unusual in such a highly trained animal.

Fifth, I learned about sacrifice, part of Raider's DNA. He would give his last drop of energy to accomplish the task. Whatever we asked of him, he seemed more than ready to tackle the job.

Strange, is it not, that one can learn so much from a simple, black fire dog? These are all natural traits for a sweet dog like Raider. In many ways they've been bred into him.

By the same token, as Christians we have a certain spiritual DNA. We learn from the Lord how to be faithful in every situation. As the Scripture teaches us, we strive with one another in teamwork. Kindness is a fruit of the Spirit as God works through us, as is patience. Self-sacrifice becomes normal as the Lord Jesus lives through us.

Prayer:
Help me to live out my spiritual DNA before a dying world, O Lord.

JUNE 30

Daniel A. Clegg, Rural-Metro EMT; Engineer/EMT–Indianapolis Fire Department (Retired); Fellowship of Christian Firefighters Regional Director / International Board Member

COST OF GREED
We risked our lives for twenty-five dollars and would do it again!

ON THE evening of April 16, 1980, while I was assigned to Ladder Company 27, we responded to a box alarm for an apartment fire with a reported entrapped person. Upon arrival, we were informed that one resident who lived alone in a second-floor efficiency apartment was missing. Engineer Richard and I immediately began our search-and-rescue efforts.

While Engine 27 proceeded to obtain water for the fire, we headed for the top of the stairwell. Even though the fire blazed in front of the apartment, we were able to circumvent it to search the adjoining rooms. Six minutes into the search, Corporal Tom met me at the top of the stairwell.

"Tom, I need an inch-and-a-half attack line for a water curtain so I can access this apartment blocked by flames," I told him.

Tom, recognizing the danger, quickly responded by putting a water curtain between the fire and me. With only minor sunburn on my face, I was able to enter the apartment and retrieve the victim, Paul. I dragged Paul outside the door through the protective water curtain. Corporal Tom then assisted me in picking him up. We did a two-man carry down the stairway and turned Paul over to the care of Rescue Squad 7, who rushed him to the hospital.

This tragic fire, which caused the death of two men, was set on account of a twenty-five-dollar gambling debt. It was also a waste of precious time because I, along with others who were on scene, had to appear

240

in court to testify against the arsonist. Consequently we lost an entire day when we could have been fighting fires.

We risked our lives, two people died, others received injuries, we lost time, and a man will spend the rest of his life in prison—a pretty high cost for greed, don't you think?

Would we do it again? Without a doubt! While two died, one was saved. And above all else, fighting fire is what we do.

> "He [God] gave them over to a depraved mind, to do what ought not to be done. They have become filled with every kind of wickedness, evil, greed and depravity." (Romans 1:28, 29)

Prayer:
I pray for your perspective and forgiving heart, Lord, when greed and wickedness result in a call where lives are injured, threatened, or lost, and property is damaged and destroyed. You understand the pain of the victims and the rescuers. Please comfort all of us with the comfort that can only come from you.

Dessa Patton, Paramedic, Olive Branch, MS and Horn Lake
Fire Departments, MS; North Mississippi Medical Center-
Fulton Ambulance Service in conjunction with
all Itawamba County, MS fire departments

CHIPPY: MAY HE REST IN PEACE
Laughter: a gift from God that lifts the spirit

WHEN MY friend and I compared our most bizarre calls, I think hers won. She's a paramedic with a department that doesn't go out on "cat in a tree" calls; they go out on "squirrel in a tree" calls.

You may wonder, *How does a squirrel get stuck in a tree? They live in trees!*

This special squirrel, Chippy, was raised in captivity by a kindly grandmother. She had a harness for Chippy so he could experience the outdoors in a reasonably safe manner. One day while she was walking him, he headed for a tree and began climbing. Suddenly his pleasant chatter turned to one of panic. He was tangled in the tree and stranded. She frantically called the fire department. The chief had compassion and sent an engine and ambulance to see what could be done for poor Chippy.

The firefighters, seeing Chippy hanging way in the top, knew they were too heavy for the tree to support. The chief's son, who was among the spectators, was nominated to climb to the top of the tree and assist Chippy. The firefighters, while kind enough to lend the boy one glove, neglected to instruct him to grab Chippy with the gloved hand. When the boy reached for the squirrel, Chippy bit him, the lad spontaneously jumped, and Chippy's fragile neck snapped. The chief's son brought down the lifeless Chippy. The grandmother, though distraught, thanked the boy for his brave efforts.

> "God has brought me laughter, and everyone who hears about this will laugh with me."
> (Genesis 21:6)

The chief decided the squirrel needed to be tested for rabies. My friend was elected to return to the grandmother's house to ask for Chippy's body. Lovingly nestled in a small cardboard casket, Chippy was taken to the station and placed in a plastic bag to be stored in the refrigerator with the label, "Squirrel for testing, not for eating." The following Monday, my friend found the uninfected Chippy in another cardboard casket complete with headstone and toe tag.

They felt dreadful for the grandmother and her loss, but when the stories began to circulate beginning with "Chippy, may he rest in peace," laughter followed. Laughter lifts the spirit and is often the best remedy when returning from a call filled with images we would rather not dwell on. God promised Job that one day laughter would fill his mouth.

Prayer:
*Lord, help me remember that laughter is a gift from God
and when shared in goodness of spirit it helps relieve
the pain I encounter in this career.*

JULY 2

*Lieutenant Danny Legge, Paramedic/Chaplain –
Clay County, FL, Fire Rescue*

CUSTOMER SERVICE
Through love serve one another

RECENTLY, DURING the mandatory officers' meeting, we discussed "customer service." While I did learn more about who our customers are, I couldn't help but get disgusted about why customer service is such a hard thing to grasp. What kept rolling through my head was, "Do unto others . . ." But as the meeting progressed, I realized customer service is more than, "Do unto others"; it's also, "Through love serve one another" (Galatians 5:13 NASB).

If great customer service is the goal, then you must serve, and do it through love. In order to serve through love, you're going to have to lose a couple of things: *pride* and *self*. You have to stop serving with the anticipation of something in return and start serving with the "love of Christ" in mind. You must humble yourself, which for most of us is very difficult. But if God can do it, then surely you can. God stepped down out of heaven and all its glory to this dungpile called "Earth." What a humbling experience that must have been!

Yes, God created the world and "it was good"—but people destroyed it with wants, desires, and personal agendas. As sin spread, God took on flesh in Jesus and came to save all of humanity who would accept God's gift. Jesus was human in every way; he didn't have any place to lay his head, he wept, and he washed his disciples' nasty feet. Why? Here's that word again: *love!* It's only really serving when it's done through love. You

244

don't have to love what others do (or did), you just have to see them through God's eyes, which for him is like looking into a mirror. In the beginning, in Genesis, we learn we were created in God's image. Not some of us—all of us!

"You, my brothers, were called to be free. But do not use your freedom to indulge the sinful nature; rather, serve one another in love." (Galatians 5:13)

You want people to see what Jesus is about? Then serve! Serve one another with Christ in mind. It's not the norm, so people will question it. When they do, you have an open door to discuss the God who loves them and died for a relationship with them, who then rose again so they could live forever with him.

So today is the day! Today is the day in which Jesus yells from the station kitchen: "Order up!" Take what he has prepared and serve it with the love that only can come from him.

Prayer:
Today, Lord, is the day for me to "order up" and then serve through the example of love you selflessly and unconditionally demonstrated for me.

Tommy Neiman, Author of Sirens for the Cross; EMS Training Officer – St. Lucie County, FL; Fellowship of Christian Firefighters International Regional Director / International Board Member

THE CACTUS GUY
Saved from a potentially deadly pestilence

MANY LIFE-THREATENING concerns are part of the first responder's job. An increasingly prevalent one is communicable diseases. That concern became a life threat for me on a run for a guy I call the "Cactus Guy."

Caution signs immediately flashed in my mind when we arrived at an unkempt home. Music blared despite the victim's dire condition, and an odor of drugs reached my nostrils. The victim wasn't an ordinary figure, but a bright red figure totally covered with blood, indicating the bleeding came from an artery.

"He fell through the door," a bystander yelled.

I glanced up. The huge glass window in the middle of the door was broken off at knee level; its bloody, jagged edge looked treacherous.

"This guy's been drinking all morning," the bystander continued. "I saw him crash backward through that window. His legs were caught until, like from a sling shot, he went flying off the glass, landing in the cactus bed."

With no time to worry about a potentially deadly transmissible disease, my partner and I went to work. Soon my latex gloves were completely red and shiny from his blood. As we log-rolled him onto his side, he shrieked with pain. His skin was loaded with minute, piercing, yellow cactus needles. I wondered how many had penetrated my gloves. As he drifted from consciousness, I prayed we weren't endangering our lives for naught.

At the hospital we handed him over to the nurses and the doctor. I then carefully removed my gloves praying none of the hundreds of tiny, blood-soaked cactus spines was embedded in my skin. I noticed small holes in the cuffs of the gloves and took a deep breath. The moment of truth arrived. I held my hands up to the fluorescent light. Not one single cactus needle was embedded in my skin. Praise the Lord! I found absolutely nothing. I turned to my partner. A smile covered his face. He, too, came up cactus-free.

> "I will say of the Lord, 'He is my refuge and my fortress, my God, in whom I trust.' Surely he will save you from the fowler's snare and from the deadly pestilence."
> (Psalm 91:2, 3)

On that hot, muggy summer afternoon, God's Word was truly my fortress. He did indeed save me from a potentially deadly pestilence.

The "Cactus Guy" underwent extensive reconstructive surgery and eventually recovered. I don't think he'll ever know how the Lord used his accident to strengthen the faith of this paramedic. God, in whom I trust, is truly my Protector.

Prayer:
It is you whom I trust, Lord, and because of that trust I know you'll deliver me from the devil's attacks. You are my Shield and Fortress.

246

Chaplain Gaius Reynolds, President – Fellowship of
Christian Firefighters International; Volunteer Firefighter –
Livermore, CO, Fire Protection District

DIRECTION AND DECISION

Changing the "Oh, man, I can't!"
to "Oh, man, let's get after it!"

THE FOURTH of July gives us pause to reflect on our freedoms. Are you truly independent and free?

There's only one sure way to be free—have your life grounded in our Lord and his Word. The Bible provides life-changing direction for every aspect of life, love, and relating to others. His directions are clear and simple. To be truly free, your goal should be to draw closer to God, to become more like

> "Work at telling others the Good News, and fully carry out the ministry God has given you."
> (2 Timothy 4:5 NLT)

him, to develop a personal relationship with him, and to share Christ with others.

Christian first responders have taken on an added responsibility of reaching the fire service and their communities, and taking the vision of knowing Christ to them by *evangelism, empowerment,* and *encouragement.*

How can these goals be accomplished?

First, by reading his Word. To know any author, you must read his works.

Second, by going a step further and studying what he says. Seek to know what he means. His Word is *The Word.* It is the same today as it was in the past or will be in the future.

Next comes application. As you read and study his Word, understanding his deity increases. Godly instruction from pastors, Bible teachers, and Sunday school leaders, and fellowship with others who walk with the Lord, will assist you in developing godly application. The "Great Commission" is clear. Go and make disciples of all nations. It is not a choice but a command from our Lord. And it requires action.

God's directions are clear. The decision is up to us. First responders face unique situations and see things most people only read superficially about.

Is God calling you to lead a Bible study for those in your workplace and help them, according to God's love? Is there someone God has been telling you to witness to? When you commit to him and stand on his Word, the "Oh, man, I can't!" changes to "Oh, man, let's get after it!"

Remember—with Christ, all things are possible. You may be the *encourager* your workplace needs. You may be the only Bible that your co-workers read. They read you when they meet you. They may not know your name, yet they are reading you.

What kind of "read" are you? Do you study to understand God's directions? Have you decided to follow? The decision is yours to make!

Prayer:
*I have decided to follow you, Lord, and to
complete the duties of a servant of God.*

JULY 5

*Rick Barton, Fire Safety Officer; Rick Barton Ministries,
Gunnison, CO; Fellowship of Christian Firefighters
International Ambassador-at-Large*

THOSE BOOKS

*Is the problem one of unbelievers not responding to witnessing,
or is it one of motivating believers to step
out and share God's Word?*

DO YOU remember *those books* you sent me last year?" the fire chief asked.

Of course I did. I'd served on a fire assignment in western Colorado and this chief was the incident commander. At the end of the incident I gave him an *Answering the Call New Testament* and asked him to look it over and pass it around to the folks in his department. "If the guys would like some more, just call me," I added.

Two weeks later he did call. He asked for a case of "those books."

With the help of the Fellowship of Christian Firefighters International, the box of Bibles was on its way. After that I didn't hear from the chief until I called and told him I was planning to speak in a church in his community and wanted to honor and pray over the members of the fire, EMS, and police departments during the meetings. I told him I would also like to present the department with one of the "Flag of Honor" American flags, which contain the names of the 343 first responder victims of 9/11 written on the red stripes. The chief agreed to pass the word around and then told me what was happening with "those books."

After the department received the case of New Testaments, he put them out in the station for men and women to pick up. Soon, most of the department had a copy. Since the building is used for other training, the chief noticed that other groups of emergency responders were taking copies as well! "We're kind of working our way through them, and could use some more," he said.

"The harvest is plentiful, but the workers are few." (Luke 10:2)

Lessons learned! First, we don't ever have to be reluctant about passing out God's Word. It's especially easy when it's giving a fellow firefighter an *Answering the Call*. Second, we don't always know the long-term impact one New Testament will have.

Is the problem one of unbelievers not responding to witnessing, or is it one of motivating believers to step out and share God's Word?

Prayer:
Lord, I realize the fire service provides a plentiful harvest field.
Guide me, Lord, as I reach out to them sharing your Word and love.
May I be a credible witness to your life-changing power.

249

Dwayne Clemmons, Adjunct Instructor – Virginia Department of Fire Programs; Founder – DMC Ministries; Author of Exploits, Jesus Rides in an Ambulance, and Utterances from the Throne Room; Volunteer in Fire and EMS for forty years in Virginia

YOU WILL EAT WHAT YOU SAY
What's for lunch?

AROUND THE station or on difficult calls, the language sometimes becomes harsh, to put it mildly. Just how important are those words we speak?

Matthew 4:4 reports these words spoken by Jesus: "It is written: 'Man does not live on bread alone, but on every word that comes from the mouth of God.'"

Do you get hungry? Do you ever find yourself daydreaming about a thick, juicy steak, a lobster tail, or pork chops right off the grill? If you're a vegetarian, do you have visions of cucumbers, longings for lettuce, or desires for beans? Did you know, however, that you will eat what you say?

James 3:5 says, "Likewise the tongue is a small part of the body, but it makes great boasts. Consider what a great forest is set on fire by a small spark." We can definitely relate to and understand this concept.

Hebrews 4:12 says, "For the word of God is living and active. Sharper than any double-edged sword, it penetrates even to dividing soul and spirit, joints and marrow; it judges the thoughts and attitudes of the heart." The Word of God is still the most powerful source in the universe. It still has the same power that raised Jesus from the dead.

If you're saved, born again, and filled with the Spirit of God, then you're a joint heir with Jesus, you are a duplication of the Word; therefore, you live by every word that comes out of your mouth. This is true, because your tongue has power and the words that go forth do not return to you void; thus your words penetrate you and that is how you will either live or die.

You have to make a decision whether you want to be a disciple or a rebel. Are you only interested in success or are you more concerned with the significance of what you do? Do you have confidence God is able to direct your life to a specific end? Are you willing to let go and let God?

You must have faith to believe that if your words are the Word, then they will go out and accomplish what they are meant to accomplish and not return unto you void.

What's for lunch? Remember, you will eat what you say.

Prayer:
Lord, help me study and learn your Word. Enable me to apply
it in every circumstance. Focus my attention on my mouth.
Let no vain utterance come forth. Make my words
a source of eternal life for me and others.

JULY 7

Daniel A. Clegg, Rural-Metro EMT; Engineer/EMT–Indianapolis Fire Department (Retired); Fellowship of Christian Firefighters Regional Director / International Board Member

JOE'S STORY
A night that marked the beginning of a story that continues to unfold

THE STORY began in 1972. We'd moved into a new fire station on East Tenth Street. The differences were very obvious. This noisy, smaller station had no place to get away alone. I cherish my quiet time in God's Word, so I sought out the only quiet room available, the bathroom.

One night I went to investigate a strange voice outside the restroom and found a civilian using our wall phone. He started to retreat, then muttered to me, "Can you believe it? I got put on hold while calling the suicide hot line."

"Would you like to talk?" I asked.

"Yeah!" he mumbled.

251

We began to talk about our Lord when he interrupted me. "Will you call Reverend Hamilton at the Wheeler Mission for me?"

Midnight was approaching and I didn't know Reverend Hamilton. The young man persisted. It became obvious that if I didn't call, I was going to lose Joe. I made the call. Reverend Hamilton then made a forty-minute drive across town to speak with a hurting man.

We talked. We listened. We read Scripture. The clock struck three. Joe bowed his head and accepted Jesus Christ as his Lord and Savior. When he stood to leave, he reached into his coat pocket and pulled out a loaded .38 revolver. "I planned on using this tonight to end my life. But now I have a new hope, a new life," he said.

> "Therefore, if anyone is in Christ, he is a new creation; the old has gone, the new has come!."
> (2 Corinthians 5:17)

Years later, in a Monday night service, a well-dressed man I vaguely recognized stood up. He shared a story of a cold, hopeless night when he wandered into a fire station to use the phone to call the suicide hot line and was put on hold.

Tears filled my eyes. It couldn't be Joe, could it?

"I was ready to end my life. You probably don't recognize me," he said. "I'm all cleaned up on the inside and the outside, too. I'm now a caretaker at a mission in Ohio. I came to visit my family and had to come here to tell you how amazed I am at how Jesus Christ changed my life. Thank you."

It was Joe!

Prayer:
May I always remember that my life, no matter how distraught I may feel, is in your hands and that I am precious in your sight. Because of you, I am a new creation, and even when I struggle with the "old man" and feelings of hopelessness, you help me keep my focus on you and the hope you offer, free of charge.

Chaplain Robert Osbourn, Sylacauaga, AL, Fire Department

HOW TO FIGHT FIRE

He has his hand on the nozzle
and he is in control

THE BIBLE doesn't guarantee freedom from the fires and storms of life. It does give valuable perspectives regarding trials. Times of trouble in the lives of biblical characters provide insightful lessons about faith, God, and life. The apostle Paul labored for the Lord while fighting the fire of an afflicting thorn in the flesh—a thorn God refused to remove. And don't forget Shadrach, Meshach, Abednego, and the fiery furnace.

You may feel because you serve God, you should be free from the storms of life. Have you ever asked, "Why is this happening to me? I've tried to do everything the Lord wants me to do!" Often, God takes the cream of the crop into the fire to change one's perspective on life and teach valuable lessons. When you realize God "is able," you will be comforted and strengthened in trying times. God hasn't changed one bit. He is still "able" to do anything that needs to be done in your life or mine! (Ephesians 3:20).

> "If we are thrown into the blazing furnace, the God we serve is able to save us from it, and he will rescue us from your hand, O king."
> (Daniel 3:17)

As fires or trials confront you, God has his hand on the nozzle and he is in control. In fact, if the fire comes into your life, it first passed through the filter of God's perfect plan for you. Remember when the fire is raging in your life that "in all things God works for the good of those who love him, who have been called according to his purpose" (Romans 8:28).

Unfortunately, when fires come they are often accompanied by the temptation to quit on God. If you're so tempted, remember that God promises his help. He promises not to allow you to be tempted beyond your ability to bear it (1 Corinthians 10:13).

Jesus set an example. During the worst trial he faced, he didn't quit (Luke 22:42). He endured and kept his commitment because he loves you.

The hour of temptation and trial is when the sincerity of your profession of faith is proved. It's easy to vow things to God when it looks as if the world is going to be perfect. However, when the tough times come, that's when you get to honor the commitments you've made to the Lord.

Prayer:
Fires and trials! Often I don't understand, but help me grow
from them and stand firm in my faith. For you are able,
and you will be with me in the fires of life.

Tommy Neiman, Author of Sirens for the Cross; EMS
Training Officer – St. Lucie County, FL; Fellowship of
Christian Firefighters International Regional
Director / International Board Member

SMILIN', MIGHTY JESUS
Once you're infected, he promises
to always be with you

SHORTLY AFTER joining the fire service I was sent to a new station. I headed for the dorm to stash my things. As I opened my duffel bag, one of the guys, Steve, immediately recognized my choice of reading material, a Bible. This sparked an interesting conversation and immediate bonding, for we both were children of God. From the onset of my days as a first responder, Christ, along with the comfort God's Word provides, has been my Rock. Steve and I first talked about our respective churches and even shared a few of our favorite verses before he said, "Hey, I've got a call you'll really appreciate."

The chuckle in his voice caught my interest. "Oh, yeah? Tell me."

He immediately began his story.

About a month earlier Steve had received a "weakness" call. He arrived to find an older gentleman who seemed quite illiterate and definitely hard of hearing. He walked up to the man and said, "Sir, what's going on today?"

"I got the smilin', mighty Jesus," the man responded.

"Excuse me. Could you repeat that?" Steve asked.

"I got the smilin', mighty Jesus."

Realizing he might not be hearing the man clearly, he moved closer. "Could you repeat that v-e-r-y s-l-o-w-l-y?"

254

"I . . . got . . . the . . . smilin', . . . mighty . . . Jesus," came the drawn-out reply.

Steve thought, *Oh, well. I guess we'll never figure this one out.* Then he had a bright idea. "Do you have any papers from your doctor?"

> "And surely I am with you always, to the very end of the age."
> (Matthew 28:20)

The man pointed to the table. Sure enough, he had medical papers from his home health nurse, the contents of which made Steve quiver and regret his close proximity. This man might very well have had the "smilin', mighty Jesus," for he appeared to be a man of faith, but the medical papers didn't say that. No, the papers didn't refer to what he had as "smilin', mighty Jesus" —but a very contagious *spinal meningitis!*

Do you have the real "smilin', mighty Jesus" in your life? I sure pray you do. The smile he puts on your heart, and the strength and peace of his loving presence on the funniest and the most tragic calls is contagious—and that's a contagion everyone needs to be exposed to. Once you're infected, he promises to always be with you.

Prayer:
Thank you for always being with me. What a wonderful promise!

Reverend Wayne Detzler, PhD, Chaplain (Retired) – Charlotte, NC, Fire Department; Fellowship of Christian Firefighters Regional Director

HE GIVES HIS LIFE AWAY
We keep what we give to God

HIS WHOLE career was spent in a suburban Connecticut town. His highest rank was captain of a ladder truck. For my friend, Dick, this was not just a job—it was a calling, a spiritual vocation.

Dick was the first one there and the last to leave, and he defended firefighters whenever anyone brought criticism. Dick's passion was the fire service and he expected his crew to share this. He wasn't just zealous, he was also very smart and well-informed. He knew exactly what to do, and he did it. Leading was an active verb for him. He didn't just tell the firefighters what to do, he led them by example.

When a car was crushed at the main railroad crossing in his town, Dick responded. He put his life on the line to rescue the woman caught in the crash. As he worked through the incident he went back and forth along the tracks, until his boot caught and he wrenched his knee, causing a potentially career-ending injury.

Not only did Dick serve selflessly, he stood firmly for Christ. It was Dick who introduced me to the Fellowship of Christian Firefighters International. He spearheaded the advance of FCFI throughout central Connecticut. His integrity as a fire captain reinforced his commitment as a Christian.

One day Dick came to me with a remarkable challenge: "Would you be willing to serve as a fire chaplain?"

"Tell me more," I responded with cautious enthusiasm. "I'm very interested." After serving overseas for many years, I felt a concern to invest in my community, to establish a witness by serving among civil servants.

"My Father will honor the one who serves me." (John 12:26)

"Your local department desperately needs a chaplain. I've checked with the local chief, and he'd like to meet with you," Dick continued.

When I met with the chief he appointed me chaplain immediately. He asked me to take a hands-on role. Top priority was my willingness to respond to working fires, sudden deaths, and crises in the lives of firefighters.

Dick coached me. He shared an impressive depth of experience in the fire service. He taught me how to respond, how to become an integral part of the team. One New Year's Eve my pager went off right in the middle of a hymn. I handed it to Dick, and he took the message. He briefed me about an attempted suicide in our department. Dick was always there, always serving the community with the commitment the Lord worked into his life. The example he set continues to impact my life, and I thank the Lord for the role models he places in my life.

Prayer:
Lord, make me a faithful, reliable servant like my friend.

*Rick Barton, Fire Safety Officer; Rick Barton Ministries,
Gunnison, CO; Fellowship of Christian Firefighters
International Ambassador-at-Large*

MY DAD DIED
What to say? How to feel?

THE PHONE rang early one Sunday morning. "Rick, this is Jim Barton," the voice said. "Dad died last night." What to say, how to feel? My parents divorced when I was young. I hadn't talked to him in more than ten years. He had remarried and had two sons I hadn't met until the previous year. Now one of them was calling to tell me my dad died.

> "In fact, the law requires that nearly everything be cleansed with blood, and without the shedding of blood there is no forgiveness." (Hebrews 9:22)

I'm not sure how I would have handled this during earlier years, but while in college I gave my life to Jesus, married a godly woman, and started a ministry. As our children grew, they asked, "When are we going to meet your dad?" It was becoming more difficult to reconcile my new life in Christ with the wall I'd built toward my father. Finally, the time came when that became impossible. My dad sent me a letter. "Please forgive me," he wrote.

As a follower of Jesus I really didn't have a choice, did I? I wrote him and said I'd like to see him and introduce my family. In two days the phone rang. "Rick, this is Dad," the voice on the other end said. Caught off guard I said, "Who?"

We met and began to build a relationship. I was able to share my testimony and how he could come to know Jesus. Eventually, we met his wife and sons and were able to share with them as well. His wife even asked us to write down the words to the "Sinner's Prayer" so they could pray it together.

Three years ago my dad entered an Alzheimer's unit. For the last year he didn't recognize me, but his wife noticed he always became peaceful when I sang hymns and prayed with him. And now, I believe he's in heaven. And it all started because I had a wife and kids who held me be accountable to my faith and because of my understanding that God's commandment to forgive is just that—a commandment. It's not a choice. God's law requires it.

Prayer:
Why is forgiving so hard? In your prayer, Lord, recorded in the book of Matthew, you make it clear we must forgive. In Hebrews I learned that true forgiveness came when you shed your blood for my sins. Help me, Lord, to have a forgiving heart.

JULY 12

Jeff Turkel, Firefighter/Dispatcher – North Pole, Alaska; Fellowship of Christian Firefighters Regional Director

READY TO DIE

A peace came over me like I had never felt before

IN 1989 I was serving as an Air Force crew chief assigned to Eglin Air Force Base, Fire Station 5, Camp James E. Rudder. A wildland fire was reported approximately one-half mile behind the housing area of the Army Ranger Camp. Being short-handed, we were forced to respond with only a two-man crew and the station captain on a crash truck. Forestry crews were delayed, but backup crews were en route from the main fire station twenty miles away.

This fast-moving grass fire, fueled by heavy winds, was heading for a stand of longleaf pine trees and palmetto bushes. If the fire got into the trees, it was likely to reach the housing area. I made the decision to don an Indian pump and try to attack the main body of fire. The wind shifted and before I knew it I was surrounded by fire. I heard my station captain yelling, "Turkel! Get out of there!"

I looked around. I was trapped by a wall of fire impossible for him to see from his location. Attired in crash silver, the only bunkers we had been issued, I put down the face shield on my structural helmet and tucked my chin to my chest.

My greatest nightmare seemed imminent—burning to death on a call. Fire was all around me. I sincerely started to pray, "God, it's not my will to die right now. But if it's your will for me to die here and now, it's okay with me. If you want to call me home, I'm ready. You are my Lord, and I'm willing to accept whatever you have for me."

258

As soon as I finished this prayer, a peace came over me like I had never felt before.

A split-second later the winds died down and I ran faster than I'd ever run in my life. As soon as I passed the area of fire, I looked over my shoulder in time to see the area I had been standing in explode in a wall of flame.

> "Thy will be done, as in heaven, so in earth."
> (Luke 11:2 KJV)

Who says prayer doesn't work? Not me!

Prayer:

As I see the tragedy and loss that come with this job, I realize that time is a precious commodity. Let me always use it for your glory. And when my time has come to join you in heaven, may I hear the words, "Well done, good and faithful servant."

JULY 13

Tommy Neiman, Author of Sirens for the Cross; EMS Training Officer – St. Lucie County, FL; Fellowship of Christian Firefighters International Regional Director / International Board Member

WORLDLY DIVERSIONS, OR ETERNAL COMFORT?
What kinds of diversion do you seek?

JOEY WAS six years old. He was on an adventure at the beach across the street from the fire station where I was the paramedic on duty. While happily playing in the surf, he came in contact with a Portuguese man-o-war. These jellyfish-like creatures have long, invisible tentacles with little stingers that inflict pain when they come in contact with the skin. Joey's mom grabbed the crying child, rushed across the street, and placed her howling child on our kitchen table. Together, mom and paramedic started the tedious task of calming the youngster down. I explained to the mom that the red marks were most likely man-o-war stings and, since Joey wasn't having any signs of a full-body reaction, he'd be okay.

The warm ammonia-and-water solution I gently swabbed on his sting marks seemed to alleviate some of the pain. Joey sniffed, let out a few more cries, and, upon seeing one of the guys fixing hot dogs, made his intentions clear. He whined until he acquired not only the hot dogs but the cookies the guy had reserved for dessert. With each acquisition, his pain appeared to decrease. Then, seeing one of the guys turn on the television in the adjoining day room, Joey confidently pointed to the television and asked, "Could you put on Nickelodeon?"

I looked at the guy who had not only lost his hot dogs and cookies but was going to miss his midday sports report. "Sure," I laughingly said, motioning for that slightly-angered-but-not-showing-it firefighter to turn the channel to Nickelodeon. At this point we knew our fire station had been taken over by a six-year-old. Fortunately, Joey's mom also realized this. She told Joey, since his "boo-boo" was better, it was time to tell all the nice firemen good-bye. While heading to the door, Joey noticed one of the guys with ice cream. You guessed it; his departure was delayed as he ate a bowl of ice cream.

> "Shout for joy, O heavens; rejoice, O earth; burst into song, O mountains! For the Lord comforts his people and will have compassion on his afflicted ones."
> (Isaiah 49:13)

Hot dogs, cookies, a favorite TV show, and ice cream all served as diversions for the young boy. What kinds of diversion do you seek when seized by pain? Do you turn to "things"? I hope you turn instead to the only true and lasting Source of comfort.

Prayer:
I rejoice, Lord, that you are there to comfort me and that I don't need possessions and diversions when things seem insurmountable—I only need you.

Captain Raul A. Angulo – Seattle Fire Department;
Fellowship of Christian Firefighters Regional
Director / International Board Member

CLEANSING WATER

I visualized all my junk and stupid
pettiness being rinsed off

THERE'S NOTHING more rewarding than when one of your children has an "ah-hah!" moment, and one of your pearls of wisdom finally makes sense.

On the eve of her adulthood, my daughter and I got into a petty argument. She ended the argument ten minutes before her birthday by saying, "I have to take a shower!" Half an hour later she descended the stairs and apologized with a kiss and a hug.

"Honey, you spent the strike of midnight into adulthood in the shower," I said with a note of disappointment.

"I know Dad; I did it on purpose. I realized my rants and raves are childish. As I showered, I visualized all my junk and stupid pettiness being rinsed off. Now I'm an adult with a brand new, clean start!"

Wow! I wasn't expecting that! We hugged. What started out as a disaster ended up in a special father-daughter closure to her childhood.

Water is the universal neutralizer. This clear, colorless liquid is essential to sustain all life. The Bible speaks of peaceful, quiet, raging, living, and bloody waters. It mentions walking on water and water turned into wine.

> "I will sprinkle clean water on you, and you will be clean; I will cleanse you from all your impurities and from all your idols."
> (Ezekiel 36:25)

Firefighters know the value of water for extinguishing fires. I appreciate it in another sense. I stop by the health club frequently after shift. After exercising, I head for the jetted tub. The hot water helps relax me from stress and soothes my muscles. Especially after a fire, the water helps clean my body of the contaminants absorbed into my skin.

It's therapeutic for both body and soul. I use that time to think, pray, and visualize all the impurities and sins leaving my body. Since my daughter's profound words about water rinsing off all her junk, I now think of God's cleansing waters and am thankful that through my faith in him, I'm cleansed.

Don't be discouraged when you fail. Get up, dust yourself off, and make another clean, fresh start in drawing nearer to God. The next time you shower or sit in a hot tub, reflect on scriptural references to water. Visualize your sins, faults, and shortcomings being washed away. Our purification and sanctification only happens because of the grace of God. That's his way of drawing you closer to him. The good thing about his grace is that every day is a new day to try to get it right.

Prayer:
When I'm discouraged, slipping into old, sinful patterns,
or needing a new, fresh start, thank you, Lord, for your
cleansing water that draws me closer to you.

JULY 15

Reverend Wayne Detzler, PhD, Chaplain (Retired) –
Charlotte, NC, Fire Department; Fellowship of
Christian Firefighters Regional Director

SERVANT OF ALL

Learning to serve first

OUR CITY, Meriden, Connecticut, was a graveyard of its industrial past. At one time it had been the proud "Silver City," where much of America's silverware was made. Famous names of the past had been identified with the tableware that flowed from its factories.

Alas, when I arrived, all the silver factories were closed. The jobs had been exported to other states, other countries. In the wake of their departure there remained empty factories devoid of life. Where once machines stood, now there were graves in the concrete floors. Often these old machinery wells were filled with oil, the lubricant of better days.

"Fire in the factory," the dispatcher spread the word. The oily floors had erupted in one of many fires. Our crews rushed to the scene in an effort to head off a chain reaction.

As the assistant chief entered the factory, it was dark. The thick smoke hung heavy and visibility was limited, almost lost. As the assistant chief / incident commander saw an oil slick, he assumed it was only some spilled lubricant. In reality it was a machine well several feet deep and filled with thick black oil.

262

"Help," the assistant chief called as he sank beneath the black surface. Immediately firefighters pulled him out, rescuing him from the stinking substance. He was coated in black oil, head to toe. The firefighters led him out to the street and out of danger.

> "The Son of Man did not come to be served, but to serve."
> (Matthew 20:28)

"Chaplain," an officer ordered, "quick, help the assistant chief get his gear off." So I began the process of stripping him down. Each piece of bunker gear was placed in a red bio-hazard bag. It might be saturated with cancer-causing chemicals.

The whole affair left the assistant chief embarrassed, but it left the rest of us red-faced, too. After all, how often does one strip an assistant chief right on a city street? As I processed the affair in my mind, I could hear the voice of Jesus whisper, "Servant of all." It was all part of turning me into a servant.

Sure, we call it the "fire service," but serving has its limits in our lives. We resent it when people seem to impose on us. We guard our off-duty time, our private lives. However, Jesus is intent on teaching us that all of our life is set apart for service. We are servants first, and everything else is second.

Prayer:
Lord, make me a servant first and foremost in every situation of my life.

Rick Barton, Fire Safety Officer; Rick Barton Ministries, Gunnison, CO; Fellowship of Christian Firefighters International Ambassador-at-Large

I CAN'T DO THAT
But he did, and I found a new man a man set free!

THE PASTOR looked at me with troubled eyes. "I can't do that!" he insisted. It was after the service ended and everyone else had left.

"What do you mean?" I asked. The pastor was obviously in anguish.

"I can't do what you taught on tonight. When you said Jesus tells us to forgive others or else he won't forgive us, it hit me. My brother used to abuse me when I was a child, and I've always sworn that the next time

I saw him would be at his funeral. Today they called me and he's in the hospital and may not live. I can't go . . ." His voice trailed off.

I've known this pastor many years and he's always seemed to have a cloud of despair hanging over him. He'd had family tragedies, financial struggles, and what seemed to be in many ways an unproductive ministry. Yet, he is a good brother and I care for him. As I taught on the Lord's Prayer (Matthew 6:9–13), Jesus' words immediately impacted him, especially, "For if you forgive men when they sin against you, your heavenly Father will also forgive you. But if you do not forgive men their sins, your Father will not forgive your sins" (Matthew 6:14, 15).

"Brother," I said, "I can't tell you what to do, but I can take care of things here for the next few days." Miracles followed. He went to the hospital, met his brother's wife, and was told that his brother recently came to Jesus and would want to see him. Unfortunately, his brother was in a coma. When my friend prayed beside his brother, his brother regained consciousness! They prayed together, and gave and received forgiveness. The brother slipped back into the coma and within a few days he passed into glory.

> "But if you do not forgive men their sins, your Father will not forgive your sins."
> (Matthew 6:15)

Years later when our paths crossed, I found the pastor to be a new man a man set free! The Lord had opened up a new ministry for him in the local jail with an effective outreach to inmates and officers alike. His attitude at church was transformed. He had life and purpose again.

Are you harboring an unforgiving spirit?

Prayer:
Reveal to me any areas where I need to forgive, and set me free.
Help me forgive as you forgive, and not harbor an unforgiving spirit.

Chief Lee Callahan, Burlington, MA; Fellowship of
Christian Firefighters International Regional
Director / International Board Member

LISTEN TO THIS!

*Whether on the job or at home, the same principles apply:
love, respect, and really listening with interest*

GREAT LEADERS listen to their followers and respect their input. Whether in business, emergency first response, or family situations, true leadership includes an ability to listen.

Everyone is a leader in some aspect of life. As that leader, do you listen to others? Do you listen to those you hope will follow you? Do your co-workers know you value their input? Or are you authoritarian, letting everybody know it is "my way or the highway"?

If that is your *modus operandi* I predict you won't have many followers. Clearly, you will be a better leader if you value the contributions of those around you.

Should you act on each and every thought, idea, and suggestion you receive? Of course not! If you did, you'd be jumping in a lake several times a day. A successful leader must be able to get to the substance of ideas in order to listen and reflect on whether those views might work.

Discerning the merits of others' input requires attentively listening and asking questions, especially regarding potential pitfalls and implementation challenges, and then praying. A prayer (even a quick one) can give you guidance from the Holy Spirit.

> "After the earthquake came a fire, but the LORD was not in the fire. And after the fire came a gentle whisper."
> (1 Kings 19:12)

Whether on the job or at home, the same principles apply: love, respect, and carefully listening with interest.

As first responders, effective, on-the-spot decision making is greatly influenced by how well we listen. The Golden Rule addresses this: "And just as you want men to do to you, you also do to them likewise" (Luke 6:31 NKJV). If you want to be heard, hear someone first. Lead by example!

The ability and willingness to listen is a good starting point. Getting others to feel empowered by their contribution to the cause is another trait of a leader. How can you get them involved and accept what you are trying to involve them in if they don't feel that you listen to them?

Prayer:
A good listener! Lord, that is what I seek to be. Help me lead in a way pleasing to you and therefore to those whom you place under my leadership. Help me listen to others' ideas and, as I do, to stay tuned to what the Holy Spirit is saying. God, as you communicate with me in a still (soft) voice, may I be a good listener.

JULY 18

Craig Duck, Lieutenant, Engine Co. 11 – Washington, DC, Fire Department; Fellowship of Christian Firefighters International Atlantic States Regional Director / International Board Member

APPROVED WORKMEN
Daily challenged to study and live by God's Word

OCCASIONALLY firefighters receive orders or memorandums from the fire chief explaining a new fire department policy or procedure. Many times, as the firefighters read and discuss them, heated discussions ensue. Some simple and easy-to-understand orders regarding topics such as new hydrants, promotions, or special events, they agree with and move on. Occasionally the fire chief puts out a difficult order that creates controversy. After careful study, some accept the special order and agree with it. Others interpret it as bad or even potentially ruining the department. But ultimately the chief made the decision, and firefighters must follow those orders.

> "Do your best to present yourself to God as one approved, a workman who does not need to be ashamed and who correctly handles the word of truth." (2 Timothy 2:15)

As Christians, God's Word is our ultimate life guide. Whether we strongly agree with or struggle with some of God's guidelines and ways, he is our Chief. "For he chose us in him before the creation of the world to be holy and blameless in his sight . . . to the praise of his glorious grace" (Ephesians 1:4, 6). As his chosen, we need to read, study, and obey his Word.

As firefighters/EMTs we need to spend time studying to improve our skills, to prepare for a class, or to take a promotional test. Typically the more we study, the better we will do on that test.

The Christian life is similar to those tests we study for. The people who "pass" and do well are the ones who put honest work into their studying.

Have you ever worked with Christians who truly have their lives all together? Chances are they are students of God's Word. That's not to say they're perfect; they're just trying to live by what the Bible says. Often I feel as if I'm in the spotlight when I share who I am in Christ and refuse to take part in workplace activities that go against God's Word. Ever been there? It can be quite uncomfortable, challenging, and humbling. It is then I more fully understand my need to know the Bible. To correctly handle his Word, I know beyond a doubt I must read, study, and apply it as I would a work training manual. My life depends on it.

Prayer:
Help me to be as diligent a student of your Word as I am of my fire/EMS training manuals. May I correctly handle your Word and effectively apply the fire and medical skills I've learned.

J U L Y   1 9

Chaplain Marc Santorella, Firefighter Danvers Fire Department, MA; Public Fire and Life Safety Educator and Certified Fire Instructor Level 1

HOCUS FOCUS
At first glance they seem identical

A PICTURE PUZZLE, "Hocus Focus," once found in the Sunday comics, involved two pictures side-by-side that at first glance seemed identical. The objective was to find their subtle differences. I thought of this puzzle while returning from a men's retreat. Attendees, much like friends at home, had different levels of education, and careers varying from computer engineers, construction workers, health care professionals, to firefighters. Some struggled with finances, marriage and family problems, and/or the painful consequences caused by pornography, alcohol, and drugs. Some dealt with anger and hate issues. They were much

267

like any other random group found in your own neighborhood, social club, or firehouse.

But what made them different? I knew the obvious—they were Christians. Jesus was the difference.

What about those who don't seek God? Their struggles are real. On the surface their issues appear no different than those facing the Christians. So, what's the difference? In addition to the gift of Jesus, what is it Christians have that makes Christians different?

Hope!

The world sifts through mountains of self-help programs and books on how to deal with everything from weight loss, finance, making a marriage work, to raising children. In the end they, like Christians, seek that same thing.

> "For I am the least of the apostles and do not even deserve to be called an apostle, because I persecuted the church of God." (1 Corinthians 15:9)

Hope!

Fortunately, many Christian authors address this subject. Authentic Christian books and programs come back to the same resource: Scripture. You know they're genuine when the answers given are not the author's creation but from God's Word. As humans we don't have the answers. We'd never claim to have the inside scoop on any life-changing discovery, excepting of course a relationship with Jesus Christ. Christians continue to search and find answers from the same source: the Bible.

Remember that those we learn about in God's Word were just ordinary people like us. It's easy to fall into the trap of thinking they were extraordinary and therefore interacted with God in ways we're not capable of. This is not true.

The apostle Paul writes to the church in Rome that we have peace with God through Jesus Christ. Paul does not in any way identify himself as anyone more special than anyone else. In fact, Paul makes it very clear that he considers himself one of the last God should consider for favor.

Prayer:
*Please use me, Lord, an ordinary person, to share the
difference you make in a person's life, whether at the station,
on call, or at home. May that difference be clear and
not hidden like those in a hocus focus puzzle.*

Reverend Wayne Detzler, PhD, Chaplain (Retired) –
Charlotte, NC, Fire Department; Fellowship of
Christian Firefighters Regional Director

ONCE I WAS BLIND

His eyes were opened

TANGLED CARS and broken bodies littered the intersection in a nearby suburb. Several pieces of equipment were on scene as medics and firefighters scrambled all over.

"Get the Jaws of Life," the lieutenant shouted. He grabbed a hydraulic line, ready to make the hookup. Then he noticed what seemed to be a jam in the line, so he gently tapped the coupling on the ground. It was a standard, if not approved, practice. Usually it opened the clogged hose.

Whoosh! Fluid shot out of the hose. It sprayed hydraulic oil and dirt all over the lieutenant's face. Worst of all, it shot straight into his unprotected eyes. "I'm blind," he screamed. "I can't see a thing!"

Medics rushed to the side of our helpless leader; quickly they checked his eyes and gently covered them with sterile compresses. "Take him to the hospital," the medics ordered. "Take him now." I guided him to my car and belted him in. To combat shock and quiet his chills, we turned the heat up. Aware of the urgency, I sped to a nearby emergency room where a team had already been alerted.

Quickly nurses got him into a wheelchair and rushed us both into a special eye treatment room. In the dim light they carefully removed the compresses, while mopping the dirt and grime from his face. "Can

> "One thing I do know. I was blind but now I see." (John 9:25)

you see anything?" they asked nervously. "Try to open your eyes."

"No," he replied, "I am absolutely blind." Gently they began to irrigate his eyes with a saline solution. They persisted until he felt relief. Little by little the pain lessened. His vision returned. Finally, the doctor could examine his eyes. No permanent damage was done. His eyes would need to be covered for a day or two, but he was able to see again.

Spiritual blindness is devastating and leads to choices that damage relationships and careers, and cause folks to make eternally damaging decisions. More importantly, unlike blindness caused by physical circumstances, you have a choice. Jesus is described as "the Light of the world." He alone can give sight to the spiritually blind.

Prayer:
Jesus, thank you for opening my eyes to see you in all your glory.

Rev. Joe Smaha, Chaplain/Fire Inspector/Firefighter/EMT/
Hazmat Specialist – Paramus, NJ, Fire Department;
Fire Instructor – Bergen County, NJ, Fire Academy;
Pastor – Community Church of Paramus

CISM

The answer to haunting critical incidents

FIREFIGHTERS, police officers, and emergency medical technicians witness things in the line of duty many people cannot even imagine. Death, destruction, traumatic injuries, and devastation are part of the job. Seeing people on the worst days of their lives comes with the uniform. People don't call us when things are going well. They don't invite the fire department to a barbeque, unless the barbeque grill is on fire. When you add to this equation the times that emergency responders find themselves in the face of danger to themselves and their team members, it's no wonder the burnout rate is so high.

> "So with you: Now is your time of grief, but I will see you again and you will rejoice, and no one will take away your joy." (John 16:22)

In my position at the Bergen County Fire Academy, I, along with another fire instructor, am in charge of teaching Critical Incident Stress Management (CISM) to each Firefighter 1 class. This class warns the new recruits about the stressful incidents and situations they'll encounter in the fire service. It's also designed to warn them of the pitfalls of the job and give them some tools and resources to help get them through those difficult times.

As a firefighter, I've been through those difficult critical incidents that haunt you long after they're over. I honestly don't know how emergency responders get through these critical incidents without a personal relationship with the Lord. Not because God makes the incident easier, but because he gives us the strength and power to endure.

270

As believers, God gives us promises that assure us of Jesus' presence with us and his care for us. In Hebrews 13:5 he tells us, "Never will I leave you; never will I forsake you." Knowing that God has our back gives us confidence during the most trying and dangerous incidents.

King David proclaims, "God is our refuge and strength, an ever-present help in trouble. Therefore we will not fear" (Psalm 46:1, 2).

If you feel alone, lack confidence, or feel your own strength is insufficient, call on God. He is just a prayer away and, as is written in 1 Peter 5:7, you can give all your cares to God because he cares for you.

Prayer:
Praise God, you are bigger than all my troubles in any or all situations. God, you are my Refuge and Strength to perform my duties as a firefighter regardless of the circumstances! In times of grief, thank you for your promise that no one can take away my joy.

JULY 22

Dr. Jonathan Newell, Missionary Malawi, Africa

THE LIGHT THAT SHINES IN THE DARKNESS
His light shone brightly in my darkest moment

IT IS OFTEN in the darkest moments of one's life the light of the Lord Jesus shines its brightest. This was certainly my experience one night in 2009. Three men armed with at least one gun and other weapons, using crowbars, smashed down one of the outside doors of our house in Blantyre, Malawi, and then the door to the passageway to our bedrooms. They were probably on drugs of some kind and were very worked up. I praise the Lord, however, I was able to get my wife and three children locked away in the bathroom, where they remained silently hiding while the thieves rampaged through the house.

There were so many instances of the Lord's protection that night that it continues to amaze me. The thieves kept asking me where my wife and children were, but they never demanded an answer at gunpoint. They only tried the door to the bathroom where my wife and children were hiding once. Then they left it alone. They kept demanding that I lie down on the floor, but I never did. Unbelievably, they never forced me to do so. They shouted at me that they were going to kill me, but I was never touched

271

even once by them. The entire time I had an unusual sense of inner peace. I was able to converse with the men and try to keep them as calm as possible. It remains my conviction that these men were permitted to steal from us, but they were not able to touch us in any way—and for this we thank the Lord with all our hearts. I vividly remember one of the men actually speaking to me respectfully and backing away from me, almost as if there were others present in the room at the time. For me, the Lord was there that night. He stood beside me in a way I'd never experienced before. His light shone brightly in the darkness of that night and his light overcame the darkness for me and my family.

> "The light shines in the darkness, but the darkness has not understood it." (John 1:5)

That light is available to all. When you encounter any danger whatsoever, God's light is there in your darkest moment. Call on him.

Prayer:
Heavenly Father, help me never to despair, but to look for the light of your Son in the darkest moments of my life and the darkest corners of this world.

JULY 23

Melissa Williamson, Wife of Don Williamson, Apparatus Operator – Vestavia Hills, AL, Fire Department; Lieutenant – City of Chelsea, AL; FCFI Alabama Regional Director

WHAT WAS I DOING?
Take up our tambourines and start dancing

WHEN MY husband, Don, decided nearly two decades ago to become a full-time, paid firefighter after years of volunteering, neither of us ever looked back or questioned the decision. We knew it was exactly what God had designed for him to do. Were there adjustments and issues along the way? Absolutely!

First of all, there were my sleepless nights when he was at the station. That got easier when we got a dog and even easier when our first child came along. But then came the nights (years of them) when I had to do most of the getting up with babies and toddlers because Don was either at work, just coming off shift, or about to go back on shift.

272

But the worst of it, by far, was the "single parenting" of three kids. And trust me—I've done plenty of complaining about that. Those of you who have children know what I mean: day after day and night after night with little or no relief from settling disputes, doling out discipline, getting kids off to school and extracurricular activities, and getting kids fed, bathed, and off to bed after homework is done. There have been numerous events Dad missed in spite of his best efforts to be there. At times, I've called him at the station just to vent or cry out my frustration over the phone.

When reading God's Word and applying it to my feelings, I could feel his words change to relate to me in this way: "My child, you say you believe I'm an awesome God and everything is under my control. You trust me to take care of Don on his job. Do you think I can't meet the needs of you and your children in his absence?"

> "The Lord appeared to us in the past, saying: 'I have loved you with an everlasting love; I have drawn you with loving-kindness. I will build you up again and you will be rebuilt, O Virgin Israel. Again you will take up your tambourines and go out to dance with the joyful.'" (Jeremiah 31:3, 4)

What had I been doing? Without realizing it, I was resenting Don's job and the role I'd so earnestly desired as a mom.

Remember that God will "meet all your needs according to his glorious riches in Christ Jesus" (Philippians 4:19). God loves you with an everlasting love and wants you to stop complaining and "take up your tambourines and go out to dance with the joyful" (Jeremiah 31:4).

Prayer:
Let me take up my tambourine and start dancing! Let me be understanding of the role of a firefighter, the spouse, and the children. God, help me rest securely in your everlasting love.

*Reverend Wayne Detzler, PhD, Chaplain (Retired) –
Charlotte, NC, Fire Department; Fellowship of
Christian Firefighters Regional Director*

SAVED FROM THE FIRE

When God answers prayer

IN RURAL North Carolina, many farms still dot the countryside, adding a picturesque touch to the tapestry of the scenery. Red barns stand out against the perpetual green and tall silos often stand beside them. For city guys, these farms look rather old-fashioned.

> "You, O LORD, have delivered my soul from death, my eyes from tears, my feet from stumbling."
> (Psalm 116:8)

"Fire in the silo." The volunteer fire department received an urgent call. The highly flammable wheat chaff had exploded into an inferno. When they rolled up on the scene, the silo was full of fire. It was shooting out the top. Quickly they hooked up to the tanker truck and started to pour water on the blaze.

Finally, the firefighters were able to climb up the outside of the silo and get a clear shot on the hot spots down below. Three of the young guys fought fire, trying to hit each erupting flame. They almost had it under control, when the unthinkable happened.

One of the guys fell into the silo. It looked as if he would certainly be killed. Suppression turned into rescue. Firefighters gingerly let themselves down into the fire scene. They carefully lifted their comrade out of harm's way, but his burns seemed serious. His survival was in doubt.

The chief called for a debriefing and my team was scrambled for this mission. When we arrived, the atmosphere was grim at best, hopeless at worst. As we asked our questions, there seemed to be little earthly hope.

Midway through the debriefing the door opened. The injured firefighter walked in, and the whole room erupted in applause. The Lord had answered our prayers for our friend and fellow firefighter.

Nothing is more basic than a miracle of rescue. Those miracles come in different ways for different eternal needs. On this call, the Lord was not ready to call the man home. His miraculous entrance was a reminder the Lord is always near those in danger and as we cry out to him, he saves us.

Prayer:
Lord, thank you for being near to me in time of danger.

274

Steve Kidd, Firefighter Orange County Fire and Rescue, Florida; Central Florida Chapter of the Fellowship of Christian Firefighters; Author of the Carbusters video series

ARE YOU HUMBLE ENOUGH TO SERVE?

We all face types of alarms that simply rub us the wrong way

INTEGRITY, A quality found in most firefighters, means "honesty, sincerity, and completeness." Anyone who works day in and day out helping people they don't know must have a high degree of integrity. People trust us with their most precious possessions, including their lives. They call us heroes.

A reporter once asked a salty old fire lieutenant if he had any heroes. The lieutenant looked the young reporter straight in the eye and said, "Firefighters don't have heroes; we *are* heroes." Not a very humble reply if you ask me.

False humility is unhealthy to spiritual well-being. In reality, anything false is not good. Scripture tells us to be humble before God, recognize his power and position in our life, and serve him by loving him and his creatures.

Each day first responders are called upon to serve our fellow man. Not every call makes the morning news—quite the contrary. While we often find ourselves

> "Therefore, as God's chosen people, holy and dearly loved, clothe yourselves with compassion, kindness, humility, gentleness and patience."
> (Colossians 3:12)

shaking our heads at the petty reasons people call 9-1-1, we must always remember that it is an emergency to the caller. A humble person acting in a Christian manner does not scoff at another person's suffering. Jesus washed the feet of his disciples to teach them the importance of doing God's work by serving each other. He never scoffed when someone came to him.

The question should not be if you are good enough to be a Christian firefighter. The question should be, "Are you humble enough to serve?"

We all face types of alarms that simply rub us the wrong way. For some, EMS calls that involve someone vomiting from too much alcohol just turns them completely off, making them less than compassionate to the suffering person. Others become upset at being called for a water salvage—to assist someone because their toilet has overflowed.

What are some of the types of alarms that make you resent the person who called for help? If you are a supervisor, how can you serve those of lesser rank than you? Do you find it humbling and/or difficult to resist temptation at work and to adhere to your Christian integrity and honesty? What areas of humility do you need to develop?

Prayer:
*When calls create a sense of resentment, when humility needs
to be my calling card, not peer acceptance and earthly rewards,
I thank you for your Word that admonishes me to act
with integrity befitting one of your children.*

Dwayne Clemmons, Adjunct Instructor – Virginia Department of Fire Programs; Founder – DMC Ministries; Author of Exploits, Jesus Rides in an Ambulance, and Utterances from the Throne Room; Volunteer in Fire and EMS for forty years in Virginia

GRACE AND TRUTH: THE DYNAMIC DUO
The way to overcoming obstacles

A HUGE MOUNTAIN of sawdust burning uncontrollably and a concerned forestry department confronted us when we arrived at a sawmill. Their concern became ours. We were well aware that if this fire spread out of the compound area, it would take off across an adjacent field, posing a threat to a nearby housing area. The temperature and humidity were both in the nineties with fifteen-mile-an-hour winds. Fatigue set in almost immediately, and the initial attack didn't progress well. We knew the only way to whip this thing was with enormous quantities of water, which we didn't have. We backed into a defensive position and calculated how to get a handle on this fire, and Incident Command (IC) requested additional companies to help set up a rural water supply operation. As the fire grew, a ladder truck became the primary method of attack. A massive water shuttle operation with multiple drop tanks and about twenty tankers was initiated. After two hours the situation was marked "under control."

Overwhelming obstacles are not foreign in the lives of first responders. But, if we know where the source is, we can obtain the grace needed to make it through. Hezekiah knew where his strength came from. After he cried to the Lord, "The word of the LORD came to Isaiah: 'Go and tell Hezekiah . . . 'I have heard your prayer and seen your tears; I will add fifteen years to your life. And I will deliver you and this city from the hand of the king of Assyria. I will defend this city'" (Isaiah 38:4, 5). Hezekiah was on the verge of death when God sent the needed resource in the form of Isaiah the prophet. Hezekiah reacted appropriately, his life was spared, and God delivered and defended the entire city. A classic example of the dynamic duo: grace and truth.

> "The Word became flesh and made his dwelling among us. We have seen his glory, the glory of the One and Only, who came from the Father, full of grace and truth." (John 1:14)

Firefighters know the potential of finding themselves in difficult and precarious situations. It's the very nature of our job. I wonder how many unsaved firefighters truthfully understand the consequences of what they do.

As Christians, we've been assigned the task of illuminating this dark and dying world with the light of Christ. We have to live our lives so others understand we're not in control—he is. We must demonstrate that the glory of God is with us always.

Prayer:
*Lord, I rely on you during my difficult and challenging
calls so, in all things, you receive the praise and glory.*

JULY 27

*Bob Crum, Co-founder – Fellowship of Christian Firefighters
International (Retired) – Denver Fire Department*

WELL DONE, GOOD AND FAITHFUL SERVANT

*Faithfulness and perseverance reap
the greatest reward of all*

OUR PERSONAL suffering for the Gospel and our Lord faces a reality check when we read 2 Corinthians 11:22–29 and learn what the apostle Paul endured to preserve God's truth. Because of his commitment to our Lord, five times he received thirty-nine lashes, three times he was beaten with rods, once he was stoned and left for dead. The list continues with frequent imprisonment, three shipwrecks, hunger, thirst, extreme cold, nakedness, and weariness. Paul daily felt concern for all the churches. Those things should have been enough to make him throw in the towel, or, at least, cool his witness. In spite of all his trials, Paul ran the race to win and he persevered to the end. His commitment to the Lord Jesus Christ never wavered.

Who of us has been called to suffer as Paul did? Mostly we're comfortable in our service and commitment to the Lord. As Christian firefighters the worst things we suffer are negative responses to something we say or do, or perhaps a little isolation and ridicule when we choose not to join in things God would frown upon. Compared with the suffering of the apostle Paul, this is nothing.

We need to be obedient to the vision God has given us. Matthew 28:19 clearly states it is our responsibility to go and tell what the Lord has done and seek to glorify Jesus Christ.

"Well done, good and faithful servant." (Matthew 25:21)

How do we glorify Christ? It is a complex concern. It may take brainstorming with other local Christians and ascertaining the needs for your workplace. It definitely involves permeating it with a Christian atmosphere, so a conversation about the Lord is as acceptable in the office as a conversation about hunting, fishing, sports, family, or anything else.

And, it starts with you! You are the one who can cause it to happen in the place where you work. Your life should be a demonstration every day of what Jesus is for you. Will it be easy? No! Will there be persecution? Maybe! Will you be able to live that kind of life? Through Christ you can. Will it be worth it? When you finish the race and stand before Christ you will know your faithfulness and perseverance have been rewarded when he says, "Well done!"

Prayer:
To glorify you in the fire service and in my life—that is my goal.
I thank you that you are with me regardless of
challenges this commitment entails.

Reverend Wayne Detzler, PhD, Chaplain (Retired) –
Charlotte, NC, Fire Department; Fellowship of
Christian Firefighters Regional Director

THEY NEED A SHEPHERD

When no one seems to care

"9-1-1," the pager screamed at me. This was the signal for urgency. When the need could not be postponed, the dispatcher sent the code "9-1-1." I was speaking at a Thanksgiving breakfast in a posh suburb. But the pager persisted, "9-1-1."

Quickly, I excused myself and made for a phone. (These were the days before cell phones). "Chaplain, get back now," the dispatcher instructed me, "it's a really bad scene and we need you now."

When I arrived the officer filled me in, and he spoke in bullet points. "She missed the school bus," he spoke of the eleven-year-old girl. "When her mother looked for her, she was still in the bathroom, but she didn't respond."

The panic-stricken mother broke into the bathroom, pushing hard on the door. On the floor was her daughter; unconscious and nonresponsive. Immediately the mother dialed 9-1-1. In minutes firefighters and EMTs were on the scene.

> "He gathers the lambs in his arms and carries them close to his heart." (Isaiah 40:11)

All attempts to revive the little girl were futile, so they transported her to a nearby hospital. The preliminary diagnosis was a heart attack. Later it was discovered that the little one had ingested her mother's drugs. She had died of a drug overdose.

The mother was inconsolable as she realized her aberrant behavior had snatched away her young daughter. Legal punishments were nothing compared with the self-condemnation she suffered.

People find many rationalizations for participating in sinful activities. Key among those rationalizations is, "It's my life and as long as I don't hurt others, then what should they care?" The truth is that we do not live in a vacuum, and our sins always have far-reaching tentacles. Others are always affected, maybe not as seriously as the woman's daughter, but others do suffer from our transgressions.

What can we say about that dear little girl whose childish mistake turned out to be fatal?

279

My mind kept thinking about that child dying alone with no response from her mother and how alone she must have felt. Then I realized that only God can care for children at times like this. He gently took her home, where she could never again suffer the abuse of a sin-sick world.

Prayer:
Loving Father, care for the children in our lives today. Protect them from harm. Give me the strength I need when similar calls bring emotions too difficult for words. As I continue to process such sadness, I call on you, Lord, to comfort me and those affected by such a tragedy.

JULY 29

Daniel A. Clegg, Rural-Metro EMT; Engineer/EMT–Indianapolis Fire Department (Retired); Fellowship of Christian Firefighters Regional Director / International Board Member

DAY ONE

This job is more than adventure, excitement, serving, and job security

THE DAY I had dreamed about arrived—*Day 1* as an Indianapolis firefighter. Concern, mingled with apprehension, was the theme as I headed for the station. Questions bombarded my thoughts: *What am I getting myself into? Am I capable of handling the emergency and fire situations that lie ahead? Will I measure up to the department's high standards?*

My uncle, a forty-year veteran who went down as a line-of-duty fatality, said, "Dan, the best career any person can have is being a firefighter." My brother also took great pride in his fire career. I knew firefighting offered adventure, excitement, an opportunity to serve my community, and job security. I focused on these things as I entered Firehouse 12.

No sooner had I arrived than the alerts sounded, the bell rang, and my heart started pounding.

"Step on and hang on!" The lieutenant yelled. I was told the proper way to ride a back step is on your tiptoes (a practice no longer allowed). I never imagined that my first call would be a DOA (dead on arrival). I did my job, praying I'd never be insensitive to those who gathered at such a scene.

280

The next call of Day 1 was for a new convertible completely consumed by flames. The driver's eyes reflected that his dream car was being destroyed.

At sunset, the bells sounded for a fully involved residence fire. Sadly I watched the fire destroy all the material possessions this family had worked so hard for. "We've lost everything!" the young mother of two wept, "and we don't have insurance."

Questions flooded my mind. *Do I really want to spend my career witnessing the loss of life, the loss of dreams, and the loss of property? Am I cut out to be a firefighter?*

The answer was an undeniable, "YES!"

Day 1! A stark eye opener! A reality check! A realization my challenges lay in

> "The Spirit of the Lord is on me, because he has anointed me to preach good news to the poor."
> (Luke 4:18)

much more than fighting flames and administering first aid! This job is about much more than adventure, excitement, serving my community, and job security. It's about people, heartache, loss, and the opportunity to share a small glimmer of hope for a brighter tomorrow. Yes, this is the career for me and this is what the fire service is all about.

Prayer:
Lord, may your Spirit descend upon me. Let me do my job with you at my side and share your Good News and hope through my actions and words with all whom you bring in my path.

JULY 30

Fire Chaplain John Kalashian, Caledonia, Wisconsin; Founder/Director – Men with a Burden, a ministry to the homeless men at the Milwaukee Rescue Mission; Founder/President – Corvettes for Christ

THE NEXT CALL
May the ultimate First Responder be on your crew

AS A NEW chaplain, I was green and fresh out of the box and about to experience firsthand a day in the life of a Caledonia, Wisconsin, firefighter. To soothe my anxiety, I poured a cup of coffee and listened as the incoming and outgoing shifts conducted their briefing and debriefing.

Preparation, a central theme in firefighting, involves engine pressure testing, aerial ladder checks, drug accountability and inventory, SCBA (self-contained breathing apparatus) bleed-down tests, radio and emergency light checks, and locking and tagging of medical and narcotic trays.

Imagine answering a call without the necessary equipment or finding your instruments or tools in a state of unreadiness! People who call 9-1-1 expect a professional lifesaving response a firefighter who responds quickly and fully equipped. While testing and preparation reduce the likelihood of equipment failure, it doesn't guarantee absence of fault. There is absolutely nothing made by man that is perfect and free from failure—notice I said "made by man."

What if you had access to something that saved lives and rescued successfully 100 hundred percent of the time and was available 24/7? Sound too good to be true? Look no further—God gave that lifesaving performance and guaranteed reliability in his Son, Jesus Christ!

> "Now to him who is able to do immeasurably more than all we ask or imagine, according to his power that is at work within us, to him be glory." (Ephesians 3:20, 21)

Jesus Christ is the ultimate First Responder. He was fully tested and prepared. "Because he himself suffered when he was tempted, he is able to help those who are being tempted" (Hebrews 2:18). What's more, he is willing and able: "I have come that they may have life, and have it to the full" (John 10:10). Christ is able to give life. Additionally comforting is the fact that he is ready and waiting: "Come to me, all you who are weary and burdened, and I will give you rest. Take my yoke upon you and learn from me, for I am gentle and humble in heart, and you will find rest for your souls" (Matthew 11:28, 29). Christ says, "Come"—meaning anytime. He doesn't have limited hours of operation—he can be your First Responder 24/7. His phone line is always open. Jesus offers a successful rescue if you make your "next call" to him. He'll respond quickly, fully equipped, and always at his best. This godly guarantee is found in his Word.

Prayer:
Thank you that I can always call on you, the ultimate
First Responder, and know that blessings will follow.

282

*Reverend Wayne Detzler, PhD, Chaplain (Retired) –
Charlotte, NC, Fire Department; Fellowship of
Christian Firefighters Regional Director*

LET THE CHILDREN COME TO ME

I learned how much Jesus loves children

THEY WERE motionless. No one moved a muscle. Tough, burly cops stood silent. "Can do" firefighters did nothing. High-speed EMTs just stood there. And they were all crammed into a postage-stamp-sized, two-room apartment in a tacky house.

Motionless, a fragile baby lay on a chair. She did not move. Her color was washed out, her little face peaceful. She was dead, a victim of SIDS (sudden infant death syndrome). The room was silent. A sense of awe and sadness hung heavy in the air.

No parents were in sight. So, I asked, "Where are her parents? Are they here?" The lieutenant pointed to closed doors, doors that led to a bedroom. In the silence one could hear the sound of quiet, sad sobbing

Not knowing what to expect, I knocked quietly on the door. A soft answer came back, "Come in." I gently opened the door. Sitting on the bed was a young couple, far too young to handle the death of their little one. They were probably not out of their teens, and no family member was there to comfort them.

> "Let the little children come to me, and do not hinder them."
> (Mark 10:14)

"Can I come in?" I asked. It is always good to leave the control in their hands, especially when their life is totally out of control. "I won't stay long," I continued. "I'm a chaplain, a pastor with the fire department." The dad, almost a boy, nodded, and I knelt before them. For several minutes I wept, saying nothing at all.

"Can I pray with you?" I finally asked them. They nodded through their tears. Simply and briefly I thanked God for their little baby. I assured them she was safe in Jesus' loving arms.

"Why?" people often ask when a child dies. The story of King David's small child is helpful (2 Samuel 12:15–23). The child is an innocent victim of an evil world. But there is good news: The child passes from this world into the very presence of the Lord. The child is spared future suffering and hardship. Yes, Jesus loves them—the Bible tells us so.

Prayer:
Lord, thank you for the babies in our lives.
Thank you that you love them so much.

Captain Raul A. Angulo – Seattle Fire Department;
Fellowship of Christian Firefighters Regional
Director / International Board Member

"CIRCUMCISED FOREHEAD"

Laughter that eased the tension

WHILE WORKING Aid 5 in downtown Seattle, I was listening to a Christian radio station airing an Old Testament study on Abraham and circumcision. As I listened intently about how science validated circumcision on the eighth day, the bell suddenly hit for an alarm for a two-car motor vehicle accident. One of the cars involved contained a father and his five- and six-year-old sons. The father suffered back pain and facial and neck injuries. He was immediately transported by ambulance to the emergency room. The two boys were not seriously injured but, since they had multiple fragments of glass embedded in their foreheads from the shattered windshield, we transported in Aid 5.

As we arrived at the emergency room, an onslaught of doctors and nurses rushed to meet us. I couldn't figure out what all the commotion was about—it was only a basic life support (BLS) run. As the doctors checked the boys, I heard them say, "There's no glass embedded in the foreskin!"

> "I am about to open my mouth; my words are on the tip of my tongue. My words come from an upright heart; my lips sincerely speak what I know." (Job 33:2, 3)

"Foreskin! What are you talking about?" I asked.

"The short report came over as "transporting two kids with glass embedded in the foreskin."

As I pointed to the boys' foreheads I said, "I'm sure you're mistaken. I said glass in the forehead. Look!"

"We're doctors. We don't make mistakes like that. You said 'foreskin'!"

I couldn't imagine I'd ever say such a thing over the radio but then, this would explain all the hullabaloo at the ER on our arrival. I remained silent.

After we completed our responsibilities, I said, "Let's make a stop at the fire alarm center. I want to replay that tape."

Sure enough, there was my clear, audible voice saying, "This is Aid 5. We are transporting two young males, five and six, with glass embedded in the foreskin. ETA 5 minutes."

Thanks a lot, Abraham!

Mistakes happen and, if we're fortunate, the end result is not harmful. In this instance, it led to laughter that eased the tension of the run and hurt no one. It is, however, an example of our need to make sure the utterances from our lips are carefully spoken.

Prayer:
When I open my mouth, may my words come out upright of heart, sincere, and edifying to you and to those you bring in my path. And may my mistakes result in laughter and not harm.

AUGUST 2

*Reverend Wayne Detzler, PhD, Chaplain (Retired) –
Charlotte, NC, Fire Department; Fellowship of
Christian Firefighters Regional Director*

ALL ALONE EXCEPT FOR GOD
When no one is there to help

IT'S A FATAL fire," the pager prepared me. I made my way across the city as day was dawning. A low-income home was smoldering when I arrived. Only the charred remains of the home distinguished it from the poverty surrounding it. Firefighters stood by gazing in disbelief at the fire scene.

"What's happened?" I tried to open conversation, but the firefighters just pointed and said nothing. My eyes followed the stare of the crew members, but I saw only a burned-out children's bedroom. Then I noticed something protruding from a closet, two little feet. They looked like a doll, but they belonged to a small child.

"The family is Cambodian," the incident commander briefed me. "The parents have already been taken to the hospital, but the dead girl's brother is at another home. Could you pick him up at the neighbor's house and go to the hospital?"

I took a police officer along with me to get the child. We were astounded to find another Cambodian family with several sleeping on the living room floor.

When we arrived at the hospital the mother of the family was sitting in the waiting room, shocked and dismayed by the loss of her child. Still she wanted to explain how the little one had died. Softly, the grieving mother described that her little girl was mentally challenged. She couldn't find her way out of the fire. In an effort to escape the blazes, she hid in her clothes closet. This turned out to be her fatal mistake.

> "Though I walk through the valley of the shadow of death, I will fear no evil." (Psalm 23:4)

We went with the mother to see her husband, who was being treated at the same hospital. He said nothing, not a word, to console his wife. Nor did he touch her, or even look at her. He held her responsible for the fire. He blamed her for the death of their little girl.

In the midst of all of this, Sam, pastor of a Cambodian church in our town, arrived. His influence reached far beyond his small congregation. Gently he touched the broken lives around us, speaking softly and praying to the Lord. He truly brought the presence of the Lord into the chaotic scene of death.

Prayer:
Lord, help me to remember how near you are,
especially when children suffer.

AUGUST 3

Rick Barton, Fire Safety Officer; Rick Barton Ministries,
Gunnison, CO; Fellowship of Christian Firefighters
International Ambassador-at-Large

SEEDY CHARACTERS CAUGHT CHANGING THE WORLD

Jesus gave us the "seed" of the Word of God and salvation

CAN GOD really save my friend?" "What can I do? He's dying." All of us go through times of wondering or feeling inadequate when it comes to sharing our faith. It seems easier to just enjoy our Christian life and to hope that God sends "someone else" to help those around us who are lost in sin. This is the story of two volunteer firefighters/EMTs who didn't cop out.

This is about Deb and Ralph, two "seedy characters" who overcame those doubts and changed the face of eternity by an act of faith and obedience. You see, Deb and Ralph love their bright red firefighter Harleys. They also love the Lord. This couple picked up a motorcycle New Testament, *Hope for the Highway*, available from Biblica, and prayerfully took it to their friend, a motorcyclist, who was dying. They lay it next to his bed

> "I tell you, open your eyes and look at the fields! They are ripe for harvest. Even now the reaper draws his wages, even now he harvests the crop for eternal life." (John 4:35, 36)

and prayed for him. The man began to read the stories, eventually turning to the great news of the Gospels. In the days before his death, their friend yielded his life to the Savior! As he slipped from this world into the arms of his heavenly Father, he asked them to sing "The Old Rugged Cross" at his bedside, and once again at his funeral.

Imagine the tearful joy of these "seedy characters" as they saw the results of sharing the "seed" of God's Word with this man! They realized what Luke meant when he wrote that Jesus sent out the disciples "two by two ahead of him to every town and place where he was about to go" (Luke 10:1).

Jesus gave us the "seed" of the Word of God and salvation. Our assignment is to go to those he leads us to and share it with them. These are places and people he is preparing to come to! As Luke goes on to say, "The harvest is plentiful, but the workers are few." Can he count on us? Jesus is looking for more "seedy characters"! Will you be one of them?

Prayer:
Lord, count me among your seedy characters.

AUGUST 4

Craig Duck, Lieutenant, Engine Co. 11 – Washington, DC, Fire Department; Fellowship of Christian Firefighters International Atlantic States Regional Director / International Board Member

WHO'S DRIVING THE TRUCK?
Allowing God to have full control of one's life—especially at the firehouse

SOME PEOPLE join the fire service for excitement. Who wouldn't enjoy getting on a fire truck with lights flashing and sirens blaring?

288

The thrill of seeing people pull over as the fire truck comes by and the ability to go through red lights drives firefighters to stick around for many years. Driving a fire truck takes skill and experience; not just anyone can drive one. Fire trucks weigh in excess of twenty-eight thousand pounds and carry all sorts of lifesaving equipment that needs to be there when it counts.

As an officer, I remember the first time I rode in the officer seat of the fire truck. As we left the firehouse, responding on a box alarm, I had absolutely no control over the fire truck. I'm sure I could have screamed at the driver or barked out some order, but ultimately I had to trust the driver to get me to the emergency safely. The runs on which I tried to tell the driver what to do or how to drive usually ended with our company making a mistake. Over the years I've had to ride with many different types of drivers. There were those I felt needed more training in regards to safe speeds and road conditions, to those extremely safe drivers who got the company to the fire safely every time. Regardless, I learned I had to trust the drivers to do their job. Then the rest of our company could do our job.

> "Trust in the Lord with all your heart and lean not on your own understanding; in all your ways acknowledge him, and he will make your paths straight."
> (Proverbs 3:5, 6)

Our lives are like those fire trucks I've been riding on over the years. They are easily controlled by outside influences. Some Christian firefighters allow money, pride, selfish ambitions, or worldliness to drive them far from God. Believers need to allow God to control their lives in every way, whether at the firehouse or at home.

Jesus came "to shine on those living in darkness and in the shadow of death, to guide our feet into the path of peace" (Luke 1:79). God, the maker of heaven and Earth, knows what's best for our lives; let's give him full control of our lives. Let's resolve to let those around us know that God is driving our truck. Who's driving yours?

Prayer:
Help me, Lord, to allow you to have full control of my life so I can accomplish your perfect will in my life.

Daniel A. Clegg, Rural-Metro EMT; Engineer/EMT–Indianapolis Fire Department (Retired); Fellowship of Christian Firefighters Regional Director / International Board Member

KEYS

Unlocking the door to heaven

FIREFIGHTERS have keys: keys to fire apparatus, emergency vehicles, lockers, personal cars, homes . . . the list goes on and on. But the most valuable key to all is none other than Jesus Christ.

In Matthew 16:19 Jesus tells Peter, "I will give you the keys of the kingdom of heaven; whatever you bind on earth will be bound in heaven, and whatever you loose on earth will be loosed in heaven."

Peter was given the keys of the kingdom of heaven, which is salvation through Jesus Christ. Then he was given the command to share those keys with others, to bind them together in Christ's love, and to share the gift of salvation. Peter took this commission to heart. At Pentecost, Peter's preaching opened the door to three thousand souls. Later, in the house of Cornelius, he unlocked and opened wide the door to the Gentiles. As we read further of Peter's outreach we can only imagine the thousands of doors to heaven that were unlocked by his preaching, sharing, and example.

> "Therefore go and make disciples of all nations, baptizing them in the name of the Father and of the Son and of the Holy Spirit."
> (Matthew 28:19)

The fire service needs those keys to salvation. They need to know that whatever trials and tragedies they face, God wants to comfort them. At Jesus' ascension to heaven, he promised to send the Holy Spirit, the Comforter, who dwells in the lives of all who believe in their hearts and confess with their mouths that Jesus Christ is Lord. That is the key to having the Comforter dwell in our lives.

As Christians, God set before us a mission field of people with hearts that need our service. Let us, as Christians, by our witness and work, help unlock the door for others so they can find Christ and his gift of salvation and eternity. There is no higher calling or privilege than that.

Prayer:
You became my Lord and Savior when I learned of your unconditional love and believed in my heart that you are indeed

Lord. I know that salvation is through only you and that works will not open the door to heaven. Likewise I know that you want me to share this love with others and give them that precious key to peace and eternal life. Help me, Lord, as I allow Peter to be my example and reach out to the fire service.

Rick Barton, Fire Safety Officer; Rick Barton Ministries, Gunnison, CO; Fellowship of Christian Firefighters International Ambassador-at-Large

HE UNDERSTANDS MY HEART
He is always with you!

A TOUGH FIRE season with more than ninety days away from home, sleeping on the ground, working fourteen-hour days, eating off paper plates, and pounding up and down a hundred fire lines was nearly over. I love my job but I was beat—physically, mentally, and spiritually.

I'd fought food poisoning, bugs, spiders, sunburn, and sudden rainstorms. I'd blown two tires, had a flat in an ant pile, been stopped by corroded electrical wires, and had a muffler go out. I was ready for a real bed, inside plumbing, and most of all my wife and family. Being a wildland firefighter is one of my great joys in life, but I was ready for a break. The trouble was that I was the only safety officer on this fire. It was my responsibility, as part of the management team, to ensure the welfare of the crews and keep up with myriad meetings and materials. I couldn't leave. What could I do? I could take a hike!

> "Come to me, all you who are weary and burdened, and I will give you rest."
> (Matthew 11:28)

My primary responsibility was the safety of the crews on the line. Since they were felling dangerous hazard trees along popular hiking paths closed by the fire, I grabbed a tool, shouldered my web gear, and headed up the trail. Within an hour I reached the first saw team, chatted a few minutes, and checked out their safety awareness and qualifications for the size and type of tree they were cutting. Then, I headed on up the line.

By noon I was overlooking the small but beautiful Lake McGinnis. I pulled out a sandwich and my New Testament. In more than thirty seasons of fighting fire I've discovered I need both physical food and spiritual food. If I neglect the physical menu, I get weak and lose my resistance to sickness. If I neglect my spiritual menu, I get weak spiritually and hardships tend to drag me into loneliness and depression.

I opened to Matthew 11:28: "Come to me, all who are weary and burdened, and I will give you rest." As I read, I entered into his peace. He is with me. He understands my weary heart and body for he's been there.

As I poured out my thoughts and feelings to him, I sensed his presence and knew everything was going to be all right. Refreshed in my spirit and knowing his rest, I resumed my walk along the fire's edge.

Prayer:
*Lord, help me remember that you are always
with me and that true rest lies in you!*

AUGUST 7

*Reverend Wayne Detzler, PhD, Chaplain (Retired) –
Charlotte, NC, Fire Department; Fellowship of
Christian Firefighters Regional Director*

SERVING THE COMMUNITY
Helping a new generation to overcome

DEBRIEFING OF firefighters and medics after a run has emerged over the past few years. This process gives them a chance to talk about the stress and strain of life on the edge. In many cases this may help them avoid the high price of post-traumatic stress.

For fire chaplains this is becoming a key element in community ministry. When a high school teacher approached me, I was skeptical. She asked me to talk about the debriefing process in a high school psychology class. Colleagues within the emergency services urged me to do it. So, cautiously I agreed, praying for an opening to witness about the Lord.

The day dawned, and with it came a bombshell. A lone gunman had roamed the campus of Virginia Tech mowing down students and professors alike. The very peaceful campus snuggled in the Blue Ridge Mountains had become a killing field. As I entered the high school classroom, students were shocked. Some of their peers had actually visited Virginia Tech over the past weekend.

Cautiously I led the discussion among the students. "What did you think?" I asked. Then I delved deeper: "What did you think when you

first heard the news about Virginia Tech?"
The teens admitted that it scared them.

Then I led them even deeper, into the affective, or emotional, area of their lives. "How did you feel about the news?" I now was asking them about their feelings. Some of the students actually grieved over this

> "We can comfort those in any trouble with the comfort we ourselves have received from God." (2 Corinthians 1:4)

news. They were emotionally caught up in the events, although Virginia Tech was several hundred miles away. Finally, I led them into some suggestions for recovery. Not only did we talk about proper eating and sleep habits, but we also talked about exercise. Then, I was able to point them to prayer and spiritual ministry as a means of coping.

As Christians, we can be helpful to our communities. We can give them God's hope in time of trouble. We can reach out to care for hurting hearts. And, when we are the one in need, we can turn to God, and then to his people, who will comfort us so we can comfort others.

Prayer:
*Lord, help me to be awake and aware of the needs in our communities.
May I also be sensitive to the needs of those I work with.*

A U G U S T   8

*Chaplain Gaius Reynolds, President – Fellowship of
Christian Firefighters International; Volunteer
Firefighter – Livermore, CO, Fire Protection District*

HOT
Proactive in doing spiritual wildfire mitigation

HOT! RECORD-setting heat, little or no rain, parched land . . . These are conditions that mean it's wildfire season. Hot! That about sums it up.

When hot, dry conditions exist, they seem to occur not in just an isolated area, but across the country, afflicting large acreages. It appears as if the whole country is a tinder box waiting for ignition.

When wildfire season approaches, most fire departments go into the preparation mode as they plan for an expected emergency.

Intelligent homeowners do the same. They rid their homes of dried brush and other objects that would add fuel if a fire spread in their area.

293

How about you? Are you hot? Are you burning up? Are you parched? If so, do you seek God's Living Water? Then do you take that Living Water to your crew? Have you shared the cooling effects of Christ? Are you preparing for the spiritual "fire season" with the same amount of planning and forethought?

The spiritual fire season is here now! And it's exploding in full force! What have you done to mitigate the effects of the outbreak? Is your home defensible? How have you prepared your family for the conflagration? Are the safe zones identified? Are you wearing your personal protective equipment? Are you carrying your fire shelter? Have you practiced deploying your shelter? In other words: Are you prepared for the spiritual fires on the horizon or already here?

> "O LORD, the hope of Israel, all who forsake you will be put to shame. Those who turn away from you will be written in the dust because they have forsaken the LORD, the spring of living water." (Jeremiah 17:13)

As you peruse the newspapers and listen to the news, you become aware our country is falling further and further away from our fire shelter—the Bible. More of God's edicts are being legislated away in the name of "correctness" or "fairness." It's time to stand up for your beliefs, for your God-given rights. It's time to stand up for your Lord and Savior, Jesus Christ. The fires are burning all around; it's up to Christians to extinguish them. I've always said. "I don't do hot well."

There's a definite reason, clearly stated by Jeremiah, for not forsaking the Lord. The reason is shame. Instead of the consuming heat of shame, Jesus offers his Living Water. Have you accepted his offer? And are you willing to share that refreshing cleansing that comes from him? Are you ready to combat the spiritual fires surfacing around our nation?

Prayer:
*Help me, Lord, to stand up against the hot spots, complete the
mop-up, and become proactive in doing spiritual wildfire
mitigation. As I partake of your Living Water, I will
share it with others to help combat spiritual fires.*

294

Steve Kidd, Firefighter Orange County Fire and Rescue, Florida; Central Florida Chapter of the Fellowship of Christian Firefighters; Author of the Carbusters video series

LACK OF TRAINING IS NO EXCUSE!

There is no substitute for actual hands-on experience

THERE IS A difference between training and education. Anyone facing major surgery wants to know that the surgeon is both well-educated in all the facets of medicine, and well-trained in the manipulative skills it takes to perform delicate procedures with a scalpel or laser.

Fighting fires is much the same way. While it's extremely important that we know all the latest techniques and procedures, there is no substitute for actual hands-on experience with a nozzle, saw, pike pole, or axe. How good would an engineer be who had only read about pumping a truck in a book, but never actually practiced pulling the levers and twisting the knobs? Would you want to put your life, home, or property in the hands of someone who might or might not get water to the nozzle?

> "Flee the desires of youth, and pursue righteousness, faith, love and peace, along with those who call on the Lord with a pure heart."
> (2 Timothy 2:22)

Being a Christian is much the same way. We must take the time to practice being a Christian, not just sit around reading and talking about it. The cliché "Actions speaker louder than words" certainly applies to the Christian walk. True Christians live their life in a way that demonstrates their faith in Jesus. They are patient leaders, humble followers, and gentle parents. You can learn everything there is to know about being a Christian, but it is to no good purpose unless you train yourself to put Christ's teaching to work in your life.

One thing you can accept as total truth—Christ practiced his belief and put his faith to the ultimate test. He gave his life on the cross so we all can receive the blessing of eternal life.

Isn't it time for your next practical training session on living the life of a Christian? Start by reflecting on your last shift, call, or conversation with your spouse or children. Are there some words that would have been better left unsaid, or actions contrary to your Christian walk? Is there something you need to flee from?

Prayer:
Well-educated and well-trained in the way of you, Lord; that is my desire. With your help, I can be more like you each day.

Tommy Neiman, Author of Sirens for the Cross; EMS Training Officer – St. Lucie County, FL; Fellowship of Christian Firefighters International Regional Director / International Board Member

JOY

Not just for a moment but for eternity

SHARING HUMOROUS calls often helps pass the time when things are slow at the station. Here's one I heard that caused a chuckle and brought joy into an uneventful day just when I needed a little something to uplift my spirits.

It was 3 a.m. and my friend had finally drifted into one of those rare, but peaceful, sleeps that seldom accompany a shift at the firehouse—when a lady frantically called his station. "My pacemaker is malfunctioning," she complained. "Hurry! Please!"

When the crew arrived, they found an elderly lady living alone. She appeared all right physically. Emotionally she was distraught.

In the stillness of the night, upon entering the house, the rescue crew heard a sudden "chirp" sound. Ignoring it, they crossed the room to the little old lady, who was sitting anxiously on the couch.

"What's wrong, ma'am?"

"It's my pacemaker. I think there is something wrong with it. It keeps going off."

The guys were somewhat bewildered as they hooked her up to the EKG monitor and all looked fine. Just then they heard the chirp again.

"There it goes again!" the lady cried out. "Every little while it goes off like that! I just know my pacemaker is acting up and I need to get it fixed."

The guys looked up. Immediately they suspected where the noise came from. They felt certain it was the smoke detector on the wall that was mak-

296

ing the occasional sound to tell her the battery needed to be changed. They waited a moment to confirm their suspicions. Again, the chirp.

"See," the lady said, "it keeps doing that!" The guys looked at each other and discreetly shook their heads. From that point on the biggest challenge was keeping a straight face while explaining "that chirp" to the lady.

> "I have told you this so that my joy may be in you and that your joy may be complete." (John 15:11)

I relate this to you hoping it brings you a moment of laughter and joy as it did me. An even greater joy—one that lasts for eternity—was shared thousands of years ago by our Lord Jesus Christ. In John 15:15 he tells of his and his Father's love for you and their desire to call you Friend. (Read the verse in the sidebar above.) And as he shares from his heart, Jesus tells you how your joy will be complete.

Prayer:
*Thank you, Lord, for calling and for choosing me as your
friend. Because of you, my joy is complete and not
dependent on momentary distractions and activities.*

AUGUST 11

*Reverend Wayne Detzler, PhD, Chaplain (Retired) –
Charlotte, NC, Fire Department; Fellowship of
Christian Firefighters Regional Director*

NICE TRIP, CHAPLAIN
How I learned humility

IT WAS MY first working fire. When the alarm sounded, I jumped into my little green Volkswagen and followed the chief to the scene. The chief blazed the trail with lights and siren, but I had neither lights nor siren. So, I stuck to his back bumper like a tick on a deer.

When we came to a red light, the chief slowed and proceeded through the intersection. Afraid of losing my way in a new town, I cautiously followed him. This was my first big mistake that day! He later dressed me down for running a light without any authorization, and he never let me forget the incident.

When we arrived at the scene, the fire was contained. The residents had been evacuated to the next-door neighbor's.

"Go explain to the people what has happened," the chief ordered me. Cautiously, I made my way to the neighbor's front door. As I mounted the steps, I tripped and fell headlong onto the porch. My brand new blue helmet fell off, bouncing across the wooden porch, making an awful clatter.

Recovering my composure, and whatever was left of my dignity, I knocked on the door. The neighbor ushered me into her living room, where the fire victims were sitting quietly, weeping as they waited for news.

"It's going to be all right," I assured them. "Soon you'll be able to get into your house and pick up a few things." They asked further questions. To my amazement, I was able to answer them. Finally, before I left, they allowed me to pray with them, as I committed them to the Lord. I asked the Lord for strength as they coped with the results of the fire and rebuilt their lives.

> "God opposes the proud but gives grace to the humble." (1 Peter 5:5)

Quickly I walked back out the door. The chief was waiting with his quick wit and a cute remark: "Have a nice trip, Chaplain?" he shouted. Never did he let me forget my first fire. Two big blunders marked my first working fire, but they also stripped me of my pride and pretense of ability.

Prayer:
Lord, thank you for using me even when I am weak and very human.

AUGUST 12

Daniel A. Clegg, Rural-Metro EMT; Engineer/EMT–Indianapolis Fire Department (Retired); Fellowship of Christian Firefighters Regional Director / International Board Member

THE ROCK
The only solid foundation

ROCK AND CHURCH—two common words in Christian vernacular. In Matthew 16:16–19, Simon Peter acknowledges Jesus' deity when he tells Jesus he knows Jesus is the Christ and the Son of God. Jesus praises Peter for his insight that could only come from God the Father and then uses a play on the meaning of Peter's name (a rock or boulder) to give a foreshadowing of the foundation of Christ's church. The Rock upon which Christ says he will build his church is none other than Christ himself. Without question, Jesus is the foundation of the Christian church.

Jesus' reference to the word *church* in Matthew 16, is the first in the New Testament. As you continue to read, you'll find the word *church* mentioned repeatedly in Paul's epistles. *Church* (*ecclesia* in Greek) literally means "the called-out ones." It doesn't refer to a denomination, a building, or a religious institution. It's a people who know Christ as Savior and Lord. It's the fellowship of the redeemed, the committed—the living body of believers in Christ who allow themselves to be the minds through which Christ can share and hearts through which Christ can work. And it is built on the Rock, Jesus Christ.

> "For no one can lay any foundation other than the one already laid, which is Jesus Christ."
> (1 Corinthians 3:11)

The church is invincible; the powers of death shall not prevail against it. Kingdoms topple, empires rise and fall, ideologies come and go, and great cities are eroded by time or ravages of war, but the church endures because its foundation is Jesus Christ.

Peter's confession of the divinity of Christ is central to our faith as believers. His confession, acknowledged by Christ himself, confirms Jesus was indeed who he proclaimed to be: the one and only Messiah, God incarnated. Peter was given the keys to the kingdom of heaven, which is salvation though Christ. At Pentecost, Peter's preaching provided those keys to open the door to three thousand souls. Later, in the house of Cornelius, he unlocked and opened the door wide to the Gentiles. Everyone who proclaims Christ uses the keys of the kingdom.

The fire service needs those keys. Regardless of the trials and tragedies faced, Christ wants to comfort all. He is the Rock.

Let us, by our witness and work, help unlock the door so others can find Christ and his gift of salvation. There is no higher calling or privilege, and there is no Foundation other than Jesus Christ upon which we can build our eternal existence with God.

Prayer:

Christ, you are my Rock, the Foundation upon which I build my life. May it be one that glorifies you as I try to help others unlock the doors that block you out.

Dwayne Clemmons, Adjunct Instructor – Virginia Department of Fire Programs; Founder – DMC Ministries; Author of Exploits, Jesus Rides in an Ambulance, and Utterances from the Throne Room; Volunteer in Fire and EMS for forty years in Virginia

PRESSURES ABOUND

There will be light at the end of the proverbial tunnel

EVER FELT like you were drawn in a dozen different directions and there was seemingly no end to the pressure you felt? Then, as the pressures mounted, did it seem increasingly difficult to take your focus off the stress or the unpleasant things besieging you? Matthew 6:23 addresses this concept. *The Message* puts it this way: "Your eyes are windows into your body." It continues to say that if they become squinty-eyed, then "your body is a dank cellar. If you pull the blinds on your windows, what a dark life you will have!" Matthew preceded these words about darkness with encouraging words: If you open your eyes wide in wonder and belief, you'll be filled with light.

> "Give your entire attention to what God is doing right now, and don't get worked up about what may or may not happen tomorrow. God will help you deal with whatever hard things come up when the time comes."
> (Matthew 6:34 MSG)

Are you feeling down? Maybe the demands from your chief or your job in general are bearing down on you. Perhaps something in your personal life is askew. There is an antidote that Matthew made perfectly clear. Open your eyes and see how good our God is! Flood your spirit with his light, which gives you goodness and mercy only God can provide. Don't be concerned by the foolishness of this world. Seek first the kingdom of God and everything else will be provided you. The Bible states it this way: "Give your entire attention to what God is doing right now, and don't get worked up about what may or may not happen tomorrow. God will help you deal with whatever hard things come up when the time comes" (Matthew 6:34 MSG).

If you feel as if life is closing in on you, read all of chapter 6 in Matthew. Read firsthand of Christ's awesome, endless love for you. Allow his Spirit to flow within you and let him carry your burdens and relieve your pressure.

I don't know about you, but I long for that time when I wake up in the Spirit, walk all day in the Spirit, and go to bed in the Spirit. I know if

I continue to tackle life's pressures alone, my eyes will become squinty and my life a dank cellar. But if I open my eyes to the wonder and provisions of Christ's love, his light will shine. There will be light at the end of the proverbial tunnel.

Prayer:
I want to reflect your light, Lord, at home, at the station, during every run, and in all I do. Help me turn my cares and concerns over to you.

Bob Crum, Co-founder – Fellowship of Christian Firefighters International (Retired) – Denver Fire Department

FELLOWSHIP: A HORIZONTAL AND VERTICAL RELATIONSHIP

Our love for Jesus is our common bond as we fellowship together

WHEN THE Bible talks about fellowship, it speaks of a horizontal relationship—person with person—as well as a vertical relationship—person with God. This kind of fellowship is not an event that has been promoted. It happens when we gather in Jesus' name—gathering together just as we are, in his presence. Richard Halverson, in one of his devotional letters, says we can come together as marbles or as grapes. If we come together as marbles we bump against each other, ricochet around, and never enjoy a vital relationship. If we come together as grapes we are willing to be crushed with our egos broken in a spirit of sharing, understanding, and caring.

When we come together with this grape attitude, we're leaving ourselves open for others to see us as we really are, and that makes us vulnerable. Firefighters don't like to be vulnerable, and that's understandable given our chosen profession. Nevertheless, that is the kind of Christian fellowship the Scriptures require of us—a loving, caring, sharing openness with each other and with the Lord.

The Bible states this very clearly in 1 John 1:3: "We proclaim to you what we have seen and heard, so that you may also have fellowship with us. And our fellowship is with the Father and with his Son, Jesus Christ."

Is Christian fellowship important to the Lord? Matthew 18:20 says, "For where two or three come together in my name, there am I with them." What's more amazing is the prophet Malachi telling us that every time we come together for Christian fellowship, a written record is kept. So whether you come together with two, three, fifty, or a hundred, your fellowship is important to the Lord. Our love for Jesus is the common bond we have as we come together in fellowship to share the joy of being in his presence.

> "Then those who feared the LORD talked with each other, and the LORD listened and heard. A scroll of remembrance was written in his presence concerning those who feared the LORD and honored his name."
> (Malachi 3:16)

I urge you to fellowship in his name at your workplace or at a nearby restaurant. Share and live your faith, conduct a Bible study, and pray with your fellow believers. You will be blessed.

Prayer:
How thankful I am that when we fellowship with others in your name, you listen and hear!

AUGUST 15

Chaplain Gilbert, Captain – Indianapolis Fire Department;
President Indianapolis Chapter Fellowship
of Christian Firefighters

BE OF GOOD CHEER

Remember your friend, Jesus, is just a prayer away

WE CAN'T stop the birds from flying overhead, but we don't have to let them build a nest in our hair," states a commonly heard cliché. You've probably also been told on more than one occasion to "be of good cheer."

Do we really have the power to keep "nests out of our hair" or control our emotions? Do we have the power to bring thoughts and impulses that are not from God under submission to Christ?

Paul says we do. He tells us to "take captive every thought to make it obedient to Christ" (1 Corinthians 10:5).

With all the wantonness we encounter as first responders, our thoughts could easily center on the negative and evil. We can give harmful

302

thoughts and attitudes life by dwelling on them and convincing ourselves they're true, or we can demolish such thoughts and ask, "What am I thinking? And why?" and then turn them over to Christ. Detrimental thoughts have no place in our lives. They go against who we are in God. As we more fully understand who we are to God, created in his image, and that Jesus says we can call him Friend, then we can control our negative thoughts and imaginings. We can't control

> "We demolish arguments and every pretension that sets itself up against the knowledge of God, and we take captive every thought to make it obedient to Christ."
> (2 Corinthians 10:5)

what crosses our minds, but we can control what we dwell on, build on, and give life to.

Paul also tells us to renew our mind daily. In doing so, we allow ourselves to become more spiritual and we let Christ increase and our flesh decrease.

Satan will tempt us and beset our minds with wild imaginings, but with every temptation God provides an escape. When we are born again we have the power to subdue Satan, resist sin, and glorify our Savior with our lives. This is a process that begins with repentance, acknowledging our need for the saving grace of God, giving Christ lordship of our lives, and living for our spirit, not the flesh. It is reflected in our words, thoughts, and actions. When thoughts that set themselves against God plague you, remember that your friend Jesus is just a prayer away.

Prayer:
Lord, I turn all my pretentious arguments over to you.
May I always reflect you in my life.

AUGUST 16

Daniel A. Clegg, Rural-Metro EMT; Engineer/EMT–Indianapolis Fire Department (Retired); Fellowship of Christian Firefighters Regional Director / International Board Member

GOOD NIGHT

Life is a precious gift of God

THE LAST night of my thirty-year career with the Indianapolis Fire Department arrived. My emotions were mixed—joy for the future and unbelief that so many years had passed. As a youth I had hoped that if an emergency happened it would be on my shift. Tonight, I wanted a peaceful entrance into retirement. Instead it proved to be a sleepless night with two of the most unique runs of my career.

As I prepared for rest, we were dispatched for an O.B. run. "Where's the expectant mother?" we asked on arrival.

"She's not here. She gave birth, cleaned up, and drove off with her baby. She's a crackhead," he said.

We skeptically searched the dumpster and had no sooner returned to the station than the alarm went off again: another O.B. run.

Climbing into the driver's seat I jokingly said, "It's probably that mother and baby." On scene we found a young lady sitting contently with her newborn cradled in her arms.

"Where's the expectant mother?" I asked.

"I'm the mom and this is my baby. I delivered her myself without a problem. I had prenatal care." As she continued to speak, I realized she was the missing mom from the previous call.

I looked at the baby lying in her arms in a bright blue sleeper and smiled.

"I haven't touched any crack since I got pregnant," she proudly announced.

I inquired about the afterbirth and learned it was still attached. I gloved up, clamped the cord, examined the baby, and updated the medic en route.

> "How great is the love the Father has lavished on us, that we should be called children of God! And that is what we are!." (1John 3:1)

Back at the station, sleep evaded me as I thought about that baby delivered at home by her own mom. Had I jumped to conclusions that could have altered the care I gave this new family? I pray not! As I remembered the motherly glow on the mom's face, I thought about another birth two thousand years ago given by another woman whose character was questioned. Humbly, I asked God to help me not to judge. I prayed this birth would permanently change the young mom's outlook and lead her to God.

Life is a precious gift of God, a gift some cherish and others take much too lightly.

Prayer:
I'm a child of God and so are all those you bring in my path, regardless of age or circumstances. When I'm weary, when the things I face on this job reek of poor decisions and tragedy, may I remember the love you, God, have lavished on all of your children.

Lieutenant (Retired) Lou Dattolo,
Tallahassee, FL, Fire Department

HEAVENLY PERFORMANCE EVALUATION

Honestly evaluating ourselves

BEING FROM an urban, Northern upbringing, when I first started working for a Southern fire department, I had to make a few adjustments. The men loved to tell stories and joke around. I hadn't shared many of their life experiences, such as hunting, fishing, and farming and wasn't much of a story teller. To top it off, as a Christian, I was naturally set apart from much of the "foolishness."

Over the years, I noticed a gradual change in myself. Though on-the-job profanity was not that big an issue on my shifts, my participation in what Ephesians 5:4 refers to as foolish talking and jesting increased to where I could pretty much hold my own. All along, though, I was aware this change was not necessarily for the better.

We all know there's an ever-present danger in firefighting—from the emergency response to unpredictable conditions, to the confrontation with the fire "dragon" on its home turf. Add to that seeing people of all ages at their most helpless times (or immediately after their death), and we can get down physically, mentally, emotionally, and even spiritually. If the public knew what we go through, they'd understand why the fire station is a sanctuary. The camaraderie of fellow firefighters plays a major role in recuperating from the

> "Neither filthiness, nor foolish talking, nor jesting, which are not convenient: but rather giving of thanks."
> (Ephesians 5:4 KJV)

difficult aspects of the job. Without that shared sense of humor and levity, depression would get an even stronger hold than it already does.

But what about that fine line that's crossed from time to time when that which is healthy and accepted of the Lord becomes that which is injurious and unacceptable to him or, at the very least, "not convenient" or helpful in walking in the narrow way? In Matthew 12:36 the Lord Jesus reminds us we will have to give an account of "every idle word" (KJV) one day. This is part of our "Heavenly Performance Evaluation." That's a staggering and sobering truth.

Let's honestly evaluate ourselves in light of God's Word. Let's "give thanks" as we make adjustments that need to be made through prayer and submission to the work of God and the Holy Spirit as we are being conformed to the image of Christ.

Prayer:

Lord, help me be to be aware of all the words I speak. Help me to know the difference between good humor and harmful foolish talking. Help me not speak profanity or ever utter your name in vain. Help me to be a person of clean, uplifting, and positive speech. May all I say be pleasing to your ears.

Chaplain Marc Santorella Firefighter Fire Department, MA; Public Fire and Life Safety Educator and Certified Fire Instructor Level 1

TRIALS AND FIRES

Live fires are the best training ground

FACED ANY personal fires lately? You know—the ones that come from trials and challenges. If so, how did you view them?

Scripture indicates that trials are opportunities for God to work in the toughest situations, to show his love for you, and reveal his truth through you. When that happens it's for his glory, not yours. Do you benefit? Definitely! You emerge stronger and better equipped.

Fighting fires is hard work. You often emerge exhausted and dirty. But the experience makes you better equipped for the next one. The best way to become a more proficient firefighter is to put your training to work as you fight fires. Live fires are the best training ground. They provide opportunities to hone skills, learn from mistakes, and develop confidence.

The apostle Paul, one of the first "Christian-based authors," wrote that we "rejoice in the hope of the glory of God" (Romans 5:2), and we also "rejoice in our sufferings" (v. 3). He's not referring to rejoicing as an "object feeling" but as an "object status." We may not always "feel" joy, but we know we have it because of Jesus.

From the moment the veil in the temple ripped at the time of Jesus' death (Mark 15:38) you were given personal and direct access to God. Not because of who you are, but because of who Jesus is. By having personal and direct access to God, you're privileged to be able to bring everything to him. You're free to seek strength, wisdom, and victory over all situations. As you do this you also receive hope, because perseverance builds character, and character builds hope (Romans 5:4). "And hope does not disappoint [you], because God has poured out his love into [your] hearts by the Holy Spirit, whom he has given [you]" (v. 5).

> "God is our refuge and strength, an ever-present help in trouble."
> (Psalms 46:1)

Facing trials is like fighting fires in that the fight is not always easy. As a Christian you can emerge victorious with the assurance you're not alone. Jesus is at your side. Will the walk be pain-free? Not likely. Filled with hope? Yes. Our Lord knows about trials and hard times. Jesus walked through everything you have for he was "tempted in every way, just as [you] are—yet was without sin" (Hebrews 4:15). He understands and he offers hope.

Prayer:
Dear God, help me remember that you are my ever-present hope. I can be confident that you are able to see me through any situation I may face because you have already provided the victory and you are with me.

AUGUST 19

Captain Jim Herrington, Firefighter/Paramedic,
Poudre Fire Authority, Fort Collins, CO

HIGH-ANGLE RESCUE AND NORTHERN LIGHTS
God makes his majesty known

ON THE WEST edge of Boulder, Colorado, stands a spectacular backdrop of enormous rock cliffs called the Flatirons that attract many hikers. They are the source of numerous situations requiring technical rescue. The routes start out easy but become increasingly difficult the higher one climbs.

Our patient, climbing without proper rock-climbing equipment, fell and landed on a ledge, breaking his leg. As part of an all-volunteer search-and-rescue team, I helped carry equipment to a position above him. One rescuer was lowered to the victim to administer first aid and determined his injuries were isolated to his lower leg. He splinted it accordingly. As part of the next team I was lowered with a litter to the ledge, assisted the patient into the litter, zipped him into a sleeping bag, placed a helmet on him, and strapped him into the litter. He was embarrassed but in good spirits. We reassured him the rest of the trip would be easy, even though night had fallen.

On this pleasant, cloudless, and moonless night only a few obstructions blocked the way. Tied into the ropes on the litter and hanging from our harnesses, we pulled the litter out from the wall. Facing the wall, we were walking backward with the litter balanced between the wall and us when we noticed a glow on the northern horizon. We were high enough the Wyoming border was visible, but this glow was in the atmosphere and not from any city. Something clicked. *That has to be the Northern Lights — Aurora Borealis!*

> "The heavens declare the glory of God; the skies proclaim the work of his hands."
> (Psalm 19:1)

Excited to see this uncommon sight, I shared my discovery with my patient and team member. The patient twisted to see the lights. He was having trouble so I radioed for the litter to "stop," and ordered, "foot." There are two ropes on our lowering system, one at the head of the litter and another at the foot. "Now keep the head end stopped but let the foot end lower so our patient can see." As we paused to watch the glow in the north, the rays of lights pulsed slowly, gliding silently over the horizon. Within five minutes the display had dimmed (but didn't fade completely away).

Creation has many wonders. Even in the midst of exciting and interesting rescues, God makes his majesty known.

Prayer:
You are visible in your creation. What an awesome and mighty God you are! I praise you, Lord, for you have created mighty works for us to enjoy. I worship you, the God of Creation.

Ken Henry, Battalion Chief (Retired) –
Hillsborough County, Florida

A BAD DAY WAS GETTING WORSE—UNTIL I TOOK IT TO THE LORD

Answered prayer is a warm and wonderful gift

I WAITED FOR the traffic light to change so I could get home to figure out what to do next. My wife, Colleen, in the advanced stages of Alzheimer's, was rushed to the hospital the previous day with another seizure of undetermined cause. This was the third trip in two months Marion County Station 22 is ready to add us to their "Frequent Flyer" list. For three-plus years we've eaten evening meals in one of two restaurants. We'd go after the rush and sit in a closed, quiet section to make it easier for me to spoon-feed her. I knew the day would come when we could no longer do this, and I'd have to make other arrangements. I didn't have a clue what I'd do when that day arrived. It had arrived. The doctor and social worker talked about options for alternative care.

My answer was, "There's no option other than I care for her in our home." (It's called *commitment*—I still remember that "for better or worse" promise I made to her forty-six years ago).

As I continued to wait for the light to change, I talked to the Lord in complete despair. It was more grunts than words there aren't words when you're that far down. I can cook for myself, rice, beans, anything fried; quantity not quality. Not good for my wife. What to do? "Lord, please show me the answer. I don't know what to do. Only you can get us through this."

> "Cast all your anxiety on him because he cares for you." (1 Peter 5:7)

I looked up and noticed a gaudily painted delivery van. Large letters over plates full of food proclaimed "DoingDinner.com." I knew my prayer had been answered.

The next day I talked with Bill, the owner. I could microwave it in what it came in and throw it away when finished. The excellent variety of dishes are freshly prepared, no preservatives, flash frozen, and cheaper than eating out. Problem solved.

Bill asked how I heard about them. When I told him I saw his delivery van in our area he laughed, "Wow, we don't deliver in your county. The only reason we were over there is that one of our employees has a relative who just had surgery. As a favor we agreed to deliver a one-time order to her. Never been there before, probably won't be there again."

Prayer:
Thank you, Lord, for the privilege of prayer.
Help me to never take it for granted.

AUGUST 21

Fire Chaplain Randy S. Martin, Engineer/Peace Officer/
Arson Investigator – Camp Roberts, CA, Fire
Emergency Services/Fire and Law Enforcement

FROM BUMMED OUT TO BLESSED

Blessings that far exceeded my expectations

I WAS SUPPOSED to work overtime (OT) that weekend at the fire station. I never work OT, and why I accepted this time is still puzzling to me. I'd rather spend time with my wife and kids. I've been with my department eight years and during those years I've never volunteered to work OT. I was bummed.

There was an arson conference during that time I wanted to attend. Even though I'm the arson investigator and fire chaplain for my department, I couldn't go because the department couldn't afford to send me. Double bummer!

It turned out the guy I was supposed to work for showed up and my OT was canceled. My time with the family was preserved. But God had still other plans for me. I received a phone call from a fellow investigator explaining that the chaplain for the Arson Conference was not going to be able to make it. They were looking for a new chaplain and wondered if I'd like to go.

No hesitation on my part. When I arrived, I met with the president of the conference, who asked if I was just going to be a fill-in or if I wanted the full-time ride. This blessing far exceeded my expectations and I willingly accepted. The Arson Conference is held twice a year. I'm now

310

privileged to attend both conferences free of charge. But there is more: I have the honor of giving the opening prayer, participating in opening ceremonies, and giving the closing prayer.

> "He gives strength to the weary and increases the power of the weak. Even youths grow tired and weary, and young men stumble and fall. (Isaiah 40:29, 30)

God didn't want me to work the overtime that weekend because he had bigger plans for me. If I'd worked OT, I wouldn't have been available to be the new chaplain for the Arson Conference. Now I have the opportunity to reach out to more than two hundred investigators twice a year and share with them the Good News of Jesus Christ.

I went from being bummed out to blessed in a matter of days. It's amazing how God's hand continues to guide my life and remind me that he knows the plans he has for me, and that they are for me to prosper (see Jeremiah 29:11).

During those disappointing days, I also turned to Isaiah 40:29, 30.

Prayer:

Heavenly Father, thank you for reminding me you have a plan for my life. Thank you for raising me up when I'm down and renewing my strength so I can soar on wings like eagles. Father, thank you for all of the blessings you give to me. I pray this in Jesus' name, amen.

A U G U S T   2 2

Aaron Johnson, Fire Inspector – Martin County, FL

UL-LISTED LIFE

Can you pass the test?

PART OF MY responsibility as a fire inspector is to ensure that products are properly "listed" for their intended use. An organization called Underwriters Laboratories (no doubt you have seen their "UL" mark on household items) puts various items through a rigorous testing process to certify them for their planned purpose.

For example, if a building requires a two-hour firewall, it must be installed according to UL specifications. If there are any openings (doors, windows, etc.) in that "rated" firewall, they must have an equal UL-listed—"rated"—door, window, etc. Also, various products must be UL-listed or they are not permitted. Among those items are kitchen hood systems, surge protectors, and extension cords.

At the UL facility they have massive furnaces these various products and assemblies are tested in. If a new product wants to be accepted worldwide, it must pass all the UL tests. The product is subjected to all kinds of forces including heat, cold, pressure, and water.

Just as UL-listed products must endure a series of trials to ensure they're not lacking any manufacturer integrity, as Christians we endure many trials. Never has God promised a life "untested." In fact, James says to "count it all joy" when we go through times of hardship, trial, and testing. It is in these times God is making us mature and complete Christians. As we endure these things, our walk and relationship with Christ is strengthened, and we grow closer to him. We need a solid faith in Christ that our trials are allowed for our good and God's glory.

> "Consider it a great joy, my brothers, whenever you experience various trials, knowing that the testing of your faith produces endurance. But endurance must do its complete work, so that you may be mature and complete, lacking nothing." (James 1:2–4 HCSB)

The "believer" who lacks faith will fail these tests of endurance.

As a Christian, has your life passed the test of endurance? Have you gone through various trials and tests only to come out "mature and complete"?

Many products pass the UL process and gain the coveted "UL listing." Have you, as a believer, passed the test of endurance? Is the life you live worthy of the label "Christian"?

Prayer:
Father, complete your work in me. I desire to be worthy of the label "Christian." Give me the strength to endure.

Rick Barton, Fire Safety Officer; Rick Barton Ministries,
Gunnison, CO; Fellowship of Christian Firefighters
International Ambassador-at-Large

WHERE'S THE CHIEF?

Is there an armor-bearer in your life?

THE MODULAR home was fully involved. Local fire resources responded and soon the chief was ready to enter the structure and get at the source of the fire. Moments later the call was heard over the radio, "Where's the chief?" Everyone shifted gears. One of their own was missing, and it was the chief

> "Do all that you have in mind," his armor-bearer said. "Go ahead; I am with you heart and soul."
> (1 Samuel 14:7)

at that. Saving lives is what we do without feelings of partiality, but when it's one of our own, other emotions come into play.

A frantic search ensued until, minutes (that seemed like hours) later, the chief was located. He was trapped under part of a collapsed floor in the basement. By the time the others were able to safely enter and retrieve him, the chief had perished.

The investigation revealed that the chief had been working in tandem with another firefighter. At one point the other individual left to check another door. The chief decided not to wait for his return and entered on his own. As he stepped inside, the floor collapsed. He was trapped.

Is there a lesson to be learned here? Is it smart to enter into dangerous situations on your own? Can you do this without backup?

In our private lives it seems wise to "buddy up" with others who will "watch our back" as well as hold us accountable. In the Bible Jesus sent his disciples out two by two. Jonathan, Saul's son, had an armor-bearer there to back him up when he went into the Philistine camp. When Jonathan's father, King Saul, threatened David, Jonathan became David's backup and saved his life. David was God's anointed and went on to become king. Honoring the promise he made to his friend Jonathan, David later reached out to Jonathan's son.

Is there an armor-bearer, Jonathan, or David in your life? Do you have a close friend to help hold you accountable? Whom are you walking with? Who's got your back? Who is your accountability buddy?

Prayer:
*Thank you for my friends. May my friends
know I am there for them heart and soul.*

313

Tommy Neiman, *Author of Sirens for the Cross; EMS*
Training Officer – St. Lucie County, FL; Fellowship of
Christian Firefighters International Regional
Director / International Board Member

A SEIZURE?

One try . . . and you might die

AS A RESCUE worker, I've grown to hate some things—alcohol and other drugs directly or indirectly destroying people. They are tools Satan uses in his efforts, as recorded in Scripture, "to steal and kill and destroy (John 10:10). Abuse of alcohol and other drugs many times leads to horrific accidents and needless tragedies.

One such call involved a sixteen-year-old girl, supposedly having a seizure and shaking viciously. The house was filled with loud music and teenagers apparently undaunted by the distressed teen. Fortunately, the girl's friend called 9-1-1.

Things settled down when the police arrived, but the patient continued her wild behavior. She pulled at her clothes, face, hair—anything she could grab in the midst of her "seizure." She kept yelling hysterically, "I'm burning up."

> "You, dear children, are from God and have overcome them, because the one who is in you is greater than the one who is in the world." (1 John 4:4)

As her shaking and violent movements increased, I suspected this was not a seizure. Then her friend confirmed my suspicions: "She tried her first crack." I'd heard about first-time reactions to crack cocaine, and after seeing this girl I understood why death can happen after one try of this Satan-laced drug. Never had I witnessed a heart rate so fast—I thought it was going to explode. Sweat ran off her head and body in torrents.

Her erratic and uncontrolled behavior, coupled with the rapid beeps of my monitor recording her heartbeat, finally made the majority of onlookers aware of the magnitude of her condition. A silence filled the house. But even in the midst of the surrounding stillness, trying to get this girl to calm down was like walking through a brick wall. Many young people witnessed her potential death. Only God's grace kept her from becoming a statistic.

As we loaded her for transport, I prayed we were leaving a penetrating message behind. Maybe a good motto for crack cocaine and the evil

314

one behind it, Satan, should be, "One try . . . and you might die." Seeing the suffering and violence crack cocaine produces made the voice of Satan ring loud in my ears. But he is not the victor. Regardless of the severity of the sin or temptation in anyone's life, with Christ in their heart, they have the very power of God to make them victorious over Satan. Christ and prayer—therein lies the sure antidote. And that's a promise!

Prayer:
Jesus, I know you are the antidote for all sin in everyone's lives. I pray for those tempted by drugs and alcohol, I pray for those responding, and I turn all my sins and temptations over to you.

AUGUST 25

Dr. Jonathan Newell, Missionary Malawi, Africa

SPIRITUAL TRAINING CAN ALSO HELP
Help in times of crisis

DRIVING RESPONSIBLY, but quickly, is crucial to getting firemen to any emergency. Much effort is put into training drivers and teaching them how to negotiate their way through traffic safely. It's often said good training takes over in a crisis. There is truth in this because there's often little or no time to think. Let me suggest, however, that spiritual training can also help in crises.

> "Train yourself to be godly." (1 Timothy 4:7)

About a year ago I was driving along the only main road in Malawi, Africa, which runs from the north to the south of the country. It was at the start of the rainy season, when tropical downpours make driving extremely difficult. During this season, the rain becomes so heavy at times that visibility is close to zero. As I drove, I entered a rain storm quite abruptly and as I tried to slow down, I realized my truck was not responding to the steering wheel. In fact, the vehicle started to careen across the road. It spun completely around twice, right in the middle of the two-lane highway. Then, as I was unable to gain control, my truck slipped off the tarmac and into the bush. I vividly remember branches, bushes, and maize being thrown up onto the windscreen until I slid to a stop in a ditch. To my astonishment, the only damage to the truck was one missing hub cap.

I haven't been trained in all the driving techniques that could well have helped me that day. However, I was trained spiritually as a young boy. One story I recall hearing during my church training that came back to me as my truck spun out of control was from an old bus driver who shared how he lost control of his bus on a very wet day. Instead of panic, he sensed the Lord's help.

So what did I do as I spun around in the middle of the main road? I prayed out loud, "Lord, save us! Lord, save us!" I did not even think about doing this. I simply did it, because I'd been trained to pray from an early age both in the home and at church. Let us not forget that spiritual training can also be a great asset in times of emergency and can even complement professional training.

Prayer:
Our heavenly Father, help us to value both our professional training and the spiritual training that you offer to us. Give us the grace to see that we need both if we are to succeed in this life.

Ann Christmas, Fellowship of Christian Firefighters, St. Louis Chapter; American Red Cross, North County Citizen Corps

TEAMWORK
Jesus showed us how to love the unlovable

GOD DID NOT intend for one person to complete every task alone. We've been given different gifts, abilities, interests, and desires. Consequently, it only makes sense that we were intended to work in teams. In a team, one person's weakness may be another person's strength, thus giving an enhanced opportunity to succeed.

In emergency services, teamwork is indispensable. For instance, in a typical two-alarm fire, firefighters battle the fire; police keep people away and block the street from traffic; and the paramedics wait close in case of injuries. If there are injuries, they go into action. In an arson fire, the police and fire departments work collectively to find the person who potentially put the emergency workers in harm's way and caused the destruction.

316

Just as in high school, in the military, and in about every profession we have, there is rivalry between departments. Sometimes it's friendly words—firefighters flinging jokes towards the police, and vice versa. Other times, there is tension between the groups that leads to animosity and dislike. I'm not sure why this happens. I personally appreciate all emergency workers and can't imagine what this world would be like without them. Without team cooperation, many more would die daily and suffering would increase in number and seriousness. There would be more homelessness. Violence would escalate.

In Philippians 2, Paul shares how we are to have an attitude like Christ's. We must love one another and work together without being self-centered. We must put others before ourselves, assisting those we perhaps do not even want to be around. That is when we should look deep within ourselves.

"Then make me truly happy by agreeing wholeheartedly with each other, loving one another, and working together with one mind and purpose. Don't be selfish; don't try to impress others. Be humble, thinking of others as better than yourselves. Don't look out only for your own interests, but take an interest in others, too. You must have the same attitude that Christ Jesus had." (Philippians 2:2–5 NLT)

Is there someone in your life you don't want to be around? Is there someone you dread to work with, and when your paths cross your skin crawls, and you wish you were somewhere else? If so, it's time to take a look at yourself. God never promised it would be easy to love others; in fact, Jesus showed us how to love the unlovable. Just keep in mind, as the light shines, darkness disappears.

Prayer:
Lord, show me where in my life I can become a better team member. Help me dig deep inside to pull out anything that keeps me from loving others and hinders my growth. Teach me to have an attitude like yours: selfless, loving, and humble. In Jesus' name, amen.

*Fire Chaplain John Kalashian, Caledonia, Wisconsin;
Founder/Director – Men with a Burden, a ministry to
the homeless men at the Milwaukee Rescue Mission;
Founder/President – Corvettes for Christ*

GIFT OF FORGIVENESS
I asked and received

WE'RE ALL guilty of it, and whether we admit it or not, we perhaps do it on a daily basis. I'm referring to "falling short," or, simply put another way, "failing." Each of us falls short of expected standards, and the results are felt by those around us—on our jobs, in our marriages, and in other aspects of our personal lives.

While attempting to fill my duties as a fire chaplain, I've disappointed and failed some of those in the department where I serve—those I've grown to love and admire. My words and actions fell short of the trust and standards placed in me. Ever been there? If so, you probably understand that forgiveness is not the easiest thing to ask for, but it's always the wisest choice. I know from experience. I've sought and gratefully received the "gift of forgiveness."

> "So I say to you: Ask and it will be given to you; seek and you will find; knock and the door will be opened to you. For everyone who asks receives; he who seeks finds; and to him who knocks, the door will be opened." (Luke 11:9, 10)

Forgiveness is a gift we all possess, but it has no value and does no good unless given and accepted. Whether it's between firefighters, husbands and wives, parents and children, or friends—relationships are wonderfully changed when forgiveness is asked for and given!

Gifts intrinsically bring joy, but no joy is as great as the joy associated with the "gift of forgiveness," a gift welcomed and appreciated because it represents grace and favor. In other words—we can breathe a sigh of relief for receiving a gift we didn't deserve, and feel pleased for willingly giving it out!

We can all be gift-givers, but no one does it better than Jesus Christ. Just as we fall short and fail in our human relationships, we also fall short and fail God's standards! The well-known Scripture from Romans 3:23 clearly explains that all have sinned and therefore we all fall short of the glory of God and pleasing him. We don't deserve his forgiveness but through his example of grace and pardon, God offers it to those who humbly ask! "If we confess our sins, he is faithful and just and will forgive us our sins and purify us from all unrighteousness" (1 John 1:9). We never need to be fearful of approaching Christ, because he will always forgive. One could almost say "forgiveness" is one of God's middle names. Jesus says, "Ask and it will be given to you" (Luke 11:9, 10).

Prayer:
Thank you, Lord, that I can faithfully come to Christ as I fail and fall short of expected standards and you will not turn me away empty-handed, but instead will bless me with your "gift of forgiveness."

AUGUST 28

Reverend Wayne Detzler, PhD, Chaplain (Retired) – Charlotte, NC, Fire Department; Fellowship of Christian Firefighters Regional Director

SPEAKING OUT AND SPEAKING UP
How I learned to speak

CHAOS CHARACTERIZED the scene. A commuter aircraft crashed into the concrete apron at the local airport. All aboard were lost. The tangle of metal was mingled with the tangle of bodies. Patiently, methodically, and professionally, firefighters, FBI agents, and medics recovered remains.

From the wreckage bodies were brought to a decontamination tent, where fuel and contaminants could be cleansed from the remains. At the same time a preliminary identification emerged. Crew and passengers became real people to us. We thought of their families waiting in vain for good news.

As chaplains our main job was supporting the firefighters and the other workers. The FBI chaplain and I stood together touching emergency workers and praying for them. As they left the scene we tried to defuse their stress.

"You are having a normal reaction to an abnormal situation." We said that sentence over and over again. Later we would visit the fire stations to conduct follow-up debriefings.

"Chaplain, can you help me?" The public information officer (PIO) approached me. "Can you handle a media briefing for me?" My past experience as a morning guy on the radio had equipped me for this. The PIO briefed me on the facts and figures. He instructed me carefully.

> "You will be my witnesses . . . to the ends of the earth." (Acts 1:8)

Then we went to an unused terminal where the media waited for us. For the next hour or so I answered questions. Carefully I avoided issues of blame. Only subsequent investigation would show why the plane crashed. My job was to tell what had happened. I tried to focus the attention of the media people on the families of the victims.

I said what the PIO told me to say. No more, no less. My task was that of a spokesperson, a voice. The media did not care if I was a chaplain or a chief. Neither did they care about my qualifications either as a media person or a pastor. Their only concern was information. They wanted to know.

As Christians, we, too, are speakers of God's eternal truths. Christ calls us to be a witness for him (see Acts 26:16). The task of a witness is simple. First, he or she must have experienced something, seen something. Second, he or she must tell exactly what was seen.

Prayer:
Thank you, Lord, for calling me to speak for
you in a world that needs you so much.

AUGUST 29

Tommy Neiman, Author of Sirens for the Cross; EMS Training Officer – St. Lucie County, FL; Fellowship of Christian Firefighters International Regional Director / International Board Member

THE MAN NEXT DOOR
A man unrecognizable as the monster I'd envisioned

FROM THE time my twin brother, Robbie, and I could hold a bat, we spent untold hours playing baseball in our backyard. The older we got, the more balls sailed over the fence. We knew those balls were gone forever because our neighbor, Mr. Milner, angrily confiscated them. Each run-in with Mr. Milner frightened us and fed our imaginations, making us certain we never wanted to meet him face-to-face. We conjured up fearful images of him and successfully avoided him as long as we lived next to him.

Years later, when dispatched to an address I recognized as Mr. Milner's, I regressed to childhood, riddled with fear. Upon arrival, I glanced toward our former home, noting the carport where we'd rollerskated, our favorite climbing tree, and, of course, my first ballfield—my fenced-in backyard.

> "Finally, all of you, live in harmony with one another; be sympathetic, love as brothers, be compassionate and humble. Do not repay evil with evil or insult with insult, but with blessing, because to this you were called so that you may inherit a blessing." (1 Peter 3:8, 9)

Mrs. Milner met me at the door. She didn't seem to recognize me as I looked about the room expecting to see a big crate of old baseballs. I began to tremble as she explained her husband had advanced stages of cancer. Still harboring my childhood fear, yet confident God was in charge, I approached the now feeble, shriveled Mr. Milner, a man unrecognizable as the monster I'd envisioned when I was a child. He needed hospital care, and I knew this was one ambulance ride God wanted me to take.

"We'll take good care of your husband," I said. "You know, I'm one of the twins who grew up next door." Recognition beamed on her face. I felt a loving acceptance replace my once-smothering fear.

At the hospital I accompanied Mr. Milner to his bed, held his hand, and told him who I was. I shared salvation through Jesus Christ and informed him it was never too late to accept Jesus, and it could be done without a spoken word. Then I asked, "Do you believe that Jesus is God's only Son and that He loves you and died for your sins?" He squeezed my hand. "Do you believe and trust Jesus to be your own personal Savior?" He squeezed my hand once more.

In medical terms, this was a Code 1 call—no lights and no sirens. In spiritual terms, it was a Code 3—a lifesaving call.

Prayer:

When fear threatens to steal my peace and cause me to live in disharmony or in an uncompassionate way, I thank you for your firm reminder not to allow that to happen and be tempted to repay evil or insult in a like manner.

Suzanne Hagelin, Team Leader – FDNY Prayer Support Team

BE READY

He has equipped us

THE RIG has been inspected, the equipment is functioning, air tanks are full, and turnout gear is positioned to be put on quickly. Each firefighter's been trained, knows who is in charge, and understands the orders given. When the call comes in, the team is ready.

As Christians, we should also be ready for whatever need the Lord wants us to meet.

We "happened" to drop by a firehouse in Manhattan the day they'd heard about the suicide of a brother firefighter in another house—another uncounted casualty of 9/11. They were grieved and discouraged. One told me about the funeral the next day, pointed at me, and said, "I expect to see you there."

Another asked me what hope there was in the Bible for a man who'd died this way. The Lord brought John 6:40 to mind. "For my Father's will is that everyone who looks to the Son and believes in him shall have eternal life, and I will raise him up at the last day." The door to heaven is open and Jesus is the Way. Anyone who looks to him and hopes in him is saved, even if it's the last moment of his life.

> "All Scripture is God-breathed and is useful for teaching, rebuking, correcting and training in righteousness, so that the man of God may be thoroughly equipped for every good work."
> (2 Timothy 3:16, 17)

How precious is the Lord's sense of timing! He sent us there right when they needed us.

As the Lord's eyes roam to and fro throughout the earth, searching for those whose hearts are completely his (2 Chronicles 16:9), does he notice us? Can he count on us? Are we ready?

"Be dressed ready for service and keep your lamps burning . . . It will be good for those servants whose master finds them watching when he comes . . . You also must be ready, because the Son of Man will come at an hour when you do not expect him" (Luke 12:35, 37, 40). God expects us to be ready to share with those in need (1 Timothy 6:18), to preach the Word (2 Timothy 4:2), to do good deeds (Titus 3:1), to make a defense of our faith (1 Peter 3:15), to speak with grace according to the need of the moment (Colossians 4:6), and to forgive (Matthew 5:22–25).

Fortunately, he has equipped us for all these things and trains us to respond. And how joyful we are to serve him!

Prayer:
Father in heaven, grant me a willing spirit and a humble heart. Give me a listening ear. Equip me to serve you, and help me always be ready for your call. In Jesus' name, amen.

AUGUST 31

Sue Reynolds, Missionary – Fellowship of Christian Firefighters International (FCFI), and Chaplain Gaius Reynolds, President – FCFI; Volunteer Firefighter – Livermore, CO, Fire Protection District

DIRECTLY AND DYNAMICALLY IN TOUCH WITH GOD
Part of God's inner circle

WHEN SOMEONE joins the fire department, a distinct "pecking order" (hierarchy) is evident. The rookie gets the least desirable jobs. Other responsibilities are assigned according to seniority and rank. Access to the chief, in some departments, must go through the proper channels. Diplomacy, treading carefully, is essential.

Ever wondered why diplomacy is often required when approaching your superiors? Queen Esther certainly understood this when approaching the king with her request to save her people. Her prayerful patience, respect, caution, and diplomacy reaped great rewards and her people were saved. With rank comes privilege. A wise person shows respect to those of higher rank.

God, too, wants our respect—but rank and seniority do not come into play. He created man for intimate fellowship with him, a fellowship that was hindered when sin entered the scene. No diplomacy, no consideration of rank is needed with God. You can come to him directly just as you are—and he listens. God created you to be a part of his inner circle in a perfect love and intimate fellowship with him.

There are hundreds of references to prayer in the Bible, indicating its importance to God and to you. Prayer is your most powerful and effective direct access to God. And because of this direct and dynamic channel to God, that channel is transferred to the world. You can spend time today, wherever you are, praying with, or for, a person sitting right next to you or miles away as though you are right there in person. Whatever type of prayer—praise, worship, thanksgiving, confession, communion, intercession, requests (regardless of the severity or perceived importance of the request)—every manner and type of prayer is pleasing to God and delights him. As you pray and draw near to him, he will draw near to you (James 4:8). First Thessalonians 5:17 clearly expresses how God feels. He wants you to always talk to him, to "pray continually."

> "In him and through faith in him we may approach God with freedom and confidence."
> (Ephesians 3:12)

Prayer:
What a blessing, God, to know that I am a part of your inner circle and to know that I can be directly and dynamically in touch with you.

Tommy Neiman, Author of Sirens for the Cross; EMS Training Officer – St. Lucie County, FL; Fellowship of Christian Firefighters International Regional Director / International Board Member

OUR IMPRESSIVE VISITOR

Actions and words leave a lasting impression

ANIMALS ARE notorious for finding homes at fire stations. When they do, they seem to create a keen, yet temporary, interest on the part of the firefighters. I've seen an array of animals seek temporary shelter in a fire station, from dogs and cats to birds, raccoons, and armadillos. We even had a large python hanging out at our front door one night until a gentleman claimed it. Of all the animals the most memorable one is the Station 2 Squirrel.

My encounter with the Station 2 Squirrel occurred my rookie year when I saw this visitor in the middle of the dinner table eating a walnut. Three burly firefighters, buried in the newspaper, sat next to a munching squirrel. As I moseyed over to get a bowl of cereal, I casually said, "Who's the visitor?"

When the squirrel finished his walnut and bounced around a bit, I finally heard about this unique creature. As the weeks passed my affection grew in the warmth and delight of this little critter. Most mornings, the on-duty shift opened the screenless back kitchen window where the barbecue was conveniently located. Our fun-loving friend then jumped on it, climbed up to the windowsill, leaped down onto the kitchen counter and over to the table, and expectantly waited for breakfast. And he never left hungry. He seemed to trust everyone, at least those with blue uniform shirts. I had him walking on my arms almost immediately. Yes, he was quite the character and we enjoyed his antics shift after shift. Then one day, he didn't show up. When a call came in, we hurriedly exited the station, but *not* so quickly we didn't notice a fluffy-tailed, car-squished animal about 500 feet down the road. We hoped it wasn't our Station 2 Squirrel. As the days passed and he never returned, we feared he hadn't learned to look both ways before crossing the street.

> "This is what we speak, not in words taught us by human wisdom but in words taught by the Spirit, expressing spiritual truths in spiritual words."
> (1 Corinthians 2:13)

The Station 2 Squirrel was a neat little character. He left quite an impression on the guys and really helped lighten the atmosphere at this busy station.

Our actions and words, too, will leave a lasting impression on those we work with and serve. Words and actions, once said and done, can not be taken back. Let's make sure they are spoken to encourage and reflect our love for the Lord.

Prayer:
Fill me, Lord, with your wisdom so that my every expression, whether in word or action, leaves a lasting impression that reflects who I am in you.

SEPTEMBER 2

Richard Intartaglio, Assistant Chief of Operations – South Trail Fire Protection and Rescue Service Division, Fort Myers, FL

ATTITUDE OF CHRIST
Serving God in the workplace

THE GRACE of God works in the lives of people who have experienced it through faith in Jesus Christ. As a Christian firefighter and "child of grace" you know what it's like to feel God's love and witness his mercy and forgiveness. Ephesians, chapter 2, makes this clear by explaining that your salvation is a gift from God, and not because of works. Otherwise you might become boastful. God *did* create you to do good works, however, that he prepared in advance for you. And he wants you to do them in his grace, not in your own strength (vv. 8, 9). So why do I often hear people complain that Christians are a bunch of hypocrites whose works don't match their words?

The apostle Paul taught Christians to live a life of grace in all situations and settings. This requires having an understanding of God's grace and who we are in his grace.

The grace of God "works" in all relationships including those at the workplace. Many firefighters spend more hours at the station and involved in other responsibilities and activities than at home. It's important to spend that time for God's glory. One of the big buzzwords in the workplace these days is "attitude." It's the topic of books, calendars, seminars, and news programs. Some common phrases include, "It's your attitude, not your aptitude, that determines your altitude in life"; "The positive thinker creates a majority"; and many others.

As God's children, you're told to put off (get rid of) the old self because it's being corrupted by its deceitful desires. You are to get a new attitude, a new self, one that is "created to be like God in true righteousness and holiness" (Ephesians 4:22–24). Thus, we should have the attitude of Christ as we serve him and minister to those whom God places in our path.

> "Do nothing out of selfish ambition or vain conceit, but in humility consider others better than yourselves. Each of you should look not only to your own interests, but also to the interests of others. Your attitude should be the same as that of Christ Jesus."
> (Philippians 2:3–5)

The fire service is a unique profession in which we see the good and the bad. Thus, we can fall into the trappings of this world. No matter what position the Lord puts you in—chief, lieutenant, or firefighter—remember it's by his grace you've come this far. He'll never leave you nor forsake you. He'll empower you to be his witness.

The best person to share Christ in the fire service is the Christian who works in the same workplace. Paul instructs us to be "like-minded," having the same love, being one in spirit and purpose.

Prayer:
Lord, I pray others see my attitude as the same as yours.

S E P T E M B E R   3

Rick Barton, Fire Safety Officer; Rick Barton Ministries, Gunnison, CO; Fellowship of Christian Firefighters International Ambassador-at-Large

THE CASE OF THE TWO SEEDS

Just the little act of prayerfully planting a seed can change a life

SEED #1: My phone rang. It was an Oregon Forest Service fire manager I'd recently worked with on a wilderness fire in California. I'd come away from the fire disappointed. It was one of the few times I'd held a chapel service and no one came.

The helicopter dropped twenty-five of us off in a spike camp (remote camp near a fire line) for ten days. When Sunday arrived, I invited everyone to come over to a log for church. No one came. Ouch! The same old struggle internally—could God turn my *dis-appointment* into *his-appointment*?

Later that day I gave an *Answering the Call* firefighter Bible to one of the men. He glanced it over, expressed his thanks, and nothing more was said. I prayed it would be a seed God could use.

> "Even now he harvests the crop for eternal life, so that the sower and the reaper may be glad together. Thus the saying 'One sows and another reaps' is true."
> (John 4:36, 37)

Tonight the man called. He said he started by reading the testimonies in the firefighter Bible and then he turned to the Scripture. God touched him. Now he wanted more to give away. He and his wife started attending a local church. I could hear in his voice that God was working.

Seed #2: During a wildland fire in Colorado, only a couple of hours from my home, several homes were lost. I'd headed over to assist the local public information officer. As I left the fire that evening, I gave the incident commander / volunteer fire chief a copy of *Answering the Call*. He looked somewhat surprised and said thanks. A few days later he contacted me. "Where can I get a case of those books?" He'd given his copy to one of his men in the hospital. Now he wanted more to share with the entire department.

Just the little act of prayerfully *planting a seed*—giving away a New Testament, inviting someone to church or Bible study, offering to pray with them over a concern—can be the start of something that will change that person's life for eternity! It just takes us being willing to step out.

Bonus seed! When in Oklahoma City, I gave a motorcycle New Testament *Hope for the Highway* to a lady attending our meeting. She e-mailed me. Seems her family owns a motorcycle shop and . . .

Prayer:
Each day, Jesus, I ask you to fill me with the Holy Spirit, lead me to people where you want me to plant seeds of your truth. Give me the courage to sow so you can reap.

"Dropping on the Rat" Big Fish Fire Near Meeker, Colorado, 2002
(Courtesy of Rick Barton)

Dwayne Clemmons, Adjunct Instructor – Virginia Department of Fire Programs; Founder – DMC Ministries; Author of Exploits, Jesus Rides in an Ambulance, and Utterances from the Throne Room; Volunteer in Fire and EMS for forty years in Virginia

VALUE OF LIFE

You are an incredible creation by a magnificent God

DO YOU know the value of your life as a first responder? Do you realize God chose to use you specifically to respond to emergencies and save others from an impending tragedy? True, not all are saved, but when God has ordained it, he uses you to save people from physical loss.

Do you know the value of your life as a Christian? Do you realize there are people you know, work with, and walk by every day whose soul will never be saved unless you answer God's call to share his Word?

What if you arrived on scene to administer first aid or put out a fire and people failed to recognize who you were, so they refused your help? Jesus met with this rejection: "He came to that which was his own, but his own did not receive him" (John 1:11).

Good news follows in verse 12, where we learn that everyone who receives Christ and believes in him will become children of God, and thus they will be saved.

Jesus came for his own people but they rejected him. Yet God, in his infinite wisdom and incredible mercy, gave more people a chance to experience his love, plan, and salvation.

> "He was in the world, and though the world was made through him, the world did not recognize him. He came to that which was his own, but his own did not receive him. Yet to all who received him, to those who believed in his name, he gave the right to become children of God—children born not of natural descent, nor of human decision or a husband's will, but born of God." (John 1:10–13)

You are of value as a Christian. John 13:1–17 explains that you, as a Christian, are born of God, and consequently all your witnessing efforts and soul-winning crusades are an incredible gift from God. God made a conscious decision to choose you and to use you in his plan. You are all his idea.

Are you living each day, serving each day, sharing his love each day with the awareness that the only reason you're alive is because of God?

You are an incredible creation by a magnificent God. He needs you, whether you believe it or not. You've been selected to participate in a training evolution called life in which you are being prepared for what you'll be doing for eternity. If you go to bed each night knowing you've done all you could do that day to serve God, I assure you, your life will never be the same again.

Prayer:
Lord, I thank you that I'm born of you. May I be sensitive to the Spirit each day to be more productive and zealous in sharing my faith.

SEPTEMBER 5

Chief Lee Callahan, Burlington, MA; Fellowship of Christian Firefighters International Regional Director / International Board Member

A FOOL'S PERSPECTIVE
Discerning what is foolish in God's sight

WHEN PERFORMING equipment maintenance, I picked up a can of spray paint, and as I shook it I started to sing, "Shake it up baby, now, Twist and shout." This flashback to an early Beatles tune enticed two other crew members to join in. We had a ball singing and making fools of ourselves until the painting, and consequently the singing, were done. We had a good laugh as we thought about what the scene would look like if someone had seen us. We were supposed to be performing maintenance on important firefighting equipment. Instead, we were singing, shaking, grooving, and carrying on—making fools of ourselves.

Perhaps you've played the fool's role by butting into a conversation with your very important insight only to find out the conversation was on a different topic. Maybe you were so sure of a fact you got into an argument only to find you had the facts messed up. Maybe it's not you, but someone you work with or socialize with, who ended up looking like a fool.

Society doesn't take kindly to fools. Fools make us uncomfortable. They have few, if any, friends, and are often shunned. In the fire service we tend not to have much patience with fools.

331

The Bible has a lot to say about fools. It describes them, among other things, as contentious, hypocritical, materialistic, self-confident, wasteful, wordy, or even blasphemous. Now obviously there are contexts to look at when finding out why God's Word uses those words to describe fools, but I think the message is clear: God is not pleased with

> "The plans of the foolish and the thought of foolishness are sin, and the scoffer is an abomination to men."
> (Proverbs 24:9 AMP)

fools. Other characteristics the Bible assigns fools are self-righteous, hating knowledge, despicable, disappointing, and a form of sin. A form of sin? Affirmative, but who fools us to fall into sin? Who fooled Eve way back in the Garden of Eden? I think you know the answer: Satan.

Let's work, with the Holy Spirit's help, to keep Satan at a distance by staying away from being a fool involved in the foolishness of this world.

Does singing and "goofing off" a little have to be obliterated? Of course not! God wants us to have fun and enjoy life. It does mean you must be discerning of what is foolish in God's sight and what is foolish in the sight of the world.

Prayer:
May my singing and dancing, fooling around and enjoying life, be in a manner to lift spirits and most of all may it always be honoring to you, God.

SEPTEMBER 6

Reverend Wayne Detzler, PhD, Chaplain (Retired) –
Charlotte, NC, Fire Department; Fellowship of
Christian Firefighters Regional Director

WHERE'S THE PILOT?
When the Lord saved his life

NEAR CHARLOTTE is a remarkable missionary center. It's called JAARS, Wycliffe Bible Translators' Jungle Aviation and Radio Service. Their research and development work is legendary, but their most obvious interest is missionary aviation. Pilots and service personnel are based there. These pilots and mechanics are some of the best in the world. In fact, they're really geniuses at what they do.

One evening a test pilot took off for a routine flight. He cleared the base and started to climb, but power failed. The plane lost altitude. The pilot brought it down for a relatively soft landing in a nearby field.

Immediately the volunteer fire fighters based at JAARS responded. The landing site was very near their station. In minutes they were on site and located the wrecked plane. Mercifully, it had not burned. Also, it was close enough to the road that firefighters could readily access the wreck.

But where was the pilot? They found the plane, but the pilot was not there. He'd vanished from the site. Quickly they secured the wreck, as they continued to puzzle over the pilot.

They asked the neighbors, but no one knew the pilot's whereabouts. Finally they checked with the JAARS base. "Where's the pilot?" they asked. "We can't find him."

Immediately, JAARS checked with their flight operations and discovered the answer.

> "In you our fathers put their trust; they trusted and you delivered them."
> (Psalm 22:4)

The pilot walked away from the wreck and the short distance back to the JAARS base. He was safe and sound and trying to plan recovery of the plane so they could discover what had gone wrong.

"I don't get it!" the firefighter shared with me. "How does this kind of thing happen?" As an amateur pilot, I was as shocked as my firefighter friend was. Few people walk away from a plane wreck. Even fewer planes are able to be recovered.

This remarkable escape became a Christian witness to the whole fire-fighting community. Missionary pilots are missionaries first, pilots second. They gladly gave God the glory for this event.

Prayer:
*Lord, your protection is a powerful witness
to the world around me, and I thank you.*

Sue Reynolds, Missionary – Fellowship of Christian Firefighters International (FCFI), and Chaplain Gaius Reynolds, President – FCFI; Volunteer Firefighter – Livermore, CO, Fire Protection District

OPTIONS

To accept or reject, that is the question

WHEN FLAMES rise to take lives and consume property, firefighters step in to save them from destruction. Many biblical parallels can be drawn regarding being saved from destruction, especially when you consider saving a soul from eternal flames. Revelation 20:14, 15 describes those eternal flames as a "lake of fire." Not a pleasant image. Turn now to the first chapter of Revelation, verse 1, which describes the alternative to a lake of fire: a new heaven (and new earth). Two eternal options for eternity are clearly presented. If a person's name isn't found in the Book of Life, their destiny is the lake of fire.

> "Then death and Hades were thrown into the lake of fire. The lake of fire is the second death. If anyone's name was not found written in the book of life, he was thrown into the lake of fire."
> (Revelation 20:14, 15)

You have a choice of where you spend eternity, a decision that must be made in this lifetime. You can choose to accept Christ and the salvation he offers that leads to the new heaven and earth, or to reject him, which leads to the lake of fire. The choice to be saved from eternal destruction, to avail yourself of the safeguards against destruction (your personal protective equipment), is up to you.

There are skeptics who insist there is no life after we leave this world, and there is no God, heaven and new earth, or hell. Similar beliefs were held in Jesus' day by the Sadducees (they were "sad, you see" because they didn't believe in resurrection and life after death). Jesus addressed these false views by sharing the parable of Lazarus and the rich man (Luke 16:19–31). Other illustrations of heaven and Satan's tactics fill the pages of the New Testament. None, however, compares to Romans 6:5's succinct preview of what's in store for those who believe on Christ: "If we have been united with [Christ]

> "Then I saw a new heaven and a new earth, for the first heaven and the first earth had passed away, and there was no longer any sea."
> (Revelation 1:1)

like this in his death [a sacrificial death for the forgiveness of your sins], we will certainly also be united with him in his resurrection." Paul affirmed this truth when he said to be absent from the body is to be present with the Lord (2 Corinthians 5:8), and "to live is Christ and to die is gain" (Philippians 1:21).

I pray you have made a decision for eternity with God and pledged to be a witness of his truths and love.

Prayer:
Thank you, God, for the assurance that through Christ I have an eternity with you that started the day I accepted you as my Lord. While I know this part of my life on Earth will not be free from tears and hurts, I know one day I will be with you in a perfect heaven and new earth.

S E P T E M B E R   8

Chaplain Marc Santorella; Firefighter Danvers Fire Department, MA Public Fire and Life Safety Educator and Certified Fire Instructor Level 1

GPS
God's Positioning System

GPS DEVICES are showing up on pieces of firefighting apparatus. From Day 1, we're told it is important for first responders to know our streets. So why would we be given devices to encourage us *not* to learn? With a GPS we just need to turn it on and it provides directions. The job's done for us.

On the other side of the coin, have you ever been in an emergency situation and suddenly forgotten where a once-familiar street was? In a non-emergency moment, you could probably drive there blindfolded, but pressure can cause a mental lapse, making you forget where you're headed. Maybe it's good that GPS devices are available.

These navigational tracking systems use three separate satellites, which cross-reference the GPS unit. By taking three points of reference they're able to give a proper geographical position.

Just as we reference our positions geographically, it's important to get a fix on where we are spiritually. There will always be a danger of veering off course if we walk through our daily lives without a spiritual GPS. God provides three sure points of reference for us to obtain our daily spiritual position. We just need to consider the Trinity. We might even call this a "Three-Person" reference.

They are God's Word, Jesus' example, and the Holy Spirit's presence.

God's Word existed from the very beginning (John 1:1), it was given by inspiration of God, it is profitable (2 Timothy 3:16), and it's the food of life (Matthew 4:4).

The second GPS reference point is Jesus' example. In his own words, he said, "I have set you an example that you should do as I have done for you" (John 13:15).

> "It was the LORD our God himself who brought us and our fathers up out of Egypt, from that land of slavery, and performed those great signs before our eyes. He protected us on our entire journey and among all the nations through which we traveled."
> (Joshua 24:17)

Finally, and without fail, we can rely on the Holy Spirit's presence. Believers live by a faith that is unseen and at times unfelt. Even so, we're assured he is always with us and available to us. When Jesus ascended to heaven, he sent the Holy Spirit. He has also promised, "Never will I leave you; never will I forsake you" (Hebrews 13:5).

God's Positioning System (GPS) is aligned and true. No matter which of life's journeys you're traveling, the GPS that Christians rely on is always operating and without error. God has mapped out your next course. Remember, he guided and protected the Israelites on their journey, and he'll do the same for you.

Prayer:
Thank you, God the Father, the Son, and the Holy Spirit,
for guiding my path. What an awesome GPS you are!

SEPTEMBER 9

Craig Duck, Lieutenant, Engine Co. 11 – Washington, DC, Fire Department; Fellowship of Christian Firefighters International Atlantic States Regional Director / International Board Member

ORDER OUT OF CHAOS
Restoring peace and hope in a world gone wrong

I REMEMBER THE day as if it were yesterday. I reported for work that autumn day as I had many others before it. As I hung my gear in the officer's position, I marveled at the clear blue sky and the warm temperature. Like many firefighters in America, we were sitting around the television that September day when we first saw the images of the planes hitting the towers in New York. We began to discuss the tactics and strategies the New York City firefighters would be using, not realizing we would be going to our own disaster within minutes. When the box alarm was sounded in our firehouse, we were on our way to assist the Arlington Fire Department with a plane that struck the Pentagon. As one could imagine, as we approached the Pentagon, it was a very chaotic scene. Cars were stopped on the highway with people walking about, civilians were just wandering around the Pentagon dazed and confused, and the fire units on the scene were doing their best to organize the rescue and firefighting groups.

> "The LORD is my light and my salvation—whom shall I fear? The Lord is the stronghold of my life—of whom shall I be afraid?" (Psalm 27:1)

The Pentagon was the largest disaster any of us had ever responded to in this region of the country. The radio was abuzz with priority messages and firefighters trying to explain what they needed. The scene was one of chaos. I will never forget how one chief changed all that.

When this chief arrived, everything changed on the radio. We became more organized as we listened to him, and people seemed to calm down. The chief's calm voice reassured us it would be all right, and that he was in control. That chief reminds me of God, and how he always reassures his children during times of trouble. Isaiah knew this kind of reassurance when he wrote, "For I am the LORD, your God, who takes hold of your right hand and says to you, Do not fear; I will help you" (Isaiah 41:13). God is in control—we need to listen to him during times of trouble.

In the midst of your next trial just remember that God, our Incident Commander, always makes order out of chaos.

Prayer:
*Help me, Lord, to live my life for you so I can be used
by you in times of trouble, and be calmed by your comfort.*

*Reverend Wayne Detzler, PhD, Chaplain (Retired) –
Charlotte, NC, Fire Department; Fellowship of
Christian Firefighters Regional Director*

RESCUING THE PERISHING
Learning to reach the unreachable

THE BARBAROUS attacks of September 11, 2001, changed American life forever. Perhaps they changed the role of first responders most of all. No one will ever look on us again as they did before 9/11. Likewise, many will never look at their careers the same again.

Before that sparkling September morning, first responders were almost part of the scenery in cities and towns across America.

"Why do you do it?" my lead pastor asked me. "I just don't know why you're so deeply involved, so passionate about the fire service." He urged me to take it easy. "After all," he added, "at your age you have earned a rest."

All that changed, however, on September 11, 2001. Now the community commenced to understand. They knew just how dangerous it all was. They saw those unforgettable images of firefighters rushing *into* the twin towers, just as civilians were rushing *out*.

> "Whoever enters through me will be saved." (John 10:9)

A whole new emphasis was born on that day. I remember how we commenced training for Urban Search and Rescue (USAR). Day after day I stood by as firefighters drilled through concrete, shifted huge slabs of cement, and learned to lift collapsed walls and roofs.

There was a new motivation. We knew it might well happen again. Or it might be an earthquake in Haiti, or even in China. The task is as daunting as it is desperate. Finding the trapped and the injured is Job Number 1.

Rescue is what we do as first responders. For years we've cut people out of crashed cars. For a long time we've combed through the ashes of burned-out homes as we hunted for people and rescued them. We've rescued people who fell off cliffs. Saving the helpless is top priority.

We learn this from the Lord Jesus Christ. His very name is Savior. After all, he left the glory of heaven to seek and save those who are lost. He gave his very life so we might have *eternal* life.

September 11, 2001, brought to the forefront of the public's mind the dangers first responders encounter. Perhaps it also made first responders a little more cognizant of their own mortality. Three-hundred-forty-seven fell that fatal day. Did they know the Lord? For some we may never know. For you personally, you can know for sure. Because all who believe in Jesus and confess that belief, through him, will be saved.

Prayer:
Thank you for teaching me how important
it is to be saved, O Lord our Savior.

S E P T E M B E R   1 1

Rev. Joe Smaha, Chaplain/Fire Inspector/Firefighter/EMT/
Hazmat Specialist – Paramus, NJ, Fire Department;
Fire Instructor – Bergen County, NJ, Fire Academy;
Pastor – Community Church of Paramus

THE DARKEST OF DAYS

The impromptu prayer meetings
and expressions of thanks were a ray of hope

ON SEPTEMBER 11, 2001, less than five hours after the first plane struck the North Tower of the World Trade Center, the Paramus Fire Department Hazardous Materials Team was at Ground Zero.

Several things made a marked impression on me. First was the enormity of the disaster area. It was a vast sixteen acres and everything was still burning, including several surrounding buildings. Dust, rubble, and papers were strewn everywhere. It was like a war zone with debris and crushed emergency vehicles everywhere. Second, knowing the immense loss of human life that lay in the ruins added heavily to the enormity. The next was the quiet. I was born in New York City, so I'm used to the busy, noisy pace of downtown. Today, there was no pedestrian traffic, and the only vehicle noise was the sound of an occasional siren. The normal busy downtown pace was replaced by an ominous quiet.

Then the ground trembled, people ran, and a column of dust rose where Building 7 once stood. Our hazmat team was there to back up the FDNY Haz-Mat 1 Team in case chemical or biological weapons were discovered. Thank God none was. For eleven hours we unloaded trucks of food, water, equipment, and supplies into the Manhattan Community College gymnasium, now a staging area. I couldn't grasp the startling reality of this horrific situation. I kept hoping to wake up and find it a terrible dream.

339

That night people gathered in the streets outside Ground Zero praying. Around 9:30, under the glow of emergency lighting, hundreds of FDNY firefighters involved in search and rescue withdrew. They marched out, weary, worn, dusty, dirty, and solemn, like soldiers emerging from the heat of battle. Some rode out on partially crushed dust-covered fire apparatus so badly damaged, it's a wonder they could be driven. As New York City's Bravest emerged from the rubble, the crowds cheered, applauded, and shouted gratitude.

The impromptu prayer meetings and expressions of gratitude gave a ray of hope that Romans 8:28 still holds true God can still bring good to America out of the ashes of despair. Many Americans gained a new spiritual interest—evidence that God can bring victory out of the most horrendous disaster.

"Do not store up for yourselves treasures on earth, where moth and rust destroy, and where thieves break in and steal [or terrorists threaten and destroy]. But store up for yourselves treasures in heaven, where moth and rust do not destroy, and where thieves [terrorists] do not break in and steal. For where your treasure is, there your heart will be also."
(Matthew 6:19–21)

America will never be the same. I know I've changed. Perhaps America is wiser and less naive. Maybe we realize our trust in "things" was misguided. Jesus said,

Prayer:

Thank you for light on the darkest days. I pray you'll revive, heal, and bless the United States of America. May my heart dwell on heavenly, not earthly, treasures.

Ten House (Courtesy of William Garvey)

*Tommy Neiman, Author of Sirens for the Cross; EMS
Training Officer – St. Lucie County, FL; Fellowship of
Christian Firefighters International Regional
Director / International Board Member*

AFTER THE ATTACK

I urge you to continue to pray

SEPTEMBER 11, 2001, my wife met me at the door with a stricken look on her face. Panic gripped my emotions when, hardly able to speak, Alicia asked, "Tommy, did you hear what happened?" Trembling she said, "The Twin Towers in New York City, they're on the ground! Planes hit them. A plane also hit the Pentagon. Another, possibly targeting the White House, crashed to the ground. I can't believe this."

Neither could I as I stayed glued to the news and wondered what part God would allow me to play in this world-changing event. Would it be as

341

a rescuer, chaplain, pastor, or what? What could I do? Obviously, the first thing was to pray! And pray I did, along with millions of Christians around the country. But would there be more for me to do?

The days went by and my prayers continued until a call came from the president of the Fellowship of Christian Firefighters, Gaius Reynolds. He was in New York City. They needed more chaplains to present ceremonial urns and flags to the victims' families.

Wasting no time, I arrived the next day. After a Blue and White Service to honor first responders, our group of chaplains headed to Liberty Island to honor the victims' families. From young children to mature seniors, each touched my heart. Family groups wore pins or screen-print photos of their lost loved ones. The victims were not impersonal names in the paper—they were cherished loved ones. As each family came forward, I experienced sadness and a powerful desire to comfort them. So deep was their loss, many had to be held up as they received their urn. I prayed they knew the only lasing comfort comes from Jesus. In the forefront of my mind was the realization that a life without Jesus is a life without promise, hope, or healing.

> "For just as the sufferings of Christ flow over into our lives, so also through Christ our comfort overflows. If we are distressed, it is for your comfort and salvation; if we are comforted, it is for your comfort, which produces in you patient endurance of the same sufferings we suffer. And our hope for you is firm, because we know that just as you share in our sufferings, so also you share in our comfort." (2 Corinthians 1:5–7)

I only had a little over a minute with each family, but my prayers will always be with them.

As another year passes since that tragic day, September 11, 2001, I urge you to pray for the families affected directly and indirectly by that attack of terror. Pray that, if they don't know the saving love of Jesus, they will turn to Jesus to deal with whatever emptiness, meaninglessness, lack of hope, or pain they continue to harbor in their lives.

Prayer:
May you continue to heal those lives forever changed in September 2001. If they don't know you, Lord, may they come to a saving knowledge of life as a child of God.

FDNY Memorial Wall (Courtesy of William Garvey)

Bob Macchia, Federal Aviation Administration,
Real Estate Contracting Officer, New York

I AM HERE AND
I LOVE YOU, DAD!

"Behold, I am with you" (Genesis 28:15 NKJV)

LIEUTENANT John P. Napolitano, one of America's heroes, started as a rookie in the Lakeland, New York, Fire Department in 1991 and worked his way up to chief, then became a commissioner. He worked at Rescue 2 in Brooklyn. Fellow firefighters said they followed John into fires so loud you couldn't hear a thing, yet Johnny never took a step back. He was a friend to many, and loved firefighting and his wife, Anne, and two little girls, Elizabeth and Emma Rose. He'd do anything for them and in return earned nontarnishing medals—the ones that come in the form of smiles and hugs.

343

On September 11, 2001, John entered one more burning building to save another life. He did it because that is the way heroes live their lives. On September 11, 2001, my nephew, John Napolitano, gave the ultimate gift. He gave his life.

> "Oh, the depth of the riches of the wisdom and knowledge of God! How unsearchable his judgments, and his paths beyond tracing out!" (Romans 11:33)

After the tragedy my daughter Dina received an e-mail message from Sergeant Joe Jackson, NYPD, who'd purchased a magazine from Dina titled "Through the Ashes." It was dedicated to our nephew. Joe had volunteered for a couple of years with Johnny at the Lakeland Fire Department. After the Attack on America he was called to Ground Zero.

Johnny's dad and close friend Lenny Crisci visited Ground Zero repeatedly to conduct their own search. Lenny, a retired police officer, who lost his brother, spent days traversing the dust that covered the ground where once the majestic towers of the Trade Center stood. Johnny's dad wrote a message to his son. In the fine, thick dust of Ground Zero, he wrote: "Johnny Napolitano, I am here and I Love You, Dad."

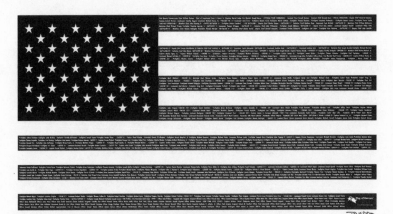

Flag of Heroes™

This flag contains the names of the emergency services personnel who gave
their lives to save others in the terrorist attacks of 9.11. *
Now and forever it will represent their immortality
We shall never forget them

A Loving Tribute

It was through that message, written in dust, Sergeant Joe Jackson first learned of the loss of his friend and comrade. Joe related in his message to Dina that while stopping to rest after spending several hours at Ground Zero he spotted Johnny's dad's message. He was saddened to find out his friend had perished, yet he was touched by the scribbled and loving message from Johnny's dad.

I am forever awed by the amazing and strange ways in which God works.

Prayer:

Your ways are wonderful. Thank you, Lord, for those who have given so freely to serve others. I lift up their family and loved ones to you that they may know your comfort and peace. Help them as they continue to process the losses suffered while serving as first responders.

SEPTEMBER 14

Tommy Neiman, Author of Sirens for the Cross; EMS Training Officer – St. Lucie County, FL; Fellowship of Christian Firefighters International Regional Director / International Board Member

GROUND HERO AND THE CROSS
The cross will always be standing

THE TERM *Ground Zero* suggests many different things: terrorism, attacks on our freedom, lost loved ones, destruction, and the strength and solidarity of the American people and way of life. To many, it is not *Ground Zero*, but . . . *Ground Hero*, for on those New York City grounds, where the stately 110-story World Trade Center towers once stood, many of America's true heroes gave their lives. It is to those heroes who "laid down" their lives the tragic morning of September 11, 2001, to the ones they were unable to save, and to all who serve as first responders this tribute is dedicated.

When God allowed me to enter Ground Hero to visit and pray for, and with, recovery teams, my eyes focused on the still-smoking debris piles and massive amounts of twisted steel and concrete. No computer image or magazine can portray the immensity of the destruction that surrounded me. Jolted to the core by the destruction, I sensed the evil that caused this.

345

I felt Satan was taunting me and trying to crush my spirit by implying, "See the evil and death I can do."

Our Fellowship of Christian Firefighters' chaplains' group's earnest prayers were to be able to provide spiritual comfort, encourage, thank, and present small tokens of appreciation (in the form of Bibles and books) to the firefighters and emergency workers who

> "And having disarmed the powers and authorities, he made a public spectacle of them, triumphing over them by the cross" (Colossians 2:15).

relentlessly and selflessly searched for their brothers' bodies, victims' bodies, and restoration. We were overwhelmed by the warm reception and privileged to have people share their experiences with us. With God's direction, we were allowed to share Jesus' love.

Upon leaving, my focus changed from evil and loss to promise when I noticed something I'd missed when entering. It was the now-famous steel-beam cross cut out during the collapse. Seeing this perfectly cutout cross instantly took away the jolt of death and destruction Satan was using to try to suppress my spirit.

How did I miss this steel-beam cross? Probably because, just as in life, when the world comes crumbling down, my attention was drawn to the destruction and not the cross. My physical eyes simply did what my spiritual eyes often do. But regardless of the surrounding damage, destruction, and death, the cross will always be standing!

Ground Zero? Maybe for the media, but to me it is *Ground Hero.*

Prayer:

Jesus, the bearer of that cross, thank you that you will never leave me nor forsake me! May the heroics and selfless demonstration of what America is really about never be forgotten. May I always keep my focus on you, and may you, God, bless our country.

USA Flag Overlooking Cross at Ground Zero (Courtesy of William Garvey)

Tommy Neiman, Author of Sirens for the Cross; EMS Training Officer – St. Lucie County, FL; Fellowship of Christian Firefighters International Regional Director / International Board Member

THE LAST ALARM

All of us will someday encounter our "Last Alarm"

ONE PRIMARY fire service publication contains a section called "The Last Alarm" devoted to the recognition and honor of those who recently died in the line of duty. As I look over the names, I think about their families, the children they left behind, and the people they worked with. I wonder if they knew the Lord, then I pray for those left behind.

God placed a heavy burden on my heart for my lost brothers and sisters in fire departments all over this nation. But the burden extends even further; it extends to the lost who don't know Jesus, and consequently don't have the assurance that when their last alarm sounds they'll spend eternity with Jesus.

One call on which that burden was foremost in my mind was for a twenty-six-year-old woman in the later stages of AIDS. Barely able to move, she collapsed at her converted motel room apartment. Weighing less than fifty pounds, it was nothing to single-handedly place her on our stretcher. I knew God called our crew out of our normal zone and sent me to minister to this deathly weak and trembling woman. I took her shaking hand and delicately, but straightforwardly, said, "You know you haven't got long, don't you? Do you know Jesus loves you? Have you trusted him as your Savior?"

> "This is how God showed his love among us: He sent his one and only Son into the world that we might live through him."
> (1 John 4:9)

She nodded her head and said, "Yes." Fear still covered her trembling face.

I next said, "You don't have to be afraid; Jesus is right there holding you as you pass with him into glory."

She smiled and closed her eyes as if immediately sensing God's presence. As she slipped from this world into eternity, I told her I'd see her again someday because of what Jesus Christ did for us two thousand years ago.

Whether due to a fatal illness, an accident, or the natural process of aging, or in the line of duty, all of us will someday encounter our "Last Alarm."

Prayer:
God, you've done your part, you sent your only Son to die on the cross for my sins. Christ, you, too, did your part; you came to Earth in the form of man, died a brutal death on the cross, rose from the dead, ascended to heaven, and prepared a place for me in eternity. Thank you, Lord. When my final alarm sounds, because of you, Lord, I can be assured of my destiny. Help me be bold enough to share your promise and truth with my crew and those I encounter who are ready to hear of your love.

SEPTEMBER 16

William Garvey, Writer/Photographer; Damage Prevention Supervisor – Gas Company, Michigan

GOD BLESS OUR HEROES!
Please know that many folks like me say, "Thank you"

WHAT IF you could tell your thoughts to the heroes in your life? What would you say? How would you say it?

The idea for sharing my appreciation with heroes came after September 11, 2001. I knew that many firefighters had given their lives, and I wanted to express my appreciation. An idea crossed my mind to shoot a photo of our daughter praying as a thank you. A few years later, a friend told me about a New York magazine that was looking for a photo that expressed the same gratitude I felt. The next day our paper's front page featured a photo of a soldier standing proudly in uniform with an American flag flying respectfully in the background. The accompanying story told how he was one of the first to die fighting for our country in Iraq.

What if he was my son? How did his parents feel? The hurt from those thoughts stuck with me all day. Then I thought about those in the military and fire service who gave their lives or are currently putting their lives in danger serving others. Those folks are my heroes as well and I wanted to say, "Thank you."

349

Photography is one of my hobbies. Remembering my earlier idea, I told my daughter I wanted to say, "Thank you" to America's heroes through a special photo of her praying. The result was a silhouette of a little girl praying with a brightly lit flag in the background.

No doubt many times as they serve our country, first responders wonder, *Why did I choose this profession? My life schedule is haphazard; the events of the days are obscure. Will I face danger? Will my life or that of my co-worker be in jeopardy? . . .*

Please know that many folks like me say, "Thank you." When we see flashing lights and hear sirens blare, many of us offer a prayer for safety. And, if you see a photo of a young girl praying in front of our nation's flag, please know that I am one of the many folks across America who say, "Thank You" every chance I get.

"Grace and peace to you from God our Father and the Lord Jesus Christ. I thank my God every time I remember you. In all my prayers for all of you, I always pray with joy." (Philippians 1:2–4)

Prayer:
When a call puts me and my co-workers in danger, I thank you that there are Christian men and women who pray for first responders. I, too, Lord, lift up all my brother and sister first responders to you that you will protect them with your shield of protection.

God Bless Our Heroes

"Thank You Lord" Praying for our Nation (Courtesy of William Garvey)

*Rev. Joe Smaha, Chaplain/Fire Inspector/Firefighter/EMT/
Hazmat Specialist – Paramus, NJ, Fire Department;
Fire Instructor – Bergen County, NJ, Fire Academy;
Pastor – Community Church of Paramus*

HURRICANE FLOYD

*I'm humbled and grateful to be counted
as a member of "America's Bravest"*

SEPTEMBER 17, 1999, Hurricane Floyd, forecast to miss our state, unexpectedly terrorized New Jersey for more than twelve hours with a relentless barrage of heavy rain. The Paramus Fire Department, like many local fire departments, received an onslaught of calls ranging from false alarms, downed power lines, odors of smoke or natural gas, to stranded and terrified motorists and residents. The usually lazy Saddlebrook Stream swelled and engulfed the surrounding area under water eight to twelve feet higher than normal. Fire Company 3, where I was stationed, responded to more than two dozen such calls.

> "But thanks be to God! He gives us the victory through our Lord Jesus Christ. Therefore, my dear brothers, stand firm. Let nothing move you. Always give your-selves fully to the work of the Lord, because you know that your labor in the Lord is not in vain."
> (1 Corinthians 15:57, 58)

On scene, bizarre, surreal sights met our eyes. Cars bobbed along the flooded highway. Fish and crawfish swam across the usually dry roadway. Electrical flashes, accompanied by the sounds of arcing wires and exploding electrical transformers, illuminated tragic casualties. With hand lights and rescue tools, and aware of our perilous footing, we waded into the chest-deep water. Victims were carried to large front-end loaders that were waiting to transport them to buses to take them to emergency shelters. Sixteen infants, a young woman in a cast from her thigh to her foot, elderly men and women with oxygen tanks, as well as numerous children, composed the diversity of victims. Yet they all shared a commonality. They were frightened, and the sight of rescuers brought relief.

Paramus Emergency Service Responders, made up of police, EMS, and fire and rescue responders, helped rescue more than a hundred families from homes damaged by a hurricane that was not supposed to hit New Jersey at all.

Hurricane Floyd was extreme. Daily, throughout our great land, similar tragedies occur that both challenge and require the expertise of our country's emergency responders, who are prepared to help twenty-four hours a day, seven days a week.

It is rewarding and satisfying to be a part of a team that makes a difference in people's lives. When fellow Americans share their thankfulness, that satisfaction multiplies. Most of all, I'm humbled and grateful to be counted as a member of "America's Bravest."

Prayer:
I give thanks to you, God, that I have victory through Jesus.
Help me stand firm and always give 100 percent
to the work you've set before me.

SEPTEMBER 18

William Garvey, Writer/Photographer; Damage
Prevention Supervisor – Gas Company, Michigan

DID THEY KNOW?

Lord, take me where you want me
to go and keep me out of your way

WHAT A SIGHT we were as we pulled into Manhattan, New York, September 11, 2006, the fifth anniversary of the Attack on America! In the back of our truck was a five-hundred-pound pumpkin. My wife, Lorraine, and I came to say thank you, we're praying for you, and we'll never forget what you do and your losses from America's dreadful attack.

When Ten House regretfully said they lacked a safe place, they sent us to the 7 & 1 House on Duane Street. I headed there thinking, *Now I know how Mary and Joseph felt.*

Surprised when they saw us, one yelled, "Is that a pumpkin or what?" As they examined the five-hundred-pound carving I explained, "We came 650 miles to give it to

> "I will never forget your precepts, for by them you have preserved my life. Save me, for I am yours." (Psalm 119:93, 94)

352

Five Hundred Pounds of Gratitude (Courtesy of William Garvey)

you and say thank you." Carved in the pumpkin's eyes were a boy and girl praying, each surrounded by a heart. The nose was firefighters putting up the flag at Ground Zero. The mouth was the word AMERICA, shaped to make a smile.

"But you spelled America wrong!" the captain said.

My heart sank. "Oh, no!" I looked closely, spelled it in my head three times, and then responded, "I spelled it right!"

He started laughing. "Yeah, I know, but I had you going!"

Laughter followed. New friendships were made.

God brought us to that firehouse to say thanks, and that truth was reinforced when we received a card of thanks, dated 09-11-06, with a prayer card from the late FDNY Fire Chaplain Father Mychal Judge, who died on 9-11-01. This prayer summed up our trip: "Lord, Take me where you want me to go. Let me meet who you want me to meet and keep me out of your way."

God had done just that with the firefighters of the 7 & 1 House on 09-11-01 when the Twin Towers came down. The important thing to us was, as the dust cleared, they all made it out alive. Their story gave us hope and is the same gift we wished for our youngest son, Tim, who was then on his way to fight for our country in Iraq.

FDNY, you didn't know we were coming, but in our hearts we were always there. Thank you—we will never forget you.

Prayer:
Serving you, Lord, I often reap so much more than I give. Thank you for those blessings. I am yours. May I never forget those who served and lost their lives, whether at Ground Zero, in other LODDs, or in other ways of giving of themselves to serve others.

SEPTEMBER 19

Ken Cofiell, Dispatcher/Firefighter/EMT (Deceased) –
Anne Arundel County, MD, Fire Department

QUIET HEROES
Some must die for life, but there are others who must go on living for life

ON SEPTEMBER 11, 2001, during the dreadful Attack on America, hundreds of firefighters and law enforcement officers faced their "Last Alarm." In the history of America, they shall rightfully be acclaimed heroes. Yet, there is another group of heroes who quietly and humbly walk the streets of our country. It was my blessing to meet one of them.

> "Therefore, since through God's mercy we have this ministry, we do not lose heart."
> (2 Corinthians 4:1)

On my last day working the Fellowship of Christian Firefighters booth at the Firehouse Expo in Baltimore, Maryland, a year after the Attack on America, the effects that attack had on firefighters was evident on the faces those who stopped at or passed by our booth. Everyone was quick to share their personal stories of where they were at that time. One person, however, stood out among the others. It was a young woman perusing the items we had on display.

"Are you with the fire department?" I asked.

"No," she replied with a touch of reluctance in her voice, "but my husband was."

"Is he retired?" I asked hoping he took an early retirement.

In a solemn but strong voice she answered with the one answer I was hoping not to hear. "No, he died in the towers on 9/11."

What do you say to someone who lost a loved one so tragically? As I faltered for words, I realized I was standing in front of one of America's quiet heroes—a surviving victim of 9/11. As I noticed the pendant around her neck with a picture of a family of four, two bubbly children approached. They were excited about the things they'd collected. My eyes were drawn to their necks adorned with necklaces identical to the one their mom wore—necklaces that displayed a picture of days forever gone, days when their dad was still with them. The pain and sadness she carried deep inside was revealed as she spoke of the void that was once filled with her husband's presence.

As this family walked away, I watched in awe. They represented the countless quiet heroes who silently paid the ultimate price. This husband died for life, but his family goes on living for life.

Prayer:
Let me "Never Forget." May I never become insensitive to the hurt of the families who suffered loss because of the Attack on America. May I show compassion to those I respond to on each and every call, sharing your mercy and love.

S E P T E M B E R   2 0

William Garvey, Writer/Photographer; Damage Prevention Supervisor – Gas Company, Michigan

EXCUSE ME, MISTER! WERE YOU THERE?

His grave a nation's heart shall be,
His monument a people free.

CAROLINE ATHERTON BRIGGS MASON

I HAD MANY childhood heroes who were examples of superhuman strength going where *no man has gone before!* Time expanded my knowledge of what a hero really is. What's more, heroes are easy to pick out, for they usually have the letters FD, PD, or US on their clothing.

One hero made that tragic day of September 11, 2001, is my friend and co-worker, Lieutenant Tim Wren, a Troy, Michigan, firefighter. Tim was in charge of the 2001 Fallen Firefighters' Memorial.

Coordinating the 2001 Fallen Firefighters' Memorial in the aftermath of 9/11 was very challenging. The growing number of concerned people planning to attend made it necessary to postpone the ceremony several times. Despite the trials, the ceremony went well. When President Bush made an unscheduled appearance to thank everyone and pay a special tribute of honor to all the fallen that year, he turned toward Tim as if to say, "Thank you." Tim saluted and President Bush saluted back!

On the ride home, still dressed in firefighter uniforms, Tim and Lieutenant Jack Spreyer stopped for dinner. They selected a table in the back in hopes of just relaxing and regrouping.

Soon, they were approached by a five-year-old blond. Ever so quietly, her hands clasped behind her back, she said, "Excuse me, mister. Were you there?"

> "Therefore, I urge you, brothers, in view of God's mercy, to offer your bodies as living sacrifices, holy and pleasing to God—this is your spiritual act of worship." (Romans 12:1)

Tim answered, "Sweetheart, where do you mean?"

"You know!"

"Do you mean the World Trade Center in New York?"

"Yes!" the little girl replied.

"Yes, honey, we were there, along with a lot of our friends."

The little girl pulled her hands from behind her back and handed them a piece of paper. With a smile she asked, "Could I please have your autographs?"

Humbly, the two firefighters signed the paper. As they did, her parents stood and started applauding. When Tim and Jack felt that life doesn't get any better, everyone in the restaurant rose to their feet and applauded them as the heroes they didn't know they were!

While the two were standing to thank everyone, a man came up behind them, put his arms around them both and said, "It is about time America had some real heroes!"

Firemen have always done the things they do, and they have done them every day of their lives, but today these two discovered something different! America was finally as proud of them as they were of America.

Prayer:
When others look at me as a hero, may I remember that all things I do are because of you and may my actions be holy and pleasing to you.

Ken Cofiell, Dispatcher/Firefighter/EMT (Deceased) –
Anne Arundel County, MD, Fire Department

BOLD HUMILITY

True heroes are humble and they walk remembering

I KNOW THIS man, I thought as I searched my mind for some flicker of remembrance of how I knew him. As he approached the booth where I was working, I asked, "Do I know you?"

"No, I don't think we've met before."

That overwhelming feeling of knowing the man continued. The few moments we visited were special and ended all too soon. The fire convention hall was packed with firefighters and emergency service workers and the Fellowship of Christian Firefighters' booth at the Baltimore Firehouse Expo had been surprisingly busy.

"Are you sure I haven't seen you somewhere before?" I just had to ask him one more time. He just smiled and shook his head before turning and continuing to visit other booths. There was no haughtiness about this man as others greeted him as if he were a man of "position."

Then the young man paused, raised his head, turned around, and asked, "Do you remember the firefighters who carried the American Flag to the roof of the Pentagon and hung it over the side?"

"Of course I do!" I responded.

A warm smile came across his face as he departed.

> "Therefore, whoever humbles himself like this child is the greatest in the kingdom of heaven."
> (Matthew 18:4)

I've read other stories about this young man who found and raised the American Flag above the Pentagon on that fatal day terrorists tried to destroy America's patriotism, honor, and property. In every account, he is consistently portrayed as a giving servant. To me he represented what makes America the great country it is—a country made of people who willingly give of themselves out of love.

I watched him as he walked away and began interacting with others, and at once I remembered. True heroes are humble and they walk remembering.

Many firefighters were given a new title in the aftermath of 9/11—the title of "hero." But true heroes don't have to broadcast their status. They live it.

Likewise, a Christian should not have to tell others, "I am a Christian!" Their words, actions, and attitudes should be their witness.

Prayer:
Lord, may I walk humbly before you and all men. May others know I am yours by the way I walk and live my life.

SEPTEMBER 22

Bob Crum, Co-founder – Fellowship of Christian Firefighters International (Retired) – Denver Fire Department

TO GROW OR TO GRUMBLE?

It all depends on your response

CHANGE! Is it good? Does it present a seemingly insurmountable challenge? Is it detrimental? On a more personal level, how can I as a Christian firefighter effectively minister to a constantly changing fire service? City administrators attempting to balance the budget are reducing fire department funds, causing manpower cuts, freezes on buying needed equipment, and a drastic lowering of morale among firefighters. What is my responsibility as a Christian firefighter in dealing with critical issues facing the fire service today?

The apostle Peter was no stranger to critical issues. First Peter 4:12 (using the paraphrase from the Living Bible) reads, "Don't be bewildered or surprised when you go through the fiery trials ahead . . . Instead be really glad—because these trials will make you partners with Christ in his suffering, and afterwards you will have the wonderful joy of sharing his glory." In other words, you have a choice. Persecution can cause you either to grow or to grumble in the Christian life. It all depends on your response.

The same is true in your job as a firefighter. Your response to situations can be positive or negative, but ultimately the decision is up to you. Those you work with will be watching for your response and will be influenced by your words and actions.

> "Dear friends, do not be surprised at the painful trial you are suffering, as though something strange were happening to you. But rejoice that you participate in the sufferings of Christ, so that you may be overjoyed when his glory is revealed."
> (1 Peter 4:12, 13)

358

God provided the way for a Christian to live that kind of lifestyle. First Peter 1:3 says that through Christ's resurrection you have new hope and new birth. Verses 6 and 7 continue by saying you should greatly rejoice even though for a time you may have seen trials and suffered grief. No one understands this better than a first responder. Grief and trials are part of the normal work routine. The good news is that the end result will be praise, honor, and glory when Christ is revealed. God's children are victors in the end.

The non-Christians you work with will be checking to see if your faith is genuine. Your prompt and cheerful obedience to God's Word will be an example to those around you. Your character and conduct should be above reproach as an ambassador for the Lord Jesus Christ. The result will be actions rooted in submission, obedience, and cheerful service. The choice is up to you.

Prayer:
*Lord, I know the final chapter. You're the victor. May I show
an attitude of gratitude and reflect the joy I have in
knowing you, regardless of the trials ahead.*

S E P T E M B E R   2 3

*Daniel A. Clegg, Rural-Metro EMT; Engineer/EMT–Indianapolis
Fire Department (Retired); Fellowship of Christian Firefighters
Regional Director / International Board Member*

VALUE OF A PENNY
While talking to Nick I learned a valuable lesson

WHILE TRANSPORTING patients from nursing homes to hospitals, I noticed Nick, a patient from a previous ambulance run, sitting in a wheelchair with a "Yield" sign attached to it.

"How are you today, Nick?"

He looked me straight in the eye. "Not that good. I just feel like a dirty piece of copper!"

"Gee, that sure was an interesting comment. Tell me Nick, what does a dirty piece of copper feel like?" I asked.

"Well, let me ask you a question, do you know what a penny is made of?"

"Of course I do. It's made of copper!"

"Do you see pennies tossed along the side of the road from time to time?"

"Sure."

"Do you ever go out of your way to bend down and pick one up?"

"Sometimes I do, but not always."

> "Indeed, the very hairs of your head are all numbered. Don't be afraid; you are worth more than many sparrows." (Luke 12:7)

"That's what I'm talking about. Most people don't take the time. To them a penny has no value."

Here before me sat an old gentleman, trapped in a nursing home, and feeling so dejected he equated himself to a dirty piece of copper.

What a tragedy for another human being, living in the greatest and richest nation, to feel his life is of no value to anyone!

I tried to cheer him up. "Nick, I'm sure there are people who really do care about you and would be willing to help you."

"If that's so, my friend, they sure have a funny way of showing it."

"Nick, I care about you and so does God. Not a sparrow falls to the ground that God doesn't know about and He knows about you and He loves you."

Nick listened as I told him how much value he had in God's eyes. Then he allowed me to pray with him.

"Dan," he said, "I believe in God, but you really need to pray for those in the world who are not willing to bend over and pick someone up. You need to pray for those who are so busy they refuse to take time to help another human being. Those people are the ones who really need prayer. They need God's touch and love in their hearts."

Prayer:

Lord, may I always take time to pick up a penny and remember the coin is of great worth, for it symbolizes the value in each and every person regardless of how big, little, young, old, or what their situation in life is. And Lord, as Nick requested, I pray for those who have become desensitized to the value of others.

Craig Duck, Lieutenant, Engine Co. 11 – Washington, DC, Fire Department; Fellowship of Christian Firefighters International Atlantic States Regional Director / International Board Member

MUSIC—MAKING A JOYFUL NOISE

Singing God's goodness and grace in the fire service

MUSIC IS an emotional and powerful tool. People going through tough times often listen to their favorite songs in order to forget their present circumstances. Search the Web and you'll find thousands of images of hurting people singing their hearts out. I'll never forget images of September 11, 2001. During one of the worst times in firefighting history, when 343 firefighters died, many firefighters were confused, saddened, and didn't know where to turn for help. Many, who were not in New York or Washington, DC, watched countless hours of news reports on television. I vividly remember watching one report of congressmen and senators on the steps of the U.S. Capitol telling what their response to the terrorist attacks would be. I'll never forget when one of the senators began singing "God Bless America." Unscripted, unrehearsed, and yet the sound of those voices singing was very moving and powerful.

> "Come, let us sing for joy to the Lord; let us shout aloud to the Rock of our salvation." (Psalm 95:1)

The Bible has a lot to say about music and its therapeutic effect on the soul. Paul encouraged the Christians in Ephesus to be filled with the Spirit and to "Speak to one another with psalms, hymns and spiritual songs. Sing and make music in your heart to the Lord" (Ephesians 5:19).

Try doing a word study in the Bible on music. You'll discover why it is so important, and why it is one of the core elements at the heart of worship. Sadly you don't hear firefighters singing praises to God very much. Perhaps they don't know how. Maybe they're afraid of how they sound. I'm thankful God never calls us to sing perfectly, just to sing.

During a Fellowship of Christian Firefighters International (FCFI) event my son, Christopher, and I decided to break out our guitars and start singing. At first folks were reluctant to sing. I wondered if we should stop, but we kept singing praises to the God who has done so much for us. By the end of the night our group was making a beautiful sound, and I am confident God was well-pleased.

Can you imagine what the fire service would be like if we sang at more of our events? What a joyful noise that could be!

Prayer:
*Help me, Lord, not to be afraid to sing praises
to your name within the fire service.*

SEPTEMBER 25

*Rick Barton, Fire Safety Officer; Rick Barton Ministries,
Gunnison, CO; Fellowship of Christian Firefighters
International Ambassador-at-Large*

MAYDAY! MAYDAY!

He never tunes us out

MAYDAY! Mayday!" my radio suddenly crackled.

The universal call of someone in distress came across the forest service frequency loud and clear. The problem was I had no idea who was calling, the nature of the emergency, or where it was. Even though the call was being picked up on our frequency, they apparently couldn't hear us responding.

With a prayer for wisdom, I called the police dispatch center and they joined me in trying to locate the party in need. Search-and-rescue units were assembled and after an intent discussion with logical reasoning, they were rightly dispatched to a popular hang-gliding area. Before long the injured party was located and first aid administered.

I can only imagine the feeling of helplessness the injured person experienced calling for help and not knowing if anyone could hear. Was the radio working? Was help on the way? How long would he feel alone and isolated before someone missed him?

> "Who shall separate us from the love of Christ? Shall trouble or hardship or persecution or famine or nakedness or danger or sword? As it is written: 'For your sake we face death all day long; we are considered as sheep to be slaughtered.' No, in all these things we are more than conquerors through him who loved us"
> (Romans 8:35–37)

Sometimes I feel that way. I'm in trouble, I know it, and call out to God for help. Yet, it feels as if there's no answer. Is my "radio" working? Does God hear me? Is help on the way? When I start wondering, I remember how Daniel was assured God heard his cry and that a "search-and-rescue" operation was begun the minute Daniel's humble prayer was heard (Daniel 10:12–14). God keeps his promises and he promises to never leave us or forsake us (Hebrews 13:5). He promises that nothing can ever separate us from him—not death, life, angels, spirits, or anything now or in the future or in the whole world can separate us from God's love. He leaves nothing out (Romans 8:35–39). Wow, what a blessing and assurance! Keep those communication channels open. God is listening. So shout out that "Mayday!" to the Savior—he never tunes you out.

Prayer:
I am so blessed, for when I cry out to you, you never tune me out.

SEPTEMBER 26

*Captain Raul A. Angulo – Seattle Fire Department;
Fellowship of Christian Firefighters Regional
Director / International Board Member*

WHEEL OF FORTUNE
A night of friendly rivalry

A FRIENDLY RIVALRY exists between the engine (pumper truck) crews and the truck (the trucks with long hook and ladders) crews. The bantering never stops. Whether it's a water fight or playing practical jokes, the crews are always trying to "one up" each other. This was especially true in Seattle and Engine Company 6, B shift's lieutenant.

Frequently, after the dinner dishes are done, the two crews of Station 6 watch *Wheel of Fortune*. As the TV contestants buy vowels and pick consonants, the Engine and Truck start competitively yelling their guesses.

Ladder Company 3 was pretty good and not shy about letting the Engine know. They kept score, and when ahead (which was most of the time), they'd chant, "Truck! Truck!" while dancing and pointing to the engine crew. This drove Lieutenant Donny nuts!

One night everything changed. The Engine started winning every night for weeks. Now the chants changed to, "Engine! Engine!" They never lost.

Finally, it was time for Donny to play his final "ace" and humiliate the Truck, forever ending the debate on whose crew was smartest.

The first round of *Wheel of Fortune* started. It was a long title. As the first contestant asked for a vowel, Donny waited a couple of seconds, just long enough to concentrate, and correctly yelled out, "Gettysburg Address!"

> "Be devoted to one another in brotherly love. Honor one another above yourselves."
> (Romans 12:10)

The Truck yelled in protest! "This must be a re-run!" They quickly checked the TV guide but no, it was regular programming.

Donny's crew, aching from laughter, finally couldn't contain their secret any longer. "Did Donny ever tell you that his daughter's favorite show is *Wheel of Fortune?*"

There was a moment of silence, followed by the loudest roar of laughter ever recorded at Station 6. Newspapers flew across the table along with anything else that wasn't nailed down.

As the rigs pulled out of the station to respond to a fire call, both crews were still smiling and shaking their heads. Donny had the biggest smile because he had truly "one-upped" the Truck. You see, his daughter lives in New York City—on Eastern Time.

It's times like these the "brotherhood" bonds in yet another way. We bond as we face danger together and that bond strengthens as we sit around the station and enjoy the camaraderie that comes from being a firefighter.

Prayer:
Lord, thank you for those I work with, and bless them. May we continue to bond and may I always be there for them whether on call, in the station, or out reflecting your love so they see you in me.

Reverend Wayne Detzler, PhD, Chaplain (Retired) –
Charlotte, NC, Fire Department; Fellowship of
Christian Firefighters Regional Director

RED BEANS AND RICE

Reaching out to each other

THE NEIGHBORHOOD is tough. Gunshots often punctuate the night air. No one is safe outside the fire station, but it's still one of the best assignments in our town. Locally, it's called "Fort Apache"!

> "I tell you, I will not drink of this fruit of the vine from now on until that day when I drink it anew with you in my Father's kingdom."
> (Matthew 26:29)

"Time to eat, Chaplain," the guys welcomed me as I settled in for an all night ride-along. The meal was simple. It was a pot full of rice and red beans. Next to it was the signature Southern cornbread. And for desert, there was a huge banana pudding.

The food came in second, however. The real center of our attention was the relationship between firefighters. These guys had seen everything, and they'd worked together for a long period of time.

Around the table is where firefighters are joined in heart and mind. In actuality, however, the kitchen is the real heart of the fire station. Very often it's the place where friendships are forged and lives are changed. One night a Christian brother was hanging out in the kitchen when another firefighter came in with a startling question. "Can you tell me how to accept Christ into my life?" the young firefighter asked his friend.

No sooner had the Christian commenced to explain the Gospel than the tones went off. Together they went for the pole and slid to the equipment room. In a few minutes they were back in the station. My Christian friend wondered if the chance had passed him by. But, he didn't have to wait long to find the answer.

"Now, will you tell me?" the other firefighter asked him. "Now, will you tell me how to accept the Lord?" Mercifully the station was silent. Quiet enough for the believer to lead his friend to faith. So, the kitchen is where the Bread of Life is also served up at times. Sometimes, it's the place where people come to new life in Christ.

In the Scripture, the Lord spent his last night before the Crucifixion with his men around the table. Jesus promised them there was a day coming when they would again meet around the table in Glory. What a feast that will be, second only to the heart-and-mind union and fellowship of those seated at Christ's table.

Prayer:
I thank you, Lord, for those times of rich fellowship around the table.

SEPTEMBER 28

Rick Barton, Fire Safety Officer; Rick Barton Ministries, Gunnison, CO; Fellowship of Christian Firefighters International Ambassador-at-Large

DIS-APPOINTMENT OR HIS-APPOINTMENT?

I almost missed the blessing of this special appointment

EVERY FIREFIGHTER knows that a key word in our business is *flexibility*. When deployed to the Florida hurricanes in the fall of 2004, hundreds of us found "frustration" superseded our feelings of flexibility. We'd been sent to Atlanta for two days of training before being assigned to a disaster zone. As the training was ending, another hurricane reared its ugly head. So, instead of being out helping disaster victims, several thousand of us were stuck in a hotel. The agency in charge was overwhelmed by the number of people it had suddenly acquired. As a result, it had a difficult time implementing the Incident Command System. Tempers grew short as directions changed almost hourly. Soon, many left and returned home.

> "But he said to me, 'My grace is sufficient for you, for my power is made perfect in weakness.'"
> (2 Corinthians 12:9)

After five days we were loaded onto buses for a six-hour ride to Jacksonville. Hope began to spring up. But again, it was hurry-up-and-wait while hundreds of us milled around as the hurricane played out its fickle dance. Frustration increased as day after day was filled with mostly meaningless meetings. Finally, someone spoke what all of us felt: "We've been here almost two weeks without fulfilling our mission."

366

Then it hit me: As a disciple of Jesus, my mission is whatever he places in my life each day. As I reflected, I realized that every day he'd been bringing us people who needed counsel, prayer, and encouragement. We weren't missing our mission—it just wasn't the one we'd imagined. As we looked at what the Lord was doing in and through us, we recognized our "dis-appointment" was actually "his-appointment." It's funny how just changing one letter can make such a difference. His Word tells us he guides the steps of his righteous followers (Psalm 37:23).

And I almost missed the blessing of this special appointment by grumbling in frustration. The next time I start to feel disappointment, I pray that I will look for "his-appointment."

As disciples of Jesus, our mission is whatever God places in our life. If we fret, become rigid in our scheduling, or allow frustration to control our actions, our Christian witness suffers. What's more, we lose the peace God offers us. We are told in 2 Corinthians 12:9 his grace is sufficient for us and that his power is made perfect in our weakness.

Prayer:
Help me rely on you and not my own strength when disappointment threatens to steal my peace. Allow me to change dis-appointment to "his-appointment" (your appointment), God.

Tommy Neiman, Author of Sirens for the Cross; EMS Training Officer – St. Lucie County, FL; Fellowship of Christian Firefighters International Regional Director / International Board Member

WHY?

Little compares to a brother or sister in the Lord when encouragement is needed.

I HAVE NO doubt about God's all-powerful, all-knowing, and all-loving nature. I do realize, however, that God sometimes chooses for us not to understand his reasons for allowing things to happen as they do. I know he has a plan for us, a plan far more wondrous than our human minds can conceive, and yet, when I see a child face injury or death, my heart still cries out, "Why"?

367

I'll never know the answer to many of the "Why?s" in life, but I do know God is faithful and that I can turn to him for strength and peace. It is through him, and those he places in my path to share his love with, that I find comfort during and after distressing calls.

One such call was for an eight-year-old boy called home to be with the Lord when hit by a car. His motionless body left a deep impression on me. The other guys in the rescue team didn't seem phased. Maybe they just didn't show their feelings. I don't know. But I was hurting, I cried, and I honestly had doubts about continuing in this type of work. But praise God for his strength and comfort! How people can deal with tragedy without the Lord, I'll never know.

> "As the heavens are higher than the earth, so are my ways higher than your ways and my thoughts than your thoughts." (Isaiah 55:9)

Several months later I experienced the loss of an eight-month-old child whose head got stuck between two broken bars of his crib and was strangled to death. For a futile two hours our guys and the emergency room staff tried to bring life back to this little one. But the whole time, this little child was already giggling and smiling in the lap of his heavenly Father.

Unlike the first call, my partners were visibly hurting. We talked, questioned, and pondered—"What if . . .?" We encouraged one another, prayed, cried, and knew that the real source of strength was the common denominator of knowing God was in control, that God's ways are not ours, and that he has a purpose we may never know or understand in this life.

These were two of many tragic calls. As we continue to serve, we also continue to share and encourage each other. As we do, our bond of friendship grows. Little compares to a brother or sister in the Lord when encouragement is needed. And believe me, in this business, one doesn't go very long without needing encouragement.

Prayer:
I know your ways and thoughts far exceed mine, and when you choose not to reveal your plan to me, I thank you for fellow believers I can share with and that we can mutually encourage each other.

Reverend Wayne Detzler, PhD, Chaplain (Retired) –
Charlotte, NC, Fire Department; Fellowship of
Christian Firefighters Regional Director

WHEN HOPE TURNS TO SIGHT

He answers our heart cry

WE WERE summoned to debrief a volunteer fire department. A morning alarm had scrambled the volunteers. As they tried to weave their way through traffic, a distracted driver pulled out in front of the engine.

There was too little space and too much speed. The engineer couldn't stop. He slammed into the car. Extrication became the immediate task. As fast as possible, the firefighters released the driver. She looked lifeless as they lifted her into an ambulance and sent her to a nearby hospital.

The chief gathered his firefighters at the local station. Then he called for a debriefing team. That's where I came in. The atmosphere was serious; gloom hung in the air as firefighters thought they had actually killed the driver.

> "Before they call I will answer; while they are still speaking I will hear."
> (Isaiah 65:24)

Carefully we worked through the incident. "What was your first thought?" I asked. At first no one spoke, and then someone expressed grief and disbelief. In the rush and tumble of morning traffic, the accident appeared to be unavoidable.

Second, I asked, "How did you feel? What did your gut tell you?" They let it all out. Tears are not unusual at this point, as firefighters talk freely, safe in the company of their fellows. Still they assumed that the woman was dead, victim of this unavoidable accident.

Third, we began to teach them coping strategies: how they can combine exercise and healthy food, and how they can draw strength from each other. We also urged them to seek spiritual support in their church.

The phone rang and the chief excused himself. When he came back he was smiling, a smile of relief. The woman would recover from the accident. She would make a full recovery. Together, we thanked the Lord for this powerful intervention.

Identifying your thoughts, processing your emotions, and examining your "gut feelings" are important steps in moving forward. Coping strategies keep many first responders from sleepless and haunted nights. We mustn't try to go it alone. We must seek God, and the people he uses—chaplains, Christian counselors, and CISM (debriefing) teams—they're there for us.

Prayer:

Lord, give me and all first responders safety as we try to help our community into a place of safety. Thank you for those we can share with from our hearts.

Tommy Neiman, *Author of Sirens for the Cross; EMS Training Officer – St. Lucie County, FL; Fellowship of Christian Firefighters International Regional Director / International Board Member*

GOING BACKWARD

The truck was in reverse and moving right toward us!

HUMOROUS, yet potentially tragic, incidents occurred my rookie year that opened my eyes to the seriousness of operating emergency vehicles.

Upon arrival at a minor accident, I slammed on the brakes, jumped out of our truck, briskly walked to the scene, and intuitively glanced back at the ambulance. It was slowly moving right toward us and the two accident vehicles. I'd left the truck in reverse! I ran, opened the door, jumped in, and slammed down the brake. A precious few feet remained between the heavy rescue truck and the closest vehicle, in which the victim was still seated wide-eyed and thankful to not be a victim twice in the same day.

The second occurred while transporting a senile gentleman. He had multiple health problems coupled with severe mental illness. The trip proceeded smoothly until we reached the outer city limits when, without warning, a motorist ahead stopped abruptly, causing a chain reaction. We were the next in line and destined to impact the car in front of us! My brakes locked. Miraculously, we veered just to the right of the car ahead, which had already struck another car.

> "When I smiled at them, they scarcely believed it; the light of my face was precious to them."
> (Job 29:24)

But wait! We weren't through skidding. Instead, we hit a guardrail at just the right angle to cause our ambulance to roll over. As I checked the patient, what I saw caused me to chuckle. Our patient, locked-in and seatbelted securely, was lying sideways on the stretcher and smiling ear to ear.

"Are we there yet?" he asked.

"No, not yet, and you know what? You're gonna get to ride in another ambulance!"

"All right," he cheerfully said.

When the media arrived, I thought, *My career is done. Lawyers will be all over this in a heartbeat.*

Fortunately, the highway patrolman's honest report stated I wasn't at fault and deserved commendation for avoiding a crash.

When I went to see the patient, two lawyers were questioning him. "Sir um, sir? Will you try to concentrate and explain what happened?"

"Absolutely! You see, the accident was out on the battlefield. I was lying low in a foxhole and . . ."

I smiled. Guess my rookie days weren't over.

Those experiences helped me realize how serious the repercussions could have been. I thank God for making sure I had the right kind of patients for those rookie days.

Prayer:
Thank you for watching over us. When actions made in haste could lead to danger, I pray you'll guide and protect all involved. May the light on my face be precious to others.

OCTOBER 2

Rick Barton, Fire Safety Officer; Rick Barton Ministries, Gunnison, CO; Fellowship of Christian Firefighters International Ambassador-at-Large

DYING ON ICE MOUNTAIN!
Nothing too small or large for prayer

MIDNIGHT approached as several fire crew members enjoyed the quiet summer's evening singing in a closed café at a small resort, high in the Colorado Rockies. Suddenly, Bob, the owner of the nearby Boys' Camp, barged through the door. "My climbing instructor, Jim, is dying on Ice Mountain!" he exclaimed. "He and our camp counselor were climbing Ice Mountain."

This peak wasn't technically difficult but the climb involved steep, exposed areas of large boulders. Storm clouds rolled in before the men reached the summit and against their better judgment, they continued the climb. When they started their descent, Jim slipped and fell twenty feet. The counselor administered what first aid he could to the semiconscious and bleeding climber and then ran for help.

With limited information we prepared for the search, hoping we faced a rescue, not a body recovery. I called the police dispatcher and ordered a rescue team even though I knew it would be dawn before they could arrive. Next, gathering headlamps, blankets, and first-aid gear we started our trek.

> "Give thanks in all circumstances, for this is God's will for you in Christ Jesus."
> (1 Thessalonians 5:18)

After more than an hour of hiking in the dark we reached a crisis point. The trail forked and various spurs broke toward the summit. To add to our dilemma, a heavy fog had settled on the mountain. We shouted, "Jim, Jim! Can you hear us?" No response. Someone suggested we pray. With heads bowed we asked for divine intervention. Moments later a breeze shifted the fog ever so slightly and we saw a feeble flicker of light. Was it a star, a reflection of a headlamp off the wet rocks? We didn't know. But it was the only lead we had.

After what seemed like an eternity, we found him. He'd lost blood and suffered a concussion, but he was alive.

As we attended to Jim we noticed the source of the guiding light. It was a small candle jammed into the rocks. Jim, having regained consciousness, had taken the candle out of his pack, lit it, and passed out again.

After patching Jim up and rigging a stretcher from saplings and blankets, we began the slow descent to the base of the mountain. It was daybreak and the fog was clearing. Halfway down the trail we met the rescue team and gratefully placed Jim into their capable hands.

Over breakfast we marveled at what we had experienced and remembered that there is nothing too small or too large for prayer.

Prayer:
No matter how small or large my circumstances appear, may I always remember to call upon you and give thanks.

OCTOBER 3

Chaplain Marc Santorella, Firefighter Danvers Fire Department, MA; Public Fire and Life Safety Educator and Certified Fire Instructor Level 1

SAID AND GONE!

Restoration through an act of forgiveness

IT HAS HAPPENED to us all. The "Oh! I wish I hadn't said that!" moment. The sting of regret can be overwhelming. It may take years before we find the courage, or even the opportunity, to say, "I'm sorry." Still we must pray for that opportunity. God instructs us, "With the tongue we praise our Lord and Father, and with it we curse men, who have been made in God's likeness . . . My brothers, this should not be" (James 3:9, 10).

At an educator's conference, I ran into an old high school teacher I had tried to impress when I was a youth by saying something really boastful. It had made me look like a real jerk.

The thought that my former teacher would never know how sorry I was stayed with me for years. It wasn't until this conference I was able to personally apologize.

God knows our heart; he also knows those regrets we carry from our sin. We may not always get a chance to take back our words, but we know God's forgiveness for the repentant heart is immediate and full.

> "In him we have redemption through his blood, the forgiveness of sins, in accordance with the riches of God's grace." (Ephesians 1:7)

When appropriate, we should always take the opportunity to make restitution. Not for forgiveness—God's forgiveness is immediate in repentance. Still, going back to the source and acknowledging our misplaced words is a way of honoring God and glorifying the Lord for the grace he gives us.

In the heat of battling a fire, emotions can flare and words we should leave unsaid may surface. In the aftermath, we may do the same, whether at home or at the station.

Take time today and ask, "Are there words I regret saying that are hanging in the air, that I need to bring before you, Lord? Is there anyone I can be a witness to by showing your glory through the humbleness of apology? Is there a relationship which could be restored through an act of forgiveness?"

God's grace! Given not because of what we do, but because of his amazing love for us.

Prayer:

God, I thank you for grace and the forgiveness of sins made available by the blood of the Lamb. Help me remember, Lord, that a repentant heart is all that is required no matter what I do. I could never earn forgiveness on my own efforts; your love for me is so great you forgive unconditionally and any effort on my part should not be to appease you but to glorify you and, Lord, I do seek to glorify you.

Chief Steve Parsons, St. Albans, WV, Fire Department

JESUS, BRING THE REIGN

Send me every difficulty I can handle so I will walk closer to you

EVER BEEN on scene when danger lurked close and one of your non-Christian crew members called out to God in a positive way? How about you? Have you let your prayer life slack and then called to God when challenged or threatened? When have you felt closest to God?

It appears to be a common occurrence to cry out to Jesus for help when facing difficult situations. Many nonbelievers as well as Christians seek God in the worst situation, then place him back on the shelf when the tribulation passes. This would suggest people are closer to God when facing trials. If this holds true in your life, I encourage you to pray for life's difficulties. If this is the only time you seek or feel truly close to God, then I say, "Jesus, bring the rain. Send me every problem I can handle so I will walk closer to you." Jesus, "reign" on my life.

A contemporary song by the group *Mercy Me* talks about a life changed, before rainy days, and how the thought of turning away from the Lord never crossed the mind. Instead drawing closer to God and praying were foremost. The lyrics continue with "I know there'll be days when this life brings me pain, but if that's what it takes to praise you, Jesus, bring the rain."

God's ultimate purpose for us is to grow into the image of his Son (Romans 8:29). In 1 Peter 1:6, 7 this is explained: "In this you greatly rejoice, though now for a little while you may have had to suffer grief in all kinds of trials. These have come so that your faith—of greater worth than gold, which perishes even though refined by fire—may be proved genuine and may result in praise, glory and honor when Jesus Christ is revealed."

> "Then I heard what sounded like a great multitude, like the roar of rushing waters and like loud peals of thunder, shouting: 'Hallelujah! For our Lord God Almighty reigns. Let us rejoice and be glad and give him glory!'" (Revelation 19:6, 7)

James says to consider it a joy when trials come. Trials test your faith and help develop perseverance. But there is more—those who persevere will receive the "crown of life" promised to those who love God (James 1:2, 3, 12).

Have you been refined by the fire and made more precious than gold? Do you have joy from having persevered through trials? Has your faith increased as a result? If so, Hallelujah! God is "reigning" in your life. You can truly rejoice.

Prayer:
Gracious Father, thank you for the trials I've endured. May I forever grow closer to you through tough times. I praise you even in bad times, for you are mighty, forgiving, loving, and compassionate.

O C T O B E R   5

Chaplain Robert Osbourn, Sylacauaga, AL, Fire Department

HOW TO MAKE YOUR WALLS FALL
You have a choice!

EVER FELT as if your life hit a brick wall, seemingly going nowhere, and making you feel as if everything is against you?

First responders face trauma and hurting victims. They work long shifts away from family, and are clueless about what the next alarm has in store. Sometimes that brick wall seems impenetrable.

No doubt, the Israelites felt that same way when needing to conquer Jericho, the oldest city in the world, surrounded by a system of two massive stone walls. To top it off, between the walls was a guarded fifteen-foot walkway presenting a seemingly insurmountable obstacle.

The walls first responders face may come as a lost victim, sadness over the loss of a victim's home, decisions poorly made, family trouble, financial trouble, or maybe a besetting sin that constantly crops up.

You can look upon your obstacles as a dead end, or you can realize they are opportunities for the Lord to work in your life—a chance to grow and allow God's power to be revealed in and through you when you're unable to handle things on your own. You have a choice!

God is more clearly visible when you're totally out of the picture. That's what he did with Israel in Jericho. He completely removed them from the equation! The victory at Jericho was all God's!

God is always in control, even when it doesn't seem like it. God promised Israel the victory before they attacked Jericho. As you face obstacles, you can do so with similar confidence because you have his promises as banners to march under. Your weapons are loaded with God's power (2 Corinthians 10:4, 5). Whatever you face, God determined it for your good and his glory! (Romans 8:28). Your ability in Jesus is limited only by your own faith (Philippians 4:13). As you face your Jericho, you can do it in his strength (Ephesians 6:10), and you can trust him for victory (Romans 4:21).

> "Shout! For the LORD has given you the city!"
> (Joshua 6:16)

Whatever the obstacles, you don't have to face them alone or in your own strength! Israel experienced victory at Jericho because they believed, acted in faith, and did it God's way. You, too, have a choice—your way or his way.

Prayer:
Thank you for your promise of victory and that I can bring all things to you, the One who excels in doing the undoable! Help me tear down those walls in my spiritual life and to continue steadfastly in my walk with you.

OCTOBER 6

Jeff Turkel, Firefighter/Dispatcher – North Pole, Alaska; Fellowship of Christian Firefighters Regional Director

HEADS-UP CRASH
Some may call it luck—I call it an answer to prayer

IT WAS 10 o'clock on a dark night in 1996. I was an Air Force fire protection crew chief assigned to Eielson Air Force Base in Alaska. I was ready to retire for the night when the dispatcher's voice blared over the PA system, "Heads up crash! We have an in-flight emergency on a huge C-5 aircraft, eighty-eight souls on board. Nature of the emergency is left main landing gear stuck in the up position. ETA is twenty minutes."

My initial reaction was to pray, "Lord, let the gear come down." In my twenty years in the Air Force I'd been on countless emergencies where aircraft reported they couldn't get their gear down, yet prior to landing the gear came down. But somehow I felt this one would be different.

Four crash trucks, one rescue, one engine, and the assistant chief's truck were deployed to our pre-designated runway standby positions. Base agencies prepared for the worst, the hospital recalled medical crews and ambulance buses prepared for multiple casualties.

Ten minutes before landing, when a flyby of the tower confirmed that the gear was still in the up position, I continued praying. I got strange looks from my driver, but eventually he joined me in praying specifically that the gear would come down and all aboard would be safe. When the tower crew again confirmed the gear was in the up position and the aircraft made its final turn to the runway, the fire chief gave instructions for final preparations. I prepared for the worst.

Darkness surrounded us. We were unable to see the gear area as the aircraft approached. The closer it got to landing, the louder I prayed, not only for the safety of the passengers and crew, but for the strength to deal with the inevitability of a crash.

Crews stood ready as this giant of an aircraft touched the runway.

I blinked. I looked again. Is this real? The left main gear was down and the aircraft smoothly touched the ground. Aircraft rollout was normal. The C-5 came to a safe stop.

Some may call it luck—I call it an answer to prayer.

Prayer:
When darkness surrounds me and situations appear insurmountable and headed for disaster, Lord, I know that nothing is impossible for you. And therefore I pray, Lord, for your divine intervention.

OCTOBER 7

Chaplain Gaius Reynolds, President – Fellowship of Christian Firefighters International; Volunteer Firefighter – Livermore, CO, Fire Protection District

GOD'S MESSENGER
What are you doing for Christ?

WE ARE NOT human beings going through a temporary spiritual experience. We are spiritual beings going through a temporary human experience. Our sojourn on the planet Earth is temporary. Eternity is just that—forever. So, let me ask: What are you doing for Christ during your temporary human experience? Are you reaching out to your co-workers with the love of Christ? Are you acting like Christ? Can those at your workplace tell you are a believer by your words, actions, choices, and attitudes? Are you different, or do you go with the flow? Do you put on Christ at church and then leave him there?

What you do, what you say, and how you react to situations reveals who you are. Can people see you're a child of God, or do you have to *tell* them you're a Christian?

Being different is not a bad thing. Neither is being an alien. God's Word clearly states that a Christian's true citizenship is not here on Earth: "But our citizenship is in heaven. And we eagerly await a Savior from there, the Lord Jesus Christ" (Philippians 3:20).

I challenge you to mull this question over as you fulfill the duties of your job. Is your experience honoring to the Lord?

You are a vital member of God's ministry team. You have contact with a special and exceptional segment of the world's population: your co-workers. Only other personnel in your field can truly identify with the unique experiences you encounter. God needs you to be the messenger he directs you to be. And, you need to be that messenger wherever you are, in whatever he inspires you to do.

> "He makes winds his messengers, flames of fire his servants."
> (Psalm 104:4)

Are you a servant of the Lord? Do you want to share him with your co-workers? Resolve today to be a better, more active servant of Christ and to continue until he returns. Be like the wind and flames of fire as you share God's love and as you continue to reflect on this question: What are you doing for Christ?

Prayer:
Lord, you made the winds your messenger and flames of fire your servant. I know you can do no less for me. I am here, Lord. Use me.

Rick Barton, Fire Safety Officer; Rick Barton Ministries, Gunnison, CO; Fellowship of Christian Firefighters International Ambassador-at-Large

SAVED BY THE LEAF BLOWERS

Different conditions call for different methods

IT WAS THE end of October; the 2000 forest fire season finally came to an end. After dispatches from Texas to Montana, I'd stored the red bag for the winter and was ready for a reprieve. Then the phone rang once again. This time the fires were in North Carolina and Tennessee.

On the way out the door my fire management officer yelled, "Don't forget, Barton—that stuff burns in the rain," referring to the leaf litter, downed trees, and debris common in this area, especially during the fall season.

Surely not, I thought.

A day later I arrived in Asheville, picked up an Alaska smokejumper as a trainee, and drove to the fire. Before long we heard a strange sound coming toward us through the hardwoods. The Mescalero Hot Shots burst into view with leaf blowers and swatters! Our jaws hit the ground. What kind of fire line was this?

But it worked. The fire was being carried by leaf litter, and the blowers cut a swath quickly and effectively with minimal resource damage.

I guess we learned a lesson that day: Different conditions call for different methods. Whether we're starting a conversation with an unbeliever, choosing a style of music to reach our audience, or even picking a spot to hold a Bible study, we need to be prayerful and flexible in our approach. As someone

> "God, who knows the heart, showed that he accepted them by giving the Holy Spirit to them, just as he did to us."
> (Acts 15:8)

once told me, "God's principles and truths never change, his methods always do!" The Hot Shots were stopping the fire more quickly and efficiently with leaf blowers than they ever could with Pulaskis (fire axes) and combi-tools (hoe/pick/shovels).

Maybe meeting in a coffee shop might be more effective in reaching our unsaved and unchurched friends than using the church's facilities, who knows? Often the impromptu meetings where you are open to God's whispered methods are as effective as planned meetings. The key is to be open and flexible.

Oh, yeah, that stuff really does burn in the rain!

Prayer:
God, you know our hearts and thoughts and have accepted them. Help me to be flexible, accepting, and loving enough to reach people where they are. May I be a faithful witness of your truths wherever I am and whoever I am with.

Reverend Wayne Detzler, PhD, Chaplain (Retired) – Charlotte, NC, Fire Department; Fellowship of Christian Firefighters Regional Director

THE STEAMY SAUNA
When water is all we need

"FIRE IN A furniture warehouse." The dispatcher called me to a working blaze. It was confined to a warehouse above a furniture store in our small town. When I arrived, it was well under control.

No one knew how it all started, but almost immediately a sprinkler system had sprayed the flame. When firefighters arrived, the sprinklers were still spraying the scene. Smoldering furniture filled the space with acrid smoke and steam.

Outside it was a blistering hot summer day (ninety degrees plus). While the sprinkler extinguished the fire, it also created a sauna-like atmosphere in the warehouse. Still, the firefighters worked their way through the warehouse searching out hot spots and remnants of the fire.

What should I do as chaplain? As a relatively new member of the fire department, I often asked myself this question. Then it dawned on me. As crews came out of the fire scene, they were absolutely wrung out by the heat and humidity.

"Have you got any Gatorade?" I asked the clerk in the convenience store next door. "I need to buy all you have." In those days we didn't yet carry drinking water on fire trucks. So, my request was really a stab in the dark.

381

I returned to the scene with an armful of Gatorade. As crew members came out of the building, I handed them a bottle. They eagerly grasped the refreshment, gulping it down to rehydrate themselves.

It all reminded me of the Living Water the Lord promised to a soul-thirsty woman in Samaria. Her life was a mess. She was alienated from others in her community and isolated by her sin. Physically she craved water, and she came to the well at the worst time of the day, at noontime.

> "Whoever drinks the water I give him will never thirst. Indeed, the water I give him will become in him a spring of water welling up to eternal life." (John 4:14)

As always, Jesus met her at her time of deepest need. He offered her water that really satisfies—Living Water. He promised her absolute relief from her thirst. And the water worked. She invited others to taste this life-giving water.

Dehydration, despair, hopelessness, anguish, or misery—there is only one true remedy: Living Water. And you don't have to run to the local convenience store to purchase it. It's free and available by knee-mail.

Prayer:
You are Living Water in a dry and parched place,
and I thank you, O Lord.

OCTOBER 10

Dr. Jonathan Newell, Missionary Malawi, Africa

OFFERING WHAT WE HAVE
The Lord, Jesus, works with whatever we offer

IN MALAWI, Africa, where I live and work as a missionary, the fire services have almost no equipment at all compared with firemen in the United States. At times in Blantyre, which is a city of about 1.3 million people, they don't even have one working fire engine. Nor do they have proper breathing apparatus. There is not even one computer at the fire station, and there are insufficient uniforms for all the personnel. Spare parts for vehicles frequently cannot be sourced within Malawi and there are no funds available to purchase them. Training is extremely difficult in such circumstances and procuring finance for international examinations often impossible.

How should we react to circumstances like these? One option is to simply give up. This is what Jesus' disciple, Philip, did when he saw the huge crowd of perhaps fifteen thousand to twenty thousand people coming toward Jesus one day. His only answer was the magnitude of the problem and the impossibility of even beginning to solve it (John 6:7). Andrew, however, looked not at the enormous crowd, but at what was at hand—a small boy's lunch of five loaves and two fish. Andrew could not see how such meager resources could help, but he did understand that it was right that it should be offered to the Lord. Interestingly, the moment Andrew finished speaking, Jesus gave a command and the people were fed (John 6:8–11).

> "Jesus then took the loaves, gave thanks, and distributed to those who were seated as much as they wanted. He did the same with the fish."
> (John 6:11)

The point is that the Lord Jesus works with whatever we offer him in faith. It's not the size, value, or importance of what we offer him that matters—it's the manner in which it is offered. Faith, in the face of apparently impossible odds, is everything. To all of us who think like Philip, let us remember Andrew's question: "But how far will they go among so many?" (John 6:9). If the Lord is present then whatever we offer him will go as far as he wishes it to go, because his power is unlimited.

Will you offer your life to him? He can use it to work a miracle and make a difference.

Prayer:
Dear Lord, help us not to lose heart when we see the huge needs around us in this world, but help us to have faith in your Son and to offer ourselves and all we have to be used by you to make a difference.

OCTOBER 11

William Garvey, Writer/Photographer; Damage Prevention Supervisor for a Michigan gas Company

TO HELP A FIREFIGHTER
Let them know you care

ONE MONTH after the Attack on America, as I toured the New York City Red Cross Family Assistance Center, I saw a uniformed fireman walking out of an enclosure that contained playing children.

When I asked about them I was told, "Many adults are here for assistance. They need someone to watch their kids while they go through the red tape. Several kids have no place to go because their parents aren't here anymore. We're trying to find someone to help them."

As I walked through the corridor of offices separated by curtains, I learned families came here for counsel to help them get through the loss and subsequent hurt. My eyes met those of a young woman being counseled. Her tear-streaked face cut through to my soul. I thought to myself, *Dear God, please help us to dry some of these tears!* Then I pondered what I could do.

> "There should be no division in the body, but that its parts should have equal concern for each other. If one part suffers, every part suffers with it; if one part is honored, every part rejoices with it."
> (1 Corinthians 12:25, 26)

As I humbly ate lunch alongside firefighters still dusty and tired from a hard day of searching, I knew I sat among the best of the best in America. What a blessing! While eating, I was startled by a crashing sound. Turning quickly, I saw the firefighter who'd thrown his helmet against the lockers. Concerned, I asked why.

"Today is the last day of searching. Many of the missing haven't been found. Tomorrow the big equipment comes in and to the fireman, it's his job to find his brothers and sisters."

Another person said, "You couldn't have come on a better day. The firefighters need to know others are praying for them."

As I left, I stopped by a life-sized photo of the firefighters raising the "Flag at Ground Zero." The wall was decorated with pictures and words of thanks to the first responders—most drawn or written in crayon by children. With tears in my eyes, I read "thank you" and "I love you" notes, wondering the whole time how others could help these firefighters smile again.

While driving home, I found the answer. To help the firefighters find peace, we needed to let them know we cared. Just like they did and were doing as they caringly searched for those lost in the rubble.

Prayer:
May I forever remember the sacrifices made after the Attack on America. May I rejoice when others are rejoicing, be compassionate to those who are suffering, and turn my suffering over to you.

Natalie Garvey Helps Turn Tears to Smiles (Courtesy of William Garvey)

OCTOBER 12

*Reverend Wayne Detzler, PhD, Chaplain (Retired) –
Charlotte, NC, Fire Department; Fellowship of
Christian Firefighters Regional Director*

CAUGHT IN THE MIDDLE

Where do I turn when I am caught?

"CHAPLAIN," the supervisor called me. "Can you come up and meet with the dispatchers?" It was one short month after the attacks of September 11, 2001. The dispatchers had worked overtime covering the dozens of panic phone calls. The whole city was on edge. Every package looked like a bomb. White powder might be anthrax.

"They're all on overload," the supervisor reminded me. "The calls never stop, and the firefighters can't keep up with them all." In those post-9/11 days every call was urgent. Each caller suspected terrorist activity. It was impossible for the dispatchers to sort out the real from the imagined threats.

It took time, lots of time to listen carefully to the dispatchers. They were decompressing from their frustrating shifts. In the quiet of a debriefing they were also trying to make sense of the barrage of calls crushing them. They were trapped in the middle between a panic-stricken public and frustrated firefighters.

The firefighters were also stretched to their limit. With some of the major banking institutions in our city there was always the fear of terrorism. What if a bomb was planted in a headquarters building? What if poisonous powder like anthrax was sent to a manager's office?

"What do we do, Chaplain?" The dispatchers vented their frustration. "We have to take every call seriously, and we know what happens if we become lax." They felt very keenly that they were on the front line of an unwelcome war in our own country, our own city.

> "He alone is my rock and my salvation; he is my fortress, I will never be shaken." (Psalm 62:2)

A special focus of this frustration was our one hazmat (hazardous materials) team. Dispatched at the beginning of each shift, they seldom got back to their station throughout the shift. By visiting the station right at shift change we could assess the stress level of these frontline warriors in the anti-terrorism battle.

As Christians we know that the Lord is our strong Defender. We can flee to him in times of stress and know we are safe. This liberates us from the crosswinds of pressure, when we are caught in the middle.

Prayer:
My Rock and my Fortress, hide me safely in times of stress and tension. Strengthen me to do your will.

386

Rob Hitt, Firefighter/EMT-I – Greenville-Spartanburg
International Airport Fire Department; South Carolina
Fellowship of Christian Firefighters International
Regional Director

SMOKE SHOWING!
BUT WHERE IS THE FIRE?
Do we always see the smoke?

WE HAVE heard all too often upon arrival on scene at a structure fire, "Smoke showing, will advise!" Do you also remember the old saying, "Where there is smoke, there is fire"? But do we always see all the smoke?

Sometimes, even when the best of incident commanders performs a textbook size-up, things like unseen smoke are missed. Likewise, even after we perform a spectacular suppression, concealed heat, embers, and flames can hide from our sight. Today we have excellent advanced technology including thermal imaging cameras, yet fire can still play a game of hide and seek.

Hidden flames in an attic, crawl space, wall, or basement are like some of the burdens we carry in our lives. The exterior appears "under control" and we may even have gone through spiritual "salvage and over-haul," but still those personal burdens can flare up in our lives and refuse to be extinguished even with our best efforts.

The only way to extinguish these personal flames is to turn command over to Jesus. He is the Incident Commander who won't miss one single thing. He already sized up everything on Calvary. The suppression of sin and burdens was not accomplished with water—they were cleansed by the blood of Jesus. But you have to do your part; you must allow him to remove those hidden fires before they "fully involve" your life.

> "You have shattered the yoke that burdens them, the bar across their shoulders, the rod of their oppressor."
> (Isaiah 9:4)

Burdens come in many and varied forms, such as an illness you don't understand, the loss of a loved one, or perhaps the death of a dream. Maybe your burdens are related to secret sins in your life, such as pornography, gambling, hate, a marital affair, or a chat room romance. Maybe it's a spirit of rebellion or an unforgiving heart that plagues you. Whatever the burden burning within you, Jesus is the answer.

Jesus' sin payment for you was no cakewalk, so you need to take it seriously. He took all your burdens and sins and then some, and nailed them to his cross. Remember the old hymn, "Burdens are lifted at Calvary . . ." Jesus will surely bring those burning desires and sins under control. Let him do that for you today!

Prayer:
Lord, it is unfathomable in human understanding what you did for me. I thank you and praise you that all my burdens were lifted at Calvary.

OCTOBER 14

Sue Reynolds, Missionary – Fellowship of Christian Firefighters International

REAL MEN DON'T CRY— OR DO THEY?

Thoughts that too often lie too deep for tears.

WILLIAM WORDSWORTH

W AS THAT *a tear in my husband's eye?* I wondered when my husband returned from his second suicide call of the week. "Want to talk about it?"

"Not yet! But the family would like you to be with them."

He needed time to process and reflect in hopes of making some sense of it all. I headed to the family's home.

This was the second suicide in four days for our small rural fire department that covers more than 360 square miles with mostly dirt roads. The first occurred the previous Thursday night when a young man burrowed himself in his bedroom and fatally took a gun to his head. My husband was among the responders.

My husband, Gay, was also among the first responders on this second suicide call in one week. While barely identifiable, there was no doubt the man was the father of two teen girls from our church. He'd ranched and raised his family in the area before an accident made ranching impossible. The marriage ended, the mother and girls remained in the area, and the girls saw their dad on visiting days.

388

Searching for answers is natural, but often leads nowhere. The mindset that the world and all loved ones are better off without you is hard for those who remain to comprehend, especially as the tentacles of pain reach out further and further. I saw

> "Hear my prayer, O Lord, listen to my cry for help; be not deaf to my weeping." (Psalm 39:12)

those tentacles extended each day as people surrounded the survivors. Feelings of guilt caused them to question and blame themselves and wonder what they could have done to keep the suicide from happening. But most of all I experienced secondhand the repercussions in the lives of the responders.

Each day my husband shared more of his feelings. People like him volunteer to help others because of their innate kind and empathetic nature, a nature that prods them to help others. It's that same sensitivity that makes the processing of such a tragedy take a long time, often causing memories of other calls to flood the mind.

As memories flood your consciousness and someone sees a tear in your eye, that's OK. Real men do cry. I know—I'm married to one.

Prayer:
Lord, each tragic call I've made has left indelible imprints on my mind. Many calls cause thoughts sometimes too deep for tears. I thank you that you are there to listen and comfort me and that you have placed others in my life who I can share with and help me process what I've seen.

OCTOBER 15

Tommy Neiman, Author of Sirens for the Cross; EMS Training Officer – St. Lucie County, FL; Fellowship of Christian Firefighters International Regional Director / International Board Member

YOU'D BETTER PRAY THAT PRAYER
Dealing with God in the face of trouble

MY RAMPANT imagination went into high gear, as it does every time a call for a shooting comes in. We arrived to find a young man with two bullet holes, lying in a pool of blood. He was going downhill fast. Pressure bandages were applied, and we placed him in a military anti-shock suit to improve his blood pressure and oxygenate his vital organs. While we were wheeling him to the ambulance, a lady called his name and yelled words I'll never forget: "Listen, man, you remember that prayer I told you to pray? You'd better pray it!" Sobbing, she repeated her demands as we loaded our patient and she probably wondered if he could hear her.

This paramedic did hear her and wondered what prayer she was talking about. Could it be a prayer for salvation? At first I thought if it was a prayer for salvation, this was good. The more I pondered, the more judgmental I became. Did she think her friend could live the way he wants and then call God at the last moment for a bailout?! Living the life he pleased probably got him shot, anyway. After all, the shooting was drug-related. Now that he's dying, she's reminding him not to forget to get saved. Sort of like "get into trouble, face death, and then call upon God"!

Who would ever do something like that?
Certainly not me, right?

Wrong!

A few months later while crawling into a smoldering inferno of suffocating smoke searching for the seat of the fire, I felt parts of the roof land on the back of my air pack and helmet. There was imminent danger of a backdraft causing a life-ending explosion, the danger of suffocation was great, and the possibility of burning to death wasn't far-fetched. I began dealing with God. "Lord, if you'll just get me out of here, I'll serve you better, just don't let me die!"

> "He [Jesus] replied, "Blessed rather are those who hear the word of God and obey it." (Luke 11:28)

The Lord wasn't ready to take me home that day. I escaped by crawling out along that precious hose line before the structure was totally consumed. After catching my breath, I realized I was dealing with God in the face of trouble just like I assumed the woman thought the shooting victim should be doing.

The man survived his shooting, I survived that burning inferno, and I learned a valuable lesson in the process.

Prayer:
Thank you, God, for your great forgiveness, awesome mercy, and unfathomable love. I know your desire is for me to obey you without making deals and judging others.

*Reverend Wayne Detzler, PhD, Chaplain (Retired) –
Charlotte, NC, Fire Department; Fellowship of
Christian Firefighters Regional Director*

FATAL MISTAKE
He didn't know

IT WAS A business conference, a sales meeting for one of America's biggest corporations. Representatives from all over the region met at a Charlotte hotel; Sunday was an arrival day for settling into the hotel.

Charlotte was a perfect place for the young sales representative. He'd been a standout on the local university baseball team. Charlotte was definitely his town, and he had wonderful connections across the community.

He went out with his friends for a night of socializing. Later, they came back to the hotel. That's when it all went wrong. Most of the partygoers went back to their rooms and got some sleep before meetings began the next day.

For one man, however, it was different. He was confused by alcohol. He couldn't comprehend that the hotel room was paid for by his company. In anger and despair he went back to his car to sleep off the effects of the evening. Before going to sleep he smoked a final cigarette—his fatal mistake.

> "In this world you will have trouble. But take heart! I have overcome the world." (John 16:33)

The cigarette butt smoldered and burst into flame. The smoker was trapped in his own car. He broke the back window, tried to crawl out, but the escape failed.

When the fire department was summoned, it was already too late. The young man with so much promise was dead. Quickly the fire crew doused the blaze, but the body hung out the back window, almost free from the burning car.

As chaplain, I accompanied the incident commander. First, we briefed the sales manager and his colleagues. They connected back to the company headquarters and we discovered a next of kin: the dead man's parents. A phone call informed the family of their son's sad demise.

Such loss is incomprehensible in human terms. The grief could lead to a life of bitterness without God. It is only through God that peace and healing can replace loss and bitterness.

Questions often linger in our minds after such a loss. What if . . .? What if he had gone to his room? What if he had not been confused by alcohol? In my mind there was one further question: What if someone had shared the comfort of the Lord with him?

Prayer:
*Lord, help me to reach out to the confused and the broken people
in our world. May I never make an eternally fatal mistake
of missing an opportunity to share your love.*

OCTOBER 17

Dwayne Clemmons, Adjunct Instructor – Virginia Department of Fire Programs; Founder – DMC Ministries; Author of Exploits, Jesus Rides in an Ambulance, and Utterances from the Throne Room; Volunteer in Fire and EMS for forty years in Virginia

ARE YOU ON FIRE?
Consumed by God's fire

WE KNOW from Firefighter 1 class it takes three things to have a fire: fuel, heat, and oxygen. We also know that when fuel is heated sufficiently to give off vapors that will ignite, a chemical chain reaction occurs resulting in the completion of the fire tetrahedron. I know you have probably seen a fire that grows so much in intensity that it literally becomes all-consuming. This type of fire is better known as a *conflagration*.

Throughout history we've experienced this phenomenon in famous instances like the Great Chicago Fire, reportedly started by a cow kicking over a lantern, or in movies like *Backdraft*. The devastation is incredible, the costs enormous, and the pain and suffering tremendous.

However, God has a better idea. His desire, plan, and purpose are for you to be consumed by *his* fire so you can become a consuming fire for his people. His fuel is your soul, mind, will, and emotions. He is the fire and the Holy Spirit is the oxygen. God desires for those who fight fire in the natural to also be a fire in the Spirit. He wants to cleanse us, purify us, and make us vessels of honor for his use.

When this process occurs, then a supernatural chemical chain reaction follows. We become a conflagration for him, consuming the Enemy, destroying obstacles, and healing others through the power of salvation. WOW! What an awesome God we serve!

How great it is that he desires to use you for his work! How fabulous it is that he loves and trusts you enough to call you by name to be his witness! How humbling it is that you have the power, authority, and responsibility to represent him on this earth!

So, are you on fire? Are you constantly pouring the gasoline of the Word on yourself so you can grow even hotter? Or are you just sitting around smoldering because you lack the oxygen to continue to burn? Open the door of your mouth, ask the Holy Spirit to come in and re-ignite you, become a backdraft that grows into a conflagration for God. People are waiting and are in desperate need to receive the fire you carry.

> "Therefore, since we are receiving a kingdom that cannot be shaken, let us be thankful, and so worship God acceptably with reverence and awe, for our 'God is a consuming fire.'"
> (Hebrews 12:28, 29)

Prayer:
Lord, may my fire spread effectively for your kingdom. Help me be effective in the ministry you have for me. Use me to ignite others.

OCTOBER 18

Bob Crum, Co-founder – Fellowship of Christian Firefighters International (Retired) – Denver Fire Department

A SOGGY HEAP, A LIFETIME OF MEMORIES, OR AN OPPORTUNITY TO SHARE CHRIST?
It's all a matter of perspective

WHEN YOU sit back and contemplate your role as a Christian, have you ever wondered about new and innovative ways you could minister to the community? Have you come to the realization nothing happens by chance and that God has placed you here by divine call to be an ambassador for Christ? Are you taking advantage of every opportunity that calling presents? Challenging questions for sure, but the frequently stated "If not you, who? If not now, when?" takes on a new urgency as you see the need for Christ so vividly.

God has provided emergency responders with many unique ways of ministering to the community. A residence gets burned out and as part of the job the fire department hauls all the trash into the yard and wets it down until it is a soggy heap. What we might view as a pile of trash is actually a lifetime of memories for the families involved: picture albums, cherished keepsakes, financial records, and their earthly possessions.

Christian firefighters need to be sensitive to the hurt of these people and find an opportunity to support and encourage them in their grief. We can be instrumental in putting them in contact with local agencies available for help. At medical emergencies there are opportunities to minister to the family with words of comfort and hope as well as acquainting them with procedures. Having a card to hand out with phone numbers for the Red Cross, Salvation Army, local hospitals, poison control, and other helpful information could prove to be a good way to support grieving families.

> "A new command I give you: Love one another. As I have loved you, so you must love one another. By this all men will know that you are my disciples, if you love one another."
> (John 13:34, 35)

A family is stranded in a foreign neighborhood when their car is totaled in an accident—what can you do? Have you networked with local restaurants, churches, or motels to provide for their immediate needs? Have you stopped to reflect on what Jesus would do?

Missionary outreach starts at home. The possibilities are limited only if we limit our innovative approach.

Prayer:
Lord, help me to see and to seize every opportunity you put in my life to share you.

OCTOBER 19

Tommy Neiman, Author of Sirens for the Cross; EMS Training Officer – St. Lucie County, FL; Fellowship of Christian Firefighters International Regional Director / International Board Member

THE NIGHT OF THE CHURCH FIRE
No one can snatch them out of God's hand

WHILE THE action at my station was steady and invigorating, it seemed as though the "Big One" was eluding us. I didn't wish for

394

disaster, but the firefighter inside me longed for action. Then came the call that still stands out in my mind, not because of its size, but because the Lord's peace and ever-assuring presence were exceptionally real. I call it "The Night of the Church Fire."

"We finally got a big one," I yelled, jamming the pedal to the floor as we saw heavy smoke coming from a large, wooden, country-style church. Hidden almost entirely by the smoke was a hamburger restaurant a few feet away. The restaurant was open and operating. That meant the possibility of people being near the dangerous burning structure. Fortunately, a fire hydrant was on the next block, only yards from the church. We quickly drove to it, hung a U-turn, and dropped off a large hose line. As soon as it was wrapped around the hydrant, I headed for the fire.

> "And God placed all things under his feet and appointed him to be head over everything for the church, which is his body, the fullness of him who fills everything in every way."
> (Ephesians 1:22, 23)

Evacuation of the restaurant became necessary as the fire flared. For a solid hour-and-a-half we relentlessly tackled the flames. Another half-hour passed. Progress, at last. The hamburger restaurant was saved from internal damage, but the church fire, while contained, continued to burn for several more hours.

During the efforts to control this fire, a flood of thoughts swept over me. Was Satan on the warpath mocking the church, taunting me with his deception, and calling out to me, "See how I'm destroying your Lord's house?" I even felt as if I heard his evil chuckles in the crackles of the flames.

Then I focused on the Lord, remembering that the church is the people, God's people, people indwelled with "the fullness of him who fills everything in every way" (Ephesians 1:23). As a part of the church, the precious body of Christ, I counted my blessings. I praised God that nothing can destroy the real church.

A genuine peace and thankfulness began to flow over me as the exact words of God's promise came to mind: "I give them eternal life, and they shall never perish; no one can snatch them out of my hand" (John 10:28).

The building that housed the church was totally destroyed, but since then the body of believers who make up the church have greatly increased in their new building.

Prayer:
*I praise you, Lord, that I am part of the church and
that nothing can snatch me out of your hand.*

Daniel A. Clegg, Rural-Metro EMT; Engineer/EMT–Indianapolis
Fire Department (Retired); Fellowship of Christian Firefighters
Regional Director / International Board Member

A WAY OF ESCAPE

*Do we play down the extent of
concern for our own life?*

ON MY THIRD multiple-alarm fire of the day while stationed at Ladder Company 27, we were dispatched to a rubber company that designs battery shells for domestic cars. They had a dangerous habit of stacking thousands of highly combustible cases outside the building.

Our ladder operation was instructed to put water on the fire. One firefighter manned the top of the ladder. Another handled the controls. We also handled a hand line to cover the exposure between the building and where the battery casings were stacked. The narrow walkway between the structure and the battery casings was less than eight feet wide. While working this area my lieutenant said, "I don't like the looks of our position. I have no intentions of dying on the job." I didn't either, so we opted to create an escape route in the event the casings collapsed and trapped us.

> "Let us throw off everything that hinders and the sin that so easily entangles, and let us run with perseverance the race marked out for us."
> (Hebrews 12:1)

It turned out the escape route wasn't needed and the fire was extinguished without causalities. Still, I sensed something extraordinary was troubling the lieutenant. Once inside the station he said, "Dan, you're in charge. I'm going to my office."

Hours passed before he approached the crew. "I've decided to retire," he stated. "Effective immediately!"

Why now? I thought. Then I wondered. *Do we sometimes play down the extent of concern for our own life and safety?* Maybe the lieutenant, after years of risking his life for others, came to that realization while risking his life because of someone else's disregard for safety procedures. Regardless of his reasoning, he decided it was time to retire.

While risks are standard operating procedure, we have no desire to become dead heroes. The need to give our lives for others is a possibility we often prefer to ignore, but it always looms in the air.

Few careers require a person to contemplate the extent to which they're willing to risk their lives. All first responders address this question as they serve their communities. Some come to the conclusion the only way to escape is through retirement. Others continue to fight the fight and run the race.

Prayer:
Risk and danger are part of this job. As I run the race and serve my community may I do so with perseverance and as a witness of your love. When it's time for me to run another race, may it be clearly your will for my life.

Reverend Wayne Detzler, PhD, Chaplain (Retired) – Charlotte, NC, Fire Department; Fellowship of Christian Firefighters Regional Director

DARKNESS TO LIGHT
From worst to wellness

IT WAS A cool, autumn Friday night, and I was engrossed in a counseling ministry when the shrill scream of my pager interrupted. "Excuse me," I explained. "It's the fire department."

"Respond immediately," the friendly dispatcher instructed. "There's been a bad accident on the turnpike." Leaving my pastoral ministry in the safe hands of a fellow pastor, I dashed off in my car. When I arrived on scene, an eerie quietness permeated the air. No fire apparatus was in sight, just the arc lights illuminating a car crushed beneath a flatbed semitrailer.

"It's a one-car wreck," the helpful cop began, as we walked toward the scrambled mess of steel. "By the way, Chaplain," he continued, "the driver is still behind the wheel. The accident sheared his head off. You're supposed to wait with us until the medical examiner comes. Then the fire department will come back and remove the body."

A long two-hour wait began. I tried to comfort the police officers. We paced back and forth until the medical examiner arrived. Soon a ladder truck showed up. Carefully the firefighters lifted the lifeless body from the wreck and covered it on a gurney.

397

"Hey, Chaplain," the lieutenant called. "Go around and sweep up brain tissue from the road surface." He gave me a hand broom and a clean dustpan. Patiently, I began sweeping up the bits of gray brain. "Put them in the body bag," the lieutenant added.

Back at the station we debriefed each other. This was long before the formal debriefings we now employ. We prayed together for the heartbroken parents of that young man.

> "I will give them comfort and joy instead of sorrow." (Jeremiah 31:13)

Time passed, pain lessened. Finally the report came back. Detailed study of the tissue revealed a serious brain tumor, the probable cause of this tragic accident. It was a comfort to the young driver's family and our firefighters.

The Lord had given us light on a very dark night. As part of the fire service, all-night calls are not unusual. In the middle of the night one often encounters the Lord in a new and fresh way. The Lord often turns disaster into a teachable moment for us.

When all seems to be lost, it is good to remember the old hymn, "God is still on the throne and he will remember his own." We are never off his divine "Global Positioning System."

Prayer:
Lord, I praise you for the light of your love and mercy. Thank you for your comfort and joy when sadness seems to over take my heart.

O C T O B E R   2 2

Daniel A. Clegg, Rural-Metro EMT; Engineer/EMT–Indianapolis Fire Department (Retired); Fellowship of Christian Firefighters Regional Director / International Board Member

HE HELPS CARRY OUR BURDENS
We never know what the day has in store

WHILE SERVING as an engineer for the Indianapolis Fire Department I was dispatched to an automobile fire. The Lawrence Fire Department was on scene when we arrived at the service station dividing our departments. They'd extinguished an automobile fire and were attacking the burning pumps. Sizing up the situation, we knew we needed to change our hats from fire to emergency service workers.

398

Four victims suffered severe burns. A two-year-old was declared dead on arrival. Two women suffered critical burns, one an expectant mother. As we prepared her for transport, she went into labor and the child was stillborn.

We continued packaging our burn victims and sped toward the hospital. The second lady died during transport.

After packaging and sending all victims to their intended destinations, my captain asked, "Dan, are you up to changing hats again from firefighter turned EMT to chaplain? The parents of the expectant mom, grandparents of the small boy, just arrived."

I was the only chaplain present. I nodded a tearful yes.

Telling a family about the tragedy their loved ones endured is never easy. Their two-year-old grandson was dead. Their daughter had miscarried, and their son-in-law fled the scene and was nowhere to be found. It wasn't a hat I wanted to wear, but it was a needed one. I prayed for the right words and strength before approaching the family.

I learned later the son-in-law fled the scene because of an outstanding arrest warrant. He was brought into custody after seeking first aid for minor burns incurred in the accident. The expectant mother succumbed to her injuries two weeks later.

> "I will come down and speak with you there, and I will take of the Spirit that is on you and put the Spirit on them. They will help you carry the burden of the people so that you will not have to carry it alone."
> (Numbers 11:17)

When firefighters arrive at their stations, they never know what the day has in store. We all have our own repertoire of stories. Fortunately, not all end as tragically as this one. Not all calls require us to don several hats, but if we are so required, we can be thankful God says he will not give us more than we can bear, and that he will help us carry the burden.

Prayer:

Thank you for not giving me more than I can bear. Thank you that you are there to help carry the burden just as you helped Moses so long ago.

Chief Lee Callahan, Burlington, MA; Fellowship of Christian Firefighters International Regional Director / International Board Member

SECOND CHANCES— DO WE TAKE THEM?

Submitting to authority is not always easy

AFTER BEING appointed chief, my friend shared that his promotion left an opening that three candidates vied for. The former chief always promoted the candidate with the highest scores, regardless of the person's experience or ability. My friend felt if he continued that policy it would negatively affect the long-term health of the department. After much deliberation, and believing that the candidate with the second-highest score would bring the most talent, skill, and enthusiasm to the job of company officer, he promoted him.

This decision was met with skepticism by some department members. This wasn't the way things had been done before, and they didn't like changes in past practices. However, the passed-over candidate, while disappointed, did not lose his focus despite peer pressure to file a grievance against the chief. Instead he asked the chief for a meeting to find out why he'd been passed over. The chief agreed and began by positively listing the candidate's strongpoints. Then he explained what he viewed as some of the candidate's weaknesses, stating they were the reasons he was not given the officer's job. After this frank discussion, the candidate immersed himself in the day's workload at the fire station.

> "Everyone must submit himself to the governing authorities, for there is no authority except that which God has established. The authorities that exist have been established by God."
> (Romans 13:1)

Several days later, after mulling over what the chief said, he met with the chief again. "After thinking over what you said," he stated, "I want you to know I'm going to change my ways and try to develop a better attitude and improve my skills. Hopefully when another promotion opens, I'll be Number 1 on the list."

The chief encouraged his new attitude and offered his assistance. A year later, when another promotion opportunity arose, the chief promoted him without hesitation. Today, the chief considers the once passed-over candidate as one of his best and most trusted officers.

Submitting to authority is not always easy, but God has ordained it. Only if we are asked to do what is contrary to God's law should we refuse to submit to the authorities placed over us. We may not always agree with or like their orders, but we are clearly told to follow them: "Everyone must submit to the governing authorities. . . " (Romans 13:1).

Prayer:
Lord, instead of looking at the difficult challenges that come
my way and rebuking the authorities I don't agree with,
I will look to you and your grace.

OCTOBER 24

Craig Duck, Lieutenant, Engine Co. 11 – Washington, DC, Fire Department; Fellowship of Christian Firefighters International Atlantic States Regional Director / International Board Member

REVIVE US AGAIN
Allowing God to reign supreme in the fire service

I'VE BEEN serving the citizens, workers, and visitors of the District of Columbia for the last twenty-four years. Before serving in the District, I was a part of several volunteer fire organizations. Many changes have occurred in the fire service since my initial involvement. Some for the best, others unfortunately not.

Recently, I was ordered to go to our training academy to attend an Emergency Medical Technician (EMT) training class. When I first entered the fire service, there was no such course. In fact, the fire departments I was accustomed to didn't provide ambulance service at all.

Attending the EMT class was a new experience requiring me to learn many new terms. The instructors threw around terms like posterior, mid-clavicle, fowler's position, and zygomatic bones. These terms, as well as common medical practices associated with them and other terms, are needed in order to revive a patient. Changes toward better patient care are definitely in the category of "for the best." The EMT's greatest joy is bringing an unresponsive patient back to life. I've seen this happen on the fire ground and on medical locals. Witnessing the survival of a person who would have died without the fire department's intervention, and then seeing that person become ambulatory and walking around, is extremely satisfying. It's one of the things that make what we do worthwhile.

God is in the business of reviving people and restoring lives. Since Creation, when God "breathed into his nostrils the breath of life" (Genesis 2:7), he has been reviving people and providing life. God not only revives individuals, as evidenced by his saving grace, but he also uses people to proclaim his Word, bringing revival to areas around the world. The fire service is in desperate need of revival—our signs and symptoms clearly indicate a need for intervention.

> "Will you not revive us again, that your people may rejoice in you? Show us your unfailing love, O Lord, and grant us your salvation."
> (Psalm 85:6, 7)

The only way revival within the fire service and a return to the "good ol' days," when firefighters praised the name of God and served him, can happen is through Christian first responders. They need to respond to the call for action and begin to share Christ with other emergency personnel.

Some change is good, but any change that takes us away from our Creator will lead away from life to death.

Prayer:
Help me, Lord, to not only pray for revival within the fire service, but to proclaim and demonstrate your mercy and grace to every firehouse and first responder I come in contact with.

OCTOBER 25

Reverend Wayne Detzler, PhD, Chaplain (Retired) – Charlotte, NC, Fire Department; Fellowship of Christian Firefighters Regional Director

WHEN NO ONE'S LOOKING
Who are you?

"CHARACTER IS who you are when no one sees you." It's an old adage, but it's absolutely true. We try to explain our way around this one, and we pretend appearance is everything, but the Bible says it's true: Character is a God thing.

It had been a long day and an even longer night for me. I'd been at the hospital helping the emergency crew through a nightmare. It was almost Christmas when they received victims of a traffic wreck on the old Merritt Parkway, New England's oldest freeway.

First, we received the body of a young surgical nurse from Bridgeport, Connecticut. Then the body of her boyfriend arrived. They were dressed for a Christmas party in middle Connecticut. As they drove through the bitterly cold night, a car catapulted over the barrier between lanes. It landed on their car, snuffing out their young lives in an instant. Their poor, broken bodies were brought to us because the highway back to Bridgeport was blocked both ways.

About midnight, I headed home for a clean shirt and quick nap. We still had to help parents identify the bodies. Then the light at our corner turned red. So, I stopped behind another car. He paused briefly before cautiously creeping into a left turn. After all, it was midnight. No one was on the road, except for me behind him.

> "The Lord is a God who knows." (1 Samuel 2:3)

Blue lights erupted like a volcano! A local cop pulled him over and ticketed him. As a fire and police chaplain, I was so glad I hadn't followed him through the red light. Despite the darkness and the early morning hour, I was glad my instincts were to stop at a red light.

Life's like that. God knows—even when no one else is looking at us. It was Hannah, Samuel's mother, who said: "The Lord is a God who knows" (1 Samuel 2:3). She knew it well, that God sees when no one else is looking. This explains her character, a spiritual legacy she passed on to her son, Samuel. "Man looks at the outward appearance, but the LORD looks at the heart" (1 Samuel 16:7).

When God looked at David, he knew David was a man after his own heart. When he looked at Hannah, no doubt he saw only her inner beauty. When he looks at you, what does he see?

Prayer:
Help me never to forget, my "Knowing Lord,"
that my life is lived before you.

Captain Raul A. Angulo – Seattle Fire Department;
Fellowship of Christian Firefighters Regional Director /
International Board Member

O ABSALOM, MY SON, MY SON!

The essence of unconditional love

THREE FATHERS crossed my path who caused me to reflect on the relationship of a father to his son. Regardless of where the responsibility lay, these fathers' hearts ached for their sons. One was at a loss on how to guide his son through a painful divorce. Another's son returned from Iraq with a drug addiction. The last father suffers from a painful estrangement from his son over political differences.

The Bible relates stories of father-son relationships filled with pain. Can you imagine how painful it was for God to give his only begotten Son for our sins? What about the pain King David experienced? (2 Samuel 13, 15, 19). David, a brave warrior, superb military leader, the greatest king of Israel—a man described by God as a "man after his own heart," and an ancestor of Jesus—had father-son problems.

Two years after David's first son, Amnon, raped his half-sister, Tamar, his brother Absalom took revenge and killed him. David wept for his sons. The pain continued when Absalom rebelled, built a great army, and forced his father to flee. As the rebellion continued,

> "We love because he first loved us."
> (1 John 4:19)

so did David's heartache, reaching a climax when Joab, commander of David's army, killed Absalom. When news reached King David, he cried, "My son, my son Absalom! If only I had died instead of you!"

Why was David so upset over his rebellious son's death? Why did David love his son even though Absalom did nothing to deserve this love? Perhaps because he knew he was partially responsible. But almost certainly because that is the nature of fatherhood—the essence of unconditional love.

Firefighters may not be kings, but the parallel to mighty warriors is evident and our heavenly Father loves us unconditionally. So does his Son who, through his sacrifice on the cross, paid the price for our sins. Though he may not remove the consequences of our sins, we are forgiven and like David, our God is able to see past all the faults and shortcomings of his children because he simply loves us!

Is there a relationship, be it between you and a child or perhaps someone at your place of work, in which you need to exhibit God's love unconditionally? It may be one of the most difficult steps you take, but as you contemplate your next step, remember—out of love, God gave his only Son. He took the first step.

Prayer:
Dear Lord, thank you for your unconditional love and forgiveness. Your love is a perfect example. Help me to reflect your love in all my relationships.

OCTOBER 27

Chaplain Marc Santorella; Firefighter Danvers Fire Department, MA Public Fire and Life Safety Educator and Certified Fire Instructor Level 1

EVEN THE BEST JOB HAS STRUGGLES
Leaning on one another for encouragement

BECOMING A firefighter created feelings of "arrival" coupled with pure adrenaline and adventure. Most firefighters, like me, regarded our new career as "the best." We absorbed as much job knowledge as possible, were "ready" when the bell rang, time was irrelevant, sleep gave way to conducting inspections, assisting with medical aids, putting out fires, waiting for the "big one," or getting breakfast. Regardless of the call, we were happy to be doing what we had waited so long to do.

Then something happened. The excitement began to fade, the newness tarnished, and it became what it is—a job. Combine that with financial cutbacks making it difficult to acquire new equipment with updated technology, thus requiring us to do more with less. Who wouldn't be frustrated? This is when we need to look at our situations through God's eyes.

Two thousand years ago people were experiencing similar struggles when Jesus came and opened the eyes of the faithful. These people listened to him teach, watched him perform miracles, and ate with him. Regardless of their circumstances, they were thrilled to be in Jesus' presence. Then things got tougher. Political rulers seemed to have it in for them. Discouragement set in, excitement waned. During this time Peter, compelled by God, wrote to Christians scattered throughout the nations telling them not to lose heart. Even though they knew many of the things Peter was going to say, he told them anyway, "I think it is right to refresh your memory" (2 Peter 1:13).

The fire service has its naysayers and enemies; always has, always will. Let's be sure to keep our opponents outside our ranks by encouraging each other not to forget our original love for the job. Every day that we put on that uniform is a good day. Every shift is an opportunity to be available to serve.

God knew hard times would come. We can trust that he is in them with us. Let's also be in this together and able to lean on each other for encouragement and support.

> "Cast all your anxiety on him because he cares for you." (1 Peter 5:7)

Like the early Christians, it's easy to forget our commitment. We can feel like the world is against us. But if you believe in God, then take heart from what God says and "cast all your anxiety on him because he cares for you" (1 Peter 5:7).

Prayer:
Jesus, you suffered every kind of trial, so you understand the trials I face. I will lean on you and, through your comfort and grace, encourage those around me. May your hope and glory shine through me as a light in dark times.

OCTOBER 28

Rick Barton, Fire Safety Officer; Rick Barton Ministries, Gunnison, CO; Fellowship of Christian Firefighters International Ambassador-at-Large

CURIOSITY KILLED . . .

If only the residents had followed the evacuation orders

AS THE fierce Santa Ana winds pushed the fire onto the stalled fire engine, the windows exploded, filling the cab with flame, heat, and smoke. In a matter of moments, four firefighters and one juvenile civilian were seriously burned. One "hitchhiking" civilian tragically perished.

What were two non-firefighters doing "hitchhiking" on the engine during this conflagration? According to the Cal Fire "Green Sheet," which gives a preliminary summary of the event, the civilians were instructed to evacuate the area. They ignored the warning and instead they followed the fire engine back into the fire on their ATV. When the ATV broke down they had to be picked up by the engine crew. As the engine approached a turnaround, they found themselves unable to back up due to another civilian on a tractor. The ATVers' curiosity led to disobedience and ultimate tragedy, for at that point the flame front hit them resulting in the injuries and fatality.

If only the residents had followed the evacuation orders! The insistence of the adult to re-enter the fire zone, and allowing the juvenile to follow, cost him his life and caused the juvenile to be critically burned. In addition, that selfish act of curiosity, in combination with the third civilian blocking the engine's egress, caused four firefighters to be burned and their engine destroyed.

Are you sometimes like those civilians? Do you allow your "curiosity" to lure you into disobedience and then places of danger—places God's Word tells you to evacuate? Pornography, lust, gambling, and harboring bitterness are all areas the Lord clearly tells you to evacuate. For example: "Flee from sexual immorality. All other sins a man commits are outside his body, but he who sins sexually sins against his own body" (1 Corinthians 6:18). If you don't flee, not only are you sinning against your own body, but you're placing your family, friends, and perhaps innocent servants like those firefighters in imminent danger. Your sin never affects just you. There are others always watching, and when you ignore God's "evacuation orders," they suffer as well.

> "Flee the evil desires of youth, and pursue righteousness, faith, love and peace, along with those who call on the Lord out of a pure heart."
> (2 Timothy 2:22)

In what area is your curiosity tempting you? Is there something in your life that God says you should flee from?

Prayer:
Lord, may my heart be pure in your sight
as well as to those around me.

407

Reverend Wayne Detzler, PhD, Chaplain (Retired) –
Charlotte, NC, Fire Department; Fellowship of
Christian Firefighters Regional Director

RUNNING WELL TO THE END
Learning how to finish well

USUALLY THE seminary classroom is a quiet place and the professor is almost always in control. So I felt especially calm that December evening. The students were well into the subject, and we were
discussing exciting lessons from missionary work worldwide. It was my
last semester as a resident professor in Charlotte.

The vibrating pager seemed like an unwanted, unwarranted interruption. I checked it briefly, but decided to wait. But, the pager would not
wait! So, I excused myself and called dispatch.

"Respond to the hospital." The dispatcher was terse and urgent.
"We've got a firefighter down, and it's serious." I went back to class and
dismissed the students; then I rushed to my car and headed uptown.

When I arrived a member of our firefighter support team briefed me.
The firefighter had been running outside his station, his normal exercise
routine. Suddenly, he fell, and a passing driver found him. He was deeply
unconscious, unresponsive.

"He's dead," they briefed me. "He was pronounced dead on arrival
here at the hospital. His family is on the
way." I moved among the assembled crew
members, and we prayed for the family.

Out of breath his young wife dashed
into the waiting room. Carefully, the chief
explained what happened. Her husband was
running as usual and he just dropped dead.

> "Precious in the sight of
> the Lord is the death of
> his saints."
> (Psalm 116:15)

Then we accompanied the young wife as she went to view his body. Quietly I led the family in prayer as we began a long, hard evening.

Quickly the waiting room filled with firefighters and family members. Members of the pastoral staff from their church joined us. The
church's campus abuts the fire station where he died. Members of their
Sunday school class came to support his wife and family in this dark
hour.

Over the weekend we prepared for the funeral. My last duty in Charlotte was to accompany this brave young firefighter to his final rest.

Because of his strong and verbal witness for the Lord, we had a celebration of his life. He died as he had lived, a courageous witness for Christ.

We never know the hour God will call us home, but when he does what a blessing it is for those left behind to know that their loved one is with God!

Prayer:
Thank you, Lord, for the witness of believers young and old
who finish well. Thank you for the knowledge that this
young man and all believers are with you in Glory.

O C T O B E R   3 0

Captain Raul A. Angulo – Seattle Fire Department;
Fellowship of Christian Firefighters Regional
Director / International Board Member

ENTERING WITH CONFIDENCE
Approaching the consuming fire with confidence

SEVERAL OLD Testament accounts illustrate the importance of obeying and taking God's warnings seriously. One incident occurred when seventy men of Beth Shemesh were killed by God for looking into the ark of the Lord (1 Samuel 6:19). After defeating the Philistines, who had captured the ark of the covenant, King David brought the ark back to Jerusalem on a new cart guided by Uzzah and Ahio. When the oxen stumbled, Uzzah took hold of it. The Lord's anger burned against this irreverent act and God struck him down.

Our reverence for God should be no different today. When we come into God's presence we should not take it lightly. The end result will be disastrous.

It's also disastrous to hand untrained, unprotected recruits a nozzle and send them into a burning structure. Without training, firefighters never develop the confidence to do this dangerous job safely. Whether fighting a structure or dumpster fire, we need to learn that fire has no favorites; it consumes every unprotected thing in its path. Fire must be respected and feared.

Training on hose and ladder evolutions, knowledge of fire behavior, building construction, strategy, and tactics gives firefighters the ability to confidently approach a fire. Helmets, coats, and our personal protective equipment (PPE) protect us from the effects of fire. With advancements in PPE technology, some feel we've become over-confident. Modern encapsulating PPE may give a false sense of security, allowing us to enter deeper into a structure since we no longer "feel" the warning signs of a pre-flashover fire.

Are you fully trained and equipped? Or are you too confident to heed the signs of God's warnings?

Through faith and acceptance of Jesus' sacrifice for us on the cross, we have immediate forgiveness for our sins past, present, and future. Being covered by the blood of the Lamb is like donning our PPE and self-contained breathing apparatus. We are fully encapsulated with his righteousness so we can approach the consuming fire with confidence. Now we have unlimited access to God. He welcomes us right where we are, just the way we are. He desires our fellowship, our praise, our worship, our prayers, and even our eternal presence—with him!

> "Yet, to all who received him, to those who believed in his name, he gave the right to become children of God." (John 1:12)

Prayer:
I am thankful for the advancements in technology that help protect me from the danger of fires. Even more so, Lord, thank you for sending your Son to protect me from the dangers of sin.

OCTOBER 31

Joel Kelm, Firefighter/EMT – Gallatin Gateway, MT; President – Big Sky Chapter of Fellowship of Christian Firefighters

A SELF-CHECK FOR LEADERSHIP
Straight from God's Word

EVER CONDUCTED a self-check and asked, "What makes or qualifies me to be a spiritual leader?"

The Bible clearly explains that a good spiritual leader must walk closely with the Lord. Doing this requires an internalized knowledge of God's Word, the kind that comes from diligent study. But what is it that qualifies you, as an individual, to be an effective and godly spiritual leader?

The third chapter of the book of Titus in the New Testament provides us with a biblical "self-check" guide. Memorizing and applying Psalm 101:2–7 to your daily life, as you struggle in this decaying world, will also provide an excellent "self-check." This psalm emphasizes the need to lead a blameless life, turn away from "vile" things, not allow faithless men to cling to you, keep men of perverse heart far from you, have nothing to do with evil slanderers with haughty eyes and a proud heart, and not allow anyone who practices deceit to dwell in your house. Obviously, God is concerned about who you fellowship with.

To be qualified as a spiritual leader, you don't need a degree. You need a lifestyle that sets an example for everyone you come in contact with, including your families and co-workers—a lifestyle clearly delineated in God's Word.

> "So do not fear, for I am with you; do not be dismayed, for I am your God. I will strengthen you and help you; I will uphold you with my righteous right hand." (Isaiah 41:10)

The battle for purity is a battle that will never be totally won until Christ calls you home. Many chosen by God as spiritual leaders did and still do struggle with the issue of purity. David committed adultery and murder, yet God called him "a man after my own heart." A worthy ambition for the day you meet our Lord face-to-face is to present yourself as a strong, faithful, uncompromising person who desired to live a righteous life here on Earth. Change begins when you set righteousness as a goal.

Is it time for change? Is it time to seek repentance before a just God, to pray for a renewed heart and a consequent fresh start? Has God called you into his service? If so, be honored and happy as God has handpicked you to be his ambassador. Then study to show yourself approved (2 Timothy 2:15) and don't fear or be dismayed—God will strengthen and help you.

Prayer:

As a firefighter, saving lives and property are proud moments that stimulate and motivate me to be the best firefighter I can be. May my even prouder moments be based on sharing your love and saving others from eternal flames.

*Reverend Wayne Detzler, PhD, Chaplain (Retired) –
Charlotte, NC, Fire Department; Fellowship of
Christian Firefighters Regional Director*

FLIPPED BY THE HOSE
It's tougher than it looks

THE PAGER roused me from a deep sleep. Automatically I grabbed and silenced it. When I phoned dispatch, I was instantly wide awake. "Working fire." The dispatcher was short. "Chaplain, there's a huge working fire and they need you now."

Fumbling for my turnout gear, I stumbled down the stairs and into the car. As I pulled out of our driveway bright orange flames illuminated the sky. This was the biggest fire I'd ever seen.

When I reached the site it was a vacant building torched by a malicious arsonist. The cause was irrelevant. The fury of the fire was the issue. Several units poured water on various parts of the building. Progress was negligible.

An hour later firefighters still struggled to get the conflagration under control, but there was so much fuel in the old building. Acrid black smoke soared into the night sky. All available units were on hand, trying to get a grip on the flames.

> "I can do everything through him who gives me strength.
> (Philippians 4:13)

"Chaplain," one of the firefighters shouted. "Chaplain, come here." I worked my way along the fire line. A crew was pouring water onto the flames, and they were getting weary.

"We want to go to the Red Cross truck and get some coffee," the lieutenant shouted over the roar of the blaze. "Can you hold the hose while we go for a break?" they asked.

"Sure!" My bravado outstripped my experience. "Give me the hose. I'll do it!" The rookie handed the hose to me. Unfortunately, I was not secured in its cradle. The loose nozzle whipped backwards and flipped me with it. The next thing I heard was my helmet hitting the concrete. Firefighters claimed that I did a pretty perfect back flip. It took a couple of firefighters to get a hand on the hose. Then they handed it over to me and took their well-earned break.

Did you ever notice how we overestimate our own strength? We often think we have more strength, more experience, and more ability than we

413

really have. It is comforting to know that the Lord's strength is perfect when we are weak (2 Corinthians 12:9–10).

Prayer:
Mighty Savior, my strength is weak.
Please work in and through me today.

N O V E M B E R 2

Daniel A. Clegg, Rural-Metro EMT; Engineer/EMT–Indianapolis Fire Department (Retired); Fellowship of Christian Firefighters Regional Director / International Board Member

ABIDE

Trusting his decision

EVER HAD one of those calls where there was nothing you could do? Such a call came while I was running on Rescue Engine 12 to a personal injury with extrication. The man had been drinking, lost control of his car, and ran it under a semi, resulting in his decapitation.

Calls such as this, while not uncommon, cause questions difficult to handle, let alone answer. Sometimes we just throw up. Other times feelings of depression bother us for days, weeks, or months. There's no doubt they remain forever embedded in our minds.

In your spiritual life, do you ever feel like that person in the car? Do you ever feel like Satan ran you over and there is no hope? Many times there are no understandable or logical answers for what we encounter. Joseph did not understand his trials; but God brought him to the point where he told his brothers, "You intended to harm me, but God intended it for good to accomplish what is now being done, the saving of many lives" (Genesis 50:20).

No matter what's said or done in your life, "If you hold to [Jesus'] teaching, . . . you will know the truth, and the truth will set you free" (John 8:31, 32).

If we abide in Christ and let him be in charge when we reflect on tragic calls, we can rest in the knowledge God is in control. His ways are not our ways, but he does have everything under control.

In dealing with the emotional aspects of our job and tragic scenes, we need to keep in mind there are consequences to poor behavior and that

414

what took place was according to the Lord's will. He was the one who made the final decision. Then we need to make the choice to trust his decision, whether we want to or not. Only then can we move forward and experience his peace, which surpasses all understanding.

> "Trust in the LORD with all your heart and lean not on your own understanding; in all your ways acknowledge him, and he will make your paths straight." (Proverbs 3:5, 6)

Do you want to know peace? Then accept his gift to us of his Son, Jesus, and get to know him. Read his Word! Pray! Trust in his plan! Develop a personal relationship with him.

Is it easy? I think not. Is it worth it? Yes! Eternally!

Prayer:
When calls that continue to haunt my memory cause me to question you, Lord, may I turn to your Word and not trust in my own thoughts and understandings.

Tommy Neiman, Author of Sirens for the Cross; EMS Training Officer – St. Lucie County, FL; Fellowship of Christian Firefighters International Regional Director / International Board Member

PRECIOUS IN HIS SIGHT
Deepened bonds of friendship

ARE THE fatalities we encounter good? Not the ones I've witnessed. Can good result from them? God says yes. Most Christians are familiar Romans 8:28, which clearly explains that if we love God and are called according to his purpose then good will be seen.

One call that made this clear was a tragic accident involving a van carrying a family of seven. The van's driver lost control, and the van flipped over numerous times and landed upside down. Three people were ejected. Four were trapped inside. My friend and co-worker, David, and his rescue truck crew were first out. Our engine followed and was governed for a top speed of sixty-five miles-per-hour, delaying our arrival. When David arrived he issued multiple trauma alerts as he worked a two-year-old in critical condition. Our engine arrived amid confusion, chaos, destruction, and loss. A blood-stained sheet covered one body.

I headed toward a teenage girl, covered with road rash and suffering multiple fractures. Others went to work on the remaining injured. The southbound lane was cleared and Air One touched down. After a secondary triage or assessment, it was decided that David and his patient would fly.

> "And we know that in all things God works for the good of those who love him, who have been called according to his purpose." (Romans 8:28)

Despite desperate efforts on the part of David, his crew, and the ER staff, the little boy went on to be with the Lord. We returned to the station overwhelmed by the tragedy and needing mutual encouragement. I found David sitting dejectedly on his bunk. "You did all you could," I calmly affirmed, placing my hand on his shoulder.

"Yeah, but . . . why? Why the little one, Tommy?"

"All I know, David, is that the Lord has little ones he specifically chooses to take home, and this was one of them. This child must be so precious to God that he called him home early for a purpose we may never fully understand in this life. We just have to trust and believe."

What good came from this?

A deepening bond of friendship grew between my already close friend, David, and me. David, more like a brother than a fellow worker, had drifted far away from the Lord and recently rededicated his life. God was working in his life and using me for spiritual encouragement. Without question God had placed us together for spiritual strength and comfort on this particular call.

Prayer:

Lord, I know your promise in Romans 8:28. Help me to see the good that comes from tragedies with no seemingly intrinsic good.

NOVEMBER 4

Robert M. Winston, District Fire Chief (Retired) – Boston, MA

CAMARADERIE UNDER FIRE
Healing could begin

DECEMBER 3, 1999, the Worcester Cold & Storage Warehouse an abandoned cavernous warehouse in Massachusetts, became the scene of fiery collapse, death, heartache, heroism, and camaraderie under the most extreme firefighting conditions. This fire was started when two homeless people argued, knocked over a candle, and fled. The fire escalated, resulting in the worst line-of-duty deaths in the history of the Worcester Fire Department.

Heavy smoke turned to visible flames as the fire ate through the nearly windowless ark of a structure. The interior, a maze of darkened rooms and corridors six floors of them with scattered debris, added to the firefighters' blind search for the seat of the fire. When the building started to collapse, the fire-chief-in-command ordered all firefighters to stop rescue attempts and vacate the building. Six Worcester firefighters perished despite the herculean efforts of a small army of rescuers. Recovery lasted an arduous, somber eight days and nights.

> "Be devoted to one another in brotherly love. Honor one another above yourselves."
> (Romans 12:10)

I was dispatched by the Boston Fire Department as a safety operational sector chief to look for safety hazards. When the warehouse roof, floors, and two exterior walls fell, the danger of additional structural collapse and of firefighters falling through burned-out floors haunted us. As I surveyed a section in danger of collapse, I issued a warning to a Worcester fire lieutenant who was in a dangerous location. He responded with anger. It's not unusual for tempers to flare under extremely stressful circumstances.

After eight days, the pile of smoldering debris was fully extinguished. Tragically five bodies of Worcester's bravest were recovered. One was still buried in the remaining mounds of twisted steel, burned wood, and bricks.

Recovery operations continued into the night until firefighter Paul Brotherton's body was located. Among those showing respect was the now-gaunt lieutenant I'd had the angry encounter with. He'd been at the scene from the fire's start, refusing to go home. These were his brothers. As we hugged, as only firefighters do at a time like this, the lieutenant literally collapsed into my arms.

It was cold, dark, and quiet as Firefighter Brotherton's body was removed. The sad task of recovery was finally over. Healing could begin.

I never again saw the exhausted lieutenant, but I think of him whenever and wherever I see the word "camaraderie."

Prayer:
I praise you for the special camaraderie among the fire service. Thank you for the way fellow first responders exhibit that love in difficult times, a love that sustains us even when confronted with enormous loss. Even more sustaining, Lord, is your ever-present love.

Aaron Johnson, Fire Inspector –
Martin County, FL

GOD'S VAPOR

Have we reached our ignition point?

ON A COOL November night in Florida, as our men's Bible study group sat around the campfire, our conversation turned to the topic of influence. How can we best impact those around us for Christ? As I listened to the conversation around me, and watched the flames lick at the logs, my mind went back to a lesson I had learned in the fire academy.

While the general public considers that fires are "things" burning, those in the fire service are well aware that "things" do not burn. Logs or wood pallets thrown on the fire do not burn. What actually happens is that the wood reaches its ignition point and the molecules start to break down; in the process, the item turns to vapor. It's this vapor that actually burns. This can be plainly seen by looking closely at the wick of a burning candle; you'll see the flame is actually not touching the wick.

Mesmerized and warmed by the flames of our campfire that evening, my mind drifted to thoughts about my walk with the Lord, and the church in general. We, the people, are God's church. Paul first referred to us as Christians two thousand years ago. But as Christians, have we reached our ignition point? Or are we still cold? Are we on fire for Christ in such a way that we're releasing his "vapor"? Is our relationship with him evident to those around us because we're emitting the love of Christ and things of the Kingdom?

> "But thanks be to God, who always leads us in triumphal procession in Christ and through us spreads everywhere the fragrance of the knowledge of him."
> (2 Corinthians 2:14)

When new in our Christian walk, we are on fire for God. But, as time goes on, it's easy to slip into a more lukewarm state. Many are not as fervent in their walk as they once were. They start to get cold. Their flame starts to dim.

Our purpose on this earth should be to impact those around us with the love of Christ. The best way to accomplish this monumental task is to live the Christian life. We need to stay connected to God through prayer and his Word, so the "vapor" of his love is emitted from our lives, touching and warming those around us.

NOVEMBER 6

Reverend Wayne Detzler, PhD, Chaplain (Retired) – Charlotte, NC, Fire Department; Fellowship of Christian Firefighters Regional Director

DRIVING THE TILLER
A guiding hand

TIME TO drive the tiller," the captain called early one Saturday morning. "Report to the station, we want you to drive the tiller," he continued.

"Tiller trucks" are old-fashioned and most departments no longer use them. They are large semitractors that, in order to navigate through narrow city streets making tight corners, haul a ladder behind them as a trailer. High on the back of the ladder is a driver's seat and a huge steering wheel. No power steering aids the tiller driver, and there was a trick to this. Your driver must steer in the opposite direction, counteracting the huge swing of the ladder. The objective? Avoid slamming into parked cars.

Despite the danger, or perhaps because of it, it was great fun to drive a tiller. "Get up into the seat," the captain ordered me. "Strap yourself in." A lap seatbelt was provided. After all, some guys did fly off the seat.

With the captain strapped in beside me, we eased our way onto the streets of our small town. We made the first turn okay as we weaved in and out through the parked cars and the tight corners. "Go gently," the captain suggested. Sometimes he put a steadying hand on the wheel.

After two hours we headed back to the barn. "I'll let *you* back it in." There was a plea in my offer.

"No, Chaplain," the captain answered. "You drove it. You back it in." Slowly, very

> "I will instruct you and teach you in the way you should go." (Psalm 32:8)

419

slowly, I backed the tiller into its bay. Relief and joy marked my mood as I climbed down from the tiller. Most of all, I was thankful for the captain's guiding hand. He knew the truck, and he knew my limitations.

As a Christian I am so thankful for the Lord's guiding hand. He not only rides with us when we have a new experience, he is with us every day to guide us. "All the way, my Savior leads me," an old hymn says. The Lord puts his steadying hand on ours as we walk through life. We can rely on this, for Psalm 32:8 tells us as much in plain, straightforward language.

Prayer:
Lord, guide me through the day today. Help me to feel your steadying hand. Help me to allow you to direct my response.

NOVEMBER 7

Chaplain Robert Osbourn, Sylacauaga, AL, Fire Department

GET BUSY
No one knows how many days we have left

MANY TRAUMATIC events caught my attention in the world news. One item told about recovery crews who found a body authorities believed was that of a sixty-seven-year-old Montgomery man whose car was swept into a large concrete drainage ditch by floodwaters. First responders tried without success to get the driver out of the vehicle when it went into the ditch. Another reported that swine flu had sickened thousands of people in thirty countries. Still another related that storm debris blocked roads and damaged houses when six tornadoes touched down. The firefighters made at least fifty water rescues. Other news reported thefts, murders, domestic quarrels, abuse, and other ungodly events.

As I was reading of these tragedies, I was overcome with the realization of our earthly mortality and how fleeting life is. I bowed to pray for these victims and as I did, God's warnings came to mind. God clearly states that no one, not even angels, or his own Son, knows when the coming of the Son of Man will be. He related that the people of Noah's day were so ignorant and immoral that "they knew nothing about what would happen until the flood came and took them all away. That is how it will be at the coming of the Son of Man" (Matthew 24:39). Then he clearly warned, "Therefore keep watch" (v. 42).

This passage is a warning about a storm that is coming upon this earth. Not a small storm in which we can run outside and fix things, but the wrath of God. It's a reminder that the end is coming and we need to be prepared. Will a good friend of yours, or someone God brings into your life, be left? Will *you* be left?

> "Therefore keep watch, because you do not know on what day your Lord will come."
> (Matthew 24:42)

I was challenged and I challenge you: Get busy! No one knows how many days we have left in order to get our lives on track and get right with Jesus.

Prayer:
Your Word is clear, God, that your Son, Jesus, will return. No one knows when that will be, but I accept the challenge to get busy. Guide me as I seek to know your will for my life, to live according to your Word, and then to share your love and truth with others.

NOVEMBER 8

Rick Barton, Fire Safety Officer; Rick Barton Ministries, Gunnison, CO; Fellowship of Christian Firefighters International Ambassador-at-Large

SICK AND TIRED
I learned a powerful lesson that day the need for humility

IT WAS THE longest, most difficult fire assignment any of us had so far encountered. Twenty days of fighting forest fires in northern California were behind us. Still, there was no end in sight. The hills were steep. Each day we spent hours on "Klamath Death Marches" just to reach the fire line. To compound matters, an inversion held the smoke over the fires, not allowing the air to clear. As a result, no aircraft could fly to help slow the fire's spread or bring us fresh food. Worst of all, the smoke made us sick. Sixteen- to twenty-hour workdays and unclean air combined to afflict each of us. We were run down, irritable, and coughing continually. We were sick and tired, and tired of being sick and tired! Not a pleasant sight, for sure.

I was the crew leader for a twenty-person hand crew that built the fire line day after day. This crew was not composed of regular firefighters but of men and women from my home forest in Colorado—folks who normally manned a desk, drove trucks, or built hiking trails. None of us was accustomed to this level of severity, and none of us escaped the sickness.

> "Humble yourself in the sight of the Lord, and He will lift you up."
> (James 4:10 NKJV)

In camp one night a tough decision was made. Our sickest crew members and the sickest of an adjoining crew would be sent home. The "survivors" would be combined into one team with me acting as the crew boss. Coughing, I hacked in agreement, "Sure, that's a great idea."

The next morning things changed again. A healthier person on the other crew was appointed as the leader. To me, that added insult to injury. "I'd rather go home than lose control of 'my' crew," I mumbled to myself.

Then, a strange thing happened. The new boss, someone I barely knew but already resented, came over to where I was standing. "Would you pray for me?" she asked. "I need all the help I can get."

Fires Consume Home (Internet Resource)

Talk about feeling about six inches high. I prayed with her and inwardly committed myself to being the best helper I could be.

I learned a powerful lesson that day the need for humility.

Prayer:
Lord, help me to remember that you alone are in control. Thank you for those you place in my life to teach me powerful lessons. May I walk humbly and not out of pride.

NOVEMBER 9

Ann Christmas, Fellowship of Christian Firefighters, St. Louis Chapter; American Red Cross, North County Citizen Corps

EAGLE OR TURKEY?
Rise above the storms or hide

EVER HAVE one of those friends who just never give up? You know the kind, the ones who have about anything tossed at them and just keep on moving forward? God blessed my son and me with a wonderful friend who never gave up, who became an example for us throughout our own battles. Dennis Foshe was the regional director for the Fellowship of Christian Firefighters in the state of Missouri. He went home to heaven in April of 2009 where, if it is at all possible, he will find a way to annoy and amuse God.

> "But those who hope in the LORD will renew their strength. They will soar on wings like eagles; they will run and not grow weary, they will walk and not be faint." (Isaiah 40:31)

Throughout his battle with cancer, Dennis always remained positive and uplifting around my ill son. I believe my son is the person he is today partially because of Dennis. He was filled with peace, hope, and joy throughout the years, always giving others a hand, and never lost his sense of humor. Dennis stood strong because of his love for Christ.

It's easy to give up on things when times are tough. But for those who stand by God and his Word, there is hope and strength. We are walking testimonies for Christ through the tough times, whether it's our health or our actions at a disaster scene. Dennis's journey was a living example of what most Christians desire to reflect. Instead of focusing on our trials, we must focus on the fact that God is walking through those trials with us. No matter what we're going through right now, God is right beside us. He's our refuge and our strength—always there to comfort.

When I think of Dennis, I'm reminded of Isaiah's encouraging words (Isaiah 40:31). When problems come, we can soar like eagles and rise above the storm clouds, or, as I once heard, we can be like a turkey and run and hide. Dennis soared high above the storm clouds.

Prayer:
Jesus, I thank you for what you've brought me through in my past and will bring me through in my future. When times get tough, I'll remember you are there to comfort and guide me. Please forgive me for the times I didn't place my total trust in you. Open my eyes to show me how to surrender to your will and follow the path you've planned for me. Some days it is hard, Lord, and I thank you for the lessons I've learned from all my experiences. Help me to be a walking testimony for others. You are my strength, God; I thank you, in Jesus' name, amen.

NOVEMBER 10

Sue Reynolds, Missionary – Fellowship of Christian Firefighters International (FCFI), and Chaplain Gaius Reynolds, President – FCFI; Volunteer Firefighter – Livermore, CO, Fire Protection District

A SAD SCENARIO
Too often repeated

PLEASE PRAY for me!" the woman pleaded. "My husband is headed to a fire conference and I don't want him to go. I know the training is needed, but when he gets with the guys . . ."

There was a long pause with intermittent sobs before she continued, "He's just so susceptible to peer pressure. Recently, he recommitted his life to the Lord after seeing the movie *Fireproof*. Our marriage has been so much better. But after long shifts at the firehouse, he quickly falls back into his old patterns. Now he's going to be with thousands of firefighters for a week."

We prayed together and talked a while longer. I was trying to seek words of encouragement for her to share with her husband before he left that wouldn't offend him—touchy ground requiring wisdom.

Have you put your spouse through a similar anguish? Is your relationship often like a roller coaster? At home does it take a while to shake off the influence from your stint at work? Maybe you're blessed with a workplace where Christians have stepped up and are willing to share and live their faith. Maybe like many workplaces I've visited, the Christians offer an apology before I enter, for

> "My son, if sinners entice you, do not give in to them. If they say, 'Come along with us; . . . my son do not go along with them.' "
> (Proverbs 1:10, 11, 15)

the language and behavior I'm likely to face. Maybe when you attend a conference you're one of the few who take advantage of praise-and-worship programs instead of joining the thousands who attend the multitude of beer-drinking celebrations?

Calls like the one above, unfortunately, are not few and far between. What a sad scenario for the people who are dedicated to serving!

Choices are a constant in life: Stand firm and risk feelings of being an outsider—or join in with things you know aren't pleasing to your spouse or God? Head for hiding—or share your faith and create a new standard for your workplace, one in which a Bible can proudly lie on a table? Seek the Christian organizations that attend most conferences—or head for the beer bash? Only you can make the choice. God and family? Or superficial acceptance?

Prayer:
Forgive me, Lord, if I have brought similar anguish and concern to my family. Help me walk in your light and bring others to you. May my station be a place where you, Lord, are welcome.

NOVEMBER 11

Tommy Neiman, Author of Sirens for the Cross; EMS Training Officer – St. Lucie County, FL; Fellowship of Christian Firefighters International Regional Director / International Board Member

PLENTY OF TIME
Laughter—what a gift!

OFTEN THE calls that invade our sleep at night are the ones with outcomes we'd rather forget. But one night I woke up laughing.

Curious as to what would wake me smiling in the middle of the night, my wife said, "Let's hear it!"

"Well, you know how you're always telling me I have a tendency to procrastinate and say we have plenty of time?"

"Do I ever," she replied.

"Well, today I said it once too often." Then I told her about my call.

We were transporting a woman in labor whose water had broken. Her contractions were five minutes apart and lasted only a few seconds. This was going to be her fifth child. Her relaxed manner indicated she was a pro. While assessing her status I commented, "You have plenty of time."

We loaded her into the truck, I threw an IV in per OB protocol, witnessed another brief contraction, and we took off for what I thought would be an uneventful ride to the hospital.

Within a minute she had another brief contraction. No big deal, it wasn't much of a contraction—no need to rush.

"The next two intersections are raised and we're in a weight-sensitive rescue truck," I casually explained, "so you'll experience two little bumps." As we approached that first bump, her casual demeanor changed, culminating in a yell. I checked her and was I surprised to see a head! I excitedly grabbed the suction bulb, rushed it to the protruding infant's head, suctioned out the nose and mouth, and witnessed the first breath of life.

Aware of the urgency, my driver stepped up the pace, hit the second bump, and this baby was practically shot-putted into my hands.

As I wrapped the little one in a towel and handed her over to her mommy, I said, "Here's your wonderful gift from God."

My wife joined me in laughter as she said, "I guess you bumped this one right into the world."

Truly this baby was a multiple gift: a gift of life from our awesome Creator, and a reminder God does great things. Laughter is surely a gift from God, as well, to help ease the strain caused by those calls we wish we could forget.

> "Our mouths were filled with laughter, our tongues with songs of joy. Then it was said among the nations, 'The Lord has done great things for them.' The LORD has done great things for us, and we are filled with joy."
> (Psalm 126:2, 3)

Prayer:
Thank you, Lord, for calling me to this profession and for your reminders of the many gifts that come from you, and you alone.

*Reverend Wayne Detzler, PhD, Chaplain (Retired) –
Charlotte, NC, Fire Department; Fellowship of
Christian Firefighters Regional Director*

NEVER ALONE

He is there when no one else is

AT 4:30 in the morning the call came. A tiny house on the edge of our city was on fire. When the first responders rolled up, it was fully involved. Fire shot out of every window.

Brave neighbors rushed to rescue the man and his little ones. They dragged the father out of the house, realizing he was seriously injured and unresponsive. They also snatched one child and rescued her.

Medics rushed to the aid of both victims. Quickly they stabilized both father and daughter. They prepared them for transport to the fine trauma center in our city. It seemed as if all was well.

As the public information officer later wrote: "Fire conditions in the rear and smoke conditions banked down to the floor as they worked to make rescues." The bravery and persistence of these firefighters was epic.

> "God has said, 'Never will I leave you; never will I forsake you.'"
> (Hebrews 13:5)

Finally, firefighters knocked down the fire. They made a second pass through the burned-out house. It was then they made a horrifying discovery. In a baby bed was a second little girl. She was dead, unable to survive the inferno that had engulfed her home.

Fire investigation found the apparent cause of the fire. It was a discarded cigarette. The pile of beer cans behind the house attested to alcohol abuse. The poor little girl never had a chance.

How do parents, friends, neighbors, and rescuers process the discovery of such a horrific situation, caused by negligence? Without the Lord, anger, bitterness, and perhaps a hardness of the heart are certain to control one's outlook in life. For all, it is good and important to know that even in the chaos, with such purposeless loss, the Lord is still there. He is still near, even when we feel as if we are all alone. Only with him, can you find peace, hope, and comfort. He will never leave you. Just call and he'll answer.

Prayer:
*Lord, help us to be a ready help for
the helpless, hope for the hopeless.*

Steve Kidd, Firefighter Orange County Fire and Rescue, Florida; Central Florida Chapter of the Fellowship of Christian Firefighters; Author of the Carbusters video series

STAY CLEAR OF THE HOT ZONE!

Reduce your chances of becoming a statistic

WE ALL know the hazards of working on or under a truss roof involved in fire. Without warning it can collapse in a sudden catastrophic crash that will kill or maim anyone within the danger zone. Any rescue that requires working underneath a burning truss roof becomes more dangerous with every second we remain in the perilous area.

We've been warned for years to remain clear of the danger area around a hazardous event. On the hazmat scene, we're told of the "Hot Zone." At a large, well-involved building fire we are told to remain clear of the collapse zone while mounting a defensive attack on the fire. If a patient is infected with a communicable disease, we speak of and establish isolation zones. One thing all these events have in common is that in order to remain safe from harm, we must limit our time in the dangerous area.

> "No temptation has seized you except what is common to man. And God is faithful; he will not let you be tempted beyond what you can bear. But when you are tempted, he will also provide a way out so that you can stand up under it." (1 Corinthians 10:13)

Time, distance, and shielding—all three work for more than just radioactive emergencies. By avoiding the danger altogether, we greatly reduce our chances of becoming a statistic in next year's death-and-injury report. None of us wants to be that kind of statistic.

Sin is more dangerous than all the fire ground, hazmat, and biohazard incidents put together. It's always around because Satan remains busy 24/7. He's waiting, ready to seize our weak moments and to shove temptation in our path. For example, consider the immediate danger to life and health an alcoholic faces if lingering in the "hot zone" called a bar.

We are all sinners. We are human. However, Christ died for our sins, and we must not dishonor his ultimate sacrifice by lingering around areas known to produce temptation. Reduce the time you spend in life's hot zones. Before sin starts gaining momentum, distance yourself from temptation by avoiding things that weaken you. And remember that through prayer and belief in our Lord Jesus Christ, God will provide a way of escape from all temptation—but you must do your part.

Prayer:
Help me reduce the time I spend in life's hot zones and distance myself from temptation by avoiding things that weaken me, before the sin starts gaining momentum. Thank you that you provide my escape route.

NOVEMBER 14

Reverend Wayne Detzler, PhD, Chaplain (Retired) – Charlotte, NC, Fire Department; Fellowship of Christian Firefighters Regional Director

THE HARDEST VISIT
Support when we cannot stand

CHAPLAIN, I need your help today." Our department chief paged me to the headquarters. As a chaplain my first responsibility was that of staff officer to the chief. He appointed me, and his needs came first.

"Chaplain," he continued when I reported for duty, "I need to visit Josh's family today, and I want you to go along." Josh had been a young firefighter, courageous and highly skilled. He had entered a burning building and fell through the floor. He landed in a cauldron of fire. Three days later the burns took his life.

Now the chief needed to visit Josh's parents. The chief was a consummate incident commander. He understood firefighting extremely well. In fact, he served for some years as president of the International Association of Fire Chiefs. In my experience, he was really a chief's chief.

Today's assignment was new to the chief. There had never been a line-of-duty death during his tenure as department chief. He'd never had to make that heart-wrenching visit to a firefighter's family. So, he called on me to go along.

As we drove to the suburban home he asked me questions. "What shall I say?" "What should I do?" "How can I ever comfort these dear folks?" The questions were many, but the answer was one: Just show your love and concern for them.

The meeting went well. We laid plans for a semiprivate funeral and a larger memorial service for the firefighter community. At the service, as I challenged our firefighters to make commit-ments, they responded. I urged them to recommit to the task of protecting our com-munity. They placed their hands on their badges as a sign.

> "Let us not love with words or tongue but with actions and in truth." (1 John 3:18)

Second, I called those present to commit to their loved ones who share the risks of our service, and they grasped hands as a sign of understanding and acceptance.

Third, I challenged firefighters to commit their lives to the Lord Jesus Christ. Then I asked them to stand as a sign of their new or renewed com-mitment to the Lord. At first no one moved. Then hundreds of firefighters signified their commitment to the Lord.

Prayer:

Help me, O Lord, to live out my commitments today in every aspect of my life. I recommit to protecting my community, loving my family, and I recommit my life to you.

NOVEMBER 15

Dwayne Clemmons, Adjunct Instructor – Virginia Department of Fire Programs; Founder – DMC Ministries; Author of Exploits, Jesus Rides in an Ambulance, and Utterances from the Throne Room; Volunteer in Fire and EMS for forty years in Virginia

DO YOU GET GOD?
Do you realize God is your friend?

SAUL OF Tarsus certainly did not understand God when he set out to destroy God's people. After his conversion, however, he became known as the apostle Paul and among his many writings is Titus 1:1–3. In these verses, it is evident his understanding of God is inspired and deep. Paul "got God."

Do you get God? Here's a short test. Replace Paul's name with yours, substitute "joint heir" for "apostle," and replace "servant" with "friend" in Titus 1:1–3 and I think you'll understand:

> "[Your name], a [friend] of God and [a joint heir] of Jesus Christ for the faith of God's elect and the knowledge of the truth that leads to godliness—a faith and knowledge resting on the hope of eternal life, which God, who does not lie, promised before the beginning of time,

and at his appointed season he brought his word to light through the preaching entrusted to me by the command of God our Savior . . ."

Wow! This is a powerful, timely, and essential statement you must commit your life to. God calls you "friend" and "joint heir." This means that everything he has, does, and is, you have, do, and are. Don't walk around moping as if you lost something. You are a valuable asset to the kingdom of God.

> "When Jesus saw their faith, he said, 'Friend, your sins are forgiven.'" (Luke 5:20)

Your faith and knowledge are resting on the hope of eternal life. This contract has been in existence from before the beginning of time. It's been guaranteed by a Man who can't lie. It's been sealed by the blood of Jesus. God exalts his Word above his name. Do you get it?

The appointed season is now. The right place is exactly where you are. You are on loan from heaven and God is waiting on you now to preach the Word he's entrusted to you. The times are evil, people are in trouble, and suffering abounds. The need for God's light to shine is unequivocally evident. Use your training, gifts, talents, and abilities, your friendship with God, for his glory. Get off the bench and get into the game. Do you get it? I ask again, "Do you get God?" His love? His plan?

Prayer:
Lord, you called Abraham your friend because he believed. When you saw the faith of a paralytic on a mat and those who carried him, you called them friend. You've entrusted me with the knowledge of your love for me as a friend and servant. As your friend, Lord, I will share your light and friendship. I do get you, God!

NOVEMBER 16

Chaplain Gilbert Gaddie, Captain – Indianapolis Fire Department; President Indianapolis Chapter Fellowship of Christian Firefighters

A SOLID ANCHOR
A reason to be truly thankful

NOVEMBER: a month to focus on giving thanks. As I prepare for another Thanksgiving feast, I'm reminded of many things to be thankful for. Highest on that list is another day of God's mercies and my escape from damnation since, like all people, I was born into sin. While the way to salvation is a narrow one, it's available to all. John 3:18 makes it clear that if we believe "in the name of God's one and only Son," we're not condemned. Inherent in that promise is our choice. We can choose life or death—heaven or eternal fire. We *do* have to choose.

Once we choose, we need to understand that the Christian life is not one-dimensional. It has ministry attached, the ministry of reconciliation. "All this is from God, who reconciled us to himself through Christ and gave us the ministry of reconciliation" (2 Corinthians 5:18). We are to go out and minister and share this truth.

Spiritually, we come to Christ as children, apt to be easily tossed to and fro and carried about by false worldly doctrines that can and will deceive us if we fail to grow into mature Christians. Jesus warns against being easily deceived. He says that in the last days many will be deceived and carried away with false doctrine: "Watch out that you are not deceived. For many will come in my name, claiming, 'I am he,' and, 'The time is near.' Do not follow them" (Luke 21:8).

> "We have this hope as an anchor for the soul, firm and secure."
> (Hebrews 6:19)

As Christians we're not only reconciled to God, but we're his vessels so others can be reconciled to him. God's Word repeatedly instructs us to be light in a world of darkness and to be an encourager showing others the real Word of God. We are to warn others not to stray, succumbing to new and deceiving fads.

To be successful in this ministry of reconciliation, to lift others up in encouragement, to avoid the deception of false teachings, we need to have the solid anchor of Jesus Christ. He gives us strength to not be deceived, boldness to be a vessel for him, and a reason to be truly thankful. God made Abraham a promise of blessings that holds true for eternity. Those blessings are there for all who choose God.

Prayer:

Thank you for being my solid anchor when I feel tossed to and fro. You have reconciled me to you, now as I mature in you I will carry out the ministry of reconciliation you have given to me.

Craig Duck, Lieutenant, Engine Co. 11 – Washington, DC, Fire Department; Fellowship of Christian Firefighters International Atlantic States Regional Director / International Board Member

THANKSGIVING AND FIREFIGHTERS

Complaining stations to thankful ones

WALK INTO most any firehouse in America and it doesn't take long for something to occur—something in regard to today's firefighters that I don't understand. It seems that when two or more firefighters sit around with nothing to do, this "something" is bound to happen.

"What's that?" you might ask.

I've noticed that firefighters are notorious for complaining about . . . well, just about everything. The fire trucks are the wrong color, the station's design is terrible, the chief makes lousy decisions, the company up the road is pathetic, and on and on it goes. In fact, you don't even need other people. Firefighters can go online to several different Web sites designed to allow you to voice your opinion about how bad things are in your department. You don't even have to sign your name to these ugly comments—comments that tear down rather than build up. How did we ever get to this point in the fire service?

The Bible tells us that complaining and whining should not be the characteristics of a godly firefighter. In fact, we are called to be opposite what the world is like. God has given the fire service many things to be thankful for. Equipment that is far superior to that of twenty-five years ago, grants to help pay for that equipment, training that is second to none, and dedicated firefighters who love to serve their communities. Go visit departments in Africa or South America and see how they operate with very little equipment and manpower, yet they are thankful for what has been given them.

> "Be joyful always; pray continually; give thanks in all circumstances, for this is God's will for you in Christ Jesus. Do not put out the Spirit's fire."
> (1 Thessalonians 5:16–19)

Christians need to be the example and begin to shout from the rooftops just how thankful to God we are for the good things he has given us. "Give thanks to the LORD, for he is good; his love endures forever" (Psalm 107:1). Let us resolve to change from complainers to thankful people.

Prayer:
Help me, Lord, to get a hold of my tongue and use it for edification, for encouragement, and for thanksgiving within the fire service.

*Fire Chaplain John Kalashian, Caledonia, Wisconsin;
Founder/Director – Men with a Burden, a ministry to the
homeless men at the Milwaukee Rescue Mission;
Founder/President – Corvettes for Christ*

A THANKFUL HEART
With Christ, we can all have
and enjoy "A Thankful Heart"

IN A MOMENT filled with honor, I humbly stood in front of the village board as the chief introduced me as "Chaplain," but even more significant is the thankful heart I've received in serving firefighters and witnessing firsthand their camaraderie. They are truly a family.

I've observed their heroic duties and can truthfully say—firefighters represent the finest! The life of firefighting is one of confronting immense hurdles and challenges. As citizens attempt to live happy and successful lives, they can find assurance knowing that first responders strive to fight the enemy the enemy of death, injury, danger, and destruction, which threatens and looms over all of us! A wailing siren is a welcome sound of hope and rescue as emergency responders are only a phone call away from willingly placing their lives in danger, and first responders do it 24/7.

With a "Thankful Heart" I serve first responders, whose daily duty is in the battlefield serving and protecting our communities. I've learned that responding to medical, fire, and other alarms is only part of what they do. Some of the other more challenging responsibilities of the workday involve sweeping bay floors, washing dishes, polishing trucks, engines, and squads, and making an occasional bag of perfectly popped popcorn (just a little attempt at humor here—perhaps very little!).

I'm also thankful to the ultimate First Responder, Jesus Christ, who himself said, "Whoever wants to be first must be your slave—just as the

Son of Man did not come to be served, but to serve, and to give his life as a ransom for many" (Matthew 20:27, 28). Notice here what Christ is saying: His duty was to "serve" by sacrificing his life on the cross for you. Like the firefighter, Christ offers his life in "service" and is available 24/7.

> "Let the peace of Christ rule in your hearts, since as members of one body you were called to peace. And be thankful." (Colossians 3:15)

It's good to know each of us can faithfully and personally call upon him, our Deliverer and Savior. He promises, "Never will I leave you; never will I forsake you" (Hebrews 13:5). For that reason alone, we can all have and enjoy a "Thankful Heart."

Prayer:

Lord, I'm thankful for my families at home and at the station, and for the family of God. May your peace rule in my heart.

NOVEMBER 19

Chaplain Gaius Reynolds, President – Fellowship of Christian Firefighters International; Volunteer Firefighter – Livermore, CO, Fire Protection District

THANKSGIVING AND TEAMWORK

Multiplying our efforts

NOVEMBER: that time of year when a renewed emphasis is placed on being thankful, reflecting on our lives, and giving thanks for our Lord's intervention on our behalf. Yes, Thanksgiving is around the corner.

Are you thankful for what the Lord has given you? Scripture reminds us of many of those things to be thankful for.

Your inheritance is guaranteed forever! As 1 John 5:6–13 tells us, that inheritance is eternal life with God if you "believe in the name of the Son of God" (v. 13).

You are saved by your faith and belief in Christ as clearly promised in Acts 16:31, "Believe in the Lord Jesus, and you will be saved". That should give you confidence about your future, and for that you must be thankful.

When you fall short and deserve punishment, God extends his unending mercy, grace, and forgiveness. Do you "always thank God . . . because of his grace given you in Christ Jesus" as 1 Corinthians 1:4 indicates you should? Paul goes on to say, "I always thank God for you because of his grace given you in Christ Jesus."

Then there's the direct line of communication with God. Any time night or day, he wants you to bring all things to him and not be anxious, but to bring your petitions, requests, everything to him "with thanksgiving" (Philippians 4:6).

Are your actions reflecting your thankful heart? We're informed in 1 John 3:18 to show our gratitude in more than words, "but with actions and in truth." We need to show his love to those we are put in contact with. That's thankfulness in action.

> "All this is for your benefit, so that the grace that is reaching more and more people may cause thanksgiving to overflow to the glory of God."
> (2 Corinthians 4:15)

Individually we have a great responsibility to God, but we need to also work with others to take the Word of God, the love of God, to the fire service. Teamwork divides the effort and multiplies the effect.

What an awesome opportunity we have! We can be missionaries in our homes, in our communities, and in our workplaces. We do not have to go to a different country to be missionaries; we can minister wherever we are. All believers can, with a thankful heart, be warriors in the battle—any time, any place—and have an important influence on this country.

Prayer:
Lord, I lift up my fellow brothers and sisters in Christ
with thanksgiving that together, through teamwork,
our effort continues and, moreover, multiplies.

NOVEMBER 20

Bob Crum, Co-founder – Fellowship of Christian Firefighters
International (Retired) – Denver Fire Department

THANK YOU

Not just once in a while, but continually

"THANK YOU"—a short phrase, but loaded with meaning. The apostle Paul didn't take appreciation lightly in any sense. To the Thessalonians he wrote, "We always thank God for all of you, mentioning you in our prayers. We continually remember before our God and Father your work produced by faith, your labor prompted by love, and your endurance inspired by hope in our Lord Jesus Christ" (1 Thessalonians 1:2, 3). To the Colossians he wrote, "We always thank God, the Father of our Lord Jesus Christ, when we pray for you, because we have heard of your faith in Christ Jesus and of the love you have for all the saints—" (Colossians 1:3, 4). Paul acknowledged that God raised up these and other churches to spread the Gospel to a lost and dying world. Paul recognized that their corporate and individual ministry could accomplish the task.

He realized the value of their love, labor, endurance, and efforts to strengthen the churches, so he continually prayed and thanked God for them. Yes, he continually gave thanks. Not just once in a while, but continually. Paul set an example that is worthy of emulating. Easy? No! Imperative? Yes!

> "So then, just as you received Christ Jesus as Lord, continue to live in him, rooted and built up in him, strengthened in the faith as you were taught, and overflowing with thankfulness."
> (Colossians 2:6, 7)

In the same way, do you thank those people God has placed in your life? Do you realize the value of your family and friends' love, labor, endurance, and efforts to accommodate the demands of your career? Do you thank co-workers and superiors? Do you thank God for a career that allows you to share his love in a unique and special way? Do you thank God for the ministry opportunities your job affords and then act on that thankfulness?

Why not start an ongoing list of the things you are thankful for? Then start each day thanking God first and then extending your thankfulness to those God has placed in your life.

Prayer:

As I fill my mind with thankfulness, may my words reflect my heart. As Paul admonished, may I never cease to remember to "always give thanks."

Sue Reynolds, Missionary – Fellowship of Christian Firefighters International (FCFI), and Chaplain Gaius Reynolds, President – FCFI; Volunteer Firefighter – Livermore, CO, Fire Protection District

GIVING THANKS
A way of life

FIRST RESPONDERS (like those in any occupation) sometimes grumble and act as if they have nothing to be thankful for. Maybe they're facing personal problems or have seen one too many tragedies that are difficult to comprehend. Difficult challenges can be overwhelming and thrust a person into despondency or even a full-fledged depression. Holidays can be the happiest, or the saddest, time of year depending on your focus. Paul must have understood this, for in 1 Thessalonians 5:18, he admonishes us by saying we should "give thanks in all circumstances, for this is God's will for you in Christ Jesus."

Paul says in "all circumstances"! Nothing is excluded. What if you're asked to restock the engine or ambulance when you had other plans for your shift? Do you give thanks? What if you're asked to work overtime for a friend and it isn't convenient, but you owe him? Maybe that's the shift where God needs you to minister to someone.

"And we know that in all things God works for the good of those who love him, who have been called according to his purpose." (Romans 8:28)

Maybe you sustained an injury and were put on leave or a desk assignment. Did you give thanks? Did you think about how God might have other plans for you, and seek to understand what those plans are?

Have budget cuts caused a decrease in your income because of the economy? Did you give thanks? This might be the time God wants you to take a look at your life-style. Are you living above your income? Are you building up too much debt from too many "toys" you think you can't live without? This may be the time to look at your priorities. Are "things" the source of your happiness, or have you found that your true joy is in the Lord?

Happiness is frequently described as a state of being that is dependent on happenings. Joy is described as putting

Jesus first, then
Others, and finally
Yourself.

Thankfulness needs to become a way of life. You may not always understand what God has in store or why he allows "bad things to happen to good people," but God said everything will work for good for those who love God and are called according to his purpose (Romans 8:28).

Has he called you? Do you thank God for your very life, your health, your family, your home, your income, your church, your mate, your Bible, the cross, your salvation . . . for everything?

Prayer:
*Lord, this Thanksgiving, and every day, help me to remember
to thank you for all things—all things, not just
those things that make me feel good.*

N O V E M B E R   2 2

*Reverend Wayne Detzler, PhD, Chaplain (Retired) –
Charlotte, NC, Fire Department; Fellowship of
Christian Firefighters Regional Director*

THROUGH THE ICE

He never heard us

WHILE I was waiting in the dentist's office, the pager sounded: "It's a man who has fallen through the ice." The dispatcher's tone was urgent. "Respond immediately, Chaplain, we're trying to save him."

When I arrived at the small pond all eyes were focused on the form of a man. He was partially lying on the ice and partially in the ice-cold water. "Stay still," the firefighters shouted. "We're coming to help you." But he didn't seem to hear. The man kept moving around trying to get out of the water, despite our pleas for him to remain motionless. He tried to pull himself free, but couldn't. For some reason he seemed too weak to crawl out onto the ice.

In the meantime firefighters tried to walk across the ice, but it was too thin and they kept falling through. Finally, they crawled across the ice toward the man, who was now flailing wildly, trying to save himself, in spite of our warnings. They pulled a rescue sled behind them, hoping to get the man into it.

Then it happened. The man fell into the water. He tried to swim, but the water was too cold. Hypothermia stopped his efforts almost immediately. He stopped moving. He was dead.

439

Rescue efforts changed to recovery. The firefighters finally reached the form and wrestled it into the sled. They waded back through the icy water pulling the sad cargo behind them.

Soon we identified the victim and contacted his family. Then the sad news became known. The victim was Polish—he didn't speak any English. Never did he understand that we wanted him to remain quiet and wait for rescue.

> "For what the law was powerless to do in that it was weakened by the sinful nature, God did by sending his own Son in the likeness of sinful man to be a sin offering." (Romans 8:3)

It reminds me of the Gospels. The Lord came to "seek and to save the lost" (Luke 19:10). He saw our desperate need, or peril. From the foundation of the earth God had designed to send his Son to save us. In the Lord Jesus he came.

Although the man in the icy pond could not understand, we can understand. God sent his Son as a man so we could understand and respond.

Prayer:
God our Father, thank you for sending Jesus
to rescue me when I was so lost.

NOVEMBER 23

Captain Raul A. Angulo – Seattle Fire Department;
Fellowship of Christian Firefighters Regional
Director / International Board Member

THE SNOWMAN
The most important part of that experience

I CAME ACROSS a rare letter I wrote to myself shortly after I accepted my first job. I was preparing to leave Los Angeles, California, for the rural town of Farmington, New Mexico, to join their fire department. Reluctantly, I was taking my younger brother, Danny, with me.

A series of false starts followed. Not allowing enough time for travel and failing to anticipate snow, I missed my first day. The effort to find an apartment while trying to access my money from a California-based bank, attend my academy classes, feed my brother, and deal with the snow, convinced me I was ill-prepared. Then, I overslept and was late for the third time. I was forced to resign and felt defeated, discouraged, and embarrassed. That fiasco was my most valuable life-lesson in personal responsibility, even though it felt like the worst day of my life.

Regardless, I never gave up on my dream of being a fireman and now serve as Captain of Engine Company 18 in the Seattle, Washington, Fire Department.

I reread the letter, this time remembering the most important part of that experience:

The Snowman:
"I came home and, right next to my door, is this neat snowman with a big smile on his face. It was saying, 'Welcome, Raul!' Danny built it. I stayed outside awhile to admire his gift. No one ever built a snowman for me before. I visualized how he made it —like a little artist busy at work and leaving it there to greet me. What a greeting it was. Oh, how I needed a smile, even if it was from a snowman. When I saw the snowman, though it was cold outside, it gave me a warm feeling inside from the little brother I love. It was saying, 'Hey, it's okay! Come on in; you're home now.'"

Things were simpler then for Danny. Life became complicated for him. Circumstances drastically changed our relationship, causing our estrangement for more than twenty years.

There are now fresh tears on this old piece of paper. I think I should call and ask my brother, "Hey, do you want to build a snowman with me?"

> "How good and pleasant it is when brothers live together in unity! It is like precious oil poured on the head, running down on the beard." (Psalm 133:1, 2)

Prayer:
Thank you, Lord, for my family—a family that has grown, for you have added me to your family; I am a child of God. I lift up my extended family—those in the fire service—whom you have brought into my life.

*Chief Lee Callahan, Burlington, MA; Fellowship of
Christian Firefighters International Regional Director /
International Board Member*

ANGELS IN DISGUISE

*To some we are heroes,
but on that special Saturday we received a new title: "Angels"*

SATURDAYS at the firehouse tend to be a day without normal training. One Saturday, special medical training was scheduled to update our skills regarding emergency childbirth. Despite the grumbling, we embarked on several hours of enhancing our knowledge of emergency labor and delivery of babies, thinking how seldom we need these techniques.

Later that Saturday, a call came in for a woman, Colleen, having a baby at home. When her labor pains began two weeks early, her husband, Kyle, reluctantly agreed to take her to the hospital, but only after he took a shower. While in the shower, Colleen's contractions came quickly. As she went to the bathroom to encourage Kyle to hurry, she sunk to the bathroom floor screaming in pain. Kyle scrambled from the shower and immediately raced to the phone to call 9-1-1.

> "Do not forget to entertain strangers, for by so doing some people have entertained angels without knowing it."
> (Hebrews 13:2)

The fire department dispatch system sounded the alert tone and said, "Wouldn't it be funny if we actually delivered a baby after just spending six hours in a refresher class on this very thing?" Little did I know how prophetic the dispatcher's words would be!

When we arrived on scene, it was obvious the child was going to be delivered in the home. Just when everybody and everything was in place for a safe delivery, a lively, screaming, beautiful baby boy entered the world.

Picture this: a bathroom with a woman, newborn baby on her chest, lying on the floor; her husband sitting in the tub, glowing in the delight of seeing his firstborn child come into this world; two EMTs sitting beside the lady, attending to mother and child; and three firefighters standing just outside the bathroom door, looking in with grins a mile wide.

A week later, Colleen, Kyle, and baby Derek stopped by the fire station to say thanks. The firefighters had placed a blue stork decal on the side of the ambulance in honor of Derek's birth. During the visit, Colleen shared that as she looked around, just after the birth of her son, she saw six smiling, rejoicing men in that bathroom and was reminded of the joy of God's angels spoken of in Scripture.

To some we are heroes but on that special Saturday we received a new title: "Angels."

Prayer:
What a blessing it is, Lord, to serve you, and if some see me as an angel in disguise, what encouragement that is to me! May I always strive to be worthy of such an honor.

NOVEMBER 25

Craig Duck, Lieutenant, Engine Co. 11 – Washington, DC, Fire Department; Fellowship of Christian Firefighters International Atlantic States Regional Director / International Board Member

FAITH AND WORKS FOR FIREFIGHTERS

Challenged to share Christ with the fire service through godly works

FIREFIGHTERS know all about work. Firefighting is hard work. Whether a big city firefighter, a small town firefighter, a wildland firefighter, medically trained, full-time, paid, or volunteer—all work hard to accomplish their mission. We all have personal stories of how exhausted we've been after fighting "the Big One."

As the Fellowship of Christian Firefighters International (FCFI) bicycle team traveled across America on a missions trip, we met all types of firefighters. What a blessing to meet fellow firefighters and to swap war stories of the "good ol' days." Many nights were spent talking to others about what they love best, their fire trucks, houses, and calls they've been on.

"Then Jesus came to them and said, 'All authority in heaven and on earth has been given to me. Therefore go and make disciples of all nations, baptizing them in the name of the Father and of the Son and of the Holy Spirit, and teaching them to obey everything I have commanded you. And surely I am with you always, to the very end of the age.'"
(Matthew 28:18–20)

443

No matter what part of the country, firefighters have one thing in common: They need to hear the Good News of God's saving grace. That was the goal of FCFI's 9/11 missions trip across America beginning in California and ending at the Pentagon on September 11, 2006, to commemorate all those who made the ultimate sacrifice on 9-11-01. As we talked to firefighters about their departments, we always talked to them about God's love for them. We were also able to hand out Bibles and literature along the way. But it wasn't always easy; the trip took lots of work by the whole team. One verse that always helped me continue on when I was tired was, "What good is it, my brothers, if a man claims to have faith but has no deeds? Can such faith save him?" (James 2:14). God wants us to share Christ with our brother and sister firefighters, and that takes work.

Throughout my career as a Christian firefighter, I've observed one thing: God will always provide opportunities to share your faith, if you are willing to be used. Could you imagine what the fire service would look like if we put as much effort into sharing Christ as we do into putting out the fire?

Prayer:
Lord, I am willing to share my faith as you provide me with opportunities to do so. Give me boldness to share Christ with my fellow first responders in the department you have called me to serve in.

NOVEMBER 26

Rick Barton, Fire Safety Officer; Rick Barton Ministries, Gunnison, CO; Fellowship of Christian Firefighters International Ambassador-at-Large

WHO NEEDS A COMPASS?!

Checking my feelings up against a compass

THE WOODS were dry, fire danger extreme. Several of us volunteered to patrol the backcountry. Equipped with water and fire tools, I drove around looking for signs of smoke. Suddenly, I saw a steady column of smoke. I decided to get a better look before calling in a report. I considered digging through my gear and pulling out my compass, but decided against it. After all, time was of the essence and I thought I had a good idea of the general direction. There were a few houses up that way, so I radioed the dispatcher to check for a trash pile burning or roadwork before getting everyone excited about a fire. "I've got a smoke northwest of my location. I think it's up Ohio Creek. Could you call the county and see if there's any burning up that way?"

Dispatcher responded. "Nothing that they know of, Rick. Do you want us to send someone that way?"

"Not yet. Let me get a better look." I went a little higher. It seemed as if it was further north than I originally thought. I asked dispatch to check the new location. Still no need for the compass; I knew what I was seeing.

Dispatch called back, "Nothing going on up that way, either."

By this time my boss was headed north to be in position to respond to my fire. I went further up the road, turned around a bend, and trouble! I could see the entire valley clearly. The smoke was the cement factory south of town.

The radio crackled again, "Barton, this is Shammy." It was my boss. How was I going to explain this? "I'm on the main road north of town. There's a paving crew working and it's putting up quite a bit of smoke.

> "Your word is a lamp to my feet and a light for my path." (Psalm 119:105)

I'm sure that's what you're seeing. Good eyes! Keep up the great work!"

You can be sure that later I confessed the truth to my supervisor about ten years later. And you can be sure I began to keep my compass at the top of my pack.

I've found in life it's often the same. Sometimes I'm convinced one thing is true and yet when I see the whole picture, it can be the opposite. I need to check my initial feelings against a "compass." For me, "God's Word is a compass to my path."

Prayer:
Let your Word be the light on the path that I travel. Help me to see the whole picture and be quick to listen and slow to speak.

Fire Chaplain John Kalashian, Caledonia, Wisconsin;
Founder/Director – Men with a Burden, a ministry to
the homeless men at the Milwaukee Rescue Mission;
Founder/President – Corvettes for Christ

SHOW OF FORCE
Ladder of success

HAVE YOU heard the expression "ladder of success"? While attending ladder training, I was amazed by the multitude of ladders. As a chaplain, I've never seen so many ladders in one place. There were thirty-five-foot and twenty-four-foot two-fly extension ladders, one-hundred-foot and seventy-five-foot bucket aerials, roof, and straight ladders. There was even a small two-foot stepladder stored to help some of "our own," with big hearts and smaller statures, make that critical first step. It was an impressive sight to behold. I called it a ladder "Show of Force."

When arriving on scene, firefighters are expected to follow four basic ladder principles: (1) quickly and safely make the correct ladder selection, (2) apply proper handling techniques, (3) work and plan with others as a team, and (4) demonstrate a skillful and keen awareness of its proper placement. Ladders help accomplish one main objective; they allow firefighters to victoriously and successfully climb to their destination! Improper use of the ladder is like adding fuel

> "Take my yoke upon you and learn from me, for I am gentle and humble in heart, and you will find rest for your souls. For my yoke is easy and my burden is light." (Matthew 11:29, 30)

to a fire. Its purpose is to help battle the danger and risk, not add to them!

God also has a ladder, but it's designed for our use, not his. It's called the "Cross of Jesus Christ," and it is God's "Show of Force." As sin and problems of this world try to consume us, the cross becomes, to those who use it, a ladder that provides a way of escape and rescue! God explains this in Hebrews 12:1, 2. He instructs us to put aside every, and any, sin, fix our eyes on Jesus, and run the race (climb the ladder) God has set before us, with endurance. In other words, your problems, the sins that hinder you, will entangle and defeat you.

God, desiring to be our First Responder, endured and provided his cross as a ladder of victory, taking us upward to his very throne! While we can pick and choose from many ladders in the world, there is none like God's. His ladder is the ultimate "Show of Force," found only in his Son, Jesus Christ. God softly and tenderly calls us to select *his* ladder so we can victoriously climb above our sins and encumbrances and successfully reach the destination—the very throne of God! He wants all to come to him.

Prayer:
Lord, what a blessing to have your ladder, your light yoke. Thank you for enabling me to reach the destination of the very throne of God!

NOVEMBER 28

Captain Raul A. Angulo – Seattle Fire Department; Fellowship of Christian Firefighters Regional Director / International Board Member

DON'T JUMP

You might be their last hope and encouragement!

AFTER YEARS on the job, firefighting can get to you. People don't call because everything's fine; they call with problems. Legitimate fire and medical calls aren't the key concern. It's the "rinky-dink" ones, like "man down" drunks and homeless, that create frustration. While their ailments may require medical attention, many of their problems are social service and not emergency situations.

One day my frustration with "rinky-dink" calls influenced my attitude. When I got home, I spewed my intolerance of people who really didn't need my services. "There was this suicidal guy last night. What does he expect us to do? He just wanted attention. People serious about killing themselves usually succeed," on I went.

My wife swiftly reprimanded me, "These people are God's children. Their only reflection of God's goodness may be through you."

I took her comments to heart.

My test came on the following shift when the bell rang for a "jumper on the Aurora Bridge."

On scene, we found him standing by the rail. He yelled, "I've had it with life. Nobody cares what happens to me." As he talked, I had flashbacks of my wife scolding me for my lack of compassion. Her words, "You might be their last hope and encouragement!" echoed in my mind.

447

"Don't jump!" I pleaded as I tackled him to the ground. My crew quickly dog-piled him to make sure he stayed down.

"Let me jump! No one cares if I live or die!" he cried.

"I care about you. You're God's creation and God doesn't make junk," I told him. "Come on, man. Life is tough for everybody. Don't quit on God. He hasn't quit on you. Why do you think I'm here? God sent me because you knocked on my door!"

The next day, I tracked him down. He said he was at his wits' end and didn't know what would have happened had I not intervened. He told me I was his guardian angel. That was the last I ever heard from him.

My wife helped me remember why I joined the Seattle Fire Department. It was to help people and save lives. I almost forgot that reason for a little while.

> "And the Lord's servant must not quarrel; instead, he must be kind to everyone, able to teach, not resentful."
> (2 Timothy 2:24)

Prayer:

Lord, may I never forget that I am a public servant. I am here not to be served, but to serve. A servant doesn't complain; a servant just serves. Help me serve with compassion and encouraging words.

NOVEMBER 29

Chaplain Marc Santorella, Firefighter Fire Department, MA; Public Fire and Life Safety Educator and Certified Fire Instructor Level 1

MORE THAN FIRST REALIZED

A moment orchestrated just for us

HAVE YOU ever looked back on something and realized it was more than it had first seemed?

One Thanksgiving my wife and I took time away just to be together. A mountain ski lodge in Vermont (even though neither of us skis) was mutually appealing. Though cold, snow had not yet fallen and the trees were bare. While touring we stopped at a small pub, relaxed, and observed the pictures of life on the slopes. Just being together brought a sense of freedom and closeness.

At the lodge, we sat in front of the big stone fireplace, enjoying privacy, snuggling, and conversation. After dinner we returned to our comfortable room with a sliding glass door overlooking the forest edge. Trails dotted with once-green trees were now bare and desolate. With the lack of snow, the ski trails looked more like forgotten hiking paths than recreational delights. Regardless, I left the curtain open when we retired.

A glaring light awakened us at daybreak. Overnight a remarkable change left an impression we'll never forget. Fresh snow blanketed the countryside and continued to fall in sheets of white. It was like being inside a snow globe just shaken.

I recently asked my wife to share her thoughts from that morning years ago. Her reply expressed what I, too, experienced in my heart: "I felt as if God's hand was upon us that morning; as if a miracle had occurred and God orchestrated it just for us."

> "And now these three remain: faith, hope and love. But the greatest of these is love."
> (1 Corinthians 13:13)

I understand now this snow was a gift. God took the barren, brown forest and transformed it into a winter wonderland as confirmation of his presence. Just as he can take a life shrouded by darkness and turn it into one shining for his glory, he can take a marriage, filled with love or struggling, and enrich it with his emanating glory. All marriages need these special moments. Add to the equation a first responder's marriage, in which long shifts often make communication sporadic, and the need multiplies.

Just as taking time to be alone with God is essential to building an intimate relationship with him, so is your precious time alone with your spouse essential to a marriage. Then, when you look back you, too, may say, "I think God orchestrated this moment just for us."

Prayer:
Just as my time with you, Lord, strengthens my faith, hope, and love, I know time with my spouse will bring us closer together. Thank you for my spouse and guide me as I set my time priorities to be sensitive to my spouse's needs.

Rick Barton, Fire Safety Officer; Rick Barton Ministries,
Gunnison, CO; Fellowship of Christian Firefighters
International Ambassador-at-Large

YEA, THO' I WALK
When danger came, God was there!

"HERE IT COMES!" someone cried out as the forecast fifty-mile-per-hour winds hit the Incident Command Post. Strong winds were pushing this lightning-caused fire directly toward us. It was in a wilderness area that was allowed to burn for more than a month to clear out thousands of acres of dead and diseased trees. It had opened areas for wildlife, new growth, and increased recreational enjoyment, but now years of below-average moisture and dry, windy conditions caused the fire to make a tragic run. Fire managers ordered extra resources to protect another resort a few miles away, anticipating the fire would take three days to reach the resort. Instead the fire erupted and raged across the distance in three hours!

We wrapped several buildings with fire-resistant sheeting. Hose lays were established around the buildings. Pumps were run from the lake to the sprinklers laid out around cabins, and engine crews were positioned in strategic locations. Then, gale force winds hit! The fire began to blow up, leaping from the crown of one tree to the next, not even touching the forest floor. Entire groups of trees simultaneously erupted into flames, creating sounds resembling a jet engine. Grudgingly firefighters withdrew.

> "Even thou I walk through the valley of the shadow of death, I will fear no evil, for you are with me." (Psalm 23:4)

Our character was tested. No firefighter I know claims to be "brave." We all have moments of anxiety filled with a sudden urge to run and hide from the danger we face. Suddenly, firefighting is no longer an adventure but a deadly serious matter of life or death. We can panic and run, be paralyzed by fear and have to be led out, or we can depend on the One who has promised never to leave us or forsake us.

As this fire leaned its column of smoke over me, I remembered the words of the psalmist, "You are with me" (Psalm 23:4). It was to his hand I clung.

Just as suddenly as the downdrafts came, they passed. The cabins stood. The sprinklers continued watering down the buildings and grass.

The engine crews discovered and put out the spot fires, hot shot crews extinguished embers, and the fire moved away from the resort.

Danger passed as quickly as it had come.

Danger will come again in different places and forms, and I know that the One who stood with me this day will always be with me.

Prayer:
Lord, when danger comes I depend on you,
and you alone, for you are with me.

Tommy Neiman, *Author of* Sirens for the Cross; *EMS Training Officer – St. Lucie County, FL; Fellowship of Christian Firefighters International Regional Director / International Board Member*

I CAN'T TELL YOU

But can others tell?

I'VE RESPONDED to some peculiar calls in my lifetime but this one ranks among the top. The origin of the call was the Coast Guard. We met them as they approached shore with a foreign refugee whose makeshift raft had split apart. For two-and-a-half days the bedraggled occupant was a captive of Florida's ocean waters.

Wasting no time, we packaged the refugee and began transporting him. He was awake, dehydrated, sunburned, and fearful. Before departing, the Coast Guard informed us the refugee wasn't speaking at all. Consequently they were unable to get his name.

As we administered first aid, I looked into his eyes and said, "No English?"

He nodded an affirmative. After we stacked blankets on him, gave him a little oxygen, and continued toward the hospital, he seemed to relax a little. I knelt next to him and asked, "What is your name?"

"I'll can tell ya," came his mumbled reply.

> "Be imitators of God, therefore, as dearly loved children and live a life of love, just as Christ loved us and gave himself up for us as a fragrant offering and sacrifice to God."
> (Ephesians 5:1, 2)

Ah, he does *speak English*, I thought. A little broken and blotched but better than nothing. I leaned over again and said, "But you can tell me, its okay. What's your name?"

"I'll can tell ya. I'll can tell ya," came the frustrated reply.

This question-and-answer routine continued until I finally gave up and resigned myself to the probability of filling out a John Doe medical report.

The next day the morning paper had a picture of us placing our sea drifter in the rescue truck. I didn't recall seeing a camera at the Coast Guard station, but apparently there was, and obviously the reporters got more information than I did, including one valuable piece—the man's name. The caption under the picture read, "Al Cantera is taken to a hospital after two-and-one-half days in the ocean."

Al Cantera! The only thing I could get out of him was, "I'll can tell ya."

When someone encounters you, can they tell you are a Christian? Do your words, actions, and attitudes reflect who you are in Christ? The nicest thing a person can say about you is, "I'll can tell ya, that person walks his talk; no doubt about it, he is a child of God."

Prayer:
Lord, I can tell you! I am thankful you are my
Father God. My goal is to imitate you in all I do.

DECEMBER 2

Reverend Wayne Detzler, PhD, Chaplain (Retired) –
Charlotte, NC, Fire Department; Fellowship of
Christian Firefighters Regional Director

CHILLED TO THE BONE
The night I learned compassion

IT WAS A warm summer night in Charlotte. Finally, we bunked down waiting for the first call. Our engine always responded to the needs of this community on the edge. Actually, it was always on the edge of chaos.

"Medical," the dispatcher woke us with our tone, "respond to the housing development. It is reported as a person in diabetic coma." With no more information than this, we sped to the site. People were waiting for us at the front door. They ushered us up steep stairs to the second floor.

In a dimly lit room we saw a figure huddled under blankets despite the warm North Carolina night. Questions remained unanswered. She was unresponsive. The medic quickly checked over the medicine bottles on the bedside table. "These are not diabetic medications," she probed gently, but no one answered. No one said anything at all.

Attempts to check the blood pressure revealed our worst fears. The poor patient's arms were so thin they looked skeletal. Her face had that familiar gaunt look. Even her legs were pencil thin. Her body seemed worn away by the disease that devastated her life.

"It looks like . . ." the words trailed off. We all filled in the blank. It appeared that the poor woman was suffering from AIDS. In the early 1990s AIDS was presumed to be a death sentence, as no medication had yet emerged to keep its victims alive.

So our task changed. We realized she needed the advanced care of a hospital. Quickly, we carried this sad little bundle of life down the stairs.

454

There was no weight at all. I remember thinking how compassionate, how kind the tough firefighters were as they gently eased our patient into the ambulance.

> "When he [Jesus] saw the crowds, he had compassion on them."
> (Matthew 9:36)

Would she survive the trip to the hospital? No one knew. We simply saw her as a neighbor in need of our care. The captain was known for his Christian commitment, and I remember thinking how appropriate that was. Who but a believer in the loving Lord could show the kindness that was needed?

Prayer:
*Lord, help me to care for those who need it
most and to show your love without limit.*

DECEMBER 3

*Captain Raul A. Angulo – Seattle Fire Department;
Fellowship of Christian Firefighters Regional
Director / International Board Member*

TRAIN UP A CHILD
*The Tommy Frankses of the
future are here in our midst*

AS A STUDENT of leadership, I like to study stressful decisions leaders have made during the cataclysmic events that defined them in history. I often ask myself, what would I have done if I were in charge of that situation?

In *American Soldier,* General Tommy Franks states, "Success in this campaign would depend more on character, sense of purpose, and value—the nation's, the president's, my own, and the troops'—than on raw military power." Yes, a four-star general, ready to embark on a global military conflict, said it was going to come down to character, values, and sense of purpose—things he had learned as a young boy.

The design of the family and the relationship between parents and the children is profound in relation to the nature of God. We are his creation. We are made in his image but the family, by design, is also made in the triune image of God: Father, Son, and Holy Spirit—father, mother, and child. The fire service is a noble profession. Most join because of a passion to serve and rescue others in times of emergency. Our jobs—coupled with other volunteer service, side jobs, and hobbies—sometimes result in neglecting our families. Many struggle with keeping these job, service, and hobby commitments in perspective with their commitment to their family. God makes the choice clear. You must put your love for God first, your family next, and then service.

General Franks is retired now. But the Tommy Frankses of the future are here in our midst. They're in the back seat of your car, they're out in the backyard playing, and they're sitting around your dinner table. Don't waste time. Start training them in character, instilling in them your values and principles. Help them develop a sense of purpose greater than themselves. If you don't do it, someone else will. Don't give up that God-given right and responsibility.

> "Love the LORD your God with all your heart and all your soul and with all your strength. These commandments that I give you today are to be upon your hearts. Impress them on your children. Talk about them when you sit at home and when you walk along the road, when you lie down and when you get up. Tie them as symbols on your hands and bind them on your foreheads.
> (Deuteronomy 6:5–8)

Prayer:
Thank you, Lord, for my family. As I set my priorities may I put my love for you first, then my family, job, and service.

Daniel A. Clegg, Rural-Metro EMT; Engineer/EMT–Indianapolis Fire Department (Retired); Fellowship of Christian Firefighters Regional Director / International Board Member

SIMPLE WORDS OF ENCOURAGEMENT

Encouragement and compassion are gifts each of us can develop and share

IT WAS AN ordinary day, or so I thought. As an EMT for a rural metro ambulance, I was making a routine patient transfer for Veronica, a single mother who recently attempted suicide. She was recovering physically and was now being transferred for counseling for emotional healing. As she began talking, I realized Veronica needed a listening ear. Our conversation turned to things of the heart, providing an opportunity to encourage and show her God's love. When departing, I handed her a business card. "Please give me a call if you ever need to talk," I said sincerely.

Two-and-a-half years passed. Then I received a letter. "Dear Mr. Clegg, You won't remember me . . ." I looked to the end of the two-page letter. It was signed, "Veronica."

I did remember her and wondered what had become of her.

It's difficult to understand the hopelessness leading to a suicide attempt. Regardless of our level of understanding, a listening heart, followed by words of encouragement spoken with compassion, are gifts each of us can develop and share.

My conversation with Veronica that evening gave me deep insights into her hurting soul, and compassion for her feelings of despair. She'd felt desperate, hopeless, abandoned, and positive her family and friends would be better off without her.

I countered with simple words of encouragement as I explained that no one could ever take her place. I talked about the love I knew her child held for her. I spoke of

> "Praise be to the God and Father of our Lord Jesus Christ, the Father of compassion and the God of all comfort, who comforts us in all our troubles, so that we can comfort those in any trouble with the comfort we ourselves have received from God."
> (2 Corinthians 1:3, 4)

God's unconditional love. Then I asked if I could pray for her. It was that conversation and prayer she remembered and used as a foundation for beginning a new life with hope.

Veronica's letter continued, "I don't remember much about that night except one thing one memory: a stranger, a kind EMT/ambulance driver cared enough to listen and pray with me. Your praying and business card have remained with me. I pray I can be there for someone as you were for me, even though I didn't know you."

An encouraging and familiar cliché states, "What goes around comes around." What's even more rewarding is when one's simple words of encouragement are appreciated, internalized, and then passed on.

Prayer:
How grateful I am that you are a God of comfort! Thank you for the comfort you bring to me. I pray, Lord, I will comfort those in need with the comfort I have received from you.

457

Rick Barton, Fire Safety Officer; Rick Barton Ministries,
Gunnison, CO; Fellowship of Christian Firefighters
International Ambassador-at-Large

INTERFERENCE OR INTERVENTION?

*What if that were I waiting at the site of a wreck,
at a fire, or at a sick loved one's side?*

THE CLEAR, crisp air of winter signaled that Christmas was just around the corner. What a special time to share the message of God's love and intervention!

While I was sharing God's Word in a small community church, a sudden cacophony of sirens interrupted the holiday message. With a sigh of impatience, I waited for what seemed like hours as every emergency service vehicle in our town responded to some emergency unknown to me. As I waited, a small voice spoke in my heart: "For you it's interference, but to those in need it is intervention."

A flood of realization washed over me. *How self-centered I was acting! What if that were I waiting at the site of a wreck, at a fire, or at a sick loved one's side? What if it were I for whom the sirens blared?*

> "The one who calls you is faithful and he will do it. Brothers, pray for us."
> (1 Thessalonians 5:24, 25)

The sirens that caused me temporary inconvenience were surely a source of great encouragement to those waiting for their arrival. I was immediately humbled. I bowed my head and led the congregation in a prayer for both the responders and those in need.

Then a second thought hit me, a thought more powerful than the first. When Jesus came to Earth, the political and religious rulers thought of him as interference. They tried to silence him, put him away, and kill him. They went to extreme measures to accomplish their evil schemes. But to those who were waiting for God's intervention, his coming was a source of great hope, an answer to years of prayer.

Once again I bowed my head. "Oh, Lord, do I see your coming into my life as interference or intervention?"

Each time I hear a siren or see emergency flashing lights, I pray for each person involved. As a firefighter, I hope those who see my emergency truck go by will do the same for me.

Prayer:
May I always see your coming into my life as intervention, not an interruption. As I hear a siren, Lord, let it be a reminder to pray for those for whom the siren blares.

D E C E M B E R   6

Chaplain Marc Santorella; Firefighter Danvers Fire Department, MA Public Fire and Life Safety Educator and Certified Fire Instructor Level 1

A COMMON ENEMY
Satan and fire—similar and dangerous

A CHRISTIAN FIREFIGHTER knows the Enemy, the devil, is as real as the fire we face. They also share similar characteristics. Among those are persistence, elusiveness, and destruction.

While camping I used my basic knowledge in fire chemistry to build a campfire able to withstand the pelting rain. When we went to bed, we left a log in the fire pit. In the morning nothing was left. Fire is persistent. It consumes! It eats and it destroys its fuel until either the chemical chain reaction is broken or nothing is left.

Firefighters approach fire from a scientific standpoint. The apostle John explains that sin like fire consumes and destroys. "The thief (Satan) comes only to steal and kill and destroy" (John 10:10). Fire, sin, and Satan steal and destroy. Satan attacks family relationships, and destroys friendships, careers, opportunities for advancement, finances, and ministries. He leaves his victims in the same state as the unstoppable alarm or barren wasteland that was once alive and thriving.

The apostle Peter warns us to be self-controlled and alert because Satan's goal is to devour (1 Peter 5:8). Peter knew what he was saying, for it was Peter to whom Jesus said, "Get behind me, Satan!" (Matthew 16:23) when Peter was tempted to try to prevent God from accomplishing his mission. Experience is a great teacher!

Like fire, Satan sometimes delays making his presence known until it's too late. In the same way that an explosive mixture of gases forms around an ignition source before fire bursts forth, Satan often keeps his presence hidden before bursting forth. A fire uses everything to its advantage—fuels, oxygen, a breeze, an adjacent property or tree line— to help it spread; it climbs over ceilings and through walls, and encompasses what it's out to devour.

> "And lead us not into temptation, but deliver us from the evil one. For Yours is the kingdom and the power and the glory forever. Amen." (Matthew 6:13 NKJV)

The advancements in fire prevention and detection have created a decrease in fires, which in turn has resulted in a degree of complacency. With their absence comes confidence. Then, when we're least expecting it, our enemy, be it fire or Satan, can explode and take us by surprise. Just as fighting fire takes knowledge, skills, and abilities, so does fighting our enemy Satan. To be victorious we need to be prepared. The Bible is our study guide. Prayer is our fireground channel; it's a direct communication with God.

Prayer:

Lord, help me when spiritual complacency sets in to remember that the Enemy is like a roaring lion looking to devour, and his attack is pending. Help me to guard my marriage, friendships, tongue, and emotions. Deliver me from the evil one.

DECEMBER 7

Rick Barton, Fire Safety Officer; Rick Barton Ministries, Gunnison, CO; Fellowship of Christian Firefighters International Ambassador-at-Large

MICROBURSTS FOR LUNCH
Be prepared!

WE'D ALREADY lost one resort and the fire was lining up for its next meal! I was the safety officer and my hands were full. Fortunately, we had a good incident management team in place including an in-camp meteorologist from the National Weather Service. The weatherman was giving us real-time updates from his satellite and computer. At our

460

noon command and general staff meeting he announced, "Microbursts of up to fifty miles per hour at 1230." Wow, a thirty-minute warning! We immediately reviewed our evacuation plan for the resort and prepared to carry it out. At exactly 1230, no kidding, the bursts hit and we rang the bell, evacuating the last of the resort workers and non-essential personnel. After a few hours of extreme fire behavior the winds subsided and the fire marched downriver away from the resort.

Jesus said, "Be dressed for service and keep your lamps burning"; in other words, "Be prepared." Because the previous safety officer had developed an evacuation plan and made sure everyone knew what to do and where to go, everything went smoothly. Secondly, because the meteorologist gave us a warning we were able to start the process early and have everyone in strategic and safe locations when the micro-bursts hit. Listening to the experts on our team and acting on their advice were wise decisions.

The Bible says there is wisdom in many counselors (Proverbs 11:14). Sure, they may miss it occasionally, we all do, but God has given them to us to round out our skills and knowledge base. I'd much rather act on their warning and be overprepared than to ignore the warning and have someone injured or killed. Ezekiel addresses the importance of heeding warnings in chapter 33, stressing, "If anyone hears the trumpet but does not take warning and the sword comes and takes his life, his blood will be on his own head" (v. 4).

> "For lack of guidance a nation falls, but many advisers make victory sure." (Proverbs 11:14)

First responders depend on many good counselors to effectively do their jobs. Likewise, God is depending on you to be a counselor, sharing his promises with those he brings in your path.

Prayer:
Thank you for those who help me with their expertise when on the job. Thank you, too, for those willing to be a witness for you. Help me to be "dressed for service and to keep [my] lamps burning" (Luke 12:25).

Sue Reynolds, Missionary – Fellowship of
Christian Firefighters International

FRIENDS BUT WE'D NEVER MET

Self-pity or service—it's a choice

I'D NEVER met Gerald Brock. I'd seen pictures of him as a smiling eight-year-old child thankful to return home from the hospital after forty-four days, pictures of a smiling adult helping others, but mostly pictures of "Fear Not," the Fire Dog, with children swarming around him. Whether at a parade, school, or fire station event, behind that dog mask is one smiling Gerald who loves life, his family, friends, the fire department, sharing fire safety tips, and serving the Lord.

When Gerald first called, my West Coast linguistically insensitive ears had difficulty understanding his South Carolina accent. Soon I understood him perfectly, especially his heart.

"How can I help with the Fellowship of Christian Firefighters? I'll help in any way I can," he said. And he meant it. When I learned what inspired such dedication, I knew he was one of God's special and humble servants.

Eight-year-old Gerald was playing baseball when his mother interrupted the game. "Gerald! Come tell your granddaddy good-bye."

As he rushed to say good-bye, a car, seemingly appearing out of nowhere, knocked him to the ground. Gerald stopped breathing. A volunteer firefighter resuscitated him. He was rushed to the hospital, where

> "I know what it is to be in need, and I know what it is to have plenty. I have learned the secret of being content in any and every situation, whether well fed or hungry, whether living in plenty or in want."
> (Philippians 4:12)

he underwent a tracheotomy and was packed in ice to maintain a constant body temperature of ninety degrees to deter brain swelling. His left side was paralyzed. For seventeen days he lay in a coma. Several times the young driver of the car that struck him joined the visitors who prayed nonstop. When Gerald regained consciousness he couldn't put words to his thoughts for more than four weeks.

When Gerald turned thirteen he accompanied his dad, a volunteer firefighter, to the station, assisting the crew by putting hose and apparatus on the truck, and his love for the fire service grew.

Today, Chaplain Gerald spends his life serving God. If you see a jaunty firedog at a parade or school, take a moment and think of Gerald. A serious accident of this kind could turn a person inward, filling them with self-pity. Not Gerald. This Darlington County Fire District 8 volunteer firefighter took an unfortunate and debilitating accident and used it to bring joy, happiness, love, fire safety awareness, and laughter to all he meets.

Prayer:
Whatever my circumstances, whatever trials and blessings come my way, may I remember to be content in all things.

DECEMBER 9

Pastor Ken Hall, Livermore Community Church; Spiritual Advisor – Fellowship of Christian Firefighters International

IN TRUTH AND GRACE

His gift of grace is not dependent on present behavior

DOES THIS sound familiar? "Physically competent individuals who take pride in their accomplishments and therefore say, 'I did it!' rather than asking for a helping hand." This phrase certainly seems applicable to the majority of emergency responders, and there's nothing wrong with that in the workplace. As a matter of fact, at times it's necessary for survival. But, let's switch our thinking to grace.

God's gift of grace is not based on earning it. Look at Ephesians 2:8: "For it is by grace you have been saved, through faith—and this not from yourselves." There is nothing in us that caused God to give us grace. It's given based on God's desire. It doesn't come from our own merit as we are clearly told in Ephesians 2:9: ". . . not by works, so that no one can boast." Grace is absolute in the Christian's life, it can't operate when we think we deserve it, and it isn't something we add to our lives to help us get saved. Grace is everything. There is no salvation apart from grace.

A lot of things in life are temporary. Rookies joining the fire service are sometimes hired on a trial basis. If they do well, they're given a permanent position. But, anyone saved by grace is not on probation. Once saved, you cannot lose your salvation. You didn't do anything to earn it, and you can't do anything to lose it. Look at John 5:24: "Whoever hears

463

my word and believes him who sent me has eternal life and will not be condemned; he has crossed over from death to life." Notice the verb tenses. We are saved and kept by grace. Salvation is a done deal for the child of God.

> "The Word became flesh and made his dwelling among us. We have seen his glory, the glory of the One and Only, who came from the Father, full of grace and truth." (John 1:14)

Have you ever been in any trouble such as unfaithfulness, stealing, or lying? When you sought forgiveness, how quickly did you regain the confidence of those you sinned against?

With Christ in your life, your past life no longer exists before God. It died at the cross; God threw your past into the deepest sea and posted a "No Fishing" sign. Once received, grace is never taken back. Christ, full of grace and truth, now dwells within you if you have accepted him as Lord and Savior of your life.

Prayer:
As one saved by grace and therefore "full of grace and truth,"
may I effectively reach out to the fire service and glorify you.

DECEMBER 10

Rick Barton, Fire Safety Officer; Rick Barton Ministries, Gunnison, CO; Fellowship of Christian Firefighters International Ambassador-at-Large

DON'T SAVE MY HOUSE!
A man's apparent lack of gratitude caused me to look at the bigger picture

HE SAID what?" our fire crew asked incredulously.

It was the end of June. The forest fire season was going strong. The previous day a fire raced through the center of a subdivision, barely avoiding a number of family dwellings. The fire crews regarded one house as a *miracle house*. When the fire reached the home and the hand crews and engines were forced to pull back, an air tanker made a low level run over the structure and saved it. But now we were hearing "the rest of the story."

464

As the crew was feverishly digging line and cutting away brush, the homeowner came out demanding, "Stop! Don't cut those trees! I had to special order them."

The crew paused for a moment shaking their heads in disbelief. To a firefighter his words sounded like, "Don't save my house." It seemed he would rather lose his expensive home than lose a few trees.

But the crews had a job to do. Hard work by these hot shots, engine crews, and the air tanker saved the day the home was spared.

A growing feeling of frustration dogged the firefighters as they left the scene. They risked life and limb to save this man's property and in return got cursed for doing so. In addition a lawsuit was filed against the air tanker pilot for dropping fire retardant on the man's white house.

> "Let the word of Christ dwell in you richly as you teach and admonish one another with all wisdom, and as you sing psalms, hymns and spiritual songs with gratitude in your hearts to God."
> (Colossians 3:16)

Most of us in the fire service don't risk our life or limbs for the money. There are far more lucrative and safer ways to make a living. Sure, we do it in part for excitement and camaraderie, but our main motivation is to help those in need. We want to be part of the answer to someone's desperate prayer. And yes, even though we appear to shrug it off, we like to be appreciated.

As I pondered these thoughts, I began to see a bigger picture. *How many people do I come into contact with every day who need a word of thanks? Perhaps a store clerk, waitress, or even one of my own family members needs some appreciation from me.*

Oh, by the way. I think the homeowner's lawsuit against the air tanker pilot for dropping red fire retardant on his white house was dismissed.

Prayer:
*Please, God, help me develop an attitude
of gratitude in all circumstances.*

*Tommy Neiman, Author of Sirens for the Cross; EMS
Training Officer – St. Lucie County, FL; Fellowship of
Christian Firefighters International Regional
Director / International Board Member*

A LEAP OF FAITH

*Our faith triumphant o'er our fears.
Are all with thee are all with thee.*

HENRY WADSWORTH LONGFELLOW

ALLEN WAS loved, educated, and also frustrated, discouraged, and without hope. Ready to check out on life, he headed up the coast from Miami with a loaded gun, stopped, cocked the trigger, and "Click!" Nothing!

"I can't even kill myself right!" He tried again. Still nothing; disgusted, he drove to a condominium and hit the elevator button for the top floor. When the elevator stopped at the seventh floor he figured this was high enough. He climbed over the railing, and jumped.

When we arrived, we found him sprawled out on the asphalt. His mangled legs, from mid-shin down, were covered with blood. Bones protruded through the flesh of both legs. The bone, as well as the artery close to the bone, was ruptured.

This guy's taken his last step, I thought as I continued my assessment and asked what happened. I caught his name but nothing else. "You need to talk to me?"

Allen said nothing.

We anatomically realigned and splinted his legs, placed him on a spine board, set up the IVs, and headed for the hospital.

> "If the LORD delights in a man's way, he makes his steps firm; though he stumble, he will not fall, for the Lord upholds him with his hand."
> (Psalm 37:23, 24)

"I can't even kill myself right," Allen grimaced. "There's nothing worth living for."

What an opportunity to share God's love! "Allen, I don't think it's a coincidence I'm on duty today. I'd wondered why I took overtime. Now, I know God arranged it so I could encourage you that life is worth living." When he allowed me to pray for him, that feeling was reinforced.

I returned to Allen's bedside many times. Several surgeries, accompanied by excruciating pain, followed. Gradually he shared the dark secrets holding his heart in bondage. A month later Allen went home, but he was not going alone. My family and I took him home. We waited for the nurses to bring Allen out in a wheelchair, but there was no wheelchair no crutches no walker no cane. He walked on his own!

When job pressures seem overwhelming, I remember Allen and the fact that what we do *does* make a difference. When I meet others who are discouraged and feel life is not worth living, I tell them about Allen and how his leap from a building turned into a leap of faith and hope for a brighter tomorrow.

Prayer:
Lord, thank you for upholding me in your hands. When I meet others who are discouraged, may you use me to share your hope and love.

DECEMBER 12

Chief Steve Parsons, St. Albans, WV, Fire Department

CAN'T SEE THE FIRE BECAUSE OF THE SMOKE

People look up to you as a hero.
Does God view you the same way?

I SEE THE smoke! Where's the fire?" Ever been in that predicament? I sure have in my thirty-one years in the fire service. Many times I've wandered through dense smoke, stumbling over furniture, running into walls, and sometimes just getting completely lost.

Life is similar to that for many in America currently. The truth is elusive because of all the smoke. Unfortunately, many Christians have turned their back on God and his biblical truths so they can feel accepted in this world. Have they ignored God's clear instruction that they "are not of this world"?

Being "in" the world means we can enjoy the things of the world, but we're not to immerse ourselves in those things the world values, nor are we to chase after worldly pleasures. Worshipping God, not pleasure, should be our calling in life. Our actions should reflect this. Not only should we abstain from, but we should be crying out against, same-sex marriages, open militant homosexuality, corporate and government corruption, and abortion, to name a few. God's Word clearly defines what is and is not sin. For instance, Leviticus 18:22 states, "Do not lie with a man as one lies with a woman; that is detestable." Yet, some Christians and denominations have now accepted openly gay ministers.

> "I have given them your word and the world has hated them, for they are not of the world any more than I am of the world." (John 17:14)

In Romans 12:2 it states, "Do not conform any longer to the pattern of this world, but be transformed by the renewing of your mind. Then you will be able to test and approve what God's will is—his good, pleasing and perfect will." As Christians we should be able to see the fire regardless of the smoke. God's design for our lives is clearly laid out in the Bible. Has America become another Sodom and Gomorrah?

As Christians, we cannot be like those who ride the fence in the name of political correctness. Christians need to know God's Word, stand up for it, and share it in our words and actions in our homes and communities. People look up to you as a hero. Does God view you the same way?

Prayer:
Father, please forgive me when I've failed to hold fast to the truth of your Word for fear of not being accepted in this world. As I read and study your Word, may I fully understand how you want me to lead my life to bring glory to your name. As the world tries to tempt me to accept things that are detestable to you, help me to please you rather than the people in this world.

DECEMBER 13

Chaplain Robert Osbourn, Sylacauaga, AL, Fire Department

CAUGHT IN THE MOMENT
Drifting aimlessly, without a purpose

SOMETIMES firefighters get caught up in the moment as they deal with excessive tragedy and chaos. They frequently feel they're expected to always have the answer when they arrive in their red engine. Couple that with never knowing what the next call might bring, and the pressure that first responders feel is understandable.

Tragedy, expectations, pressure, the unknown, and chaos can interfere with our ability to remember to put God first. Equally challenging is keeping in mind we do have an eternal destiny ahead of us.

After your earthly tent (body) dies, where you spend eternity depends on the choice you have made. You have control over your own destiny (heaven or hell). You can choose heaven, as a believer in Christ, or deny him and spend eternity in torment. Christ can be your own best friend or your own worst enemy.

Why not choose Jesus as your friend? He is alive. He died, and he rose from the grave because he loves you. If you call out to him, he'll pass over millions of people just to get to you; almost like a fire engine, passing hundreds of people just to get to the one who cried out for help. This is cause for joy, not depression and discouragement.

> "And straightway in the morning the chief priests held a consultation with the elders and scribes and the whole council, and bound Jesus, and carried *him* away, and delivered *him* to Pilate."
> (Mark 15:1 KJV)

Don't get caught in the moment. Don't allow the tragedy and pressure of the job to take your focus off God's love and eternal provision. Don't hesitate—call out to Jesus in your time of need, as his Word encourages. In Jesus' own words in Matthew 11:28–30 he urges all who are weary to come to him and take his yoke. But there is more. God shares that his yoke is easy and his burden is light.

Without the Lord Jesus in your life, you'll find yourself drifting aimlessly, without a purpose, being unsatisfied with life. But with Jesus, you'll have a sense of well-being, your spirit will rise up, and you'll find happiness, fulfillment, satisfaction, and stress release. We all, from time to time, need that stress reduction that comes only from God.

Don't bind the hands of your Savior the very hands of your own Rescuer, as the chief priests did two thousand years ago. Turn to him.

Prayer:
I seek to loose your hands, Jesus, in my life today
and to pray, study, and turn to you at all times.

Rev. Joe Smaha, Chaplain/Fire Inspector/Firefighter/EMT/
Hazmat Specialist – Paramus, NJ, Fire Department;
Fire Instructor – Bergen County, NJ, Fire Academy;
Pastor – Community Church of Paramus

FAITH VERSUS FEAR

I draw strength from three Hebrew men

THE SMOKE was so dark I couldn't see my hand in front of my face. The heat so intense, it was like walking into a fireplace. Fear as heavy as the smoke and heat enveloped my heart and mind.

I was a rookie responding to a house fire. As we forced entry and discovered the smoke came from the basement, we worked our way down the cellar stairs while the heat and smoke rose to meet us.

Descending those stairs of my first basement fire reminded me of my fire academy training regarding the extreme danger of basement fires. With only one way in, or, more importantly, only one way of escape, combined with the clutter and dangerous combustible items often stored in basements, plus the added threat of collapse, I had been told many firefighters' lives have ended in these basement tombs.

> "And so we know and rely on the love God has for us. God is love. Whoever lives in love lives in God, and God in him."
> (1 John 4:16)

I wondered, *What in the world am I doing here?* I felt like making a hasty retreat. Instead of surrendering to fear, I did something much wiser—I prayed! "Jesus, I know you called me to be a firefighter and promised never to leave or forsake me. Please give me strength to do my job." My fear fled, my training took over, and I made it down that smoke-filled stairway. We knocked the fire down, saved that house, and more significantly I learned a vital lesson that day.

Three Hebrew men faced a fiery furnace with no visible way of escape, yet they stood strong in faith before King Nebuchadnezzar. Their example of faith is a source of strength whenever I face dangerous circumstances. I place my faith and life into God's hands, knowing he is able to save and rescue me. But even if he doesn't, I have a duty an obligation to do the right thing and fulfill what he called me to do.

I've been in many fires and dangerous situations since then, including a number of basement fires, and there is something I remember to do as a result of that day. I pray for his protection, strength, and guidance. You see, my faith is not in my own ability—my faith is in the God of Creation who called me to be a Christian firefighter.

Prayer:

Thank you for listening to my every prayer. My faith is in you, Lord. Thank you that I can rely on your love in the most dangerous situations as well as my normal daily activities.

DECEMBER 15

Captain Ed Godoy Jr., Firefighter – Monroe, NY;
FDNY Auxiliary Corps

REMEMBERING UNCLE HENRY
The greatest gifts of all: his love, respect, and time

I'D JUST moved to the area known as "Hell's Kitchen" in New York and couldn't believe my good fortune: nine years old and living on the same block as Engine Company 54. Enthralled with the big red trucks, I couldn't resist heading to the station, where a blondish-red-haired man bade me to come in. "My name's Henry B. Millan Jr."

From that moment on a special relationship began. Before long I became the department's "fire buff." Henry, whom I soon called "Uncle Henry," taught me about all the things in a firehouse that wow a nine-year-old. When a call came, I watched the men slide down the poles, put their boots and coats on, and roll out the doors. Then I ran to the call, stayed with the driver, and helped. Little did I know that Uncle Henry was protecting me from the ever-growing gang culture and training me for a life in the fire service. When I was eighteen, Henry helped me through the Auxiliary Fire Corps training.

Time changes things; for me it brought a stint in the Army followed by entry into the corporate world. Health issues prevented my desired fire service career, but the Auxiliary Corps and volunteer service are still a central focus of my life.

Henry and I corresponded for years. By 1979 Uncle Henry's letters became scarce. Then his wife, Marge, started answering my letters. I never knew why. I sensed something was wrong, but part of me didn't want to know, so I never asked. I feared something physical prevented him from answering himself. I kept picturing the strong, handsome, Scottish fireman

I met many years before. In one letter, Marge mentioned moving again. Then the letters stopped and all my letters came back, unopened, saying, "address unknown." I am guessing he has been dead for quite some time now.

> "I have set you an example that you should do as I have done for you." (John 13:15)

Camaraderie remained with my brothers from 54 Engine even after they moved and became known as the "Pride of Midtown." I never entered the station without hoping Uncle Henry might show up. After several years went by with no contact, I began to assume that he had died.

Whenever I see children gazing at the trucks, I invite them to sit in the engines and give them a tour of the station. I share the importance of education, honesty, respect, working hard, staying out of trouble, and asking God for guidance and forgiveness. As I do, I see Uncle Henry's big smile and feel his hand on my shoulder. This big, gentle man, with his simple gesture of human kindness and caring, made a difference in one child's life. For that I am eternally grateful.

Engine 54, Ladder 4, and Battalion 9, the "Pride of Midtown," lost all their members who were on duty at the World Trade Center tragedy on 9-11-01. Fifteen firefighters from Engine 54, Ladder 4, and Battalion 9 made the supreme sacrifice. I lost twenty-two friends who passed through the doors of the "Pride of Midtown."

Prayer:
Thank you, Lord, for bringing "Henrys" into my life. May the examples of these giving people teach me to go and do likewise.

DECEMBER 16

Chaplain Gaius Reynolds, President – FCFI; Volunteer Firefighter – Livermore, CO, Fire Protection District

BLACK ICE

The silent warning gave way to an actual alarm

ICY RAINS, producing patches of black ice, caused conditions that set off a silent alarm in first responders' hearts. The only fully paved road in our district stretches from the Wyoming border toward Fort Collins, Colorado. This patch of highway has been featured on national television

472

as one of the most treacherous stretches in the country, a fact our department is well aware of. Black ice, often concealed by snow, contributes to this sad statistic.

As our church service ended, the silent warning gave way to an actual alarm. We arrived on scene to find that a car had hit black ice, spiraled 250 feet off the highway, and somersaulted into a field fifty feet below. A medical helicopter was launched, the car's rear window was broken, and an EMT crawled inside to hold the unresponsive victim's cervical spine and maintain airway. Extrication began, the roof was cut off, and the patient was transferred to an ambulance. Poor visibility prohibited the medical helicopter from landing on scene.

> "Give thanks to the LORD, call on his name; make known among the nations what he has done. Sing to him, sing praise to him; tell of all his wonderful acts. Glory in his holy name; let the hearts of those who seek the LORD rejoice."
> (Psalm 105:1–3)

Heads hung low as first responders departed with doubts about the young girl's destiny. So severe were her injuries, they questioned whether she'd even make it to the hospital. But God wasn't ready to bring this young girl into his presence yet. Miraculously, she not only made it to the hospital, but after weeks in the hospital and months of therapy, she recovered, returned to school, married, and started a family.

First responders are not always blessed to know their efforts are so rewarded. But this young girl was the daughter of foreign missionaries and the niece of a pastor. Prayers were sent upward from around the world and answered. Then one Sunday, the aunt and uncle visited the local church to give thanks. They knew many of the first responders were Christians and wanted to thank them and God at the same time.

Firefighters and EMTs don't do what they do for thanks, but when appreciation is shown, what an added blessing it is!

Scripture continually emphasizes the importance of giving thanks. This is one instance where many were blessed by godly people who prayed and gave thanks, to God, as well as God's people.

News of God's healing miracle in the life of this girl reached across the nations as her parents, family, and rural first responders made known what God had done.

Prayer:
Thank you, Lord, for using me. Thank you for those who remember to say thank you. What an added blessing that is to me, and I know to you as well, God.

Tommy Neiman, Author of Sirens for the Cross; EMS Training Officer – St. Lucie County, FL; Fellowship of Christian Firefighters International Regional Director / International Board Member

BOLDNESS TO SHARE

Eternal life instead of death

THERE WEREN'T many accidents on the seldom-crowded roads surrounding my assigned station, but if one occurred it was usually fatal. So when the tones sounded for an accident in a remote area, I feared it would be a bad one.

Twelve minutes later we arrived on scene to find no police cars, mangled cars, or trapped victims. There were heavy skid marks and we spotted a very dirty, mud-encrusted car in an open field across from a canal. We approached our victim. A look of frustration—or was it disbelief?—covered his face.

As we questioned and examined him, he said, "You're never going to believe what happened. For several days I think God's been trying to speak to me. I've been having confusing thoughts about who God really is. When my car went out of control, a bright flash of light surrounded me and a voice said, 'Hard to the right.' Without thinking about the light or the voice, I closed my eyes and turned hard to the right. Next thing I knew I was sitting in that field. Sounds crazy, huh?"

> "As he [Saul (Paul)] was traveling, it happened that he was approaching Damascus, and suddenly a light from heaven flashed around him; . . . and he said, 'Who are You, Lord?' And he *said*, 'I am Jesus.'"
> (Acts 9:3, 5 NASB)

"I believe that God was speaking to you," I responded, remembering how Jesus appeared in a flash of light to Saul (soon to be the apostle Paul) on his way to Damascus. Saul was on his way to persecute believers in that far-off city when a bright light blinded him and Jesus spoke to him.

I was awed at the similarity and how God continues to speak in miraculous ways to this very day. Our patient, Billy, barely missed the canal and the possibility of drowning. I have no doubts God sent that light, spoke to Billy, and kept him from death.

"Billy, if you'd gone into that canal and drowned, do you know where you'd have spent eternity?" I asked.

Billy hesitated. "I don't know, but I hope I'd be in heaven."

The door opened to share Christ's saving message, and Billy responded by accepting Christ as his Lord and Savior.

As Billy exited the back door of the rescue truck, the first highway patrolman was just arriving. *Hm-m-m . . . I wondered. Who kept him away so long?*

I'll bet that patrolman wondered why this accident victim was smiling when he stepped out of the rescue truck. There was no way he could have known that instead of death, Billy now had eternal life in Jesus Christ.

Prayer:
Lord, when you open doors for me to share your saving grace, give me the boldness and the words you would have me say.

D E C E M B E R   1 8

Chaplain Marc Santorella; Firefighter Danvers Fire Department, MA Public Fire and Life Safety Educator and Certified Fire Instructor Level 1

PREPAREDNESS
The third alarm will eventually ring

STORMS ARE amazing things to watch. If you've never stood at the ocean's edge and observed the fury of a sea in the throes of a hurricane, I highly suggest you look for the opportunity. Safety precautions are required, of course. I live in the Northeast, so I've never actually witnessed a tornado, but I've seen enough documentaries to know it's an awesome and terrifying experience. What strikes me most about these events is the suddenness with which they normally occur.

Most storms are unexpected. Here in New England we have what we call the "hurricane season," when storms could come anytime, but nothing is guaranteed. The idea is to be prepared so when the storms hit, and inevitably they do, we'll be ready.

The fire service is no different. We can go weeks without any major incidents, then without warning, that old factory building we've been watching for years goes to a three-alarm, or an explosion rocks a neighborhood, tying up resources from towns miles away. It's precisely for these reasons we maintain our equipment and do our checklists daily. When the Big One happens, and eventually it will, we don't want to be caught off guard.

Have you noticed what happens when we're prepared for the big ones? Things tend to flow a bit more smoothly when you've done the checklist and know where your tools are. You can arrive confident when you've checked your structural firefighting gear, the radio battery is charged and ready, and there's water in the tank. Sure, you still have a tough job ahead and there will be unexpected challenges, but at least when you're ready you meet those storms prepared for just about anything.

> "The LORD is a refuge for the oppressed, a stronghold in times of trouble. Those who know your name will trust in you, for you, LORD, have never forsaken those who seek you." (Psalm 9:9, 10)

Life is no different. Jesus told us we would have trouble. Consequently, we'll be wise to maintain our spiritual readiness. Read the Bible on a daily basis for training. Spend time each day in prayer. Communicate with other believers. These three simple procedures will prepare you for the personal big ones you'll face. After all, it's to be expected that storms will come, spiritual battles will ensue, and the third alarm will eventually ring.

Prayer:
Father, thank you for being honest and telling me storms will come. Whether those storms arrive today or tomorrow, I'm leaning on you for shelter, strength, and peace to carry me through.

DECEMBER 19

Reverend Wayne Detzler, PhD, Chaplain (Retired) – Charlotte, NC, Fire Department; Fellowship of Christian Firefighters Regional Director

CHRISTMAS CANDLES AND MUSIC
Sharing the story of Life

OVER THE years in our fire department, my friendships grew. Comradeship grew into deep personal affection for each other. As Christmas drew near, my wife suggested we offer an evening buffet to our firefighter friends. So, we invited the officers of our department to come to our parsonage for a Christmas buffet.

My wife set out an absolutely beautiful spread. She lit candles throughout the house to set the scene. Knowing our firefighters well, I ran around extinguishing the candles before they arrived. It was a game of cat and mouse: She'd light the candles, and I'd blow them out.

On time, the officers and their spouses started to arrive. Before long our lovely home was filled with our dearest friends, the officers and chiefs of our fire department. We chatted together as we enjoyed the buffet. There was no pressure. Our usually hectic pace slowed to a relaxed atmosphere.

On cue my wife and I invited our friends to take a seat in our living room. A musical team from Campus Crusade for Christ joined us. They were a small chamber music group, and they made our grand piano sing beautifully the songs of Christmas.

> "Everyone who calls on the name of the Lord will be saved."
> (Romans 10:13)

Glancing around the room, I couldn't imagine so many first responders relaxing together. Our spouses enjoyed seeing us in this new setting. Then the music stopped, and the pianist turned slightly on his seat as he began to speak.

Quietly he shared the story of Jesus coming to Earth to seek and to save. He showed us how Jesus set the pattern of the Great First Responder because he came into the hostile atmosphere of this world to reach us with God's grace.

At the end, the speaker held up a comment card. He said, "Please take a moment to fill out a comment card. Let us know if you have enjoyed the evening." Then he added: "If you have committed your life to the Lord, please mention that."

Afterward we went through the cards together. To our great amazement and gratitude, two of the senior chiefs indicated they had committed their lives to the Lord.

Prayer:
Your coming to Earth, O Lord, is the only way
I can go to heaven. I thank you.

Dwayne Clemmons, Adjunct Instructor – Virginia Department of Fire Programs; Founder – DMC Ministries; Author of Exploits, Jesus Rides in an Ambulance, and Utterances from the Throne Room; Volunteer in Fire and EMS for forty years in Virginia

MERRY *CHRISTMAS*
Keeping CHRIST in CHRIST*mas?*

THIS IS the month we celebrate the birth of Christ. References to our Savior and Lord as CHRIST appear in the New International Version 531 times. All these direct references are in the New Testament, affectionately known as the Good News. As you celebrate Christ's birth, it would bless our Lord if you took time to read the story of his birth in the New Testament. But don't stop there. Turn back to the Old Testament and read on with an open heart about his prophesied coming in Isaiah 9 and 53. Then return to the New Testament and read about his life, ministry, and recorded miracles. As you do, you'll more clearly understand that Christ is your hope, future, and destiny.

> "For to us a child is born, to us a son is given, and the government will be on his shoulders. And he will be called Wonderful Counselor, Mighty God, Everlasting Father, Prince of Peace."
> (Isaiah 9:6)

God said you were made by him for him and that he is the Way, the Truth, and the Life, and that no man can come to God except through Jesus Christ.

Why then is there such a push, such a fervor and immediacy, to take CHRIST *out* of Christmas? The answer is simple. Our Enemy, the devil, walks around like a roaring lion, seeking whom he may devour. His plan is to steal, kill, and destroy. He thinks by removing CHRIST from Christmas, having people legally bound to only say, "Happy holidays!", and a host of other covert plans he has underway, he can stop the work of God on Earth.

I urge you to join me in saying, "It ain't gonna happen!" Join me in your determination to say "Merry *CHRIST*mas!" as many times as you can. When someone wishes you a happy holiday, reply by saying, "Merry *CHRIST*mas."

We celebrate the birth of Christ because he transformed us from who we were to what we are. It is only by this birth and our belief, faith, and trust in him that we can claim eternity in heaven.

Don't allow yourself to be deceived by foolishness perpetrated by those who seek to destroy you. Don't allow the skeptics of unbelief to intimidate you into saying anything but "Merry *CHRIST*mas!" Remember, Jesus is the Reason for the season.

Through Christ we have hope, happiness, and joy. Through him and him alone, you can go to bed and wake up each day with hope. His birth was foretold years before he came and he is everlasting.

Prayer:

Happy birthday, Jesus! You are the Reason for the season.
With each gift, activity, and get-together, I ask you to
be present. May others see you in me.

DECEMBER 21

Captain Ed Godoy Jr., Firefighter – Monroe, NY;
FDNY Auxiliary Corps

AN EVENING OF REMINISCING, AN EVENING OF LOOKING FORWARD

I hope my grandson remembers and treasures this moment

IN 2002, my wife and I took our three-year-old grandson, Anthony, to see the magnificent Christmas tree at Rockefeller Center before heading to a firehouse party for Engine 54. Anthony stood in awe as he looked at the towering pine dressed in lights. Me? I had a tear trickle down my cheek as I thought of my comrades, fellow firefighters from Engine 54, who would never again gaze at the marvels of New York City. This was the second Christmas party since the "Attack on America." What followed was an evening to remember—reminiscing *and* looking forward.

More than four decades ago, at the age of nine, I walked into a New York City firehouse and my life changed forever. I was hooked. Tonight, amid the joy, were memories of sadness coupled with a feeling of emptiness. Surrounding us were photos and plaques for the fifteen men who lost their lives at the World Trade Center. As I talked with some other "old-timers," it felt as if time stood still. We laughed, reminisced, and reflected on our lives and the lives of those who are no longer among us.

My attention shifted to Anthony as he made his way around the firehouse, looking up at the men in their uniforms. *I hope he remembers and*

treasures this moment, I thought as I once again saw myself as a little boy and remembered how blessed I am that a firefighter cared and reached out to me.

I pray that after I leave this world, Anthony will recall how his Grandpa took him to meet these firefighters and their families at the firehouse in New York. I know if he decides to follow in my footsteps and become a fireman, these heroes will look out for him just as they always have for me.

The bright lights on the tree in Rockefeller Center, a horse-pulled wagon, Santa coming down from the roof on a fire truck, the smiles of children, sharing stories of yesteryear, being among friends, heroes; these are the things today and tomorrow are made of. These are the things I will reflect upon when tears begin to once again encompass my heart when I think of the losses sustained on September 11, 2001.

> "There is a time for everything, and a season for every activity under heaven: a time to be born and a time to die, a time to plant and a time to uproot, a time to kill and a time to heal, a time to tear down and a time to build."
> (Ecclesiastes 3:1–3)

Prayer:
Lord, your Word tells us there is a time for everything. When memories of loss and heartache plague my mind, help me look around and see your goodness as a child sees it. Help me as I shed a tear in remembrances; this is a time to heal and move on.

DECEMBER 22

Reverend Wayne Detzler, PhD, Chaplain (Retired) – Charlotte, NC, Fire Department; Fellowship of Christian Firefighters Regional Director

CHRISTMAS REALITY BURNS BRIGHT
Learning what's real

BUSY—THAT is the word for Christmastime, especially in a big-city church. To help out, I volunteered to lead the midweek prayer gathering. It was a quiet oasis in a desert of draining stress.

Halfway through the evening, my pager went off. "Working fire," it said, and the address followed. I decided to wait it out. They would be OK without me for a half-hour or so. But I couldn't wait.

Handing the leadership over to another pastor, I headed toward the fire scene. Engines and a tanker truck choked the quiet residential street. I put on my gear and hiked toward the smoldering ruins of the house. An electrical short in the lighting had ignited the Christmas tree, turning a beautiful home into a flaming inferno. The lady fled for her life as fire licked at her.

It took time to knock down the fire, and it took several fire units to finish the job. As soon as the hot spots were doused with water, we began salvage. Slowly, we pulled out the smoky-smelling remnants of their lives. With the family sheltered safely with friendly neighbors, we laid out the salvaged items in the neighbor's garage. Christmas gifts were water-soaked. Personal belongings seemed to be ruined.

> "I can do everything through him who gives me strength."
> (Philippians 4:13)

Finally, we were ready, ready to show the owners the ashes of their lives, the charred remains of their Christmas. When the lady came out, she surveyed the scene in silence. There were no tears, no complaints. She never said, "What if . . .?" Or, "Why me?" She just looked long and hard, and then she turned to me. "Wayne, is that you?" she asked.

The owners were part of our church family, and I never knew it until that moment. I sputtered some consolation before praying with the family, asking the Lord to strengthen them and soothe their hearts.

"Wayne," the lady interrupted my consolation, "Wayne, it is just stuff. We can replace stuff, and we are so happy that our family is okay." She reminded me of what we believe. We love people and use things—we do not love things and use people. That dark December night I learned a lot.

Prayer:
Creator God, I thank you for the people
around us, for they are my true wealth.

*Reverend Wayne Detzler, PhD, Chaplain (Retired) –
Charlotte, NC, Fire Department; Fellowship of
Christian Firefighters Regional Director*

CHRISTMAS SIREN OF JOY
Reaching our neighbors with hope

THE NEIGHBORHOOD was so wild we called the station "Fort Apache." Gunfire often punctuated the night air. Businesses were boarded shut, and the neighbors were known as "survivors." On one occasion, neighborhood thugs dashed in as the engine cleared the station. They stole the firefighters' wallets while the crew was making a run. This was really a tough duty assignment.

One day a Methodist lady showed up at the station. Seldom did neighborhood folks come to visit, let alone people from the community at large. But it was December, and Christmas was in the air. The church lady wanted to take gifts to neighborhood kids, but she had a problem. She was cautious of wandering into one of the toughest sections of our city.

So, she turned to the firefighters at Fort Apache.

"Could you all help me?" she asked them. "I want to take Christmas toys to neighborhood kids. I'm just afraid of wandering around the streets."

> "Rejoice in the Lord always. I will say it again: Rejoice!"
> (Philippians 4:4)

The engine company responded immediately. "Sure," the captain agreed. "We'll take you and your little girl around the neighborhood with our engine." So, they rolled out the engine and loaded up the toys, the lady, and her daughter. Soon the engine set off and distributed toys and joy to the little neighbors of Fort Apache.

Far away in an upscale suburb of New York City there is a volunteer department. Each Christmas they decorate one engine with Christmas lights and speakers for music. Then they take toys to children throughout the community. Thankful parents pay the volunteer department for this service. Children never forget the day a fire engine brought them their Christmas toy.

One of the best things about firefighters is this: They are neighbors. I learned this as a three-year-old when my grandmother took me to the fire station. I fell in love with the sights and smells of the old-fashioned fire trucks. This led me to a career of service to my neighborhoods. Scary sirens of sorrow can turn into sirens of joy at Christmas.

Prayer:
Lord, help me to bring joy all year 'round to our neighbors.
When the disaster side of this career burdens my heart,
let me remember the joy we bring and to rejoice always.

DECEMBER 24

Chief Lee Callahan, Burlington, MA; Fellowship of
Christian Firefighters International Regional
Director / International Board Member

A CHRISTIAN
STIMULUS PACKAGE
What "stimulates" the Christian firefighter?

STIMULUS, according to one dictionary, is "something that incites or rouses to action, an incentive." Insurance companies, banks, and other private segments of our national economy were invited to be "stimulated" in an effort to get the economy moving again. Other "stimulus" packages were initiated in an effort to create new jobs. Whether we like it or not, *stimulus* is a household word that provides for interesting fire station banter.

While mulling over the government's stimulus packages, a more serious question crossed my mind. What "stimulates" the Christian firefighter? Is it what we get involved with around the firehouse? That can be okay as long as what we're involved with is "worthy of full respect, so that God's name and our teaching may not be slandered" (1 Timothy 6:1).

Unfortunately many firehouses have things that stimulate in negative ways. Before getting involved in those things, I suggest you ask, "Is this what I want to be doing if Christ should come this very instant?" The Bible tells us, "And now, little children, abide in Him, that when He appears, we may have confidence and not be ashamed before Him at His coming" (1 John 2:28 NKJV).

483

Perhaps your Christian "stimulus" package includes daily Bible reading. Partner that with praying God opens your eyes and heart, and you have a winning combination. Just as spending time with them is the best way to get to know your closest friends and loved ones, spending time in God's Word and in

prayer is the best way to form a loving, strong, lasting bond with God. When you know God better, you know how to please and walk closely with him.

A third way to be a "stimulated" Christian is to serve God. Are you involved in a Christian ministry? Firefighters can develop their church's emergency evacuation plan. Do you know how to initiate first aid if needed during a service or other church activity? Have you considered organizing an outreach or special service in your community? No matter what your occupation, there are many ministries that need someone just like you.

So again I ask, "What stimulates you? Is it living for Christ? Or is it what is important to the world (man's stimulus)?"

Paul signed off his first letter to Timothy by reminding the young pastor to "turn away from godless chatter and the opposing ideas" (1 Timothy 6:20).

Prayer:
When negative influences tempt me, I'm thankful that your Word is the "stimulus package" that can turn me away from godless chatter and opposing ideas.

DECEMBER 25

Reverend Wayne Detzler, PhD, Chaplain (Retired) – Charlotte, NC, Fire Department; Fellowship of Christian Firefighters Regional Director

THE CHRISTMAS BABY
Joy for life on the edge

SHE WAS a firefighter's firefighter. Maggie was one of the best. She was incredibly fit, and she handled every challenge with skill and dedication. No matter what the emergency, Maggie was always in the middle of it bringing aid and comfort to people in need. Maggie's husband was a firefighter, too. So, we all watched with eager anticipation as they expected their first child.

As usual I made the rounds of all the fire stations on Christmas morning. Each year we went to the local chocolate factory and bought a special box of candy, one for each of the crews. It was a special treat, and it gave me a chance to chat with the guys and gals who were on duty Christmas Day.

About halfway through my rounds, the pager interrupted. When I called the dispatcher, he sent me straight to the hospital. Maggie's baby had arrived; a wonderful, healthy little one was God's Christmas gift to Maggie and her husband.

> "Then little children were brought to Jesus." (Matthew 19:13)

As chaplain, I had tried to minister to Maggie throughout the years in many complex situations, but now ministry was so simple. Together we thanked the Lord for this wonderful Christmas gift. I led in a prayer of gratitude, and the little hospital room seemed to glow with God's presence. Maggie and her husband joined with us in prayer. It's amazing how a quiet little one can soften the toughest of us.

Our jobs in the fire service are often heart-wrenching. We see the worst of nature, and we also see the worst of human nature. But a little one reminds us that the Lord is always making "all things new" (Revelation 21:5 KJV). He is always bringing new little ones into our world. As the birth of Jesus defines our Christmas, so Maggie's baby defined Christmas for that Connecticut fire department.

From time immemorial, God has sent wonderful reminders of his grace and love in the form of a baby. Little ones are so unspoiled by the world. As they are totally dependent on parents, so we are utterly dependent on the Lord. What a wonderful picture of God's good grace!

Prayer:
*Lord, I thank you for the little ones you have committed
to our love and care. May they see you in me.*

485

*Chaplain Gerald E. Brock, Darlington County, SC,
Fire District Station 8; "Fear Not," the Firefighting Dog*

SERVICE AND LOVE
We can be a vessel of Christ's love

ONE WINTER day, the Darlington County Fire District was paged out to a fast-spreading major field fire. The threat was such that three of our four fire stations were toned out. My friend, George, told dispatch he'd be standing by at Station 8 in case he was needed. I headed to the station to join him. Three hours passed as the firefighters fought to control this fire. While George and I waited to see if we'd be called out, the tone went out for another fire. A bale of hay was burning, so we figured it would be easy to put it out. When we arrived, we realized how misled we were. Instead of a simple hay fire, it was a brush fire that covered nearly two acres.

Our church's Wednesday night prayer service is a fellowship with other Christians that I seldom miss, but this call came on a Wednesday, causing me to miss the service. When friends from church mentioned how they'd missed me, I told them I felt I was serving other people by protecting life and property. This was not a lame excuse, for I do honor God's command, "Let us not give up meeting together" (Hebrews 10:25). Jesus Christ also said, "A new command I give you: Love one another. As I have loved you, so you must love one another" (John 13:34). As a fire chaplain, I take this command seriously and am blessed to join my department on calls, pray for them, assist where needed, and be a vessel for Christ by loving them as Christ loves us.

> "Here is my servant whom I have chosen, the one I love, in whom I delight." (Matthew 12:18)

Regardless of your role in life, you can be that vessel of Christ's love. Fellowship with other Christians is essential to grow in our Christian walk. Sharing his love and serving in his name is equally important. When you combine this with internalizing his Word, you will be a tool that will put out eternal fires as well as a delight to the Lord.

Prayer:
*Dear God, thank you for allowing me to have the training and
skills to help others in need. Thank you for other Christian*

firefighters who serve you and their communities. May you protect us and our families as we serve others. My prayer is that you can say you delight in me. In the name of Jesus Christ, I pray, amen.

*Ken Cofiell, Dispatcher/Firefighter/EMT (Deceased) –
Anne Arundel County, MD, Fire Department*

WE TAKE CARE OF OUR OWN

That night I more fully understood the meaning of family

WE TAKE care of our own!" This statement from training became a reality one New Year's Eve when I was on the receiving rather than serving end. I was working dispatch. Until midnight things were extremely quiet. When the New Year arrived so did the calls. Even the supervisor took calls: "What's your location?" I heard him say. "You say he can't breathe? . . . What's your name? . . . You're whose mom?" Then he turned to me.

"Kenny, it's your mom. Your dad can't breathe—pick up the phone."

I turned to push one little button like countless times before, but I kept pushing the wrong button. Finally I heard my crying mom. In the background Dad was gasping for air. I was now living "a firefighter's nightmare." The call was for my family.

While trying to calm Mom and give instructions, my emotions ran at full speed. With tears, I dispatched an engine and paramedic unit. While life-lining or directing medical units to scene, and updating patient information, I heard my lieutenant inform the responder, "This is Cofiell's dad. Ken's on duty."

The officer replied, "We understand."

The fire service is a family. My dad became their dad. We'd never give better care to him than anyone else, it's just that our emotions were different. This was family and we take care of our own!

At the hospital, I was met by one of Dad's attending paramedics. Like a brother sharing bad news with family, he put his arm around my shoulder and said, "We did all we could, but it doesn't look good. Ken, I'm sorry!"

Within the next hour my dad suffered two strokes and a heart attack. As I watched him slip deeper into his coma, all I could think was, "We take care of our own." We spend our entire career caring for everyone else, but I was beginning to understand what the saying meant. The helplessness was overwhelming. With all my training, education, and experience I couldn't help my dying father. It was at that time I remembered that "the Father of compassion and the God of all comfort, who comforts us in all our troubles, [does so] so that we can comfort those in any trouble with the comfort we ourselves have received from God" (2 Corinthians 1:3-4)

> "This is how we know that we love the children of God: by loving God and carrying out his commands." (1 John 5:2)

My first responder family was a living example of God's comfort. God used them to comfort me and give Dad the best help possible.

Prayer:
Thank you for the love of the fire service and the way we take care of others as you care for us. When others face difficult times, may I remember to reflect your love through a call, visit, or card. You take care of your own and you've shown us we are to take care of our own.

DECEMBER 28

Bill Burns, Jacksonville, FL, Fire/Rescue Department

HE IS THERE ALL THE TIME
Many times we were close to losing the battle

IN THE frigid predawn hours of a New Year, the employee charged with notifying officials when a gasoline storage tank at a petroleum facility in Jacksonville, Florida, was nearing capacity fell asleep. The tank overflowed, thousands of gallons of gasoline leaked into a diked area, and fuel vapors found an ignition source. This oversight cost the employee his life.

The Jacksonville Fire/Rescue Department (JFRD) arrived with the task of extinguishing a fully involved gasoline storage tank filled with approximately three million gallons of gasoline surrounded by a lake of burning fuel about five acres in size. This type of tank fire had never been successfully extinguished anywhere in the world. A seemingly impossible challenge faced our best officers, hazardous materials team, and firefighters.

Stabilizing the tank to avoid a catastrophic structural failure while protecting other tanks from becoming involved, was foremost. We called for assistance including asking the U.S. Navy to send us all available fire-fighting foam.

For five long days and nights, we made repeated, yet unsuccessful, attempts at extinguishing the fire. As we broke new ground, each learning experience provided insight as we prepared for what we hoped would be the final attack. All equipment was in place and properly manned. Thirteen thousand gallons of firefighting foam concentrate was on scene. But the foam concentrate was used up faster than expected and we'd done everything we could to the best of our ability, but to no avail. Our only hope was a miracle from God to give the fire its final blow.

> "But you are a shield around me, O LORD; you bestow glory on me and lift up my head."
> (Psalm 3:3)

We prayed the foam ordered on the first day would arrive. God miraculously answered our prayer with the arrival, within thirty minutes of each other, of two semis from two separate 3M plants. One came from West Virginia, nine hundred miles away, the other from Wisconsin, twelve hundred miles away.

At the time of our most critical need, God intervened, guided our actions, helped us to be successful, and provided his protection, and the fire was successfully extinguished. At one point men had to run for their lives, but praise God, injuries were minor and the most significant injury was a broken leg!

I know, beyond a doubt, that we would have failed without God's divine intervention and protection. We serve a mighty and loving God!

Prayer:
Others may not always see your hand and they may attribute success to luck or human abilities, but I know, Lord, that all praise and glory belong to you. Thank you for being with me on each and every call.

*Reverend Wayne Detzler, PhD, Chaplain (Retired) –
Charlotte, NC, Fire Department; Fellowship of
Christian Firefighters Regional Director*

NEW YEAR'S EVE ON THE EDGE

The ragged edge of a new year

IT WAS always a quiet, meditative time in our church life. Each year we watched the New Year enter with a few friends. The services were small, and the atmosphere was intimate. As pastor, I led them into a time of communion as we remembered the death of the Lord Jesus on our behalf.

During a preparatory hymn my pager went off. Sitting in the front row was my dear friend, a fire captain from the neighboring department. I handed my pager to him and asked him to check out the call. Then I tried to push the emergency out of my mind as the service continued. We sang a hymn and I prayed on behalf of our fellowship.

"It's the lieutenant." My friend was brief. "His girlfriend has attempted suicide. They're at the hospital." I explained to the fellowship that a page had come. They joined with me in prayer as I presented the need without any details.

> "For Christ's love compels us, because we are convinced that one died for all, and therefore all died."
> (2 Corinthians 5:14)

Together we celebrated the Lord's Supper and I closed the service with prayer. We took time to wish each other a happy New Year, then I excused myself to head for the hospital. When I arrived the patient had been stabilized.

I went directly to our off-duty lieutenant. "How can I help? I'm going to stay with you till we get through the night." We prayed for his girlfriend and I committed the couple to the Lord, trusting God to give us strength for that night and the year ahead. It strengthened the bond between us; a friendship that is memorable because of its depth and intensity.

Never will I understand the black void of hopelessness that drives one to suicide. Never will I fully comprehend how one can carry out this desperate act. But the love of the Lord is enough to face even these experiences. When you face similar dark nights of hopelessness, there is only one avenue for hope; it is only the hope of the Lord that can cast light on such a scene.

Prayer:
When hope seems lost, help me to bring
the warm light of your hope, O Lord.

Tommy Neiman, Author of Sirens for the Cross; EMS Training Officer – St. Lucie County, FL; Fellowship of Christian Firefighters International Regional Director / International Board Member

OUT WITH THE OLD, IN WITH THE NEW

Regardless of age, God cares

OUT WITH the old, in with the new—this describes the back-to-back rescue calls I received one Friday afternoon.

The first call came in as a "fall." We arrived to find an elderly gentleman sitting in a lawn chair in the midst of several family members and friends. He had a homemade ice pack cooling down a pretty good bump on his head. He was awake and talkative—chastising his family for calling 9-1-1.

"We just want to make sure you're okay," they told him. And he was. But the unique thing was the occasion for this get-together. The gentleman was celebrating his 107th birthday. And you'll never guess how he fell. He was dancing around the swimming pool!

We headed back for the truck, talking about how neat it must be to be able to dance at the age of 107.

The next call came less than two hours later: "a woman in labor."

We arrived to find a young lady experiencing occasional labor contractions. She was in her ninth month and within a day of her due date. I explained to her excited husband and parents that, since the contractions were rather far apart, the bag of water had not ruptured, and there was no sign of a baby's head in the birth canal, it might be a little while before the arrival of the couple's first child.

491

Since we were there already, I asked the guys to get the stretcher. I told the expectant mom we'd transport her to the hospital.

As the guys retrieved the stretcher, our mother-to-be had a very strong contraction. It was strong enough to give me an eerie feeling that something might be happening. I rechecked her. Her bag of water ruptured, and that's not all—a little head started to emerge.

> "What is man that you are mindful of him, the son of man that you care for him? You made him a little lower than the heavenly beings and crowned him with glory and honor." (Psalm 8:4, 5)

"Forget the stretcher! Get my OB kit!" I yelled.

Excitement resurfaced as family members gathered 'round. I gowned out and two contractions later, God's beautiful gift of a human life slid into my hands.

How great is God's gift of life, whether 107 years old or one second young!

As I lay in my bed that night, a new appreciation for my job, for life, and for my ultimate Provider grew within my heart. Regardless of age, God cares and provides for each and every one of us.

Prayer:
Thank you, Lord, for the wonderful gift of life now and forever. Knowing you are mindful of me, Lord, and that you care for me, while beyond my understanding of why at times, blesses and encourages me.

DECEMBER 31

Dwayne Clemmons, Adjunct Instructor – Virginia Department of Fire Programs; Founder – DMC Ministries; Author of Exploits, Jesus Rides in an Ambulance, and Utterances from the Throne Room; Volunteer in Fire and EMS for forty years in Virginia

THE DAY OF THE MASTER'S COMING

Avoid the drama that so easily plagues people

ANOTHER NEW Year is dawning. Has God indicated to you anything that will happen for sure this year?

In common, everyday English, *The Message* tells us about something that will happen for sure. Will it be in the coming year? Only God knows that, but here is what his Word says: "I don't think, friends, that I need to deal with the question of when all this is going to happen. You know as well as I that the day of the Master's coming can't be posted on our calendars. He won't call ahead and make an appointment any more than a burglar would. About the time everybody's walking around complacently, congratulating each other—"We've sure got it made! Now we can take it easy!"—suddenly everything will fall apart. It's going to come as suddenly and inescapably as birth pangs to a pregnant woman" (1 Thessalonians 5:1–3 MSG).

"Get ready; be prepared, you and all the hordes gathered about you, and take command of them." (Ezekiel 38:7)

It's amazing the number of firefighters who are more prepared for lunch than for eternity. The Word says that when Jesus comes back he wants to find us "so doing!"

So what are you going to do differently this year than you did in past years? If you're saved, born again, and Spirit-filled, then you know what needs to be done. You don't have to be concerned with people's prophecies, predictions, and intuition. You have as your manual the time-tested, completely accurate Word of the one and only true and living God. Time is short and the end is near. Don't allow yourselves or your co-workers to miss what God has for you.

I challenge you to be the light in your home and workplace. Pray, read, and study more. Get more involved in your church or ministry.

First responders have a tendency to feel invulnerable. When everything goes wrong we get the call. We go into places people run out of, deal with situations nobody wants to deal with, and sacrifice ourselves daily. Don't you think this year we should offer to others the spiritual comfort we know?

Don't allow yourselves to be caught up in the all the events of the day and drama that so easily plagues people. Guard yourself against the stress and strife that try to bring you down. Just as Gomer, in the Old Testament, was ordered to be prepared for battle, you to need to be prepared physically and spiritually.

Prayer:
I don't know what you have for me in the coming year,
but with your help and godly counsel, I will be ready.

Gaius and Sue Reynolds want you to be aware
of Christian ministries related to firefighting

**Fellowship of Christian Firefighters, International (FCFI)
(www.fellowshipofChristianfirefighters.com)**
The Fellowship of Christian Firefighters began in the Denver area in the
early 1970s, when two Christian firefighters, having a Bible study on
Hebrews 10:24-25, saw the importance and need for Christian firefighters
to support and encourage one another in their daily walk. That Bible
study led to monthly meetings of concerned and interested firefighters.

The FCFI Purpose includes glorifying God in the fire service, fellowshipping together for individual growth in the Christian life, serving the
cause of Christ through the church of one's own choice, encouraging
those in the fire service in their Christian life, sharing locally in planned
fellowship meetings, individual contact, and prayer, bringing all Christians in the fire service to a common goal of praying for the fire service
and its members, sharing on an international basis through an annual
international conference, having contact internationally with fellow
Christian firefighters and the caring for firefighters in times of need. Individual chapters and members share Christ's love in the fire service and
their communities in many other and varied ways. For more information, email us at FCFIHQ@aol.com.

Other ministries include:
- **The Federation Of Fire Chaplains** (especially their training/scholarship
  fund) could benefit. http://firechaplains.org/
- **Rick Barton Ministries.** Rick contributed quite a few devotionals, and
  he speaks at many churches, does chapel services during wild land fires,
  and his ministries gives out many materials. He is our Ambassador at
  Large and about as steadfast a Christian as we have ever met. He walks
  his talk in all ways. His web page is http://www.rickbartonministries.org/

And a Special Thank you to:
- **Tommy   Neiman** (http://www.tommyneiman.com/) (email:
  sirens4tc@aol.com) founder of Sirens For The Cross Ministries founded
  to share how powerful God is in the midst and aftermath of tragedy.
- **Dwayne Clemmons** (http://rudmc.org/) founder of RUDMC Ministries with the vision of teaching people how to be authentic in their
  faith, genuine in their service, and humble in their blessings.

Install. Inspect. Protect.

Smoke Alarms Save Lives.

United States Fire Administration • 16825 South Seton Avenue • Emmitsburg, MD 21727
www.usfa.dhs.gov/smokealarms (English) • www.usfa.dhs.gov/detectoresdehumo (Spanish)

Fire Safety Tips for Your Home

Smoke Alarms

- Place properly installed and maintained smoke alarms **both inside and outside** of sleeping areas and on every level of your home.
- Interconnected smoke alarms are best because if one sounds, they all sound.
- Get smoke alarms that can sound fast. Because both ionization and photoelectric smoke alarms are better at detecting distinctly different, yet potentially fatal fires, and because no one can predict what type of fire might start in a home, the USFA recommends that every residence and place where people sleep be equipped with a) both ionization **and** photoelectric smoke alarms, **or** b) dual sensor smoke alarms (which contain both ionization and photoelectric smoke sensors).
- Test smoke alarms monthly and change alkaline batteries at least once every year, or as instructed. You can use a date you already know, like your birthday or when you change your clocks as a reminder.

- Consider buying a long-life (lithium) battery-powered smoke alarm, which may last up to ten years with no battery change.
- Install smoke alarms away from air vents.
- Install smoke alarms on the ceiling or wall, at least 4 inches from corners or according to manufacturer's instructions.
- If a smoke alarm sounds during normal cooking or when bathing, press the hush button if the smoke alarm has one. Open the door or window or fan the area with a towel to get the air moving. **Do not** disable the smoke alarm or take out the batteries. If this happens often, the smoke alarm will need to be relocated.
- To view smoke alarm guidelines for your state, obtain the **Install. Inspect. Protect. Campaign's** "State-by-State Smoke Alarm Guide" at www.usfa.dhs.gov/smokealarms.

... next page, please ...

 FEMA   **U.S. Fire Administration Mission Statement**
We provide national leadership to foster a solid foundation for local fire and emergency services for prevention, preparedness and response.

Residential Fire Sprinklers

- If possible, install residential fire sprinklers in your home.
- Avoid painting or covering the fire sprinkler, because that will affect the sensitivity to heat.
- Do not hang decorations, plants, or other objects from the sprinkler or pipes.
- For more information on Residential Fire Sprinklers, please obtain the *Install. Inspect. Protect. Campaign's* "Residential Fire Sprinkler Fact Sheet."

Escape Planning

- Prepare and practice an escape route with all residents in the home, including children.
- Know two ways to exit from every room in your home.
- Make sure safety bars on windows can be opened from inside your home.
  - Crawl low, under smoke.
  - Feel closed doors. If hot, use another exit.
- Identify a place to meet household members outside.
- Call 9-1-1 or the local emergency number *after* you escape.
- **Never** go back inside a burning home.

Fire Safety Walkthrough

- Keep clothes, blankets, curtains, towels and other items that can be easily set on fire at least three feet from space heaters, and away from stove burners.
- Place space heaters where they will not tip over easily.
- Have chimneys cleaned and inspected annually by a professional.
- Clear away trash, flammables and decorative materials.
- Always use a metal mesh screen with fireplaces and leave glass doors open while burning a fire.
- Never leave cooking unattended.
- Be sure your stove and small appliances are off before going to bed.
- Check for worn wires and do not run cords under rugs or furniture.
- Never overload electrical sockets.
- Keep lighters and matches out of the reach of children.
- Never leave cigarettes unattended and never smoke in bed.
- Make sure cigarettes and ashes are out. The cigarette needs to be completely stubbed out in the ashtray or run under water.

For more fire prevention information and campaign materials, visit www.usfa.dhs.gov/smokealarms.